HUMAN SERVICES
IN AMERICA

HUMAN SERVICES IN AMERICA

FRANCIS X. RUSSO
GEORGE WILLIS

University of Rhode Island

PRENTICE-HALL
Englewood Cliffs, New Jersey 07632

Library of Congress Cataloging-in-Publication Data

Russo, Francis X.
  Human services in America.

  Bibliography: p.
  Includes index.
  1. Social service—United States. 2. United
States—Social conditions—1980–   . I. Willis,
George, 1941–   . II. Title.
HV91.R83 1986   362′.973   85–24435
ISBN 0–13–447467–8

Cover design: Wanda Lubelska
Manufacturing buyer: John Hall

Printed in the United States of America

10 9 8 7 6 5 4 3 2 1

ISBN 0-13-447467-8   01

Prentice-Hall International (UK) Limited, *London*
Prentice-Hall of Australia Pty. Limited, *Sydney*
Prentice-Hall Canada Inc., *Toronto*
Prentice-Hall Hispanoamericana, S.A., *Mexico*
Prentice-Hall of India Private Limited, *New Delhi*
Prentice-Hall of Japan, Inc., *Tokyo*
Prentice-Hall of Southeast Asia Pte. Ltd., *Singapore*
Editora Prentice-Hall do Brasil, Ltda., *Rio de Janeiro*
Whitehall Books Limited, *Wellington, New Zealand*

To our wives, Doris and Nancy

CONTENTS

PREFACE

The human condition requires that all people receive the help of others to live full and effective lives. Infants initially depend on their parents for life itself. Children and young adults must spend long years learning the practical and social skills necessary for adulthood. Mature adults must constantly adjust to changing social and economic conditions. The elderly especially must cope with the problems of aging. Throughout the life cycle anyone at any time may become the victim of unexpected disease or disability or may be beset by problems caused by unforeseen and uncontrollable changes in the environment. No one lives fully without encountering problems, and no one copes fully with these problems without the help of others.

All societies provide help to their members in their own ways. However, as societies grow in size and complexity helping ordinarily becomes increasingly formalized and organized into what we call in this book systems of human services. In the United States during the twentieth century formal systems of human services have grown at a phenomenal rate. Buttressed by court decisions and heavily subsidized by federal, state, and local governments, human services systems now routinely intervene in problems emerging from poverty, drug addiction, family changes, crime, delinquency, and mental illness. More than 22 million Americans now receive varying degrees of treatment, assistance, and supplementary care for a host of social problems generated directly by recent economic, political, and technological changes. Americans in increasing numbers are the direct recipients of or are otherwise influenced by Social Security, food stamps, welfare, Medicare, Medicaid, subsidized housing, veterans' compensation, unemployment compensation, and various other human services provided by public and private agencies at the federal, state, and local levels. Almost one American in three currently receives some type of direct personal benefit from the federal government alone! In addition to human services systems that deal specifically with social problems or tangible personal benefits, the formal system of education in the United States is directed toward human development and routinely provides a wide variety of basic and advanced services to nearly 60 million Americans.

All Americans are protagonists in this unfolding story. Whether directly or indirectly influenced by the expansion of human services in the United States, Americans must decide who will be recruited to implement the policies and programs that make up the human services and how these workers will select and carry out humane and effective methods. They must also decide how the rising costs of human services are to be met: for instance, whether the more than one-third of the $1 trillion annual federal budget of the 1980s spent on Social Security, Medicare, and Medicaid is too little or too much, and whether taxes or voluntary contributions to private charities should increasingly meet human services costs.

This growing involvement of all Americans in the human services and the related rapid growth of these services and their consequent impacts on social, economic, and political dimensions of national life make it imperative that Americans understand the nature, mission, role, and effectiveness of the human services systems. In this book we approach this task at three levels. First, we define the human services by placing them within a framework that organizes and categorizes the numerous and diverse programs, goods, and services provided into six clear, coherent, and distinguishable systems. We trace the history and development of human services generally and of each of the service systems specifically. Second, we examine the operation of each of the human services systems by focusing on specific programs and policies that are directed at clients with certain needs, interests, or problems. Here we trace the development of and explore possible future directions for these programs and policies. Third, we explain how the human services reflect specific social norms and ideological assumptions by identifying these norms and assumptions and how they are expressed in the operations of specific programs and policies within each of the systems. In so doing we develop two alternative human services models, the conservative and the liberal, which have been fundamental to debates, policies, and practices in the United States, and we analyze their respective ideological perspectives on the human services.

Through this approach we present students with a structural, functional, and ideological framework that we hope will enable them to attain an overview of the human services in America and understand the workings of specific programs, policies, and services. We are committed to the belief that to do something well one must understand it. High-quality professional practice is not a matter of simply carrying out routine tasks, however well that may be done. It also requires the ability to make decisions in the broadest possible context. Therefore we believe that future human services workers—regardless of their specific areas of expertise—should understand how the human services in general function, how specific systems are organized and work together, and how their policies and programs are determined by certain assumptions. We believe that only by understanding such issues can human services workers adequately choose between alternative courses of action and select policies and carry out programs at high levels of professional competence. At first the human services seem an endless array of unrelated and diverse programs. These, however, are woven together in definable systems with clearly identifiable missions and roles directed at specific clients. The book should help students sort out these issues. Additionally we have sought to introduce the student to the social and philosophical underpinnings that are critical to the evolution of human services programs and policies. We have analyzed the seemingly haphazard historical development of the human services systems in terms of the dominant social norms and values that have shaped the growth of each system.

Finally, readers should recognize that this book is primarily descriptive and interpretive and only incidentally normative. Most of our statements stop with a description of the current situation in human services in America and an explanation of this situation within the framework we have set forth. There are very few suggestions of what *should be*. This is not because we do not have our own points of view, for in fact we do and we often disagree. Instead our goal has been to provide students with a framework—particularly the conflicting conservative and liberal perspectives—within which they must thoughtfully consider significant issues and develop their own opinions. We presume a principal use of this book will be to stimulate informed discussion about the normative issues it raises. Many of the study questions and activities at the conclusion of each chapter are directed to this end.

The text is divided into two parts. Part One consists of two chapters. Chapter 1 examines the origins, history, and nature of the human services, dividing them into six systems. Chapter 2 analyzes the two basic philosophical positions of conservatism and liberalism and examines five social norms that are dominant in contemporary America. Part Two consists of six chapters that examine each of the human services systems by tracing their history and development and by selecting one or more representative areas from each system to treat in depth. The areas selected cover a wide range of programs and clients. Chapter 3 on personal social services is concerned with the abused and neglected child, the dependent elderly, and the unwed sexually active teenager. Chapter 4 on health services is concerned with the aged, disabled, and eligible poor. Chapter 5 on education services examines the idea of equality of educational opportunity and its influence on a host of specific educational programs. Chapter 6 on housing and urban environment services analyzes specific strategies to improve housing for the urban poor. Chapter 7 on income transfer services is concerned with the retired elderly. Chapter 8 on justice and public safety services discusses the juvenile court system in the United States.

As is typical with coauthored texts, this has been a collaborative effort, but each author has assumed primary responsibility for certain chapters. Francis X. Russo is primarily responsible for Chapter 3 on personal social services, Chapter 4 on health services, and Chapter 7 on income transfer services. George Willis is primarily responsible for Chapter 5 on education services, Chapter 6 on housing and urban environment services, and Chapter 8 on justice and public safety services. Although every effort has been made to ensure consistency of ideas, themes, and language, the authors apologize for the inevitable variations discernible in the text.

We wish to extend our thanks to colleagues who have provided suggestions and encouragement along the way, especially Janet Giele, Richard Gelles, Alexa Albert, Leo Carroll, John Long, Thomas Galloway, and Gail Sorenson. Their help has been invaluable as we found our way through the wide variety of materials and subjects that the book attempts to encompass. The errors, omissions, and weaknesses that remain are, of course, our own responsibility.

Thanks are also due to Mackie Robinson for typing the manuscript through several drafts, always with careful skill, and for thoughtfully attending to many of the other matters necessary for preparing the manuscript for publication.

Francis X. Russo
George Willis

1

DEVELOPMENT OF HUMAN SERVICES

If we could live in the best of all possible worlds, our lives in the mythical nation of Idealstate would be marked by no conflicts, no frustrations, and no problems. There citizens would develop their full potentials through rich educational experiences provided at no cost and designed to meet their individual needs, foster their specific abilities, and expand their personal interests. Workers would be employed in challenging jobs that provide sufficient remuneration for adequate housing, convenient transportation, proper nutrition, and ample leisure activities. Family life would be harmonious and happy; healthy children would enjoy loving, healthy parents who would provide an environment of security, care, and sharing. The elderly would live comfortably and receive complete medical care. There would be no problems of developmental disabilities, no drug addicts, no alcoholics, no handicapped children, no disabled or unemployed workers, no single-parent families, and no mentally retarded or emotionally ill citizens. The environment would be attractive, clean, and safe. Crime would not occur, juvenile delinquency would be unknown, and law enforcement agencies would not be necessary. Idealstate would have little need for human services, and few human services systems would operate there. Unfortunately in the imperfect world in which we all live Idealstate does not and never will exist.

What does exist are nations such as the United States where life for many citizens is marked by conflicts, frustrations, and severe social and economic problems. Citizens of all ages and from all types of families are confronted with difficulties caused by economic and social forces beyond their immediate control. Preschool children in families below the poverty line are victims of adverse environmental circumstances and suffer developmental attrition that may impede their physiological and psychological growth. Rather than being able to develop their full potential through education, as would the citizens in Idealstate, such children enter school unprepared and unable to take advantage of the educational opportunities offered. Adults who comprise the growing ranks of the unemployed, underemployed, low skilled, and hard to employ suffer the anguish of failure and alienation in a work-conscious and work-oriented society. Rather than receiving sufficient remuneration from challenging jobs, as would the citizens of Idealstate, they labor at the most menial of tasks for substandard wages. Along with single parents, they head families that frequently become disrupted, disorganized, and susceptible to physical, intellectual, emotional, and social damage. For these citizens it is not the life with adequate food, shelter, care, good health, and happiness of the family in Idealstate that prevails. Rather there is hunger, misery, poverty, child abuse and neglect, drug dependency, lead poisonings, accidents, rat bites, inadequate immunization and primary health care, and failure to receive early treatment for disease. Even members of affluent families, although free of economic pressures, remain susceptible to social forces causing a host of personal problems, such as alcoholism, drug addiction, and divorce, which blight many lives.

Obviously there is no Idealstate for the millions of Americans who each year find they are overwhelmed by problems that they can neither control nor resolve effectively. Among these problems are inflation, recession, unemployment, and inadequate material resources, which are generated by forces external to individuals and which may be local, national, or international in scope; marital dissension, family breakdown, and child welfare needs, which occur because of conflicts within individuals' social units or families; and aging, developmental disabilities, and physical and emotional illness, which emerge from the physical and psychic characteristics of individual human beings. Increasingly aware of the inevitability and the interrelatedness of these problems, yet unable to cope effectively with them through such informal and traditional means as personal and private initiatives, Americans have more and more come to place primary responsibility upon government to provide the necessary human services that will enable them to adjust to the economic, physical, social, psychic, and biological realities they confront each day.

A DEFINITION OF HUMAN SERVICES

Human services have been defined as "specific acts of providing to an individual or groups an economic or social good" (Miller & Horton, 1974, p. 6). This definition is comprehensive but sufficiently general to include virtually any act that produces a good effect on at least one person, regardless of whether the good effect is intended, the good outweighs possible bad effects, the good is provided only to the actor, or the act is repeatable in other situations. While in the most general sense human services can include acts that incidentally produce good, acts of self-help, or acts of spontaneous and personal caring between two people, human services in modern America are now commonly understood to comprise several major, systematic efforts to help numerous citizens cope with problems that they cannot overcome by themselves. Therefore we adopt the above definition, but with the following qualifications: human services are *intentional, organized, ongoing* efforts designed to provide good *to others.* In this light let us examine the key terms in our definition.

Specific acts.   In a complex modern society such as the United States the specific acts of human services have been left less to personal initiatives, family structures, private philanthropy, or other incidental means, and have come more and more to represent a collective national notion of what constitutes the minimal conditions for the common good. While very hazy in the abstract, this notion is now concretely embodied in the series of intentional actions, often by government officials, designed to attain specific objectives consistent with the defined needs of certain individuals or groups across the social order. Several examples may be cited. Political officeholders, concerned with the plight of constituents in single-parent households, have initiated legislation designed to provide income assistance to families with dependent children in which one parent is dead, unemployed, physically or mentally incapacitated, or continually absent from the home. Social planners concerned with the blight of slum dwellings have designed policies to provide housing for low-income families. Judges concerned with protecting the legal rights of minorities have, through judicial review, improved educational opportunities for blacks, females, and the disabled. Such actions are the general means through which American society has shaped its beliefs about equality and democracy into formal governmental policies attempting to guarantee each citizen conditions deemed necessary for full participation in the social order, conditions that permit each citizen to contribute to and share in the common good. The specific acts of providing that comprise human services are thus a primary means through which American society turns its beliefs and policies into concrete realities.

Providing.   Human services focus on providing in that they are reducible to several distinct systems, each task oriented and accountable for delivery. These systems consist primarily of publicly funded programs and agencies, although private programs and agencies are also included. They are mutually dependent upon one another as they carry out their own specific acts in implementing public purpose. Although interrelated these systems can be differentiated in terms of their basic functions and the particular characteristics of their tasks. Basic functions of human services include (1) development of human beings, (2) maintenance of their well-being, (3) prevention of problems, and (4) rehabilitation after problems occur. These functions may be shared by more than one system, and each system may have more than one basic function. For instance, the systems of educational services and health services both include all four functions, although the former focuses on human development through promoting learning of all kinds, whereas the latter focuses on prevention of disease through programs of immunization and physical fitness and on rehabilitation of the diseased and disabled through medical treatments and therapy. The system of justice and public safety services emphasizes both prevention of crime through law enforcement activities and rehabilitation of criminals through modern penal programs. In contrast, the systems of income transfer services and housing and urban environment services both focus more narrowly on maintenance of personal well-being, the former through providing financial resources and the latter through providing adequate housing.

The specific acts of providing characteristic of each system have their own standards of performance and adequacy in which the individual providers are trained, often at great length, as in the medical profession. Hence in terms of promoting the common good each system is accountable for providing in an organized and ongoing way those services consistent with its basic functions and with the specific tasks within its domain for which its workers are uniquely qualified and trained. Given the complexity of organization and training required by effective, high-quality human services systems in modern America, services are not provided incidentally or because of personal whims. Instead they are directed toward those persons who demonstrate appropriate need or who otherwise qualify.

Individuals or groups.   Persons may become recipients of human services because of individual need or because of membership in qualifying groups. In the first case a human services system provides services on an exclusive, personal, individualized level, such as counseling services directed at emotional or marital problems or child welfare services directed at child abuse and neglect or at foster care and adoption. A system may also provide services on an inclusive, general group level, such as old-age or unemployment insurance directed at workers who have retired or are temporarily out of work. In both cases a person may receive a needed service; however, the criteria for provision, the service itself, and the attitudes and values connected with it may vary considerably depending on whether the need is perceived to be personal or the result only of membership in a qualifying group.

Economic or social good.   Human services in America are intended to promote the common good by helping all citizens to participate fully in the social order. They may fulfill this goal by attending to the economic welfare and social development of people. Human services provide an economic good in that they distribute both tangible and intangible goods and services directed at meeting threats to individual or family income and economic security. Examples of services designed to promote an economic good are Old-Age, Survivors, and Disability Insurance; public assistance; job opportunity programs; food stamp programs; and home finance and rent subsidies. Human services provide a social good in that they distribute goods and services directed at meeting threats to the individual's or the family's ability to fulfill whatever social roles and requirements are needed for productive participation in society. Examples of systems providing a social good are family services and child guidance clinics, protective services, institutions for the dependent and neglected, and education and rehabilitation programs.

CHARACTERISTICS OF HUMAN SERVICES

There are several characteristics of human services inherent in our definition. First, human services are provided both selectively and universally. Second, human services include both hard and soft goods and services. Third, services are provided both directly and indirectly. Fourth, goods and services are provided by a wide variety of workers with different levels of training and professionalization. Fifth, human services are provided through public, voluntary, and private agencies. Each of these characteristics of human services in America will be discussed in order.

Selective and Universal Human Services

There are two approaches to the distribution of goods and services, and they determine the two major classifications of services available. Either human services are provided selectively, to meet the needs of relatively few people in narrowly defined circumstances, or they are provided universally, to meet the common needs of virtually all people regardless of circumstances.

Selective human services.   The selective human services approach is usually called the "residual" or "minimalist" approach and is used in case services, services provided to individuals on a case-by-case basis when need is defined by analyzing the individual's specific situation. The residual approach seeks to correct the failure of the primary institutions of society to fulfill their functions of meeting the crucial social needs of individuals or small groups. Such breakdowns occur, for example, when the poor are unable to provide their children with adequate food, clothing, and shelter or when families of varying economic means are unable to provide proper health services for the handicapped, the emotionally disturbed, and the aged. Under this approach case services are temporary and restricted solely to crisis situations of short or long duration. They are intended to help individuals weather the crisis and to restore normal functioning under normal circumstances. Selective services focus on the unmet needs of the "poor, the troubled, the dependent, the deviant, and the disturbed" (Kadushin, 1980, p. 6). They utilize means-tested programs that require all aid applicants to undergo some form of diagnosis or evaluation to establish need and eligibility for the services. This assessment may be extremely extensive, requiring clients to submit evidence of need, such as rent bills and medical bills; to open ordinarily private records, such as bank books and Internal Revenue Service forms; and to explain the causes of the crisis, such as alcoholism, spouse abuse, or divorce. The assessment may be conducted on both private and public levels by many investigators of different professions. Thus medical doctors conduct examinations in cases of child abuse and neglect, judges review evidence and determine custody in cases of adoption and foster care, psychologists conduct interviews and tests and make recommendations in cases of disturbed or delinquent children, and social work administrators and caseworkers investigate applicants and determine eligibility in cases of protective services for the aged and income assistance to families with dependent children (Horton, 1975).

The residual approach in case services has both its critics and defenders. Critics reject means-tested programs for having a stigma that discourages their use by all but the most desperate. In an American society oriented toward the work ethic, receiving any kind of organized assistance may be seen as a sign of weakness or laziness or characterized as a form of the dole. Even the thought of opening one's private life to scrutiny can itself be highly frightening, and the process of being classified as illegitimate, deserted, mentally ill, or in debt can be highly dehumanizing. Critics also view case services as intentionally failing to satisfy fully the clients' needs so as to avoid attracting large numbers of users. Defenders believe that the costs of human services have become excessive and will continue to grow unless expenditures are capped and eligibility limited. They point to income transfer payments, which alone rose from $28.5 billion in 1960 to $158.5 billion in 1975 and continue to grow. They note that the incidence of fraud and cheating increases proportionately with expanded budgets and larger numbers of clients. Thus defenders of the residual approach argue that costs will be controlled only if aid is carefully monitored and limited to emergency situations involving the sick, indigent, maladjusted, handicapped, and abused (Janowitz, 1979).

Universal human services. The universal human services approach is usually called the "institutional" or "developmental" approach and is used in public social utilities. The institutional approach seeks to meet the normal living needs of "average people facing ordinary circumstances" (Kamerman & Kahn, 1977, p. 7). It is directed at human problems that require ordinary and normal kinds of assistance, and it includes public education, day care, social insurance, and counseling for emotional problems. Under this approach public social utilities become acceptable aids for all people regardless of economic status. They are often of a quality that attracts all categories of people and are available to all people without the requirement of intrusive personal tests. Eligibility for public social utilities is determined not by means-testing but by general status, such as age and residential requirements for attending public schools, and by user option, such as voluntary submission to counseling for emotional problems (Ginsberg, 1980; Janowitz, 1979). Hence there is little or no stigma attached to their use. For instance, in the United States children are required by law to attend school, but both public and private schools are certified by states as institutions in which this requirement may be fulfilled, and families from all strata of society choose to send their children to public schools, including many affluent families who have ample financial resources to choose expensive private schools and who could do so for educational, social, or other reasons.

The institutional approach in public social utilities has both its critics and defenders. Most critics accept public social utilities such as education and social insurance as communal services that are basic components in the structure of a modern postindustrial society, but often they are opposed to expanding universal services to include family and child welfare because they fear intervention by government-supported human services may destroy family privacy and undermine individualism. Critics also stress that the increase in the supply of human services has not diminished the demand for them, but rather appears to attract more recipients who expect and even demand ever-greater services. They fear the tendency in human nature is to take the easy way out, that is, to surrender responsibilities to a government that is willing to assume them. They see the costs of these services rising astronomically, and they point to figures like the 2,200 percent increase in welfare expenditures from $10.9 billion in 1929 to $241.7 billion in 1974 as evidence of uncontrolled spending on services (Janowitz, 1979). Defenders argue that in this complex world no one is entirely self-sufficient and almost anyone could be defined as a potential recipient of assistance. The needs and problems created by the dilemmas of the population of an advanced postindustrial society have made the human services universal in their application, and the specific good created for individual recipients of these services helps create the public good from which all segments of society benefit. For instance expenditures that improve the basic levels of the health, education, safety, and material and psychic welfare of individual citizens also contribute directly to the improvement of both the general prosperity and the general quality of life for all citizens. Therefore, the defenders argue, a universal system of basic services is a necessity that must be accepted as a public responsibility.

Hard and Soft Goods and Services

Human services are expanding as they respond to the growing needs, expectations, and standards of a changing American society. In dealing with basic but evolving social processes, human services provide two types of help: hard goods and services and soft goods and services.

Hard services.   Hard or "concrete" services provide tangible goods—material benefits or specific resources—in the form of resources and technical help. These include day care services, meals-on-wheels, homemaker services, health care services, housing and rent subsidies, food stamps, and information on available assistance programs. Hard services focus upon the practical, immediate, and economically valuable help that the poor and otherwise deprived require to cope with the world and to reduce their dependency on public assistance. Such services may find day care resources for children of low-income households that allow their parents to acquire employment skills or become employed, or provide resources for home care that allow the handicapped and the elderly to remain at home rather than be confined to institutions (Ginsberg, 1980).

Soft services.   Soft or "relationship" services provide help in the form of guidance and counseling. These services are the traditional type of help that dominated human services prior to the expansion of hard services in the 1960s. Soft services do not seek to provide tangible goods or material resources, but rather emphasize helping people cope with social and emotional problems. They seek to help the individual develop self-understanding, relate successfully to others, and function effectively within the community. Included among such types of services are residential care, sensitivity-group sessions, psychiatric treatment for personal disorders, counseling for family problems ranging from managing funds to rearing children, guidance for those adjusting to retirement, and counseling for those who are addicts or have engaged in other forms of antisocial behavior. Since the good provided by soft services is intangible, soft services are not valued as highly as hard services by the poor and deprived, who are primarily concerned with receiving concrete resources and technical help to meet their survival requirements of food, clothing, shelter, and medical care. However soft services are increasingly in demand by those higher on the economic scale who do not lack the material means for survival but instead are in need of relationship and adjustment services to help them cope with the social and emotional problems generated by a competitive economic system and a complex social order (Ginsberg, 1980).

Direct and Indirect Services

Not only do the human services involve a wide range of goods and services delivered to a variety of people under diverse circumstances, but delivery is also provided both directly and indirectly and may focus on the individual, the group, or society in general.

Direct services. Services and goods such as family counseling and health care are concerned with the immediate welfare of individuals or groups and are delivered directly. As with selective human services, direct services are intended to deal with specific problems or to meet usually well defined needs of recipients. While many direct services are thus also selective, still other direct services are provided prior to or apart from any means-testing and are therefore properly classified as universal. For instance police departments may dispatch officers to the homes of victims of reported crimes prior to investigation of the veracity of the reports, and hospital emergency rooms or trauma units may provide individuals with immediate medical treatment prior to investigation of the causes, severity, or even reality of the problems for which treatment is sought. A service is direct as long as it is intended to benefit immediately the recipient individual or group.

Indirect services. Indirect services also benefit their recipients; however, the primary intent is to improve the general social welfare. The well-being of recipients becomes incidental, the definition of their specific problems and needs is often left open, and the goods and services are delivered indirectly to individuals or groups in the interest of the welfare of society. As an example, incarceration of convicted criminals may or may not benefit them, but incarceration is usually justified in terms of the reduction of crime and improvement of public safety. In some instances, the institutionalization of emotionally disturbed children is an indirect service. However, especially when the quality of institutional care is in question, debates rage about whether institutionalization should primarily benefit the children or the general social welfare. Clearly many services, such as educational services, benefit both the recipients and the general welfare. Therefore whether a specific service is classified as direct or indirect depends on the immediacy of the delivery of the goods and services, the intents of the providers, and the justifications offered for the service, all of which may vary considerably from place to place and over time within American society. As in the example of the institutionalization of emotionally disturbed children, debates about policies for the delivery of human services in the United States often focus on whether certain goods and services should be treated as direct or indirect, and the results of such debates can have a major impact on the kinds and quality of the goods and services provided.

Human Services Workers

Given the complexity of the comprehensive approach to helping that the United States has been struggling toward, the human services in America require workers with various levels of training and from many professional areas.

Training.　The degree of educational preparation needed for human services workers ranges from the limited orientation and training necessary in programs for homemakers to the advanced degrees and internships required for psychiatrists and child advocate lawyers. Human services workers collectively draw on academic areas from accounting to urban affairs and on marketplace skills from administration to testing. Individually many workers must be familiar with a variety of academic areas and most use a variety of practical skills. Knowledge and skills that at first do not seem central to the daily tasks of a human services worker may still be critical to the worker's performing at a high level of professional competence. Medical personnel use physiology and chemistry in diagnosing and treating disease but may also need knowledge of psychology, sociology, gerontology, and ethnic studies to communicate with and counsel patients, particularly in urban settings. Social workers use the latter types of information in identifying the needs of clients for support and in evaluating their progress toward self-sufficiency, but may also need knowledge of physiology and chemistry in determining whether a child has been abused or accidentally injured or whether the disorientation of a client is a result of illness or drugs. Child advocacy lawyers need more than knowledge of the law in working with psychologists and sociologists. Teachers need more than knowledge of the subjects they are teaching and skills of pedagogy in developing curricula for children from disadvantaged homes. The organization of an intentional and ongoing system of human services that equitably distributes goods throughout American society thus requires workers trained in an almost endless variety of academic areas and technical and interpersonal skills.

Professionalization. The training of human services workers is closely connected with their professionalization. Given the variety of tasks these workers perform and the variety of training they require, no united profession of human services has emerged in America, nor is one likely to emerge in the future. At one end of the spectrum are volunteers who have no permanent commitments to human services and who require little training. At the other end are psychiatrists, lawyers, and other highly trained persons whose long-range commitments are more likely to be to their specific professions than to human services generally and who may be self-employed, working for fees, rather than full-time, salaried employees of agencies. In the middle, however, is a vast range of paraprofessional, semiprofessional, and professional workers who, despite their differences, share similar concerns. These concerns focus on the problems, conflicts, and frustrations encountered as these workers attempt to increase both their autonomy and their ability to provide high-quality services while working under the direction of others and with limited resources. Such concerns lead human services workers to press for better academic and on-the-job training and for increased responsibility for professional decision-making. This move toward professionalization in part reflects the increasingly better and more comprehensive training workers have received, but it also creates both demand for still better training and circumstances under which the entire system of human services in America may improve. Thus in the future many human services in America may improve. Human services workers will tend to see themselves in less circumscribed technical roles and will increasingly engage in public deliberation about their specific tasks in relationship to the society in general, particularly about policy-making, management, and evaluation within a comprehensive human services system. Increasing professionalization not only will demand of workers greater ability to integrate academic and practical knowledge into better policies and programs, but will also demand that American society provide conditions conducive to this improvement. Increasing professionalization goes together with increasingly comprehensive training, and both may lead to more efficient delivery of higher quality services benefitting recipients, workers, and society alike.

Types of Human Services Agencies

Human services are delivered by three types of agencies: (1) public, (2) traditional and new (community) voluntary, and (3) private or proprietary. Each receives its funding from different sources and reflects different approaches to marketplace factors of distribution of goods and services, to charging fees, and to profit-making.

Public agencies.   Public agencies such as the Veterans Administration and state mental hospitals receive federal and state funding and do not charge fees for profit-making. They distribute goods and services (called entitlements, benefits, or rights) to clients whose eligibility is determined by federal or state laws. They distribute services according to such nonmarket criteria as helping the needy, controlling and rehabilitating those in difficulty, promoting concepts of social justice, and encouraging individual development.

Traditional and new voluntary agencies.   Traditional voluntary agencies differ sharply in their size and in the nature of services offered. They range from the larger agencies providing a wide variety of goods and services, such as United Way and various sectarian federations, to smaller agencies limited to specific services, such as the Muscular Dystrophy Association. They rely primarily upon contributions from private citizens, philanthropic groups, industry, unions, and various local charitable organizations. New (community) voluntary agencies such as community health and counseling centers may receive funds from federal, state, and local governments in addition to contributions from private sources. Voluntary agencies are often governed by the leadership elite of the local communities who are selected to sit on their policy boards. Such agencies have been characterized by the traditional technology of casework and by the professionalization of staff through education and training requirements. Voluntary agencies may charge nominal fees, are usually nonprofit operations, and distribute goods and services according to criteria similar to those used by public agencies.

Private or proprietary agencies.   Private or proprietary agencies such as employment agencies follow standard business procedures of charging fees, operating for a profit, and distributing goods and services according to the dictates of a competitive marketplace. While some private agencies receive only the fees paid directly to them by their clients, others receive public funds. For instance private nursing homes receive Medicare and Medicaid money directly from the federal government on behalf of patients within their care.

There exists a close working relationship and considerable interdependence among these three types of agencies. Public agencies often find it less costly and more efficient to purchase goods and services from private, independent vendors. Interagency cooperation and coordination insure better services for clients while public agencies realize considerable savings by using certain existing services of nonpublic agencies rather than attempting to develop and operate these services themselves. For example, "counseling and family services are purchased from family service agencies, child guidance clinics, rape and domestic violence centers, and shelters for teenagers in trouble with the law or in flight from their homes" (Ginsberg, 1980, p. 6). Further, public agencies can limit their purchases only to that portion of the services required to provide for their clients' needs. Since the passage of the Title XX Amendment to the Social Security Act in 1970, more than 50 percent of the annual appropriations of public agencies have been used to purchase services from nonpublic vendors. This has encouraged these vendors to expand the size of their operations and to come to rely increasingly upon public funds for their survival (Gibelman, 1980).

HISTORICAL DEVELOPMENT OF HELPING

Before examining how the foregoing definition of human services and its inherent characteristics imply that human services are social inventions that have evolved to meet changing needs and conditions, we will briefly consider the history of helping and outline the six basic human services systems that have developed in the United States. Any attempt to define human services and to explain their characteristics would remain incomplete without some explanation of changing attitudes toward helping and changing patterns of organized human services.

Helping in the Ancient World and Europe

Clearly, human needs have existed as long as there have been people, and virtually all societies have developed some means for coping with at least the most basic of these. However comparatively little is known about how most ancient societies attempted to define and to provide services to the needy, when they did so at all. In general the basic necessities of life as well as rudimentary education and health care were met for most people in the ancient world through daily labor and incidental membership in family or social group. Distribution of wealth was extremely uneven, and formal educational opportunities and adequate health care (by the standards of the place and time) were limited to the very few. In some societies organized charities and beginning forms of state-sponsored services began to take shape, but again little is known about the attitudes and motives that accompanied many of these earliest efforts.

The biblical attitude.   Much more is known about the biblical attitude toward helping the needy. The Old Testament emphasizes that nothing is more difficult to bear than poverty and that God has a special place in his

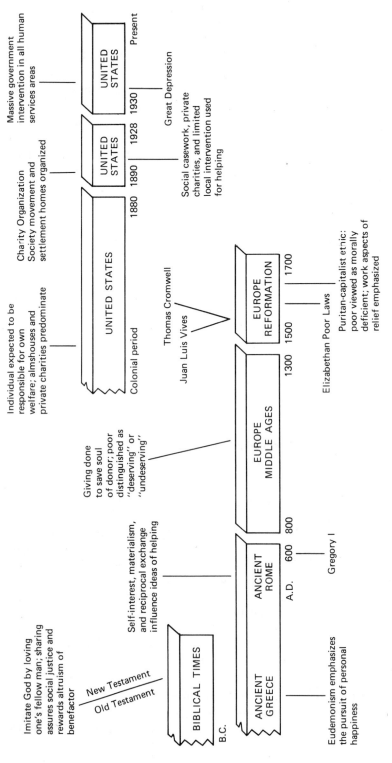

FIGURE 1–1. Timeline tracing the history of helping in ancient empires, Europe, and the United States. Key beliefs, individuals, legislation, and agencies that dominated in specific eras from the biblical period to the present are identified.

14

heart for the poor. The world is viewed as being divided between good and evil, and classical Judaism sought to imitate God's kindness and mercy through sharing. Helping the poor also became a way of imitating God by promoting justice. Charity, which is to be extended to Jew and gentile alike, is therefore a way for the individual to fulfill the wishes of God in this world. The highest good is to help the needy become self-sufficient; it is not to leave them in a situation in which inferior is helped by superior. The Christian attitude, developed in the New Testament, added to this the idea that love for one's fellows is the proper response to God's love for all people. Within the biblical attitude toward helping, which combines kindness, mercy, justice, and love, the primary reward is to the altruism of the benefactor, but, especially in the New Testament, there is also the potentially selfish motive of attempting to ensure salvation by giving (Keith-Lucas, 1972).

Ancient Greece.   The ancient Greek attitude toward helping was concerned far less with charity and far more with personal happiness. The approach was influenced by the type of society in ancient Greece, one in which a large slave class tended to the needs of a small citizen class who did not work with their hands and who for the most part were highly cultured. The emphasis on giving here was based on a sense of reciprocity, and helping one's equals was justified on the basis of what in turn would be received by the donor. There was no commiserating with the poor and the slave class because Greek citizens sought to further the development of their souls by helping others of the elite class. Eudemonism, the doctrine that emphasizes the pursuit of happiness, was the guiding system of ethics, and Greeks weighed the moral nature of actions in terms of their ability to produce personal happiness.

Ancient Rome.   The Roman attitude, like the Greek, was concerned primarily with self-interest, but was much more directly utilitarian and materialistic. The approach to helping was shaped by the nature of the Roman Empire, which generated a common culture and promoted a reciprocal exchange between the rulers, who provided material goods, and the ruled, who returned labor and loyalty. Members of the empire shared an appreciation of a common culture (the concept of *humanitas*), and the borderline between citizen and slave became blurred. The wealthy class depended on public approval to attain high offices and on recruits drawn from the masses to fill the ranks of the legions that enabled the elite to maintain and extend their power. Consequently, the rulers used helping to recruit supporters and to reward loyalty. They subsidized vast numbers of the masses with the proverbial bread and circuses, passed laws to protect the property rights of orphaned children of soldiers killed in wars, manipulated the economy to reduce poverty (for example, lowered the price of grain), and established foundations for the distribution of land and money among the poor (Hands, 1968).

European developments.   Despite the Roman accomplishment of organizing a formal system for distributing subsidies to the poor, the inevitability of poverty as a condition of life was widely accepted in Europe (and later—although to a lesser extent—in America) throughout the vast sweep of time from the early Middle Ages to the nineteenth century. Under the influence of Christianity the biblical attitude toward helping gradually subsumed elements of Greek rationalism and Roman materialism to evolve slowly into the Puritan-capitalist ethic. Throughout this period a primary impulse behind helping was the belief that giving contributed to the virtue of the donor and ensured salvation of the soul. The worldly condition of individuals was viewed as a function of their moral character. The major source of helping during the Middle Ages was the private, voluntary charity of religious and secular organizations such as the churches and guilds. Helping was directed to the poor who were morally respectable and therefore "deserving," as distinguished from the poor who succumbed to vices such as drunkenness, sloth, and mendacity and therefore were "undeserving." This distinction between "deserving" and "undeserving" became blurred during the Reformation, when God's grace became identified with worldly success. In general the poor were judged to be morally deficient, and helping was designed to make the poor as uncomfortable as possible and to force them to work in order to better themselves (Keith-Lucas, 1972).

Forerunners.   Under the influence of the evolving Christian attitude toward helping during this time there also emerged several noteworthy forerunners of modern forms of organization for human services. Pope Gregory I (c. 540–604), Juan Luis Vives (1492–1540), and Thomas Cromwell (c. 1485–1540) were pioneers in the administration and planning of helping, and during the reign of Queen Elizabeth I (1533–1605) England sought to establish a national policy for the treatment of poverty with the enactment of the Elizabethan Poor Laws.

Pope Gregory I organized and administered an effective system of distribution of aid to the masses of poor in Rome when the empire collapsed. His system efficiently collected and distributed material goods and some services. Help was given to all in need, including shut-ins, who had meals delivered to their homes, and over a period of years this system averted starvation, pestilence, and death for thousands. Juan Luis Vives conceived and developed welfare planning for the cities of Bruges and Ypres in Flanders. He called on government to teach the poor trades, to promote and sponsor employment for the voluntarily unemployed and the handicapped, and to provide medical care for the poor who were physically and emotionally sick. Thomas Cromwell proposed a welfare program for England that included a broad program of public works and relief. A nationally administered and tax-financed program would employ the poor in building highways, renovating harbors, and clearing watercourses. Medical care was to be provided to the sick poor, and begging children of the poor were to be apprenticed to masters (Elton, 1953).

Later the Elizabethan Poor Laws were designed to create employment opportunities for the poor under public auspices. They represent one of the earliest expressions of national obligation to the poor even though the workhouses they established were administered and financed by local parishes. Emphasis fell upon work, and in the workhouses the unemployed, able-bodied poor were set to work and poor children were instructed in a trade (Rimlinger, 1971). Unfortunately, the effectiveness of these laws as a means of relieving the poor was drastically blunted in practice because of the attitudes that attended them. The laws were administered extremely harshly under the prevailing belief that the poor were undeserving and that only by making them uncomfortable and forcing them to work could they be forced to better themselves. Many workhouses were run for the monetary gain of the overseers, and conditions were appalling: Families were forcibly separated, and adults and children alike might be physically and psychologically brutalized. Consequently the workhouse became a last, desperate resort for even the most destitute and was avoided by many poor who continued to beg and to seek whatever benevolence they could find in the various incidental charities that had continued to exist after the passage of the laws. Despite their original intent and the expression of national obligation they embodied, these laws codified the authority of the state to regulate the lives of the poor, actually increasingly cast many poor on their own resources, and institutionalized throughout England the Puritan-capitalist ethic into which the original biblical emphasis on kindness, mercy, justice, and love had evolved.

Helping in America

Helping in colonial America and during the first century of the United States was a continuation of the Christian attitude as it had evolved into the Puritan-capitalist ethic. While many early colonists were English and brought with them English beliefs and practices, these were gradually modified by contact with settlers from other European countries and by distinctly American circumstances.

The early United States.   Shortly after the United States became an independent nation, it widely adopted laws similar to the Elizabethan Poor Laws. These laws imposed local responsibility for the poor, liability of relatives for support of indigent family members, and restrictions of eligibility for relief to residents of the locality. They codified many informal practices of helping that had developed in colonial America. But while care of the poor was now recognized as a governmental responsibility, two other circumstances in America promoted individual initiative and independence. First, an abundance of land, easily accessible and at little cost, provided a source of potential wealth for all. Second, emerging American political institutions, laws, and social beliefs pressed toward a classless, egalitarian society. Individuals believed they could rise as high as their abilities would take them or be as independent as they wished. Such attitudes encouraged them to take responsibility for their own welfare and to feel deeply that they could better their position in society (Leiby, 1978; Schottland, 1967). Thus despite American laws much of the helping that did occur was conducted on a limited basis through local almshouses and quite haphazardly through various forms of private charity and was carried out under an ethos of reforming recipients into hard-working and morally upright members of society.

Changes in approach and attitude.   By the latter half of the nineteenth century the closing of the frontier, the increasing waves of immigrants reaching America, and the growth of industry generated a need for order and social planning to help workers and their families in expanding urban centers. The Charity Organization Society and the settlement house movement became prominent at this time. The Charity Organization Society, patterned after the London Society for Organizing Charitable Relief and Repressing Mendicancy, sought to use scientific helping processes to assist the individual in adjusting to society. It was founded on the belief that the poor could be assimilated into society through education and moral uplift. The settlement house movement, led by reformers such as Jane Addams (1860–1935), Lillian Wald (1867–1940), Florence Kelley (1859–1932), was in the vanguard of attempts to change society through social legislation and political action directly aimed at meeting the needs of people. It was established on the belief that society has the obligation to be responsive to the suffering of the poor and the vulnerable, and it advanced social programs designed to relieve distress among the working classes. As a result of these efforts, the plight of the urban poor received national attention for the first time. Laws improving housing, sanitation, and the purity of foods and drugs were passed. Services such as visiting nurses associations began to find their way into the worst of America's slums. During this time substantial progress was also made in providing universal educational services as state after state passed compulsory attendance laws and set up the legal and social mechanisms for ensuring—in theory at least—that every American child would have the opportunity to obtain an education as a means to a fruitful life. Still, despite these initial efforts at social reform and this advance in providing educational services, little change was occurring in the older, incidental forms of helping that predominated in the United States.

What served to break this pattern forever in the United States was the development in the late nineteenth and early twentieth centuries of a distinctly new approach to helping known as "social casework." It emerged from the combined influences of the writings of American philosophers and social critics such as John Dewey (1859–1952), new applications of science to human problems, and the continuing efforts at social reform. Useful especially in the growing cities of newly industrialized America as a means of coping with the problems of the urban poor and recently arrived immigrants, social casework was a method by which the helping agent, borrowing from the medical model of diagnosis and treatment, gained an in-depth understanding of the problem. The goal was to understand the circumstances pertinent to each client's particular problem, to identify and remove the specific causes of the problem, and to supply needed support as the client was restored to normal functioning. The development of social casework made feasible for the first time the provision of selective and direct human services across an entire social order. By the mid-1920s this method was complemented by a theory of helping influenced in general by the new scientific conceptions of human behavior and in particular by analytical psychology. It called for the helper's love and understanding in aiding the needy, and it rejected the judgmental attitude of the Puritan-capitalist ethic, which had dominated the approach to helping prior to this time (Fox, 1967; Keith-Lucas, 1972). The development of this method opened the door to the modern era in human services by permitting the provision on a broad scale of selective services that attack the causes of specific human problems, treat the client as a victim of circumstances, and encourage long-term resolution of problems themselves rather than their symptoms. In Chapter Two the "liberal" ideology that supports this approach is contrasted with the "conservative" ideology that supports older approaches to helping.

The United States to the present.   Until the 1930s private voluntary charity remained the primary source of helping in the United States. Federal intervention was rare, and state and local governments provided only limited assistance. With the coming of the Great Depression and the concomitant economic and social upheaval, however, these limited sources of helping proved grossly inadequate in meeting the needs of the millions of unemployed, dispossessed, and destitute. As growing numbers of Americans discovered they were unable to deal with the hazards of economic insecurity inherent in their industrial society, they turned to the federal and state governments for help in maintaining income; acquiring adequate housing; providing food, clothing, and medical treatment; and caring for the aged, widowed, abandoned, abused, and handicapped. From the passage of the Social Security Act in 1935 to the present, government intervention and the responsibility and control over human services programs thus entailed have grown dramatically. Services that did not exist during earlier eras are now taken for granted as part of the fabric of American life. Today organized helping has assumed a multiplicity of roles that affect all phases of human life, and human services organizations, heavily funded by federal and state governments, have increased in size, cost, and complexity.

THE SIX HUMAN SERVICES SYSTEMS

The general system of human services that has grown to meet the needs of complex, modern America is composed of six basic human (sometimes called social) services systems.[1] They are (1) personal social services (sometimes called general social services), (2) health services, (3) education services, (4) housing and urban environment services, (5) income transfer services, and (6) justice and public safety services.[2] (In Chapters Three to Eight the various roles and dimensions of each of these human services systems are examined in detail.)

Personal Social Services

Personal social services are personal in the "sense that they are individualized, whether in delivery, assuring access to rights or benefits, or offering counseling and guidance" (Kamerman & Kahn, 1977, p. 3). They provide goods and services directed at special groups with specific needs that are not taken care of by the other human services systems. Emphasis is on socialization and development as this system provides day care for children of working parents; homemakers for the ill and disabled; child welfare and protective services for the abandoned, neglected, and abused; social care for the aged, handicapped, and retarded; rehabilitation for persons on relief; and counseling for parents in rearing children and managing financial resources. Concern is also with prevention and with relationship and adjustive-type services as the system provides psychological counseling to aid individuals, families, and primary groups in coping with the problems generated by modern urban life. In addition to offering

[1]Kamerman and Kahn (1977) use the terms "social services" and "human services" interchangeably. They note that "the term 'social services' is internationally recognized as covering essential forms of communal provision" (pp. 2–3).

[2]In arriving at these basic human services systems we adopted part of the classification model developed by Kamerman and Kahn (1977, pp. 1–6).

family services, counseling, and information and referral programs, personal social services function as advocates for disadvantaged groups ensnarled in the bureaucratic rigidities of the services systems.

Health Services

Health services are directed at the physical, emotional, and social well-being of vulnerable groups in society such as single mothers, children, the poor, the aged, and the handicapped. They involve government, in partnership with the private sector, in attempting to redistribute health benefits among the different segments of the population. They rely on the private marketplace, and through government-financed insurance payments they permit recipients a choice of private-system medical care. Emphasis has sometimes fallen upon fee-for-service programs that allow for hospital and surgical coverage but not for primary home- and office-based physician services. Health services also seek to eliminate communicable diseases through immunization programs and to promote health awareness and self-care through education and information programs directed against alcohol, drugs, dietary fat intake, and the like. Health services include health insurance; payments and benefits for the elderly, the poor, and injured workers; biomedical research; preventive health programs for mothers and children; rehabilitation programs for the injured and disabled; and programs for veterans.

Education Services

Education services are either publicly or privately delivered and include preschool, elementary, secondary, vocational, and higher education programs. They are directed at children and adults of all levels of ability, at all stages of physical and emotional development, and from all types of social and economic background. While public education services receive considerable support from the federal government in programs ranging from Project Head Start for the disadvantaged to vocational and technical training designed to increase workers' income by raising their economic productivity, the states and local communities retain control over curricular content and educational planning. Education services are often mistakenly not regarded as part of the human services because they are usually administered by elected officials—not by appointed or civil servants—and remain separated from the other public services provided by government. The nature of education services is also unique in its universality, its legal and social foundations, and its requirement of mandatory participation. But education is an integral part of human services and provides goods and services in the form of knowledge, training, and character development that are essential to conserving and maximizing human resources.

Housing and Urban Environment Services

Housing and urban environment services are concerned with the social consequences of physical-environmental conditions on all segments of the American population. They are directed at improving housing standards; encouraging home ownership; meeting housing needs of special groups such as the poor, elderly, and handicapped; and improving neighborhoods and communities through beautification programs, clean air and water standards, and altering population density. Included among the housing and urban environment goods and services provided over the last half-century are low-rent public housing and rent subsidies for the poor and needy, mortgage insurance and loan guarantee programs for low and middle income groups, and a federal income tax deduction on local and state taxes and mortgage interest payments for homeowners of all classes. Housing and urban environment services involve a blend of federal, state, and local support and control with marketplace initiative from private enterprise. Often the federal government secures mortgage financing for potential homeowners who purchase housing that is regulated by state and local building codes and zoning rules and that is built by the housing industry in the private sector of the economy. Federal, state, and local governments have also combined with the private sector in programs to remove slums and blight through urban renewal, and to improve the general quality of life through grants for water and sewer projects, recreational facilities, open space, and beautification.

Income Transfer Services

Income transfer services are concerned with that segment of the population that has been unable to attain the necessary employment and income that will assure the minimal conditions for a decent standard of living. These services include programs of social insurance, assistance, and pensions that are directed at the aged, the widowed, the handicapped, the retired, the physically disabled, the poor child and family, and the worker who is unemployed through no personal fault. Income transfer services are supported and controlled jointly by federal and state governments; in funding the social insurance program, workers also must contribute from their earnings to be eligible for benefits. Among the goods and services provided by income transfer services are direct cash payments and benefits in kind such as food, health care, housing, and education. Direct cash payments are provided to support survivors of workers and to replace earnings lost through retirement, disability, job-related disability, and involuntary and temporary unemployment. Benefits in kind provided to the poor and needy as supplements to cash assistance take the form of food stamps, health care, public housing, rent and purchase subsidies, adult education, youth corps, employment programs, work-experience opportunities, family planning, child care, and vocational rehabilitation programs.

Justice and Public Safety Services

Justice and public safety services are concerned with that segment of the population that threatens public order and fails to observe the body of law that codifies society's rules about proper and improper behavior. This group includes juvenile delinquents (children below the age of eighteen who have violated state criminal laws and local ordinances); status offenders (children below the age of eighteen who have committed noncriminal offenses such as truancy, running away, and resisting parental control); and adults who have violated state criminal laws and local ordinances. Justice and public safety services directed at the members of this group consist of agencies, institutions, and programs involved in the apprehension, detention, trial, reform, and rehabilitation of offenders. Goods and services provided range from local, state, and federal law enforcement agents, court systems, and penal systems to halfway houses, group homes, work furloughs, home visitations, probation and parole programs, youth bureaus, and probation subsidies. Justice and public safety services are primarily the responsibility of state and local governments, which receive some assistance from federal programs and institutions such as the Law Enforcement Assistance Administration and the Juvenile Justice and Delinquency Act.

HUMAN SERVICES AS SOCIAL INVENTIONS

A comprehensive, definitive conception of human services can be drawn from the initial attempt in this chapter to define the nature and characteristics of human services and from the brief examination of the history of helping. Human services have emerged in modern America as helping-caring services directed toward meeting human needs arising from day-to-day socialization and developmental experiences. They are planned and provided by the community "to enhance individual and group development and well-being and to aid, rehabilitate, or treat those in difficulty or need" (Horton, 1975, p. 1). They are the vehicle American society uses for maximizing and conserving its human resources, and they seek to create the conditions under which people can pursue their individual goals. They are conducted under the prevailing American belief that when people are provided with optimal conditions for pursuing personal goals such as happiness or economic well-being, they also psychically, materially, and politically contribute to the common good of American society. Human services become the means to this end through their programs of "socialization and development; therapy, help, and rehabilitation (including social protection and substitute care); access, information, and advice" (Horton, 1975, p. 2). These programs are directed at people of all ethnic groups, from all levels of the social spectrum, in all stages of life, and with a variety of social and economic needs. They provide goods and services that are crucial for a particular phase of a person's life or that serve as a vital supplement for a specific period of time.

Human services have become a permanent element in the social structure of contemporary postindustrial America. The goods and services they provide are not temporary and short-lived responses to breakdowns of primary institutions, nor will they disappear as soon as certain problems are solved. Human services have assumed functions in education, health, family and child welfare, income maintenance, and community protection that the family and small community in this era of urbanization, specialization, and technological progress can no longer handle. Thus even during the early 1980s, despite the conservative political climate that brought the Reagan administration into office with its promise to reverse the half-century trend toward the establishment of "New Deal" social programs increasingly controlled and funded by the federal government, the major questions facing human services were not ones concerning their necessity and existence in modern America, but ones concerning the forms they would take and how they would be organized, financed, and controlled.

Throughout the history of human services different attitudes and values held in different societies at different times have shaped how human problems have been perceived, needs defined, and services delivered. Social, technological, and economic developments have influenced the kinds of services that could be provided. In favorable times recipients have been pitied, loved, and genuinely aided; in unfavorable times they have been rebuked, degraded, and left in want.

Yet the most basic human needs always remain the same, and as societies change new needs and means to meet them always arise. As social and economic forces have created new needs for the individual and family in the United States, for instance, human services have responded with appropriate goods and services. As Kahn has observed,

> what is not fully understood is the way in which the new circumstances create new needs which were never the responsibility of any institution in a simpler world. No earlier society ever had to provide the daily needs, retirement, leisure, and participation of tremendously large numbers of senior citizens, because no such society made the public health progress that ours has made. No previous society had to face the fact that technological progress would create unemployment and would, therefore, create public responsibility for dealing with its consequences, as ours has had to face. No earlier society built so tightly and settled man so closely in large numbers, that most people need access to transportation if they would reach places of their employment, or escape from routine to commune with nature on weekends or on vacation. (Quoted in Horton, 1975, p. 3)

In providing responses to new circumstances caused by changing social views and conditions, human services can be viewed as "social inventions which seek to meet the needs of modern man in his interrelationships and roles" (Kahn, quoted in Horton, 1975, p. 3). The human service systems that have evolved in modern America thus will continue to evolve in the future.

In this chapter we have suggested both what is necessary and what is contingent about human services in general and about the specific forms they have taken in the United States. In Chapter Two we will examine how conflicting attitudes and beliefs, which we term "conservative" and "liberal" ideologies, support alternative approaches to human services and their delivery.

STUDY QUESTIONS AND ACTIVITIES

1. Why are some human services necessary even in Idealstate? Which ones? Why will Idealstate never exist? How closely can it actually be approximated? What part do human services play in creating the closest approximations to Idealstate that now exist?

2. Why are spontaneous actions that produce good to both the recipient and the actor not considered human services? What characteristics of modern American society require that human services be considered as *intentional, organized, ongoing* efforts designed to produce good *to others*? When human services are considered in this way, what issues, problems, and opportunities arise?

3. What political theory underlies the idea that helping individual citizens or groups to participate fully in the social order promotes the common social good? Cite examples of major governmental policies or actions consistent with this theory. In what sense do individuals or groups have the right to be provided with at least minimal conditions necessary to pursue their own ends within the social order? In what sense does society provide these conditions in its own interests? What happens when citizens provided with at least minimal conditions to promote the common good still pursue selfish, antisocial, or harmful ends? Does this political theory suggest that individual citizens should be made more nearly equal or alike or merely provided equal conditions or opportunities for pursuing their own goals?

4. List as comprehensively as possible the specific ways in which each of the six major human services systems carries out different basic functions of human services: development of human beings, maintenance of their well-being, prevention of problems, and rehabilitation after problems occur. In what ways do the functions of these systems overlap? In what ways do they differ?

5. What are the basic differences between selective and universal human services? Between direct and indirect services? Why can the same service at times be classified as direct and at other times as indirect? How should needs be defined and assessed? What is the relationship between needs and values? Between needs and specific circumstances? What are the pros and cons of means-testing as a way of establishing need? What difference does it make to

individual recipients of services whether their need is perceived to be personal or the result of membership in a qualifying group?

6. Do the benefits of human services outweigh the costs? How would you go about finding the answer? How should benefits be defined? Can all benefits be measured economically? Should a universal system of human services be a public responsibility or should it be left at least in part to private initiative? Are hard services intrinsically more valuable than soft services?

7. What is the relationship between knowledge and action in providing high-quality human services? Do the demands placed on human services workers for knowledge and skills from a variety of areas indicate that their training should be interdisciplinary? Should these workers be able to formulate policies as well as provide services? What are the characteristics of a profession? Classify different human services workers according to the degrees to which they are professionalized. What is the relationship between training and professionalization in providing high-quality services?

8. What are the advantages and disadvantages of having a human services system include voluntary and private agencies as well as public agencies? List as comprehensively as possible the kinds of human services that are provided by private or proprietary agencies.

9. Compare and contrast the biblical attitude toward helping with the Puritan-capitalist ethic into which it gradually evolved. What characteristics of the Greek and Roman attitudes did the Puritan-capitalist ethic adopt? Does it make a difference whether the poor are judged deserving or undeserving as long as they receive aid? Why did the Elizabethan Poor Laws not substantially improve the lot of many poor people even though they were applied universally to the poor?

10. What circumstances in America served to change the basic approach and attitude toward helping that Americans had inherited from Europe? Describe the method of social casework. Why did the development of social casework make feasible the provision of selective and direct human services across the entire social order? Why have federal and state governments in the United States since the 1930s become increasingly involved in providing human services?

11. What human needs always remain the same? Outline the types of new human needs that have arisen in America in the last fifty years due to changes in society. In what ways do human services evolve in response to changing social conditions? In what ways in response to changing attitudes and expectations?

REFERENCES

Elton, G. R. (1953). An early Tudor poor law. *The Economic History Review, 6*, 55–67.
Fox, D. M. (1967). *The discovery of abundance* (pp. 95–104). Ithaca, NY: Cornell University Press.
Gibelman, M. (1980). Title XX purchase of service: Some speculations about service provision to the poor. *The Urban Social Change Review, 13*, 9–14.
Ginsberg, L. H. (1980). A state administrator's perspective on Title XX. *The Urban Social Change Review, 13*, 5–8.

Hands, A. R. (1968). *Charities and social aid in Greece and Rome.* New York: Cornell University Press.

Janowitz, M. (1979). *Social control and the welfare state* (pp. 1–15, 72–84). New York: Harper & Row.

Kadushin, A. (1980). *Child welfare services* (pp. 1–8). New York: Macmillan.

Kahn, A. J. (1975). What are social services? In G. T. Horton (Ed.)., *Readings on human services planning* (pp. 1–9). Arlington, VA: Human Services Institute for Children and Families.

Kamerman, S. B., & Kahn, A. J. (1977). *Social services in international perspective* (pp. 1–19). Washington, DC: U.S. Government Printing Office.

Keith-Lucas, A. (1972). *Giving and taking help* (pp. 185–199). Chapel Hill: University of North Carolina Press.

Leiby, J. (1978). *A history of social welfare and social work in the United States* (pp. 12–18). New York: Columbia University Press.

Miller, J. H., & Horton, G. F. (1974). *Alternative approaches to human services planning* (pp. 5–10). Arlington, VA: Human Services Institute for Children and Families.

Rimlinger, G. V. (1971). *Welfare policy and industrialization in Europe, America, and Russia* (pp. 18–24, 193–200). New York: John Wiley & Sons.

Schottland, C. (1967, February). Government economic programs and family life. *Journal of Marriage and the Family,* pp. 76–79.

2

BASIC APPROACHES TO HUMAN SERVICES

HUMAN SERVICES AND IDEOLOGY

In Chapter One we defined human services as specific acts of providing economic or social goods, and suggested that human services are social inventions that respond to needs that change as society changes. We further suggested that as modern American society has become increasingly complex, human services have been left less and less to personal, private, and incidental initiatives and have come more and more to represent a collective national effort to provide individual citizens with those minimal conditions necessary to maintain a decent quality of life. Although such ideas appear at first glance to be reasonably straightforward, they contain within them a series of complicated questions concerning the nature of human services themselves and American society's perceptions of its own needs and responses to those perceptions. Among such questions are: How can certain tangible objects or intangible processes be classified as goods? How are needs defined and determined? What constitutes minimal conditions for a decent quality of life? Through what specific mechanisms of providing can these conditions be obtained? How much responsibility falls on the public for providing to individuals? When does the individual good represent the common good? How does society assess and respond to change?

Answers a particular society gives to such questions ultimately depend on both the value structures and the political structures of that society. Everything rests on how the society accommodates the differing values and points of view of its various members within some kind of collective consciousness and on the processes of debate and deliberation through which its consciousness becomes the decisions or public policies that translate into the specific acts of human services the society provides. Human services in America therefore depend largely on the unique blending of values and politics characteristic of the people of the United States.

The Nature of Ideology

This collective blending of what can also be considered the philosophical and social beliefs of society is known as "ideology." Bernier and Williams (1973) define ideology as

> an integrated pattern of ideas, system of beliefs, or a "group consciousness" which characterizes a social group. Such a pattern or system may include doctrines, ideals, slogans, symbols, and direction for social and political actions. Ideologies also include objectives, demands, judgments, norms, and justifications, and in this sense they are value-impregnated systems of thought which may be perceived as sacred. (p. 27)

Bernier and Williams point out that although ideologies thus provide common systems of language and of social identity that shape the perceptions, beliefs, goals, and actions of members of the group, ideologies are also inevitably accompanied by certain internal tensions. First, they may be dogmatic or flexible and may support the social status quo or include demands for a new or radically altered social system. Second, they may admit of either little or much divergence between the collective thinking of the group and the thinking of its individual members.

In the case of the first tension, change may occur in either the system of beliefs itself or the prevailing social arrangements. For example, the general easing during the 1950s and 1960s of state laws restricting divorce was based on changing American attitudes about marriage and patterns of living, but the easing of laws led to an increased proportion of divorced persons in the population and still further tolerance not only for divorce but also for many kinds of living arrangements that earlier had been perceived as highly unconventional. However, regardless of the locus of change and of the degree of accommodation to change within the ideology, a time of rapid or dramatic change is usually perceived as a period of breakdown and crisis and is usually accompanied by calls for controls on individuals and for a return to the ways of the past. By the early 1980s increasing toleration in American society for many types of unconventional living arrangements such as group families, homosexual unions, cohabitation, and single-parent households had been countered by wide-scale demands for the reestablishment of laws supporting the sanctity of marriage and traditional family life. Another, related example is that in the early 1980s the conventional wisdom in the United States seemed to view the late 1960s as a time of excess and social chaos and not also as a time of experiments in participatory democracy and of the exercise of personal conscience, actions consistent with many long-held American values. Yet ironically this conventional wisdom supported many of the conservative emphases within the ideology of the Reagan administration on such values as laissez-faire capitalism, less federal government, and more individual self-regulation, which (so the administration claimed) had characterized an earlier and better America.

In the case of the second tension, an individual's beliefs about reality may sometimes be more adequate than the collective beliefs of society. Since collective ideologies are partly articles of faith and only partly based on empirically tested facts and careful, logical analysis, they may also serve to distort reality. In transmitting a group's beliefs, ideologies often tend to promote conventional views of reality and to discourage potentially more adequate but less easily and less widely understood views. Hence one measure of the health of any society is the degree to which its prevailing ideology can accommodate divergent points of view and gradually sort through them, rejecting those that distort reality and incorporating those that heighten or clarify reality. Bernier and Williams (1973) suggest a means of resolving this tension between individual and collective beliefs: "Ideologies can be transcended, in part, by critical thought. An individual can move beyond ideologies to perceive 'realities' from a philosophical perspective" (p. 57). Because individuals can cultivate the habit of critical thought and move toward increasingly adequate views of reality, societies that are comprised of such individuals tend to hold collective ideologies that least distort reality and most accommodate constructive change.

Although we have suggested that ideology is the collective blending of philosophical and social beliefs, we agree that both kinds of beliefs within any ideology can be critically and systematically exposed. Such exposure can reduce—if not eliminate—discrepancies between perceptions and realities, values and facts, policies and practices. In this spirit we will now examine the major ideological perspectives that have guided the two basic, predominant approaches to human services in America, looking explicitly at their philosophical and social assumptions and implications for theory and practice in human services. In so doing we will point out how these two perspectives provide differing answers to questions about how human services deal with values, social change, and the delivery of services. We will then briefly consider some major social norms within the prevailing ideology in the United States and their relation to public policies in human services. We will conclude Chapter Two by suggesting how we will use our discussion of ideology in describing the six major human services systems in subsequent chapters.

THE CONSERVATIVE PERSPECTIVE

Philosophical and Social Beliefs

Conservatism can be defined as a series of beliefs or an attitude toward life, that is, as a certain way of viewing the world. In the conservative perspective the great matters of society in any generation are influenced by (1) maintaining continuity of traditions, (2) opposing any social change that is not carefully monitored and controlled, and (3) questioning "all utopian reform movements allegedly based on reason" (Wingo, 1965, p. 28).

The conservatism that characterizes modern America has evolved, according to Wingo, specifically from the classical conservatism of the British and more generally from the "great tradition" of Western culture. From the classical conservatism of the British as expressed by John Locke (1632–1704) and Edmund Burke (1729–1797), conservatism accepts in varying degrees the following three tenets outlined by Wingo: (1) The belief in an Infinite Being or First Cause who is the source of everything that is and who determines the course of history. "Although there are various sectarian and doctrinal differences about the details of this cosmology, the thesis of an ultimate source of power and authority that transcends nature is central to this tradition" (p. 30). (2) The belief that all generations of human beings are bound by a great contract that restricts any single generation from altering and destroying the existing pattern of society. This applies to alterations attempted by nonviolent social reform movements as well as by radical or revolutionary ones. "To uproot institutions and ways of life is a breach of faith both with the generations that are gone and those that are yet to come. This is the ultimate immorality and the road to social chaos" (p. 30). (3) A conception of human nature that is both pessimistic and optimistic. It is pessimistic because it holds that all persons are tainted with original sin and thus, in their imperfect, capricious state, need to be controlled by tradition. It is optimistic because it assumes that "if the continuity of tradition can be maintained, every generation will have a source of wisdom to which it can turn for guidance" (p. 30). Although individuals can trust their initiative and judgment in the routine matters of daily life, they tend to be foolish about anything beyond the ordinary affairs and must rely on the wisdom of their ancestors. Therefore optimism comes not from faith in human nature or the abilities of individuals but from "faith in the accumulated wisdom of all the generations that is available to guide men of any generation through their own perplexities and crises if they will only take advantage of it" (p. 30).

Conservatism also embraces the foundations of the "great tradition" of Western culture. It finds its values and standards in the Hebraic ethic; the philosophy of ancient Greece, especially the Idealism of Plato; and a conception of God and human beings based on the teachings of Christ. Conservatism is marked by an unending quest for meaning in all existence.

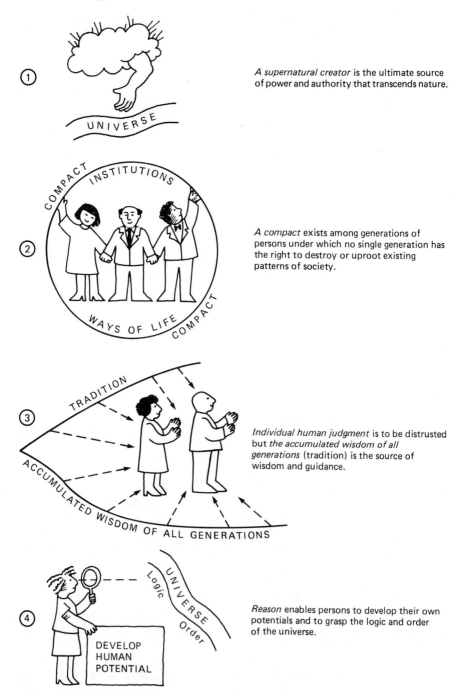

A *supernatural creator* is the ultimate source of power and authority that transcends nature.

A *compact* exists among generations of persons under which no single generation has the right to destroy or uproot existing patterns of society.

Individual human judgment is to be distrusted but *the accumulated wisdom of all generations* (tradition) is the source of wisdom and guidance.

Reason enables persons to develop their own potentials and to grasp the logic and order of the universe.

FIGURE 2–1.   Tenets accepted, in varying degrees, by conservatives.

It seeks the fullest development of the mind, which it views as the most precious and unique part of each individual. In turn its conception of the world is one in which human reasoning enjoys a preeminent status.

In embracing the "great tradition" in Western culture conservatism holds that we live in a world that is stable and understandable through reason. Because all persons possess minds, they are capable of attaining a reasonable grasp of individual nature and the stable principles on which the external world is based. Hence the mind transcends biological and social nature and is humanity's most valuable possession.

In this emphasis on the primacy of the mind and the distinctiveness of each individual, conservatives view human beings as occupying a unique place among the creatures of the earth because they possess a power of mind that enables them to discern the logic and order inherent in the universe and to recall the past and foresee the future. Other creatures are controlled by instincts and immediate circumstances, but humans, guided by reason, can move beyond passions, act freely, and develop their own potentials. Through disciplined habits they can discard their immediate animal nature and attain a distinctly human nature of self-reflection and reason. This kind of human development can be realized through the nurture and external discipline provided by institutions such as the family, church, community, and human services themselves.

The conservative perspective thus emphasizes both individual initiative and the continuity of traditional institutions, beliefs, and practices that have been developed through the sacrifices and efforts of past generations. Because most conservatives believe the world is a reflection of a supernatural creator, or at least displays an unchanging logic and basic order, and because human beings can use disciplined effort to develop the powers of reason through which the reflected, unchanging values and meanings that guide life can be discovered, conservatism attaches great importance to the individual's participation in the discovery of these values and the building of appropriate traditions. In terms of its distinctly social and political assumptions, therefore, the conservative perspective sees that the inherent worth of individuals warrants that they be free to do what they want with their lives as long as they do not infringe on the claims and rights of others who are free. At the same time it recognizes certain basic social institutions as special repositories of values: the family as the cornerstone of society, the church as the center of accumulation of core cultural values, the state as the stabilizing political force, and the school as the essential transmitter of culture and values.

For conservatism the major dilemma in all this lies in how these assumptions function as a distinct social and political ideology, because in a less-than-perfect world emphasis on individual initiative is not always consistent with preserving the best of the cultural status quo. In fact the prevailing conservative social and political ideology in contemporary America imperfectly reflects the conservative tradition as it deals with this dilemma by attempting to limit individual initiative primarily to material concerns (for instance, pursuing economic self-interest in a "free" marketplace) while at the same time encouraging individuals to accept and profess (often uncritically) commonly held political and social doctrines. Ultimately this contemporary conservative ideology assumes that when individuals work for their own economic self-interest, the common good of the whole society will be well served. Whether such a belief is warranted, it at least tends to deemphasize many traditional cultural concerns and to suggest that the political state, despite its potential as a repository for humanizing values, exists only to enable individuals to avoid overt conflicts as they pursue self-interest defined primarily in material terms. Many conservatives, of course, object to the ways they believe the contemporary ideology delimits and distorts traditional conservative concerns.

Human Services Theory and Practice

The key conservative beliefs in tradition, in the worth and integrity of the individual, and in the proper unfolding of the mind shape the conservative conception of the purpose, design, and role of the human services systems. Conservative ideology places a major emphasis on the experiences of society throughout the ages as human services have striven to preserve and transmit the essential heritage of culture and the accepted values that are the core of Western civilization. According to conservatives each of the six basic human services systems should be committed to the support and further refinement, rather than to the significant change, of those institutions and beliefs that have been erected at great cost and sacrifice by the predecessors of the present period of culture. For instance, the systems of personal social services, health services, income transfer services, and housing and urban environment services should all seek to use their various operations to strengthen the structure of family life in America. They should support such socially accepted functions as the reproduction and nurturance of children within the family unit as the primary means of socialization into the culture and its traditional values. The education services system should seek to transmit the essential principles of Western civilization through a curriculum of time-tested content, orderly sequence, structured presentations, and guided discipline. It should introduce and enculturate each generation into the socially accepted and established institutions, mores, beliefs, and practices of the Western heritage. The justice and public safety services system should seek to secure the physical safety, freedom of movement, and ownership of property of all members of society. It should be directed at ensuring that the basic American rights of life, liberty, and property are not infringed upon.

The conservative belief in order, structure, and control through established institutions leads to the development of human services marked by a clearly defined, formal, central hierarchy that carefully monitors programs designed to discourage the continual dependency of clients. The goal is the speedy return of the client to normal functioning within society without further dependency on human services systems, and in modern America conservative practices consistent with this goal include the case study or casework approach with its emphasis on individual diagnosis and evaluation.

In the specific casework approach approved by conservatives, each client is viewed as a unique person with a unique problem that must receive individualized treatment, but the caseworker must define each problem in terms of the individual's deviance from healthy norms, usually norms of the social order. For most problems clients should recognize their individual pathologies, accept blame when warranted, and cooperate in the process of their restoration to normal functioning. Although the concern for the uniqueness of each individual embodied in the conservative approach to social casework is consistent with the assumptions of modern social casework in general, the conservative emphasis on the individual's deviance from the norms of the social order as the source of problems is consistent with much older approaches to helping. Thus even in terms of contemporary casework the conservative perspective serves to encourage a role for human services of facilitating adjustment of individuals to existing situations and to discourage a role of promoting social reform.

Role of the worker. The conservative belief in order, structure, and control through established institutions also leads to a dominant role for the human services worker and a passive one for the client or recipient. The worker, as the agent of the established institutions, becomes the initiator, developer, and evaluator of the various efforts by the human services systems to assure the production and distribution of goods and services that are critical to conserving and maximizing human resources. Initiative thus lies with the worker, who must (1) identify and define the client's problem or need; (2) select what is relevant to dealing with that problem or need from among society's ideology and public policies and the vast collection of laws, agencies, and programs that make up society's investment in human services; (3) incorporate what is relevant into a program specifically designed to resolve the client's difficulty; and (4) establish criteria for assessing the effectiveness of the program imposed. Although in practice these tasks are often shared by many human services workers, it is still the worker, either individually or collectively, who is at the center of the helping process and who determines and controls the three critical ingredients of the process: (1) the nature of the aid (What kind of help should be given?), (2) the method of implementation (How should the help be given?), and (3) the form of evaluation (Has the help made a difference?). In directing this process the worker seeks to rehabilitate the client by providing solutions to problems that will support the existing social order and return the client as quickly as possible to the mainstream of the community. Conservatism recognizes that this critical role assigned to human services workers requires that they be highly qualified professionally, well balanced emotionally, and deeply committed morally and spiritually to human growth and development.

Role of the client.   In the conservative approach the client, as the human resource that remains deficient of spiritual or material norms of the established institutions, becomes the passive, conforming recipient who is expected to accept and to be grateful for any help that may be offered. The place of clients within the helping process is determined by their failure to function successfully within a social order that is, according to the conservatives, considered viable and rewarding by most of its members. This inability of certain individuals to cope with the day-to-day demands of attaining physical, emotional, and social well-being within this order places clients in a role in which they are required to defer to the judgments of human services workers and to accept the programs those workers suggest. Although the help offered may indeed represent a positive good to clients, its acceptance may also require clients to cultivate submissiveness and self-discipline and to change their thinking, personal habits, or life style. For all these reasons clients must defer to the authority of workers and conform to worker-imposed solutions or programs to be free from any future need for human services and to return to appropriate functioning in the social order.

Education services as a conservative example.   Among the human services systems education services provide one of the clearest examples of conservative beliefs. In the operating model of education that conservatives encourage, the relationship between worker and client is one in which the worker is dominant and the client is passive.

Conservatism views education as the art of transmitting an essential core of subject matter, skills, and values to a receptive but passive and uninformed learner. The worker, or teacher, selects the subject matter, sets the climate of the classroom, maintains accurate records, demands preparation and effort, and motivates the students to learn through personal example. Learning is not necessarily pleasurable, but through diligence the teacher has mastered the subject and the students are expected to follow suit. The client, or student, becomes a spectator to the teacher's presentation, and evaluation is based on the learner's ability to re-present what has been witnessed. An educational environment that includes structured courses, obedience to and respect for teachers, grades, tracking, homework, and school rules and regulations is constructed to ensure that students fully apply themselves to the subject matter at hand. Teachers exert external discipline to foster self-discipline, or the subordination of present desires for less immediate ends, among the students. The progress of students is determined by the degree to which they learn the values, skills, and bodies of knowledge essential to their understanding the world and participating in society. In this example the services provided are intended to promote the normal, healthy development of students, who thus are deemed neither pathological nor culpable for not having learned what has not previously been presented; nonetheless, onus falls on students who do not make normal progress toward the ends that have been properly presented to them by their teachers and their schools.

Analogous roles in other systems.   In other human services systems analogous roles and procedures prevail within the conservative approach. For instance, the dominant role of worker and the passive role of client define the nature of their relationship. Particularly in personal social services and health care services, but also in the other human services systems, the worker as care giver identifies the client's problems or needs and then selects or designs the program or service that will rehabilitate the client; that is, workers provide solutions that will support the social status quo and return the client as quickly as possible to the mainstream of the community. The client assumes a passive, dependent role, conforming to the worker-imposed solution or program in an effort to improve the situation and to be free from any future need for services. For conservatives the worker is considered to be normal, healthy, and socially adjusted, at least within the limits necessary to carry out a professional role and to provide a specific service. The client is viewed as being crippled by a problem and therefore damaged or deficient in some way. It is the worker who, acting as an agent for the society, has the authority, expertise, vision, and strategy necessary to identify, understand, and help resolve the client's problem. Conservatives tend to measure the success of their services and programs in terms of the rapidity and extent to which clients cease to be dependent on the services system. The conservative goal of human services is to free clients of their particular problem and in turn of the need for further goods and services. For example, the success of workers' efforts can be measured by the number of clients who no longer require AFDC (Aid to Families with Dependent Children) payments, food stamps, housing subsidies, counseling, corrective medical care, or incarceration.

Conservative Ideas about Social Change

The conservative's faith in established institutions leads to a view of human services as servants of culture, especially in passing on or adjusting people to the hard-won ideas, values, institutions, practices, and cultural forms that enhance the quality of life. Ultimately truth and the nature of the world itself are viewed as unchanging, and without this conserving and transmitting function of human services culture would tend to crumble, knowledge discovered by past generations would be lost, and people would once again be forced to rely on methods of trial and error throughout their lives. Consequently conservatives believe that the human services systems should not mirror all characteristics of the still imperfect society in which they exist. Rather they should cherish and conserve the best that a culture has produced and pass on this heritage to future generations. The task of human services is thus to strengthen, conserve, and refine those personal and social virtues that have been established over time and are critical for the preservation of society. As further search and evaluation lead to the discovery of other virtues necessary for social progress, human services will slowly incorporate, conserve, and transmit them as well.

The improvement of society therefore must necessarily be gradual. Conservatives reject attempts at rapid change through massive government intervention for fear they will result in the suppression of individual initiative and the destruction of self-sufficiency and selfhood. Consequently the various programs of the human services systems should be viewed as a means of providing individuals with only those personal and material goods necessary to permit them to attain self-sufficiency, and not as a means to some larger end such as alteration of the social order. In other words conservatives view helping professionals primarily as technicians-implementers chiefly occupied in picking up the pieces of those who break under the burdens of modern society. Rather than attempting to influence and change social policy, conservatives accept the social order with its established values and institutions, and they view the helping professions as providing an instrument of adjustment to this order for those with social problems.

Conservatives recognize that the provision of human services is not always adequate, but they do not advocate social reform because of these inadequacies. They are confident that the services will fulfill their roles of meeting specific problems and individual needs when the services are properly supported. Therefore conservatives seek to improve the services through better funding, staffing, and use of modern techniques of delivery. Their efforts are directed toward obtaining support for, coordinating, and delivering high-quality services consistent with these goals.

The Conservative Perspective Summarized

Given all these characteristics of the conservative perspective, conservatives tend to prefer selective rather than universal approaches to human services, delivery of hard rather than soft goods and services, provision of services primarily by voluntary and private rather than public agencies, and workers trained to diagnose and directly control immediate symptoms and problems rather than to engage clients in understanding and personally combating remote causes of their problems. In contemporary America these preferences certainly do not result in human services systems that can be classified as purely conservative, for only a very few conservatives actually reject the nonpreferred alternatives at all times and under all circumstances. However, these preferences tend to reflect conservative beliefs such as that the society should be assumed to represent the best of traditional culture until specific breakdowns are identified, that even then the individuals receiving aid are probably defective themselves and should receive aid only until normalcy can be restored, and that aid should be direct and should be financed and delivered as much as possible by personal and private initiatives. In short the conservative is not against the development of effective human services systems and the use of modern methods such as social casework, but rather remains skeptical and tends to see such systems as contingent rather than necessary social inventions, useful primarily in dealing with specific problems brought about by personal weaknesses, unavoidable natural circumstances, or correctable faults in a society that represents the best of traditional culture.

THE LIBERAL PERSPECTIVE

Philosophical and Social Beliefs

Liberalism, like conservatism, can be defined as a series of beliefs or an attitude toward life that represents a certain way of viewing the world. Also like conservatism it can trace its roots far back into history, but it is a perspective with a twentieth-century orientation. In fact unlike conservatism, liberalism is concerned not with tradition, authority, and stability but with contemporary society, democracy, and change. Emphasis in liberalism falls on the immediate situations in which individuals find themselves and the ways in which they can change those situations to solve the problems they encounter within them. Most liberals do not reject the wisdom of the past as a means of coping with present situations, but they stress the necessity of flexibility and experimentation and the use of what has become known as the scientific attitude with its reliance on scientific method as a way of understanding and changing the world. Hence liberalism is far more skeptical of fixed solutions than is conservatism and stresses the use of human intelligence and careful, empirical study of the contemporary world to bring about change. It emphasizes the individual's ability to discern the character of modern society and the ability of individuals collectively or democratically to restructure it for the better.

The major historical roots of the liberal perspective are found in the British and French liberal tradition of the seventeenth and eighteenth

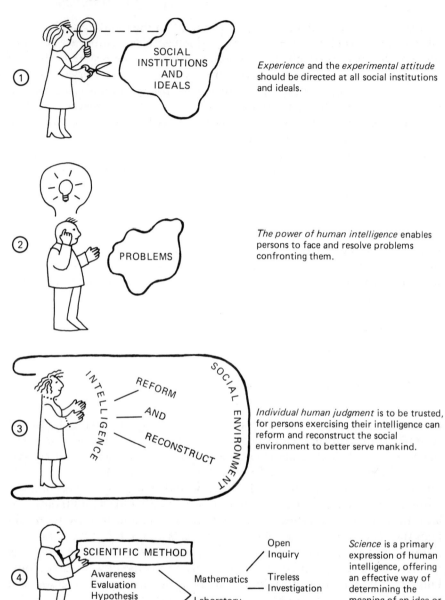

The descriptions accompanying the figure read:

1. *Experience* and the *experimental attitude* should be directed at all social institutions and ideals.

2. *The power of human intelligence* enables persons to face and resolve problems confronting them.

3. *Individual human judgment* is to be trusted, for persons exercising their intelligence can reform and reconstruct the social environment to better serve mankind.

4. *Science* is a primary expression of human intelligence, offering an effective way of determining the meaning of an idea or the plan of action for the resolution of a problem.

FIGURE 2–2.   Tenets accepted, in varying degrees, by liberals.

centuries, particularly as shaped by the writings of philosophers such as Francis Bacon (1561–1626), John Locke, and Jean Jacques Rousseau (1712–1778). Bacon's description of the inductive method laid the foundation for modern experimental science and challenged the dominance of scholastic philosophy with its emphasis on a fixed universe, which had prevailed through the Middle Ages. Locke extended Bacon's ideas by suggesting a practical psychology that held that because the mind at birth is blank, all knowledge is derived from sensory contact with the world. Locke also asserted that all people are equal and independent by nature and that the political state therefore is formed by a social contract among those governed and should be guided by a belief in their natural rights. Rousseau stressed a natural approach to living and education that would allow children to develop without interference and to be protected from the corrupting influence of established institutions. Formed around ideas such as these, the liberal tradition emphasizes the power of individuals to understand and change the world.

According to Wingo (1965), twentieth-century liberalism accepts the following tenets from this liberal tradition in varying degrees: (1) An "emphasis on experience and on an experimental attitude toward social institutions and social ideals" (p. 140). Liberals believe that all established institutions and socially accepted ideals must be subjected to regular examination and—when necessary—altered. These institutions and ideals should never be raised to such an exalted status by tradition that they fall beyond the purview of critical scrutiny. While tradition may be one of the measurements considered in establishing the worth of institutions and ideals, the most significant criterion must be how well these institutions and ideals serve human welfare. (2) "An abiding faith in the potential power of human intelligence" (p. 140). Liberals believe that humans have the ability to face and resolve the problems of their times and that through the proper exercise of their intelligence they can improve society and secure a better life for all. Acting intelligently involves embracing the spirit of scientific inquiry and using empirical evidence and logical principles to solve problems perceived by human beings as they experience the world. Intelligence is thus a means of linking individual experience and constructive social action. (3) An optimistic view of the nature of human beings. Unlike conservatives, who distrust human judgment and defer to the wisdom of tradition in all matters beyond ordinary affairs of daily life, liberals believe that people exercising intelligence—properly nurtured by education—can make the necessary decision to enjoy self-government, freedom, and development. Hence human nature in its original state is seen as essentially good and not as contaminated by original sin. "If evil is not inherent in human nature, then it must stem from the environment, particularly the social environment. Immoral society produces immoral men, and the elimination of evil from human nature must involve the reform and reconstruction of social institutions" (p. 141).

Twentieth-century liberalism is also closely associated with the philosophical position of pragmatism. Pragmatism emerged in America at the end of the nineteenth century partly in response to the changing social and cultural milieu. As Americans experienced the Industrial Revolution and the expansion of experimental science during the nineteenth century, they came to accept the values of temporal existence and to believe they could change and improve it. They stressed independence, hard work, and ability to understand and change the environment as a means to material success, and they became increasingly skeptical of institutions and religious or secular beliefs that blindly supported tradition, authority, and the status quo. Furthermore the development of democracy as both a way of life and a form of government allowed Americans to enjoy freedom of thought and action on an unprecedented mass scale and to cherish with increasing justification ideals such as social equality and the individual pursuit of happiness.

Pragmatism was greatly influenced by the ideas of American philosophers Charles Sanders Peirce (1839–1914) and William James (1842–1910), and it was developed into a complete system of thought by John Dewey. Peirce was concerned with the relation of ideas to experience. He insisted that ideas have meaning only when they make a difference in experience, that is, when they "work." Peirce believed that science offers the best method for determining the meaning of an idea because scientific method, which is based upon measurement, mathematics, and laboratory precision, deals with real things, uncovering data that can be satisfactorily explained only in terms of their meaning for human experience.

James expanded on Peirce's ideas by conceiving the distinctly pragmatic method of determining the meaning of each idea through its practical consequences. The truth of an idea, James believed, is not a static quality but is found only in the consequences of the idea when acted upon. Therefore the validation of the truth of an idea is found in the experience of the individual who determines its usefulness and meaning in terms of the specific situation of the individual. The pragmatic method of determining truth links the external world with the thought, action, experience, and meaning of the individual. The individual encounters and reacts to the external world, changing it and determining meaning and truth in terms of the consequences wrought.

During the early twentieth century Dewey, America's most influential philosopher, developed these ideas and others into a comprehensive philosophy that combined pragmatic methods, personal experience, and social vision. His philosophy both reflected much of the essential character of American life at the turn of the century, especially its energy and optimism, and further shaped that character in subsequent decades. Dewey emphasized that human experiences can be valued in terms of their influence on the development or healthy growth of later experiences; the end of healthy experiences is the growth of even better experiences. Thus as individuals interact with their environments ideas are validated as true only as they help individuals to undergo high-quality experiences within the unfolding situations. Neither truth nor value is a static quality, for both must be verified and constantly reverified within the context of individual experience as each person repeatedly reacts to and acts to alter an ever-changing world. According to Dewey the development of intelligence, as demonstrated through the solution of personal and social problems arising from interactions with the changing world, is the highest form of human growth and the clearest criterion of truth and value. The optimal conditions for intelligently directed experimentation, full growth, and active problem-solving are found only in a democratic society because there the individual has the most complete freedom to test ideas both in the interest of society and in self-interest, and because such a social structure is in itself amenable to intelligently directed reconstruction. Thus pragmatism as a philosophy emphasizes experience, intelligence, growth, and constructive social action within an ever-changing, democratic environment.

Twentieth-century liberalism incorporates the basic tenets of both the older liberal tradition and pragmatic philosophy. The major dilemma in this liberal perspective's function as a distinct social and political ideology lies in the expectation that when individuals choose and act on their own ideological beliefs (within certain limits), they also ultimately act for the general welfare. In this sense liberalism is an act of faith. It is built on the effort to extend a sense of common purpose or community beyond the individual, family, or neighborhood to the society as a whole. It does so by attempting to provide to all citizens the economic and social conditions necessary to promote maximum individual development. In then pursuing enlightened self-interest, each citizen is presumed to act for the good of all others. Individuals and society should thus improve in a tandem, ongoing relationship. The political state exists necessarily, but only to optimize conditions for individual development and to help define collective interests.

In fact although many citizens of the United States have been provided personal, social, and economic circumstances highly conducive to full growth, many have not so developed. Some have acted in ways that are clearly antithetical to the common interest. Others have never received favorable circumstances. In America's drift toward an egalitarian society and in the liberal social policies actively pursued by the federal government during much of the twentieth century lie seeds of disappointment, alienation, and rebellion when the liberal promise remains unfulfilled. Critics of liberalism can thus point to real shortcomings in society and claim that the act of faith is unwarranted, that the failure of liberal practices to reconstruct a better society has undermined liberal values, and that further liberal efforts threaten to collapse under their own weight. Defenders of liberalism are quick to point out constructive changes in society that have occurred and quite plausibly argue that although society remains imperfect, these defects may be the result of too little, not too much, liberal ideology and practice.

Human Services Theory and Practice

The key liberal beliefs in the power of intelligence, an experimental attitude, and the test of consequences and an emergent truth shape the liberal conception of the purpose, design, and role of the human services systems. Inherent in this view of a universe of process and change and of the human being as an experiencing animal is a faith in the power of human intelligence to experiment with social institutions and to build a better society and life. The role of government and the human services systems is to support individual freedom and development and to avoid constraining the individual and shaping relationships within society. The human services systems exist only to advance human welfare, and if they fail to do so they should be changed or abolished.

Education, as one of the human services systems, has as its objective the practice and improvement of the power of intelligence. Education thus occupies a central place in liberal theory, for intelligence guides the functioning of all human services systems and the development of society itself. Liberals oppose the conservative views of learning as the reception of knowledge and of knowledge as an abstract substance supplied by teachers and stored in the minds of passive students. Rather liberals believe in learning through problem-solving in which knowledge becomes an instrument actively used by involved students for controlling experience and coping with new and emerging situations. Knowledge gains significance only as it is actively acquired and welded to experience. For liberals all human services systems, regardless of their specific functions, also undertake such educational functions, for all should actively engage their clients in intelligent problem-solving. Therefore the success of human services should be measured not only in terms of the number of clients freed from problems and restored to normal functioning but also in terms of the number of clients who have profited by their experiences and learned to govern their own lives intelligently, particularly to avoid or better cope with similar problems again. Within the liberal perspective the development of this kind of individual intelligence is viewed as an integral and educational function of all human services systems.

The liberals' experimental approach toward social ideals and institutions leads to the development of human services marked by variability, informality, uniqueness, and independence. Programs are flexible and directed at promoting self-help. The emphasis is on encouraging greater client involvement in developing policy, programing, and rendering services. Worker and client become colleagues and thus develop a relationship

that seeks to uphold the self-respect of the clieι t, who, as an active participant in the resolution of the problem, avoids being ʳeduced to the potentially dehumanizing role of helpless, passive recipient. This relationship
also seeks to uphold the worth and integrity of the worker, who, as a
partner contributing to the resolution of the client's problem, avoids an
authoritarian role that might prove exploitative and self-serving.

Role of the worker.   The liberal belief in experimentation and experience and in the principles of democracy leads to the sharing of authority
between human services workers and clients. In this egalitarian view of the
helping relationship the worker is simultaneously the colleague and the
guide of the client. Both worker and client may initiate, develop, and test
human services policies and practices that will address the problems and
needs of the client. As a colleague the worker identifies with the client's
problems and treats the client as an equal. As a guide the worker uses
professional expertise, training, and experience to help the client identify
and understand problems, to serve as a resource for the knowledge and
referrals the client needs, and to suggest specific strategies and practices
for the solution of problems. In this relationship it is as if worker and client
share a common problem and both benefit from the common efforts to
resolve it. The client of course benefits directly from the solution and also
gains experience in how to avoid or better cope with similar problems. The
worker benefits professionally in refining expertise, psychically in seeing a
fellow human being through a difficult situation, and personally in sharing
in the common social good that may be created by the solution of one
person's problems.

Often, in fact, solutions to a client's problem require the worker to
identify the roots of the problem within the prevailing social situation, and
the solution may incorporate some change in or accommodation by society
itself. The role of the worker in identifying with the client's problem may
ꞏ1en become a catalyst for constructive social change, and in this case it is
ꞏ1ot necessary for worker and client to share a common problem in a com-
ꞏplete and literal sense. For example, it may be only the client who is suffering from alcoholism but both client and worker may come to understand
how certain causes of alcoholism are rooted in society itself in, for instance,
the general social attitudes about the use of alcohol, the specific images the
society portrays about drinking, and even the vested economic interests of
manufacturers and sellers of alcoholic beverages and of governments that
raise revenues through taxes derived from sales of alcohol. Although not
all members of society suffer from alcoholism, all suffer from the same
pressures connected with the social causes of alcoholism, and all must live
with the consequences within a society in which a certain proportion of its
members succumb to these pressures and become alcoholics. Therefore the
worker may help the client overcome the immediate problem with alcohol

but both may also attempt to change society to mitigate the social causes of alcoholism. While the worker may serve as a resource in terms of specific knowledge, referrals, and the like not available to the client (thus far a role similar to that of the conservative worker), basic liberal ideology about the nature of social change incorporates the specific belief that "worker and client are fundamentally in the same boat. The worker does not cease to be a resource. However, he becomes a resource *and* a political ally of the client" (Galper, 1978, p. 41 [emphasis in the original]). Our later discussion of liberal ideas about social change will identify the two groups of liberals: those who advocate indirect means of social change and those who advocate direct means. The latter group, especially when it encourages social activism, can be considered as taking the "radical" approach to human services.

Role of the client.   The liberal faith in the power of intelligence to provide people with the ability to face and resolve the problems of their times leads to a client-centered approach to the helping relationship. Clients become actively involved in the resolution of their problems by participating directly in decision-making, implementation, and evaluation. First, they help identify and define their problems. This help is based on how they see themselves experiencing problems and on what they believe the problems mean to them. Second, they review suggested strategies and approaches to their problems and may modify these suggestions into increasingly effective plans of action. Their reviews and modifications are based on the insights they have gained by experiencing their problems. Third, they team with human services workers and share in the rewards and frustrations that accompany the direction and operation of the plans selected. And fourth, they help devise and evaluate the implemented programs in terms of the resolution of their problems and the satisfaction of their own and others' long-term needs. Thus clients are cast in a role in which they view themselves not as failures and deviants outside the mainstream of a viable social order but rather as responsible and involved members of a not-too-perfect social order struggling to resolve their own problems and perhaps even the problems of others.

Education services as a liberal example.   Among the human services systems education services provide one of the clearest examples of liberal beliefs. In the operating model of education that liberals encourage, the relationship between worker and client is one of colleagues. Liberalism views education as a process of student-centered learning and activity or learning by doing. The worker, or teacher, does not direct but advises, and the interests of the client, or student, determine what is to be learned. The teacher's role is one of a colleague who places greater knowledge and experience at the disposal of the student in the pursuit of mutually agreeable ends. The teacher may present knowledge to students but the purpose is not for students to obtain knowledge for its own sake. Instead knowledge is treated as potentially changeable bodies of information for students to use in developing their intelligence and guiding their living. The emphasis is on teaching students how to think, and students enjoy freedom of movement and choice. The school becomes a laboratory in which the students, using inductive thought, seek to cope with perplexities directly, overtly, and experimentally. Through careful evaluation and the reconstruction of previous experiences students use knowledge as an instrument for resolving problems by developing their own ideas or plans of action and formulating generalizations to apply to future circumstances.

In the liberal perspective the school thus becomes a miniature community in which students are allowed to interact freely with one another in an environment that stresses partnership and cooperation over competition and pursuit of individual success. The group standards and pressures that develop in such a social environment are directed at humanizing students and promoting purposeful activity and harmonious order in the classroom. Discipline results from the educational undertaking itself (accuracy, perseverance, industry) and is based on students' commitment to rules and regulations that they have helped to draw up as members of the group.

Analogous roles in other systems.   In other human services systems analogous roles and activities prevail within the liberal approach. The interaction and relationship of worker with client are defined by their respective roles as colleague and guide or active participant. For instance, the movement to expand services to families with dependent members that will encourage the family to continue providing care is consistent with the liberal perspective. It sees the adequacy of care for the elderly as not solely dependent on the technical proficiency of human services workers but also on the involvement and active cooperation of family members who serve as the primary support system and who fulfill the day-to-day caring responsibilities. Human services workers, from physicians to house helpers, seek to work closely with the family and to support it with their skills, but the caring environment is initiated and maintained by family members who seek to respond to the developing and frequently unique needs of their dependent elderly members.

Similarly, within the liberal perspective workers should view the recipients of family counseling and planning services as actively participating in defining and solving their own problems, the residents of publicly subsidized housing as being willing to maintain and to improve their environments, and even convicted criminals as being potentially capable of rehabilitation. The goal of all human services systems is not simply to free clients from immediate problems but also, by identifying and working as colleagues with them, to help them direct their lives with increasing intelligence in the future.

Liberal Ideas about Social Change

Whereas conservatives are skeptical about social change in general and tend to view as desirable only slow, evolutionary improvement in the established order of things, liberals see social change as an inevitable result of the development of human intelligence, particularly as individuals carefully and critically scrutinize their surroundings and act to improve their lives. Although social change may be either evolutionary or abrupt, a basic issue for liberals is whether change should be primarily an incidental result of individual human development or an intentional result of collective human action. Both liberal approaches to this issue follow from basic liberal philosophical and social beliefs.

Because liberalism denies or at least disregards any supernatural influence on human nature, liberals view clients as children of nature, not of God. The liberal emphasis is on finding the causes of the shortcomings, failures, and misconduct of clients in their heredity and environment rather than in their persons. Therefore if clients continually fail or misbehave, liberalism advocates either the study of society and the related economic, political, and cultural factors or the reevaluation of the human services programs available. The needs, interests, and desires of clients are not evil in themselves; rather they are morally neutral. Liberals are optimistic that these needs, interests, and desires can be directed toward socially acceptable and useful ends and therefore that they may serve as a basis for all human services systems. As they are met society will change for the better.

The liberal perspective encourages cooperation rather than competition. People are viewed as being social by nature and as deriving their greatest satisfaction from their relationships with one another. Liberals seek to develop the higher social side of human nature, and they view love and partnership as more appropriate to the realization of this end than competition and the pursuit of individual success. All civilized living therefore must ultimately be a group experience, for the way to an ethical life is by associating and living with others in morally significant situations. This belief and its concomitant actions should suffuse all human services systems.

The liberal belief that truth and values are at best tentative and subject to individual verification within changing social contexts leads to the expectation that human services should be critical of the existing social order while at the same time being responsive to the emergent needs of society in changing times. Because change should be intelligently directed, human services should seek to cultivate an attitude of doubt and uncertainty about prevailing conditions that will encourage workers and clients to question truths held sacred by past generations and to rebuild values to meet present needs. Questioning should begin with the immediate problems and conditions that workers and clients face but then should extend into constructive criticism of society itself, including carefully observing, collecting data, analyzing, and proposing changes not only as solutions to society's most pressing and tangible problems but also as alternatives to society's most cherished beliefs about topics such as religion, politics, science, ethics, aesthetics, and social policies.

This kind of questioning of immediate circumstances and social values promotes the individual development of workers and clients as they intelligently discover and apply the most effective means of coping with the practical problems with which they must deal. However it also promotes the reconstruction of society, for the most effective means of intelligently coping may include creating new conditions by finding and implementing new social arrangements and values.

Within the liberal perspective there are therefore two basic points of view about the relationship between individual development and social change. While all liberals view individual development and social change as closely connected and individual human services as functioning as an integral part of social life, some liberals see change in society as an incidental result of the more important purpose of promoting individual development; still other liberals see the reconstruction of society as at least as important as the individual development it promotes. Hence human services may be considered as either an indirect or direct means of social change. The first group of liberals holds that the problems of many clients arise because society is changing and that the best way of helping them solve their problems is by helping them to meet this change. Accordingly as clients develop their capacities to solve their problems intelligently, they may also participate with increasing effectiveness in the process of directing social change, but constructive social change remains an indirect result of the individual development arising from human services intended to help clients. These liberals tend to focus human services on the specific needs of clients. The second group of liberals believes that many of the problems of clients cannot be solved without first changing the social conditions that cause them; therefore they argue that human services should also focus on directing social change and should not merely accept it. Of course direct improvement of social conditions also promotes the individual development of clients and increases their ability to solve their problems intelligently, because clients are often trapped by conditions they alone cannot control and cannot begin to cope with their problems until those conditions improve. This second group of liberals tends to focus human services on changing society as a means of meeting the specific needs of clients and preventing similar needs from arising for others.

The radical approach.   Within the second group of liberals there are considerable differences about what social changes are desirable, how extensive they should be, and how they should be carried out; however this general point of view, which emphasizes changing society itself, can appropriately be called the "radical" approach to human services. In contemporary American society the word "radical" has many negative connotations, usually associated with excessive or mindless activism directed at tearing down viable institutions and values. Whether such negative connotations are justified, it should be remembered that excesses can be committed by advocates of any philosophical position and that intelligence is highly prized by both conservatives and liberals alike, whatever their specific beliefs. Furthermore honest differences of opinion may exist among people about what institutions and values are desirable and how quickly or in what ways society should change. Neither conservatives nor liberals believe that society cannot be improved. Therefore the radical approach to human services should be considered as simply one point within the continuum from extreme conservatism to extreme liberalism along which people grope for the best way to live and view the world. In this light the radical approach to human services can be considered as that position within liberalism that emphasizes the faults and problems within society and advocates direct means for changing them. In general radicals find faults in the economic, political, and social power structures of America and historically have advocated varying degrees of change through political activism emphasizing redistribution of wealth, egalitarianism, and commitment of resources to building a comprehensive human services system in the United States.

In attempting to find the best way to change society, whether indirectly or directly, liberals view human services in ethical terms. Liberals consider culture as an operational construct, a means of organizing and interpreting experiences directed toward ethical living. Whether workers attempt to prepare their clients for social change by developing the knowledge and critical spirit clients will need to cope with a changing society, or whether workers prefer to become direct agents of social change by preparing clients to exert direct control over the future by promoting and managing change itself, the goal of ethical living is the same. While the first of these two points of view about social change is the more conventional within the liberal perspective on human services, the second, the radical point of view, also has many advocates. Because radical human services workers see specific social problems as traceable to the structure of society itself, these workers believe that they can effectively address the problems of clients only through what amounts to moral activism within the larger society. Thus conventional social services solutions are seen as ineffective in the resolution of problems of individual clients because these problems have their roots in the structure of the social order. The particular problems of individuals reflect ethical shortcomings in the entire society that should be changed.

In the radical view the task of human services workers in helping clients becomes twofold: first, to provide clients with whatever immediate assistance is necessary and second, to aid clients in recognizing how their particular situations relate to the larger social order. In this latter role human services workers help clients to identify the political components of their problems and the ways in which political activity can contribute to their resolutions. Doing so constructively may raise the ethical standards of the entire society. Therefore the human services systems can combine consciousness-raising with services by helping clients take constructive social actions while at the same time providing for their material welfare. Galper (1978) suggests that the radical point of view is central to basic liberal assumptions:

> If the effort to solve a given problem is to be a serious one, the individual solution toward which the person with the problem is encouraged is linked with the collective solutions which will be required to change the social order in a fundamental way. That is, the required abortion counseling is linked, conceptually and programatically, with the larger issue of women's exploitation, the larger women's movement, and the relationship between women's liberation and human liberation at large. (pp. 38–39)

The liberal perspective thus encompasses both the indirect and direct approaches to managing social change and makes ethical concerns foremost in intelligently directed living in modern society.

The Liberal Perspective Summarized

Given all these characteristics of the liberal perspective, liberals naturally have a different set of preferences about human services systems than do conservatives. In general liberals tend to prefer universal rather than selective approaches to human services, delivery of both hard and soft goods and services, provision of services primarily through public rather than voluntary and private agencies, and workers trained to engage clients actively in understanding and personally combating the root causes of their problems rather than to offer only alleviation of symptoms. As was true for the conservative perspective, in contemporary America these preferences do not result in human services systems that can be classified as purely liberal, for most liberals see the practices that conservatives tend to prefer as starting points for the practices consistent with liberal preferences. For instance, although liberals encourage the delivery of human services through public agencies (on the grounds that the government, acting on behalf of all the people, has a special duty to promote the general welfare and therefore to develop special means to ensure that the social good is fully and equitably distributed), they see little reason to discourage or dismantle private agencies that function effectively as part of the overall system of delivery and that in fact may provide conditions for the general welfare higher than those minimal conditions toward which a public agency may aim. Although ideological conflicts can and do arise, liberals often wish to deepen or extend, rather than to reform or reconstruct, the human services practices that conservatives have undertaken. Nonetheless the liberals view human services not as something appended to society only to treat its contingent shortcomings but as the integral part of society through which society improves itself and a high quality of living is attained. Although their specific forms may change with changing circumstances, human services are viewed by liberals as necessary rather than contingent social inventions.

SOCIAL NORMS AND PUBLIC POLICY

The prevailing ideology in any culture contains certain beliefs that are so widely or firmly held that they may come to characterize that culture or to guide the actions of its members. Beliefs that have become so pervasive or influential that they drastically shape basic decisions and activities of most members of the society can be regarded as social norms, those portions of the overall ideology that most graphically embody the social values by which people live. Within any society—particularly a pluralistic or culturally complex one—differing social norms are not necessarily consistent with each other. Such inconsistencies can of course create extreme difficulties for citizens in choosing their individual actions or for the society at large in determining its collective actions, for instance in creating laws and enforcing sanctions against transgressors. Their influence, however pervasive, may or may not be direct. And despite their influence social norms may or may not be clearly understood and articulated. In any case social norms are ordinarily a very strong influence on the human services systems in any society, and in so far as they guide social actions they can be considered "an unwritten blend of what a people think their society ought to be, what they wish to do collectively for the good of all, and how they prefer to act to achieve such ends" (Morris, 1979, p. 16). Social norms therefore shape what a society will permit government to do for its people.

Social norms alone do not ordinarily guide the collective decisions and actions of a society, however. Whereas social norms may function as a kind of "collective unconscious" in decision-making, a society ordinarily sets up a more overt decision-making mechanism in an effort to tease out its own operative values, to formalize sound procedures of decision-making, and to suggest how these values apply generally (although within limits) rather than to specific cases. Such formal decisions, often referred to as public policies, are made by governments and may or may not be consistent with social norms; they also influence the human services systems as they struggle to assure the production and distribution of goods and services critical to conserving and maximizing human resources.

Unlike social norms public policy does not represent the mind-set of the people on all aspects of society's life. Rather it is formed by the beliefs, attitudes, and values of individuals and political parties in government and focuses on limited aspects of society. It "provides a guide as to the aims of governing to which priority is assigned and as to the means which are acceptable to or preferred by a particular government" (Morris, 1979, p. 17), and directs government in the selection of problems to be handled and the type of action to be taken. Public policy contains a level of guiding principles that may support or differ from social norms. When these principles conflict with social norms, tension results and government may either retreat by acceding to the standards of social norms or, especially in times of economic and social upheaval, move beyond the confines of social norms and develop new social policies. Examples of this are the New Deal of Franklin Roosevelt formulated in response to the Great Depression and the New Federalism of Ronald Reagan formulated in response to stagflation and recession in the late 1970s.

The services and goals of the human services systems in America are shaped by American ideology generally but particularly by the specific forms that ideology takes in both social norms and public policy. Reviews of human services from income transfer policies to health and personal social programs reveal the impact of major social norms and public policies that reflect the liberal principles of Franklin Roosevelt or Lyndon Johnson and the Democratic Party or the conservative principles of Ronald Reagan and the Republican Party. In subsequent chapters we conduct such reviews of each of the six human services systems. In preparation, however, let us briefly consider some major American social norms, how they reflect conservative or liberal ideology, and how public policies consistent with them have shaped practices in human services. In our subsequent reviews we will extend this analysis.

Five American Social Norms

Although there are many social norms within American ideology and considerable disagreement over what these are and how to describe them, Morris has identified five social norms widely accepted by Americans.[1]

1. *The belief in the virtue of work.* This belief has its roots in the Protestant ethic that salvation comes from work and good deeds. Americans believe that individuals should receive income from the exchange of their

---

[1]We have adopted Morris's (1979) classification of social norms and some of his ideas about them. The analyses that follow reflect our own ideas, however.

services for money and that their leisure must be earned by work. Some sort of a moral base or saving virtue is derived from work, whereas the prevailing view of the poor is that they are suspect because they tend to be lazy. As ideology this belief is primarily consistent with the conservative perspective, particularly the conservative emphasis on individual initiative and the assumption that those who require human services are likely to be in need because of some personal defect, in this case probably the unwillingness to work hard or the inability to work well. However this belief is also consistent with the liberal emphasis on the value of intelligent activity that improves both society and the individual worker, although liberals usually attempt to dissociate any moral stigma from "make work" programs for the poor. This social norm has been reinforced by countless public policy decisions in America—both conservative and liberal—that have attempted to lift the poor out of poverty by providing them work or to require work in return for welfare payments.

2. *The belief that government has an obligation to assist the helpless and weak.* Americans expect government to subsidize and provide services for vulnerable segments of the population such as the handicapped, widowed, abandoned, aged, orphaned, and unemployed. This belief runs almost directly counter to the previous social norm, although both can be held simultaneously if one assumes that the "vulnerable" who deserve subsidies are vulnerable through no fault of their own. This of course is true of many people handicapped, orphaned, and the like. As ideology this social norm is primarily consistent with the liberal perspective, particularly the liberal assumption that society has an obligation to provide all people with conditions that tend to maximize individual development. However it is also consistent to a lesser extent with the conservative belief that direct aid is permissible in cases in which the ordinary functions of society have broken down because of unavoidable natural circumstances. This social norm has been reinforced by public policies that provide subsidies to people within certain categories, for example payments to the aged, blind, disabled, and widowed, or unemployment compensation to people who have lost their jobs.

3. *The belief in progress through the resolution of problems by science and technology.* As Americans in the nineteenth and early twentieth centuries realized a sense of control over their physical surroundings through scientific procedures, their faith in progress and deliberate efforts to improve the world became a kind of national religion. There remains today the optimistic attitude that actions required to meet present difficulties should be viewed as short term because science and technology ultimately will remove current problems. Combined with the first social norm on the virtue of work, this belief appears to have conservative overtones, for work may be seen as a source of progress. However conservative ideology holds that work is hard and its own reward, whereas this norm suggests that

scientific and technological progress may require relatively little labor yet be virtually inevitable. As ideology, therefore, this belief is almost purely liberal. It is consistent with the liberal assumptions that society continually improves and that experimental methods and the scientific temper guide such improvements. Public policy decisions to support basic or applied research projects in the health sciences to improve health care services are among the examples that reinforce this norm.

4. *The belief in private-party or marketplace decision-making.* This belief has its roots in a tradition of individual rights and freedom inherent in nature and institutionalized in the laws of the land. Americans prefer "allowing marketplace forces the widest and fullest expression, that is, to find the solution to problems through the interaction of many decisions made privately, if at all possible" (Morris, 1979, p. 19). As ideology this belief is largely consistent with the conservative perspective, particularly conservative emphases on the worth of the individual; individual initiative; and guidance through the use of mind, the discovery of unchanging laws, and the stability of traditional institutions. However this belief also has liberal overtones, particularly in its consistency with the liberal assumptions that humans are inherently good and that they can make sound decisions for themselves because of the power of intelligence to solve problems and refine experience. It is inconsistent however with the liberal view of government as the final guarantor of conditions necessary for the common good. This social norm has been reinforced, for example, by public policy decisions that encourage the private delivery of health care services or the redevelopment of the urban environment through urban homesteading.

5. *The belief in government of shared responsibility.* This belief has its roots in a tradition of safeguarding individual liberties from infringements by central authority. Americans prefer to distribute authority and responsibility among the various levels of federal, state, and local governments. This social norm is consistent with some conservative beliefs but is more fully consistent with the liberal perspective. It is consistent with the conservative emphasis on individual initiative (and the inherent skepticism of governmental controls) but is at least partially inconsistent with the conservative view of the authority of traditional institutions. It is more fully consistent with the basic liberal emphases on the ability of each individual to participate completely in a democratically organized society with shared decision-making and on the existence of government only to maximize conditions for individual freedom. However during the last half-century many liberals as well as most conservatives have been skeptical of the tendency of certain social policies and programs aimed at aiding individuals to concentrate power in the federal government and thus to be at least potentially destructive of shared authority. Reinforcements of this social norm have included public policy decisions to maintain a decentralized system of schools, with legal authority remaining at the state level but much real

control in the hands of locally elected boards of education directly accessible to the immediate community.

ANALYZING THE HUMAN SERVICES SYSTEMS

As these brief examples of American social norms have shown, the ideological system in the United States is clearly not a pure type either in terms of its major social norms or its operative public policies. Both conservative and liberal values are inherent within this belief system, sometimes mixed together in bewildering arrays. Different social practices are in part consistent and in part inconsistent with various norms and policies. Public policies change as political parties enter or leave office or alter their ideological bents. Yet despite this seemingly messy state of affairs the human services in America, as guided by the ideological beliefs of the people, are by no means irrational or incomprehensible. They can be understood and can in fact be shaped by careful actions consistent with deliberate thought and critical analysis. As we have suggested in this chapter, the various approaches to human services as a means of dealing with the basic social problems of America and enhancing the quality of American life can be placed along an ideological continuum that ranges from the more conservative to the more liberal perspective. Along this continuum different points of view blend into one another and gradually shift from a position of extreme dependence on conservative tenets of the tried, time-tested, established, traditional, and rational to a position of extreme dependence on the liberal tenets of experimentation, change, relativism, contemporaneity, and empiricism. An examination of the ways in which these opposing positions with their different ideological bases and sharply contrasting theories and practices apply specifically to each of the six human services systems is necessary for an understanding of the ongoing struggle in contemporary America to develop an effective approach to human services.

Our examination in subsequent chapters of the six human services systems focuses on both the general characteristics of each system and some of their specific practices and problems. We briefly describe the general organizational pattern each system has taken in the United States and then analyze in more detail one or more of the specific subareas that comprise that system. In examining both general and specific characteristics of the six human services systems in light of the basic ideas about the nature of human services raised in Chapters One and Two, we hope to provide a reasonably comprehensive description of the human services and their function in America. There are however at least two practical limitations that constrain this examination. First, there exists considerable overlap between the systems. Therefore attempting to draw well-defined boundaries between them—even for the purposes of analysis—has real limitations. Second, because most systems are sufficiently complex and diverse, examinations of selected areas within them cannot completely represent each system as a whole.

In theory the human services systems may be viewed as independent entities, but in practice there exists considerable overlap in the services provided by the systems, and complicated intersystem relationships are endemic to human services programs and policies. While each system has its own target areas, administrative procedures, and specific delivery systems, overlapping occurs because the systems are directed at the resolution or amelioration of complex human needs and problems that arise from a potpourri of closely interwoven physical, psychological, economic, social, and political causes. No one system operates totally independently of all others in the provision of any one specific service. For example the income transfer services system requires developmental and socialization services offered by the personal social services system if its programs of cash assistance and benefits in kind for the unemployed are to be effective. Similarly the personal social services system requires medical support services provided by the health services system if its developmental and socialization programs for the aged are to be effective. Thus although each system may seek to define, expand, and defend its own turf, all systems accept the vast gray areas where intersystem relationships must exist. These relationships are frequently so close that it is difficult to distinguish where one system's services end and another's begin. For example personal and family guidance and counseling are personal social services that also provide education services. Child welfare services such as protective services for abused children are personal social services that depend on health services and justice and public safety services. Our examination will consider each of the systems as an entity but the systems do not operate independently, as if in a vacuum, and the divisions of responsibility and the areas of exclusive interest and operation are not sharply defined in practice.

Each system, moreover, is composed of a network of agencies providing a broad spectrum of services to a variety of groups with differing needs. For example the personal social services system is concerned with child welfare, the aged, and family planning. Its clients include the dependent, abandoned, neglected, abused, orphaned, handicapped, deviant, and infirm. Its programs range from foster home placement to meals-on-wheels, and they include the more restricted case services as well as the broader public social utilities. We have neither the ability nor the space to examine exhaustively this or any other system, but by providing a general overview of each of the six human services systems and then examining in greater depth certain agencies, programs, policies, and affected groups within selected subareas, we hope to provide as useful a description of the human services and their function in American society as these limitations permit. Regardless of the specific subareas of the human services systems with which individual readers may be most conversant, we hope they will better understand both how their own areas function as part of a comprehensive whole and the basic premises on which policies and practices throughout human services depend.

STUDY QUESTIONS AND ACTIVITIES

1. Bernier and Williams (1965) suggest that ideologies may include doctrines, ideals, slogans, symbols, directions, objectives, demands, judgments, norms, and justifications. Identify examples of each of these that seem to be unusually pervasive or influential in American life. How do ideologies provide a social identity to members of a group? How do they sometimes hinder critical thought or obscure the reasons for group actions? Why are ideologies that are able to accommodate divergent points of view those that can best accept constructive change and that tend least to distort reality?

2. Why does conservatism place heavy emphasis on tradition and stability? Why does reason occupy a preeminent position in conservatism? Why, according to conservatives, does reason tend to promote stability instead of change? In what ways do conservatives hold an optimistic view of human nature? In what ways a pessimistic view? How, according to contemporary conservative ideology, can individuals acting on self-interest also promote traditional conservative values?

3. Why do the human services systems favored by conservatives tend to be centralized and hierarchical? Why in defining needs do conservatives tend to look more to the social order than to the individual client? Why do they view the human services worker as dominant and the client as passive? In what ways may clients contribute to the resolution of their problems? What skills are most needed by workers? Explain how education services can illustrate a conservative model of human services theory and practice. Give examples and explain in as much detail as possible the ways in which each of the other human services systems can also illustrate a conservative model. What evidence would conservatives consider foremost in evaluating the success of human services programs?

4. Although conservatives value the traditions of society, why do they believe that human services systems should not mirror society as a whole? Why do conservatives believe in evolutionary rather than rapid social change? What do they believe to be the proper role of government in promoting social change? Why do conservatives tend to favor selective instead of universal approaches to human services and the delivery of hard instead of soft goods and services? Why do they tend to see human services systems as contingent rather than necessary social inventions?

5. Why does liberalism place heavy emphasis on contemporary society, experience, and change? Contrast the liberal views about the function of intelligence and the method of verifying truth with the conservative views. How is the notion of growth inherent in liberalism? In what ways do liberals hold an optimistic view of human nature? In what ways both an optimistic and a

pessimistic view of society? How, according to contemporary liberal ideology, can individuals acting on self-interest also contribute to the common good of society?

6. Why do the human services systems favored by liberals tend to be more informal and flexible and less hierarchical than those favored by conservatives? Why in defining needs do liberals look more to the individual client than to the social order? Why does education occupy a central place in liberal theory? Explain how all human services systems carry out educational functions. Why do liberals view workers and clients as colleagues? How then can clients contribute to the resolution of their problems, and what skills are needed by workers? Explain how education services can illustrate a liberal model of human services theory and practice. Give examples and explain in as much detail as possible the ways in which each of the other human services systems can also illustrate a liberal model. What evidence would liberals consider foremost in evaluating the success of human services programs? Contrast the liberal approach to evaluation with the conservative approach.

7. Although liberals do not reject the traditions of society, why do they believe that social change is inevitable and sometimes should be rapid? Why do liberals, like conservatives, believe that human services systems should not mirror society as a whole? Why do liberals stress cooperation over competition? What is their view of the nature of ethical living? Explain the two basic liberal approaches to promoting and managing social change. Define the "radical" approach. Although Galper (1978) identifies the approach in which workers identify with clients and become politically active as radical, how is this perspective consistent with mainstream liberal thinking and potentially a means of promoting constructive social change? What do liberals believe to be the proper role of government in promoting social change? Why do liberals tend to favor universal instead of selective approaches to human services? Why do they tend to see human services systems as necessary rather than contingent social inventions?

8. What is the relationship between ideologies, social norms, and public policies? For each of the five social norms Morris (1979) has identified, list consistent examples of public policies in all six of the human services systems. For each of these examples explain the extent to which it reflects conservative and/or liberal ideology. List and explain additional social norms that seem to have a major influence on American life. Why do public policies and human services practices in American society seldom reflect purely conservative or purely liberal beliefs?

REFERENCES

Bernier, N. R., & Williams, J. E. (1973). *Beyond beliefs: Ideological foundations of American education* (pp. 19–59). Englewood Cliffs, NJ: Prentice-Hall.

Galper, J. (1978). What are radical social services? *Social Policy, 8* (4), 38–39, 40.

Morris, R. (1979). *Social policy of the American welfare state* (pp. 16–20). New York: Harper & Row.

Wingo, G. M. (1965). *Philosophies of education: An introduction* (pp. 28–31, 140–141). Lexington, MA: D.C. Heath.

3

PERSONAL SOCIAL SERVICES

SCOPE OF THE SYSTEM

The most modern, fastest growing, and perhaps most controversial human services system—personal social services—was also the most recent to develop. During the first half of the twentieth century a human services system emerged in parts of Europe and North America that sought to supplement those services initiated by the older and better established systems of health, education, income transfer, housing, and public safety. The British distinguished this system from the other social services by referring to it as "personal social services," and this label has been preferred in the United States over the terms "social services" or "general social services," which have often been identified and confused with health and education services. The word "personal" is particularly appropriate to describe these services, for they are individualized in delivery and targeted at those segments of the population with special problems. They are preventive, adjustive, and relationship-type services, operating frequently on a one-to-one basis between client and worker and directed at individuals and families struggling with needs and problems that affect their daily lives and are often critical to their very existence. These services are concerned with the private and highly personal areas of the clients' lives, intervening in various degrees in these areas by the very nature of their programs of guidance, counseling, information and referral assistance, family support services, and child and adult welfare services.

Development of Personal Social Services

Early history. Prior to the twentieth century some personal social services were provided in the United States on a limited scale and in a primitive form by church and secular charitable organizations. Organized services were aimed at addressing a limited range of needs that were not being met for some people by their family life or their community. With increasing public awareness of the pervasiveness of these unmet needs, federal and state involvement began at the close of the nineteenth century and developed throughout the twentieth century. In 1909 the White House Conference on Children recognized the need to preserve the family, and for the next two decades the Children's Bureau (established in 1912) issued reports on child labor abuses that spearheaded the movement for maternal and child health legislation. By the 1930s New Deal legislation experimented with child welfare services in rural areas and with a limited program of personal service counseling. This was followed in the 1950s with federal legislation in which the federal government assumed responsibility for supporting personal social services by matching state funds expended in this area.

Increased federal intervention. In the 1960s the federal government increased its share of support to encourage states to develop personal social services programs more rapidly. In recent decades expenditures have risen sharply, increasing from $194 million in the early 1960s to the $2.5 billion Title XX funding of the late 1970s, and delivery systems have developed that increasingly rely on services purchased from private or independent vendors as well as those provided by public agencies (Morris, 1979). Throughout the twentieth century personal social services have expanded to include programs directed not only at the personal needs of individuals but also at specific social problems that have become the object of public concern, such as "delinquency, the addictions, child abuse and neglect, runaways, developmental disabilities, emotional illness, long term and intergenerational poverty" (Kamerman & Kahn, 1978, p. 457). Hence the development of the personal social services system in the United States represents an effort by the American people to improve the quality of life of the individuals who receive these services and the general social conditions that influence the quality of life for all citizens.

Personal social services listed. Any inventory of goods and services provided by the personal social services system must remain open-ended because the boundaries of the system are unusually difficult to define and new services continually develop. Nonetheless the following list, which is drawn from the suggestions of several leaders in the field (Kamerman & Kahn, 1977; Morris, 1979) is reasonably inclusive of the primary goods and services currently offered by the organized personal social services system in the United States:

1. Child welfare services including foster homes, adoption, institutions for neglected and dependent children, and protective programs for the abused
2. Respite care for those overburdened in caring for children and the handicapped
3. Shelters for runaway adolescents and battered women
4. Community services for the aged
5. Family planning and abortion counseling
6. Protective services for the aged
7. Halfway houses for deinstitutionalized people
8. Home help and homemaker services
9. Community centers
10. Veterans programs
11. Day care
12. Alcohol and drug programs
13. Recreational services for children, the handicapped, the elderly, and average families
14. Referral and information services
15. Congregate meals and meals-on-wheels
16. Self-help and mutual-aid activities for handicapped and disadvantaged groups
17. Counseling, legal assistance, and protected residential arrangements for adolescents
18. Specialized institutions for several categories of children and adults.

General aim of personal social services.   What is perhaps most striking about this list of goods and services is the general aim of the personal social services system it reflects. Although some services provide basic necessities for maintaining people in their day-to-day living, most extend into preventing a variety of problems that may occur in people's personal lives, especially by helping individuals develop their own capacities to deal with these problems. Thus the basic functions of the system, as reflected in this list, are prevention of problems and development of persons. The specific services listed are both hard and soft, and although they are usually provided to help the recipient directly, they can also be justified as alleviating pervasive social problems and therefore can be plausibly classified as indirect as well as direct. These services are usually provided selectively to recipients, but as more and more Americans have come to believe that virtually everyone is subject to personal problems that require these services (such as professional counseling), the demand for personal social services provided on a universal basis has grown.

Controversy Surrounding Personal Social Services

Given these characteristics of the services it provides, the system necessarily developed comparatively late and is potentially controversial. Because the system frequently provides ancillary services to programs established by other human services systems that aim primarily at basic maintenance of human beings, some may view it as something of an appendage to older systems—an expensive, unnecessary, and unwarranted luxury. Also, because the system deals directly with personal lives, some may view it as not simply pervasive but also obtrusive, an invasion of personal privacy and initiative. In fact the system at it is presently constituted could not have developed in the United States without the long-term changes in the structure of American society and the attitudes of the American people that have occurred during the last century.

Luxury or necessity?   As noted in Chapters One and Two, the United States has developed from an agricultural to an industrial to a postindustrial society. Correspondingly the population has expanded and diversified, values and social structures have changed, work has become specialized, and the nation has achieved a level of prosperity that continually makes available to a mass population new kinds of goods and services that earlier may have been available only to a very few or may even not have existed at all. Although the human needs that the personal social services system addresses have always existed, most such needs were frequently ignored or traditionally met at least at rudimentary levels through the individual's family or the community or, when such informal mechanisms proved insufficient, through private or church-sponsored philanthropy. As the twentieth century has unfolded, however, first the extended family and then the nuclear family have declined in influence so that by the 1980s a large proportion of households in America have become either single-person or single-parent units. Community life has also become increasingly diverse and impersonal. Whereas at the beginning of this century families and communities tended to meet personal, human needs, they have now become places in which many needs are unfulfilled and still new ones are created. At the same time as the development of such methods as social casework have given formal personal social services agencies the ability to deal effectively with personal needs, Americans have increasingly expected and even demanded the availability of such services, and they have become increasingly tolerant (although still skeptical) of government sponsorship of services that directly touch their private lives. Thus by the last decades of the twentieth century the personal social services listed above have come to be viewed by most Americans not as luxuries but as integral parts of modern American life.

Supportive or intrusive?   Although as a practical matter most Americans have openly embraced the rapid and wide expansion of the personal social services system, the United States as a whole still regards the system with ambivalence. On one hand the system is seen as a means of patching up some of the unfortunate consequences of the major social changes in America and as otherwise providing services that enrich personal lives; on the other hand some citizens fear that the system may foster and legitimate undesirable social change and not merely patch up the consequences. Some feel, for instance, that the availability of counseling about sexuality and abortion may encourage activities that further erode traditional family life and values; that the willingness to seek advice about highly personal matters from strangers, however well meaning or well informed, may erode the individual's ability to make personal decisions; and that the growing role of government in making decisions about parents' fitness to raise their own children may represent an unwarranted intrusion into rights heretofore reserved to individuals. Ultimately some Americans harbor the belief that in a better world the personal social services system would not need to exist at all and that efforts should therefore focus directly on creating such a world, not on expanding a system that may delay its creation.

Americans have dealt with their ambivalence about personal social services by developing a wide-scale system while at the same time expressing reservations about it. Most of the services within the system are provided by private, local, and state agencies. Although federal influence is growing, this influence is due more to federal funding of these agencies than to the development by the federal government of its own agencies. This arrangement is consistent with the American social norm expressing belief in government of shared responsibility; however, in so far as this belief safeguards the tradition of individual initiative and liberty, it also accounts for skepticisms about the potential intrusiveness of personal social services. To the large extent that the system incorporates private agencies, it is also consistent with the American belief in private party or marketplace decision-making. In addition, to the degree to which the system has been a national effort both to solve pervasive social problems and to extend at least minimal conditions for high-quality living to every segment of the population, it represents the belief that government has an obligation to assist the helpless and the weak, but ambivalence develops when publicly sponsored services are made available to nonvulnerable or nonneedy segments of the population as part of the normal conditions of American life. The ways in which specifically conservative and liberal beliefs are reflected in the system itself and in ambivalence toward it is described in the three representative areas of the system analyzed in this chapter.

Purpose of the Chapter

The personal social services system in the United States is large and ever growing as social conditions change and as new services are developed and incorporated into the mainstream of American life. The boundaries between the formal system of services and the informal mechanisms of personal helping are obscure and shifting as services that traditionally were provided incidentally have become formally established in the American consciousness and social practice. We cannot exhaustively describe and analyze this system nor even smaller, less diverse systems. Therefore we have selected one or more representative areas from each system to treat in depth. For the personal social services these areas are programs for the abused and neglected child, the dependent elderly, and for the unwed sexually active teenager. We define the mission and role for each area, trace its origins and history, analyze its programs and policies from conservative and liberal perspectives, and explore its future directions.

THE ABUSED AND NEGLECTED CHILD

Mission and Role of Personal Social Services

Problem of definition. Reliable estimates suggest that between sixty thousand and two million cases of child abuse occur each year (Gelles, 1978; Newberger & Hyde, 1975); that half of the approximately two million children who run away from home annually have been physically and sexually abused by relatives and other adults; and that at least six children will be beaten to death by adults on an average day (Hobbs, 1982). Unfortunately, as abhorrent as these figures may be, they can only approximate the extent of child abuse and neglect in the United States. Statistics that precisely reflect the full extent of child abuse and neglect are difficult to compile because the children, families, and medical personnel most directly involved frequently fail to report occurrences for reasons such as shame, helplessness, ignorance, indifference, and fear of legal punishment or social censure. Also, those researchers and human services workers who attempt to identify and assess cases of child abuse and neglect and develop programs and policies to reduce their occurrence are unable to agree both on a definition of what constitutes abuse and neglect and a method for measuring the frequency of such cases. Despite this inadequate reporting and evaluation child abuse and neglect have become an increasingly visible social problem that has attained national significance within the past twenty years and consequently has become the object of growing federal and state intervention.

The problem of defining child abuse and neglect is complicated by the extremely difficult task of identifying those situations in which parents are either unwilling or unable to nurture their offspring effectively and thus endanger the child's social, emotional, and physical growth and development. Although there is some controversy as to whether a distinction should be made between the "abuse" and "neglect" of children and whether both types of situations should be subsumed under the more encompassing terms of "maltreated child" or "endangered child," there is general agreement that the statutory definition of maltreatment includes the following:

1. Physical abuse.
2. Malnourishment; poor clothing; lack of proper shelter, sleeping arrangements, attendance or supervision. Includes "failure to thrive" syndrome, which describes infants who fail to grow and develop at a normal rate.
3. Denial of essential medical care.
4. Failure to attend school regularly.
5. Exploitation, overwork.
6. Exposure to unwholesome or demoralizing circumstances.
7. Sexual abuse.
8. Somewhat less frequently the definitions include emotional abuse and neglect involving denial of the normal experiences that permit a child to feel loved, wanted, secure, and worthy. (Kadushin, 1980, p. 158)

There is also general agreement that incidents of neglect, which are often triggered by social pressures accompanying poverty and inadequate food, clothing, shelter, health care, and education, are reported more frequently than incidents of abuse. However incidents of abuse, which are often triggered by psychological pressures accompanying emotional stress and internal conflicts, receive greater public attention.

The extremes of child abuse and neglect range from infanticide to abandonment. Within these extremes the damages resulting to the child are both physical and psychological and include battered and sexually assaulted children requiring medical attention; beaten children who have sustained moderate injuries such as bruises that do not require medical attention; children deficient in cognitive and language abilities and motor skills; and children deficient in socialization skills. Although injuries from physical abuse may heal on the surface, problems with emotional development frequently have long-term and wide-ranging consequences. Abused children suffer from low self-images, express generalized unhappiness, score below normal on IQ tests, tend more than normal toward self-destruction, display highly aggressive behavior, and have difficulty relating to peers and interacting with parents (Berkeley Planning Associates, 1978; Kadushin, 1980).

Abusive parents reflect the agonies of their own childhood and the failures of their adult existence. Frequently they themselves were abused as children, became delinquents as adolescents, and have had difficulties in sustaining a marriage, earning a living, supporting a family, and relating to the community as adults.

Government response: "parens patriae." Government response to child abuse and neglect has been to provide programs of protective services through child welfare agencies and supportive and supplementary programs through other agencies within the personal social services system. Operating on the concept of *parens patriae,* or "the state's paternalistic right of guardianship of minors" (Markham, 1980, p. 182), protective services workers directly defend the rights of the child while other human services workers provide supportive family services such as casework counseling, referral services, and individual and group therapy and supplementary family services such as homemakers, crises nurseries, and extended day care centers. These family services seek to strengthen the home by identifying and treating the causes of child abuse and neglect and by rehabilitating abusive parents to their proper roles in child rearing. Although the primary emphasis of the protective services is on the immediate welfare of the child, secondary emphasis is on the preservation of the unity of the natural family in a preventive and nonpunitive way through the aid of the supportive and supplementary family services. Protective services workers will nonetheless remove the child from the home and place him in another home when the child's life is in danger or when other major threats are present.

Summary. The mission and role of programs for abused and neglected children are thus twofold. First, these programs are directed at freeing abused and neglected children from immediate threats to their health and safety. Second, having secured the safety of these children, the programs are aimed at creating conditions within the families of abused and neglected children that will prove conducive to the full, normal development of the children.

Origins and History

The Mary Ellen case. During the first century of this nation's history Americans did much as they pleased with their children, and no protective services were available to intervene on behalf of abused and neglected children. But all of this changed in 1875 when concerned citizens in the city of New York, outraged by the brutal beatings and gross neglect of a child named Mary Ellen, were able to bring her abusive guardians to court and have them imprisoned. Their appeal to the court was made through the Society for the Prevention of Cruelty to Animals, which was the only protective organization available at the time. Mary Ellen was thus viewed as an

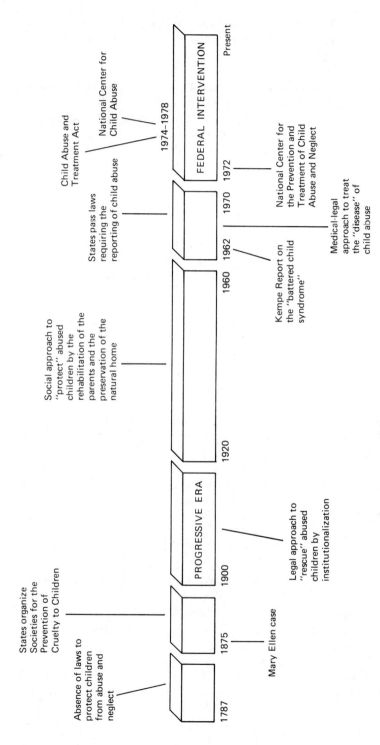

FIGURE 3–1. Timeline tracing the programs and policies relating to child abuse and neglect from the founding of the United States to the present. Key legislation, institutions, and individuals that have shaped the personal social services approach to the abused and neglected child are identified.

"animal" and spared further suffering because existing law protected animals from abuse.

Different approaches to child abuse and neglect. The successful prosecution of the Mary Ellen case was followed by the formation of the New York Society for the Prevention of Cruelty to Children. Over the next twenty-five years similar organizations were established in other large cities throughout the United States and focused on the enactment of laws to protect children and the use of courts to enforce the laws. Specifically, reformers of the Progressive Era of the early 1900s were eager to "rescue" abused and neglected children by removing them from "inefficient and disorderly" homes and placing them in institutions. The period from the 1920s to the early 1960s witnessed limited growth of protective services as the social approach of family services developed at the expense of the legal approach to protection. During this period child welfare workers deemphasized institutionalization of the abused and neglected and sought instead to rehabilitate abusive parents and preserve the natural family. But in 1962 a group of physicians headed by C. Henry Kempe at the Denver Medical Center revived public interest in the maltreated child by conducting a survey of children hospitalized because of abuse and by coining the term "battered child syndrome" to describe the pathology of their condition (Antler, 1978; Kett, 1978).

Emphasis then switched from a social approach to a medical-legal approach, and within five years after the Kempe study most states had passed laws requiring physicians, schoolteachers, and social workers to report all incidents of—or even their suspicions of—child abuse to state agencies. Physicians assumed a leadership role and sought to treat the "disease" of child abuse through a medical approach that emphasized the "physical effects of maltreatment" and the "psychopathology of abusers" and that developed hospital-based programs that reached a limited number of clients. Child welfare workers countered this approach with a social one that called for the elimination of the economic and social conditions such as poverty, unemployment and substandard housing that they associated with abuse and neglect (Kempe & Helfer, 1972; Markham, 1980).

Federal government intervention. Beginning in the early 1970s the federal government responded to the growing public outcry over the maltreated child by intervening directly with funds and regulations. In 1972 federal funds helped to establish the National Center for the Prevention and Treatment of Child Abuse and Neglect at the University of Colorado Medical Center. This center promoted both research and professional training in the areas of child abuse and protection. In 1974 the federal Child Abuse and Treatment Act was passed. This act both funded and accelerated the development of state programs to aid the maltreated child.

It also established a National Center for Child Abuse that distributed information and engaged in research on the nature of abuse and on effective intervention into it. As extended in 1978 this act continued to provide direct assistance to states that enacted legislation that would

> protect all children under age 18; cover mental injury, physical injury, and sexual abuse; include neglect reports and abuse reports; guarantee confidentiality of records; guarantee legal immunity for reporters; and provide for a guardian *ad litem* for children whose cases come to court. (Kadushin, 1980, p. 156)

Conservative and Liberal Perspectives: Social Norms

Role of government.   In their approaches to child abuse and neglect both the conservative and liberal perspectives identify with the social norm that government has an obligation to assist the helpless and the weak. Both embrace the concept of *parens patriae* and expect government intervention to protect the rights of the vulnerable even if protection requires removal of the child from the home and placement in a foster home or institution. Both conservatives and liberals are eager to strengthen, preserve, and restore the natural family unit by helping abusive parents to return to their proper roles in child rearing. But although there is wide agreement on the above points, the conservative and liberal perspectives find little else in common.

The Conservative Perspective Examined

The beliefs of conservatives in tradition, established institutions, and the viability of the existing social order built out of the sweat, tears, and sacrifices of previous generations lead them to look to the nature of persons rather than to the socioeconomic system to explain child abuse. In their view parents, although endowed with a potential to develop their minds and reason clearly, may allow their brute instincts or animal selves to predominate and thus not develop this potential. This failure is reflected in their yielding to the pressures and strains of daily living, abandoning their proper roles as parents, and inflicting abuse and neglect on their children.

The medical model.   Conservatives take the physicians' position of defining this "aberrant behavior" as a medical problem in which "both injured child and abuser are viewed as 'sick'—the one physically, the other psychologically or socially" (Newberger & Bourne, 1980, p. 418). In their approach to the maltreated child conservatives adopt a medical model that makes available to both the abuser and the abused a highly trained, hospital-based, professional staff that would provide prompt, effective, in-depth medical services (e.g., counseling, therapy, treatment, and hospitalization). The conservative position then would center on diagnosis of the behavior of abusive parents as a "sickness" or one expression, among others, of their "infantile personalities" and their "need for sympathetic mothering denied them in their own childhood" (Antler, 1978, pp. 59–60). The "cure" of their illness is contingent upon their return to effective parenting through their acquiescence to their proper place in the existing social order.

Summary. This identification of child abuse as a disease and the consequent focusing of treatment on the abusive parents fits perfectly into the basic conservative position. It follows from their beliefs that programs for child abuse should be both residual in scope and rehabilitative in purpose. They should be residual in scope by being selective of individuals for treatment. They should be rehabilitative in purpose by being of limited duration and designed to restore ill, deviant, damaged clients to a healthy and normal status within which they can cope with the challenges and problems of the established social order.

The Liberal Perspective Examined

The faith of liberals in the power of human intelligence and their belief in experience and the experimental attitude toward social institutions lead them to look to the nature of the existing socioeconomic system for an explanation of child abuse. Liberals recognize that social institutions and ideas are impermanent operational constructs designed by persons exercising their power of intelligence to meet their needs and that they may sometimes prove ill-conceived, producing injustice or inequities that result in the poverty and suffering of many. Among the victims of these inequities are the parents who succumb to the pressures and strains of a daily existence without adequate food, clothing, shelter, and education by abandoning their proper roles as parents and inflicting abuse and neglect on their children. From the liberal perspective abusive parents are then seen as the product and not the source of the shortcomings of the socioeconomic system.

The social reconstruction model. Liberals believe that because all social arrangements exist to serve human welfare, they may be altered to suit this purpose. Therefore liberals seek to remove social and economic conditions such as poverty, inadequate housing, and unemployment, which they view as straining the family's "emotional and environmental resources" (Markham, 1980, p. 181) and providing the breeding ground for child abuse and neglect (Gill, 1971). In their approach to the maltreated child they adopt a model of social reconstruction[1] that would promote a positive

---

[1]We have used this phrase to label the liberal model because we believe it accurately describes a position predicated upon fundamental changes in the political, economic, and social structure of the nation.

nurturing environment in the family through programs of income transfers such as negative income tax, AFDC, and food stamps; housing assistance such as rent subsidies and public housing; and support services such as child care, homemakers, parent counseling, visiting nurses, and medical and psychiatric services. These programs would be universal in scope and holistic in purpose. They would be public social utilities that are available to all who have need of them, would be of extended duration, and would be designed to meet the needs of the child and the family and to integrate the family into the community.

Summary. These universal programs for the treatment and prevention of child abuse accurately reflect the basic liberal position. They are based directly on the liberal assumptions that the root causes of social problems are found in the environment, that such causes and problems may be eliminated by intelligently, experimentally, and democratically rearranging the environment, and that such reconstruction promotes the full and healthy development of all individuals, particularly their ability to redirect their own lives intelligently.

Opposing Views of Maltreated Child Models: The Conservative Position

Conservatives offer the following arguments in defense of their approach to the maltreated child: (1) The medical model has made the nation aware of the problem of child abuse and has recruited the most qualified professionals in the identification and treatment of the abused. (2) The medical model provides a therapeutic approach in which the identification of child abuse as a sickness results in an emphasis on treatment and rehabilitation rather than on retribution and punishment. (3) The medical model maintains a healthy balance between the public and the private sector; it is based on the concept of *parens patriae* but still promotes the privacy of the family, parental control, and children's rights.

Opposing Views of Maltreated Child Models: The Liberal Position

In response to conservatives liberals offer the following three arguments in defense of their approach to the maltreated child: (1) The social reconstruction model attacks and seeks to eliminate the very causes of child abuse (inequities in the socioeconomic system) rather than confining itself to the treatment of some of its consequences (those abused children and abusing parents affected by medical model programs). (2) The social reconstruction model ensures and strengthens the privacy and independence of the natural family unit by emphasizing home support services designed to supplement and encourage normal parenting while eliminating conditions contributing to abuse and neglect. (3) The social reconstruction model produces those fundamental changes in the political, economic, and social structure that are necessary if a national family policy committed to the protection and welfare of all family members is to be realized.

Future Directions

The historical development of programs for abused and neglected children, the twofold mission of promoting the welfare of both children and families that has been widely adopted in the United States, and various long-term social trends suggest that future programs will incorporate both some conservative and some liberal practices and will represent a compromise between extreme expressions either of family privacy and the right of parents to raise their children without interference or of *parens patriae,* that is, the right of the state to intervene to protect the lives and welfare of children. These programs may involve early state intervention to protect the child and help the family, but if the current trend continues they will also seek to preserve family integrity by working closely and cooperatively with the family to effect change.

State intervention: first stage.   State intervention would take two forms and occur at two different stages in the cycle of abuse and neglect. In the first stage there would be early, limited intervention in which public agencies—not private voluntary ones—would have the responsibility of providing in-home support services before family conditions deteriorate and necessitate removal of the child to ensure safety. During this period counseling and other services would be intended to relieve specific stresses and to restore parents to effective roles in child rearing. Throughout this stage programs would be designed for "maximum exposure of the child to normal developmental relationships and activities at home, at school, and in the community" (Advisory Committee on Child Development, 1976, p. 89).

State intervention: second stage.   State intervention would take place at the second stage if family conditions continued to degenerate and the child's safety became endangered. At this level intervention would be directed at specifically identifiable harms and stresses and the child would be removed from the home and placed with substitute families or in small residential institutions, foster homes, or group homes. If the child suffered severe neglect and abuse during this stage, programs would provide for specific developmental needs such as speech therapy and psychotherapeutic needs such as psychiatric aid. Treatment for physical injury would include medical care and therapy for accompanying emotional problems. The maltreated child would have someone with whom to interact and communicate, be this the psychologist at the clinic, the teacher at the day care center, or the visiting therapist at the foster home. Abusing parents would continue to receive family support services, and psychotherapy would be extended and supported through self-help types of client organizations such as Parents Anonymous. Throughout this stage, although the child would be in a residential program, the "child should remain as close as possible to its [sic] normal life setting—both in space and in the psychological texture of the experience provided" (Advisory Committee on Child Development, 1976, p. 89). The ultimate goal would be to reunite the child with the family and return everyone to normal living. If this goal proved neither feasible nor appropriate, parental rights would be terminated and the child placed up for adoption.

Such programs are based primarily on the conservative medical model, which emphasizes treating abuse as a disease and restoring normal functioning within the social order; however they also incorporate liberal practices to the extent that they emphasize eliminating the socioeconomic causes of abuse and neglect and encouraging parents to understand and choose autonomously how to be good parents. In these ways the medical forms of treatments encouraged by conservatives can be consistent with the reconstruction of the social order emphasized by liberals.

The success of the above programs will depend on more than their technical adequacy, and a number of key developments will probably have to occur to ensure their effective functioning. First, some consensus will need to be reached on norms relating to "standards of adequate care that would permit identification of those situations warranting community intervention" (Kadushin, 1980, p. 223). Without such consensus intervention will be neither widespread nor consistent nationally. Second, human service workers—many of whom are women—will need to enjoy more nearly equal respect, support, and peer status with their coworkers in law, medicine, and psychiatry—most of whom are men—and will need to become involved on a more equal footing in planning and implementing programs. This development will reflect the growing professionalization of human service workers. Third, government at all levels will need to enact whatever legislation and provide whatever resources (financial, personnel, and the like) are necessary to support the above programs and to establish a national policy to ensure the well-being of all children and the integrity of all families.

If such developments come to pass, child abuse and neglect will not be eliminated in the United States but increasingly effective programs that substantially reduce the negative consequences of abuse and neglect throughout all of American society may be developed.

THE DEPENDENT ELDERLY

Mission and Role of Personal Social Services

Every twenty-four hours approximately five thousand Americans celebrate their sixty-fifth birthday and join the more than 10 percent of the nation's population who are classified as the elderly. These senior citizens have become one of the fastest growing segments of the population, increasing by 28 percent between 1970 and 1980. They reached the 25.5 million mark, or 11.3 percent of the population, in 1980, and they will comprise approximately 16 percent of the total population in the twenty-first century (Barbour, 1982). There is also aging within this elderly population. Those over the age of seventy-five have increased to over 38 percent of the total aged population, reflecting the benefits of developments in health care that prolong life. It is projected that by the year 2000 average Americans will be expected to live to the age of eighty, which is almost thirty-five years longers than their grandparents lived in 1900 (Broder, 1985; Callahan, Diamond, Giele, & Morris, 1980).

Problem of definition. This general aging of the American population has resulted in a growing number of impaired and disabled individuals who must receive long-term care either at home or in institutions. The home bears the major burden, caring for between 2.5 million and 7.8 million of these dependent elderly, while a significantly smaller number, 1.7 million, are institutionalized (Congressional Budget Office, 1977; U.S. Department of Health, Education, and Welfare, 1978). As the spread in these estimates indicates, present research can provide only the most approximate figures on the numbers of dependent elderly; however it is generally recognized that at least 17 percent, or 3 to 4 million, of the aged can be identified as functionally dependent. The functionally dependent elderly are defined as "those individuals over 65 whose illnesses, impairments, or social problems have become disabling, reducing their ability to carry out independently the customary activities of daily life" (Schorr, 1980, p. 34). Perhaps one-third of this group are institutionalized while the remaining two-thirds—including the housebound, bedfast, and severely impaired—are cared for in the home.

Although any discussion of programs for the dependent elderly will focus on the above group, it is not the only segment of the aged population that requires care. There are many among the elderly who are not fully disabled and therefore not identified as functionally dependent but who still suffer from impairments that are partially disabling and require care. Reliable estimates suggest that within the aged community in general as many as one-third of its members "express a need for services at any given moment," while one-half complain of "very serious or somewhat serious health problems" (Schorr, 1980, p. 34).

Needs of the dependent elderly. The needs of the dependent elderly derive from their efforts to retain a quality of life that allows them to maintain to the highest degree possible physical and personal independence. Most strive for maximum functional independence, which is predicated on respect for their worth, dignity, and integrity as individuals and which ensures them a role in those decisions affecting their welfare, but they recognize that the quality of life they will enjoy is contingent on the quality of care they receive. Fundamental to such care is access to needed technical and professional services, humane treatment from family and community, and the availability of opportunities for self-fulfillment.

The type of help the dependent elderly require ranges from assistance with the simplest of grooming tasks (washing, combing hair) that can be performed by the untrained and nonprofessional to complex, sophisticated services and treatment (counseling, therapy, medical and legal aid) that require highly skilled technicians and professionals. Much of the assistance needed arises from the demands of day-to-day living and involves tasks relating to the most basic requirements of food, clothing, shelter, and personal well-being. These are the kind of tasks that nondependent people perform for themselves with little thought and effort, but that may prove impossible for the dependent elderly and in turn threaten their very survival. The help required includes

> Assistance or supervision in bathing, grooming, walking, feeding
> Cleaning of incontinence, toilet training
> Shopping, planning meals, cooking, laundry
> Errands, correspondence, managing cash, advice on personal and financial affairs
> Companionship, sitting services, escort for outside excursions
> Advocacy and intermediation, summoning medical or social help as needed. (Gurland, Dean, Cook, & Gurland, 1978, p. 12)

The remainder of the assistance the dependent elderly need arises from the demands of specific illnesses or impairments that threaten their health, ability to function, and safety and that require periodic services given directly by specialists and professionals. Included in this type of help are various forms of health care (dental, medical, nursing), nutritional advice, educational programs, counseling, therapy, and recreational programs.

Children's response.   The dependent elderly generally prefer to live by themselves in their own homes within visiting distance of their children, who can provide whatever assistance is necessary for the aged to retain their independent existence. When their needs are such that they cannot live alone, most elderly prefer to live with their children. What they seek to avoid and strongly resist is being placed in an institution or nursing home, which they view with dissatisfaction. Most children respect the wishes of their parents and, as indicated by the relatively small increase in the number of elderly institutionalized (from 4 percent in 1966 to 5 percent in 1980) despite the large growth in the aged population, have elected to care for them in the home (Schorr, 1980). The home bears the bulk of the burden of ensuring continuing attention and assistance over long periods of time with the family providing help "in a significant way" to between 60 to 85 percent of the disabled and impaired elderly (Callahan et al., 1980).

Children responding to the needs of their dependent parents provide care in four different but interrelated ways: (1) providing financial support; (2) sharing a household; (3) attending to personal needs and providing physical help and care in sickness; and (4) offering emotional support, affection, and concern. Financial support is given least frequently and usually by children earning high incomes. The segment of the elderly population in general receiving such assistance declined from between 5 percent and 10 percent in 1961 to between 2 percent and 3 percent in 1975 (Louis Harris and Associates, 1975; Schorr, 1961). Sharing living accommodations is another approach used infrequently. It tends to occur in low-income families and often reflects financial necessity. The segment of the general elderly population living with adult children has declined from 33 percent in 1951 to less than 17 percent in 1980 (Schorr, 1980). Attending to personal needs, especially by providing care in sickness, and offering emotional support and affection are the two ways of providing care most frequently used and in turn most widely appreciated by the elderly in general. Children routinely provide assistance ranging from household help to meet daily personal needs to nursing care in times of illness. They also offer psychological and social support by remaining in close contact through periodic visits characterized by encouragement, counseling, and recreation. Thus only one in ten among the elderly complain of loneliness and more than two of three elderly parents see their children weekly (Louis Harris and Associates, 1975; Shanas & Hauser, 1974).

Government response.   The response of both state and federal governments to the needs of the dependent elderly has been to attempt to provide them with a decent standard of care and with the necessary support to enjoy a quality of life that ensures their individuality and allows for their self-fulfillment. Government is also concerned with maintaining the family in its role as the primary caring agent for the dependent. In an effort to achieve both these ends, government has developed programs and policies to provide income support, medical care, residential care, and family support services. Income maintenance programs for the elderly in need of long-term care include the Supplementary Security Income program (SSI) and the disability payments program of the Social Security Administration. (See Chapter Seven for an extended discussion of programs in the income transfer services system.) SSI helps to lighten the financial burden on the family by providing resources for food, shelter, and related living expenses for the dependent elderly. The disability payments ease the family's financial responsibility by providing the dependent elderly with early retirement income or payments to cover their basic living costs. Medical care programs for the dependent elderly include Medicare

EXHIBIT 3–1   *A PROMISING ALTERNATIVE TO NURSING HOME CARE*

Adult day care centers have emerged as an appealing alternative approach to caring for the elderly. Although senior centers have long provided the healthier elderly with opportunities for socialization and recreation, there has been no similar caring services available for the elderly who are mentally and physically disabled. Elderly who suffer from arteriosclerosis, arthritis, Alzheimer's disease, and mental retardation, among other infirmities, have usually been placed in nursing homes by families whose working members are not available to care for them throughout the day. But since the early 1970s many families have been enrolling their disabled elderly in adult day care centers that provide a broad range of health care and social services eight hours a day for five days a week. Their offerings include medical, nursing, education, speech and hearing, counseling, physical therapy, recreation, administration, occupational therapy, mental health, group activity, and nutrition services. Most centers have low client-to-staff ratios (usually less than nine to one); have been designed to provide ease of movement for persons in wheelchairs or with walkers; have cafeterias to provide at least one hot meal daily; have rooms designed for crafts, sewing, and recreation; have nurses on duty part of each day; and have made provisions for emergency medical care and transportation.

For families with members on 9-to-5 work schedules the centers have enormous appeal, for keeping the elderly at home becomes manageable when family support is needed only on nights and weekends. For the disabled elderly the centers enable them to enjoy pleasant social activities during the day and to return to the love and security of the family in the evenings and on weekends. For those who pay for elderly care (government or client), the centers bring considerable savings because their fees are less than half those charged by nursing homes. By the mid-1980s some nine hundred centers served more than twenty-five thousand people nationally, and the National Council on Aging had formed a special division, the National Institute on Adult Day Care, to conduct research on the centers and to promote them as an alternative approach to caring for the elderly.

and Medicaid. Medicare is a program primarily concerned with the purchase of hospital services. (See Chapter Four for an extended discussion of programs in the health services system.) It provides limited funding for nursing home services and home health care services. Medicaid is a program primarily concerned with reimbursing costs that arise from institutionalizing the dependent elderly. It is a major source of funding for nursing home services, but provides only limited financial support for home health and personal care services. Residential care and family support programs for the dependent elderly include the Title XX program and the agencies on aging under Title III of the Older Americans Act (OAA). The Title XX program provides a major source of funding for in-home services that help with tasks such as housekeeping, shopping, personal care, preparing meals, transportation, and advice and counseling. The agencies on aging under Title III provide funding for in-home services directed at the minority and isolated elderly. Included among these services are transportation, outreach, referral, and information services, advocacy, counseling, advice, legal assistance, and protective services. Although such residential care and family support programs provide some aid to the family as caretaker, their total contribution remains small and their impact is marginal at best. The burden of in-home care for the dependent elderly remains for the most part with the children, spouses, other relatives, or even friends who routinely provide up to 80 percent of the above listed in-home services (Callahan et al., 1980).

Summary. In general the mission of programs for the dependent elderly in America has been to maintain the elderly in their ordinary living arrangements as long as possible and to provide financial support when institutionalization becomes necessary. Although programs have increased significantly in number and scope in recent decades, they still remain only partially successful in fulfilling both parts of this mission.

Origins and History

Filial responsibility. Since the first colonists settled in America, responsibility for the care of the dependent has oscillated between family and community. Initially colonists adopted the Elizabethan Poor Laws that required local responsibility and liability of relatives for support of needy family members (see Chapter One). Local intervention took the form of workhouses and almhouses that provided protection and a minimal level of care for a small number of the dependent. The family accepted its liability for the support of its members and routinely provided all the care for the majority of the dependent. However, although the Poor Laws implied a concept of filial responsibility that recognized the claims of needy parents on their children, the sociopolitical environment of the colonies stressed the importance of the "individual in and of himself." When the individual matured "not even family ties interfered with his full exercise of independent choice" (Schorr, 1980, p. 7). This contradiction between the demands of filial responsibility based on the Poor Laws and the egalitarian definition of the child that emerged from the social environment did not become a source of conflict until the twentieth century. Prior to that time the nature of the economy allowed aging parents to remain independent and in control of their own situation. They retained ownership of property, controlled family income, and did not need to rely on financial help from their children. Also, because the average life expectancy was only forty-seven years, the number who lived long enough to need help was relatively small (Keniston & the Carnegie Council on Children, 1978).

During the twentieth century parents had difficulty controlling their own situation because wages and ownership were separated as the economy changed. Elderly parents lost control over family income as children became independent wage earners with the freedom to do what they wished with their income. Also, as life expectancy increased, the aged population expanded along with the number of dependent elderly. Various states responded to the needs of this emerging group of dependent elderly by passing "family expense acts," which were common laws that assigned responsibility to nuclear family members—not to extended family members as under the Elizabethan Poor Laws—and made such assistance obligatory. Once again the concept of filial responsibility was defined and in some states clearly established.

Public responsibility.   However, beginning with the Social Security Act in the 1930s and continuing into the 1980s, the federal government gradually set aside the concept of filial responsibility and shifted the burden of meeting the needs of the dependent elderly to the public sector. To achieve this end, the federal government enacted legislation, such as SSI in 1974, that eliminated the requirements that relatives provide financial support, and initiated entitlement programs that replaced filial responsibility with public responsibility. These programs freed the dependent elderly from total reliance on the voluntary help of their children or others by guaranteeing or "entitling" to them certain rights in the form of services and income apart from any responsibility by members of the family or by others. With these entitlement programs the dependent elderly came to enjoy specific rights to health services and residential care under Medicare and Medicaid, to social and personal support services under Title XX and Title III of OAA, and to income maintenance under SSI and the disability payments program of OASDI.

Conservative and Liberal Perspectives: Social Norms

Role of government.   In their approaches to the dependent elderly the conservative and liberal perspectives embrace the same social norms while differing sharply on their meaning. They agree that government must assist the vulnerable segments of the population such as the dependent elderly, but they disagree as to the form this assistance should take. Conservatives seek to limit government intervention to services that will substitute for the care that the family is unable or unwilling to provide. They believe public responsibility and assistance should begin when ordinary functions of family break down due to unavoidable natural circumstances such as the death of the caretaker or the severity of illness of the dependent elderly. Liberals on the other hand seek to expand government intervention to services that will support the care that the family normally provides. Accordingly public responsibility and assistance should be continuous with and supplementary to the ordinary functions of the family at all times.

Role of the marketplace. The conservative and liberal perspectives also agree that private party or marketplace decision-making will ensure the privacy, integrity, and independence of all parties involved in the care of the dependent elderly, but they disagree on the extent of expression such marketplace forces should be allowed. In the same vein they agree that only a government of shared responsibilities can support individual liberties essential to free choice and self-fulfillment, but they disagree as to when such a government should be allowed to intervene in respect to these liberties. Conservatives seek a public policy that will avoid government intervention by allowing free play to individual initiative and the fullest operation of marketplace forces. Each family should therefore enjoy privacy and independence in confronting, negotiating, and resolving the unique problems of its specific dependent elderly. Liberals seek a public policy of limited government intervention that allows for some expression of individual initiative while delimiting the operation of marketplace forces. Each family's privacy and independence in providing care and in related decision-making should thus be subject to the government's role as final guarantor of conditions necessary for the common good of all concerned.

The Conservative Perspective Examined

Family as caregiver. The conservative beliefs in individual initiative, in the guidance of the individual by the wisdom of tradition, and in the continuity of traditional institutions lead them to look to family members rather than government for the support and care of the dependent elderly. Conservatives believe that throughout the history of the human race the family, as the cornerstone of society, has remained the key traditional institution providing the nurturing sustenance, care, love, and support that is so critical for the very survival of the human species. This nurturing function has been determined by biological factors such as the total vulnerability and physical dependency of the infant and by psychological factors such as the awareness of the developing child of "utter helplessness and his dependence on those around him, and their good will, for his survival" (Gaylen et al., 1978, p. 12). In the natural development of the family this function continuously unfolds as members progress through life's cycle, trading the dependency of infancy for the adult responsibility of caring for others, only to return to a state of dependency in old age. The family experience then reflects "an inclination to caring that is an essential part of the nature of [the human] species," although there are "occasional abnormalities" such as a few parents who will not care for their children

(Gaylen et al., 1978, p. 19). This inclination is an expression of an altruism deeply rooted in the very existence of human beings, and hence it must remain central to any definition of the family as a traditional institution.

Conservatives are eager to avoid any inroads by other social institutions into this conception of the family as caregiver. Specifically they are concerned that various forms of government intervention designed to assist the dependent elderly also reduce the traditional responsibility of the family to provide for its members' needs. The conservatives' fear is that the more government meets the social and economic needs of the dependent elderly the less inclined family members will be to continue to contribute to such needs. In effect they view government as exceeding its appropriate role with such intervention and unintentionally weakening the family as a major social institution. Ultimately continuing and expanding government intervention could result in an end to expression of altruism common to home care because family members might abandon their traditional caring role with its constant drain on their economic, social, and emotional resources, and defer the responsibility to government or other social institutions. When this change occurs, the family as a social institution would become anachronistic.

The reactive model.   Conservatives seek to ensure the continuation of traditional family patterns of care by adopting a reactive model in their approach to the needs of the dependent elderly. Under this model the family would bear the major responsibility for caring and would be expected to play the primary role in meeting the needs of its dependent elderly members. This role would include providing long-term home care with all the social, economic, and emotional support it entails and, when necessary, contributing toward the costs of institutionalization. Government in turn would avoid interfering in the family's exercise of this care and it would seek to respect traditional concern for the privacy and independence of the family. However, when a crisis or a breakdown occurs in which the family is unwilling or unable to fulfill its role in providing care, government would react and intervene. This government reaction would have two characteristics. First, it would be residual in approach in that all benefits would be targeted at the specific individual with the problem and that no attempt would be made to provide for the needs of the family or to strengthen and support its capacity to care. The individual would be required to meet various criteria for eligibility and to establish clearly inability to meet personal needs through the normal mechanisms of the market. The focus would be on resolving the problem to guarantee the individual a minimum level of care. Second, government reaction would be substitutive and not supportive in that it is designed to transfer the responsibility for care from the family to government rather than to attempt to strengthen and support the family in its usual role. The basic purpose for government's providing these benefits and services—whether they be home ser-

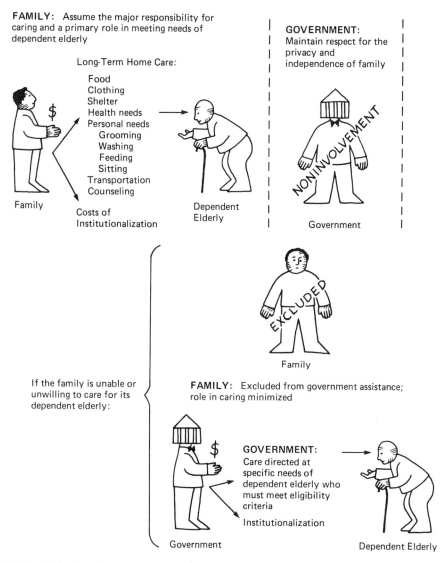

FAMILY: Assume the major responsibility for caring and a primary role in meeting needs of dependent elderly

Long-Term Home Care:

Food
Clothing
Shelter
Health needs
Personal needs
Grooming
Washing
Feeding
Sitting
Transportation
Counseling

Family

Costs of Institutionalization

Dependent Elderly

GOVERNMENT:
Maintain respect for the privacy and independence of family

NONINVOLVEMENT

Government

EXCLUDED

Family

If the family is unable or unwilling to care for its dependent elderly:

FAMILY: Excluded from government assistance; role in caring minimized

GOVERNMENT:
Care directed at specific needs of dependent elderly who must meet eligibility criteria

Institutionalization

Government

Dependent Elderly

FIGURE 3–2. Chart mapping the roles of family and government under the conservatives' *reactive model.*

vices, visiting health services, or other forms of care—would thus be to allow government to substitute for the family. Frequently, when such government intervention would take the form of institutionalizing the dependent elderly, government would assume the role of a surrogate family. It would provide residential care of room and meals and employ human services workers to ensure a total caring environment of health, protection, counseling, personal care, and social and emotional support.

Summary. This reactive model with its emphasis on a residual approach and substitutive services fits perfectly with the conservative belief that government intervention must remain marginal at best if individual initiative is to be allowed to operate freely; if the privacy, independence, and self-determination of the family is to be assured; and if the family is to exercise its traditional rights and responsibilities by providing for the health and welfare of its dependent elderly. The government substitutes for the family only as a last and temporary resort.

The Liberal Perspective Examined

The liberals' emphasis on experience and their experimental attitude toward social institutions and ideals lead them to propose fundamental changes in the traditional care provided to the dependent elderly by their families. Although recognizing the family as "the primary support system, the social institution most suited to carry the major caring responsibilities, and the most natural social environment" (Moroney, 1978, p. 51), liberals believe that government has a responsibility to intervene and share the burden of care with the family. They therefore do not view government as undermining the family or interfering unnecessarily in established social roles when it initiates programs that attempt to (1) lessen the social, economic, and physical burdens of the caretaker family; (2) support the dependent in home care settings; and (3) delay the placement of the dependent elderly in institutions providing long-term care. They recognize that the family and government will be altering their traditional roles as social institutions when the family shares with and hence transfers to government some of its responsibilities for providing care such as nursing, home help services, transportation, and meals. However liberals believe that such change, particularly the assistance and relief it brings to the family, is essential if the family is to continue to survive under the demands placed on its time, energy, financial and social resources, and physical and mental health by the needs of the bedridden and house-bound dependent elderly. For liberals, concerns for tradition must be superseded by practical concerns for how well social institutions serve human welfare by maintaining a decent quality of life for both the dependent elderly and the members of their caretaker families.

The constructive model. In their approach to the dependent elderly liberals adopt a constructive model that would be basically supportive in attempting to strengthen the ability of the family to care for its members but would also be substitutive in attempting to assume the family's role when necessary. Under this model government would intervene with services that would supplement the family's efforts to provide the dependent elderly with a decent standard of care. These services would support or

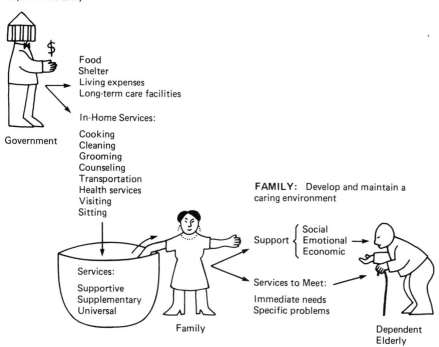

GOVERNMENT: Lessen the social, economic, and physical burdens on the caretaker family by supporting the dependent home-care setting and delaying the institutionalization of dependent elderly

Food
Shelter
Living expenses
Long-term care facilities

In-Home Services:

Government

Cooking
Cleaning
Grooming
Counseling
Transportation
Health services
Visiting
Sitting

FAMILY: Develop and maintain a caring environment

Support { Social
         Emotional →
         Economic

Services:

Supportive
Supplementary
Universal

Services to Meet:

Immediate needs
Specific problems

Family

Dependent Elderly

FIGURE 3–3. Chart mapping the roles of family and government under the liberals' *constructive model.*

encourage the family to continue providing care and would include income maintenance programs to ease the drain on family budgets by contributing money for food, shelter, and related living expenses of the dependent elderly; and in-home services to afford relief to family members from time-consuming caretaker tasks such as cooking, cleaning, grooming, visiting, counseling, and nursing. These services would be universal, not residual, and families would enjoy their benefits at all times and not only when crises threatened the continuation of the care provided by families. Such services would seek to move beyond merely ensuring a minimum level of care itself and toward improving the quality of life for all involved.

The constructive model would offer families the choice of a variety of specific services designed to supplement the care they provide. These services would range from substitutive ones such as long-term care facilities for the elderly who could no longer be cared for at home to supportive services such as financial assistance, rent subsidies, home health services, homemaking assistance, counseling, transportation, and family aides that would provide family members with temporary relief for recreation and holidays. Although liberals recognize that resources are scarce and that the price of these services would be high, they fear that without supportive services the family would increasingly abandon its function of providing care and that the costs for the dependent elderly in human suffering and for the taxpayer in supporting institutions of long-term care would become prohibitive.

Summary.   In emphasizing government intervention into the family's role of providing care, an area that has traditionally enjoyed considerable independence and privacy, the constructive model fits well with the liberal belief that social institutions and socially accepted ideals must be subjected to regular scrutiny and when necessary altered to serve human welfare more effectively. It also reflects the confidence of liberals that government intervention can be restrained to provide needed assistance without destroying the individual initiative of family members to develop and maintain an effective caring environment for their elderly dependents.

Opposing Views of Dependent Elderly Models: The Conservative Position

First argument.   Conservatives offer several arguments in defense of their approach to providing care for the dependent elderly. The first argument is that the reactive model is a practical and workable approach that will ensure the most humane, equitable, and economically efficient distribution of the limited resources available to the dependent elderly. By providing services selectively and not universally, by addressing the specific needs of the dependent elderly rather than those of the caretaker family, and by focusing on only those dependent elderly living away from their families and not those who enjoy family care, the reactive model confronts the problem of allocating scarce resources in a just and realistic manner. It makes the difficult but necessary decisions that establish priorities, introduce a hierarchy of needs, and in effect ensure that something is done for the dependent elderly who are in greatest need.

Second argument.   The conservatives assert that the alternative to the reactive model is increased government intervention, which leads to far-reaching negative consequences. In addition to undermining the willingness of families to provide care, such intervention tends to raise expectations and increase demands for new and costly benefits and services. When this intervention takes the form of financial incentives, it reduces the relationship between the caretaker family and its dependent elderly members to a cash nexus that demeans the value of the services provided by the family. It also leads to the massive intrusion into private lives by a potentially insensitive government bureaucracy. Government's growing involvement and investment of resources are always accompanied by an even more expansive development of administrative and implementative agencies, laws, and regulations needed to monitor and control the distribution of these resources. Thus the policies and services designed to support the family and assist the dependent elderly may prove more abusive of their rights than protective of their welfare. They may require divulging confidential information (marital status, legitimacy of children, medical history, personal belongings, savings, investments), restricting acquisition of wealth (amount of savings, value of car, type of housing), and limiting employment and mobility (amount of income, residence requirements, and the like). Consequently human services workers who act on behalf of a powerful government by enforcing regulations attached to the distribution of benefits are frequently restricting and violating the client's freedom, privacy, right to property, and equality before the law.

Third argument.   A corollary of this second argument is the conservative position that increased government intervention tends also to discourage home care and to facilitate extensive and increasingly costly institutionalization. Specifically programs such as Medicare and Medicaid have created "an intricate web of eligibility requirements, scope of benefits, and income formulae" that favors institutional settings over home care (Callahan et al., 1980, p. 43). Family resolve to suffer the economic and social burdens of caring for their elderly therefore is seriously eroded when government programs are readily available to completely reimburse the costs of institutionalizing the eligible dependent elderly.

Opposing Views of Dependent Elderly Models: The Liberal Position

First argument.   In response to the conservatives, liberals advance several arguments in defense of their approach to providing care for the dependent elderly. The first argument is that the constructive model offers the most effective blueprint for coping with future problems of caring for this group. The projected growth of the elderly population to over 16 percent of the total population by the year 2000 coupled with large-scale demographic changes relating to the family will result in a declining pool of caretakers at the very time the number of care receivers is expanding. These demographic trends, which will be reflected in dramatic changes in the family's willingness or ability to provide home care for the dependent elderly, include the following changes. There will be a growing participation by women, who have traditionally taken care of the dependent elderly, in the labor force. More than 50 percent of adult women have abandoned full-time housekeeping for gainful employment, and this number is expected to continue to grow (Lebed, 1984). There will be a decrease in the number of children available to help in family care. The average lifetime births per woman, which was 3.3 in the 1950s, is expected to decline to 2.2 or less by 1990 (Norton & Glick, 1976). There will be an increasing number of divorced people and single-parent families whose commitment to home care for the dependent elderly will be weakened by demands made on them as part of the labor force. Between 1960 and 1975, for example, the number of single-parent households headed by a divorced woman nearly tripled (Schorr & Moen, 1979). The constructive model cannot alter these demographic changes. However, through its universal approach and consequent increase in government intervention, it can make available to all the financial assistance and various in-home support services that will ease the family burdens of cleaning, preparing meals, nursing, grooming, counseling, and transporting the dependent elderly. This assistance will thus remove the pressures and demands on families that might otherwise become overextended and seek to terminate home care responsibilities. Rather than institutionalize their dependent elderly, these families will be able to continue providing home care while still enjoying financial solvency and the opportunities for privacy, independence, social interaction, and self-fulfillment that make up day-to-day living.

Second argument.   A corollary of this first argument is the liberal position that because a major increase in institutionalization carries a prohibitive price, family support services needed to maintain home care of the dependent elderly remain the only economically feasible approach. Proof of this can be seen by the comparison of the small growth in the population of institutionalized elderly with the rising costs of institutionalization during the 1960s and 1970s. While the institutionalized elderly only increased from 4 percent to 5 percent of the total population over sixty-five between 1966 and 1977, the costs of nursing-home care increased dramatically from $800 million in 1967 to $6.4 billion in 1977 (Callahan et al., 1980, p. 31). In contrast several studies (Sussman, 1985; Sager, 1977; Sussman, 1979) have found home care to be far less costly than institutional care. Furthermore "10 percent of the aged—twice as many as are living in institutions—are confined to bed or otherwise housebound" (Schorr, 1980, p. 33). Thus a sizeable number of dependent elderly rely on "free" home care, and any substantial shift of responsibility from home to institution must result in an astronomical rise in long-term care expenditures and a budget-breaking strain on federal and state resources.

Third argument.   A third liberal argument is that the constructive model is nonjudgmental in its universal approach that seeks to support and promote the dignity and self-sufficiency of all families caring for their elderly. In contrast the reactive model is highly judgmental in its selective approach of substituting only for those families that are experiencing problems in social functioning and thus are no longer able to care for their elderly. The reactive model has its roots in the Elizabethan Poor Laws and in an American myth that holds to an idealized conception of the "self-sufficient, protected, and protective family" (Keniston & the Carnegie Council on Children, 1978, p. 11). It assumes the family has a moral and in part legal responsibility to care for its members. Failure to do so is a "symptom of some moral inadequacy" and an admission to a "form of family bankruptcy" (Moroney, 1978, p. 119). In turn government intervention is an acknowledgment and condemnation of this inadequacy that tends to stigmatize recipients. Some families that are unable to care properly for their dependent elderly may hide this inability from government authorities out of fear of being stigmatized, and thus in some cases the reactive model may be unable to provide for the basic needs of the dependent elderly.

Future Directions

Future directions in the care of the dependent elderly will have to reflect the demographic trends described above, particularly the unprecedented growth of the elderly population. In absolute numbers there will be more elderly than ever by the year 2000, they will live longer and consequently more of them will be frail and dependent. At the same time families will be smaller and increasingly unable to provide in-home care without assistance. These demographic trends alone will probably require the United States to develop programs largely consistent with the liberals' constructive model. However, the social beliefs of the American people and the long history of family care for the elderly appear to indicate that in the future the family will remain "the deepest well of altruism in the nation" (Schorr, 1980, p. 37) and will continue to provide the bulk of care for the dependent elderly.

Government intervention: supportive services. In all probability government will continue to respect the independence and privacy of the family but also will recognize that demographic changes have diminished the family's capacity to provide care and that the family will turn away from home care and toward institutional care if it becomes overextended. Consequently in the future government will more often intervene with supportive services that do not replace but merely substitute for the family. These services will be designed to allow the family to enjoy its normal social functioning while encouraging it to continue to meet the needs of its dependent elderly members. Programs will be universal and services will be flexible and innovative. They will include financial assistance in the form of (1) benefits in kind such as food stamps, rent subsidies, and health care or direct cash payments to compensate the family for immediate costs arising from food, clothing, housing, and health services provided to the dependent elderly; (2) monthly cash allowances for the dependent elderly to help defray the costs of regular aid or assistance provided by the family or purchased from outside agencies; and (3) indirect income-maintenance subsidies such as tax deductions and income tax credits to compensate the family for the lost income of the potential wage earner who must remain at home to attend to the dependent elderly. Support services will also be provided to the family to relieve the strain of providing full-time care and to help it overcome a feeling of social isolation. These will include not only aides that will assist the family with homemaking, nursing, transporting, and other tasks but also day care centers and nursing homes that will provide the dependent elderly with temporary residential accommodations and thus free family members for short periods to pursue leisure activities or other matters.

Establishing such programs on a wide scale in the United States probably depends on two key developments. First the federal government must recognize the demographic, financial, and social factors creating the need for these programs and must take the initiative in their establishment. The individual states cannot establish effective programs without federal coordination and initiative. Federal recognition of the demands for such programs at a level sufficient to instigate their establishment may require, among other things, a thorough national study of the nature, type, and distribution of needs, problems, and resources of the dependent elderly, their families, and the agencies that provide services. Additional research must be undertaken to determine the expectations families share about the management of the dependent elderly and the conditions they require to remain as caretakers rather than placing their dependent members in institutions. From this study a national consciousness must evolve that will clearly establish the family as a critical object of social policy, and legislation must be passed that will provide appropriate support systems required for the family to continue its role in providing care.

The second key development necessary for the establishment of such programs is the adoption by the federal government of an ideological perspective that reconciles the conservative and liberal points of view. It can do so by unequivocally affirming the primary role of the family in providing care to the dependent elderly (on which both conservatives and liberals agree) and the aim of government intervention to strengthen that role. Regardless of whether programs are then based primarily on the reactive or constructive models, they at least will not undermine American beliefs about the family and reduce the dependent elderly and their family members to the status of dehumanized "commodities" serviced by impersonal government agencies. Rather families will be able to serve as the mediators between the dependent elderly, whose needs they understand, and the bureaucracy of government agencies, which can be made responsive to these needs. Families must also demand of these agencies policies that are comprehensible, that is, "to the extent possible rights ought to be available (or not) on the simplest grounds—age, employment status, and so forth" (Schorr, 1980, p. 4). To the extent that these two key developments occur, the probability of the United States establishing long-term, comprehensive, and effective policies and programs of care for the dependent elderly increases proportionately.

THE UNWED SEXUALLY ACTIVE TEENAGER

Mission and Role of Personal Social Services

Despite the elaborate moral codes and attending attitudes and mores developed by social, cultural, and religious groups to govern sexual activities, decisions to engage in sexual activities are ultimately highly personal decisions made for a wide variety of sometimes very different reasons. Ordinarily the consequences of decisions to become sexually active—even outside of marriage—are also personal, the most immediate ones being confined to the sexually active partners themselves. However, when sexual activity takes place between persons who lack the maturity to anticipate and cope with potentially negative consequences, their decisions cease to be purely personal, for society has an interest in minimizing the negative effects of sexual activity both for participants and for society itself. In the United States the largest single group of persons who fail to anticipate the potentially negative consequences of their otherwise personal decisions to engage in sexual activities are unwed teenagers, including those who become or are at risk of becoming pregnant. Our discussion focuses on personal social services directed at this group.

Extent of sexual activity.   Of the 29 million teenagers thirteen to nineteen years old in the United States in 1978, some 12 million were sexually active, with eight in ten men and seven in ten women experiencing intercourse by age nineteen (Alan Guttmacher Institute, 1981). Such a high rate of sexual activity has not been accompanied by an equally high increase in medical family planning, however. Of the 4.6 million sexually active females aged fifteen to nineteen who did not desire pregnancy, four in ten failed to get medical family planning services and either did not take any precautions or depended on the occasional use of over-the-counter contraceptives or on the "highly ineffective folk methods—withdrawal, douche, or rhythm without any medical supervision" (Alan Guttmacher Institute, 1981, p. 49). Estimates suggest that between their fourteenth and nineteenth birthdays, four in ten American girls will become pregnant, two in ten will give birth, two in five will have out-of-wedlock babies, one in three will obtain abortions, and one in nineteen will have at least one miscarriage or stillbirth (Alan Guttmacher Institute, 1981; Phipps-Yonas, 1980). This growth in sexual activity has included teenagers from all economic, ethnic, and social groups. Between 1963 and 1978 premaritally conceived births increased 250 percent for white teenagers and 50 percent for black teenagers. This meant that between 1975 and 1978 six of ten children born to white teenagers and nine of ten born to black teenagers were premaritally conceived (Phipps-Yonas, 1980).

American females aged thirteen to nineteen have one of the highest birthrates in the world, with one in ten becoming pregnant and about 5 percent giving birth each year (Alan Guttmacher Institute, 1981). The number of out-of-wedlock births to teenagers has reached epidemic proportions, and teenagers currently account for half of the one-in-seven births that are illegitimate (DeSilva, 1981; Parachini, 1982). Although the 5 million sexually active, fertile females aged fourteen to nineteen comprised only 18 percent of the 28.5 million sexually active, fertile women aged fourteen to forty-four, they gave birth to "46 percent of the 543,000 out-of-wedlock births and only 11 percent of the 2.8 million marital births" (Alan Guttmacher Institute, 1981, p. 21). For more than one in seven of these unwed teenage mothers the birth of the child will be followed by a second premarital pregnancy within one year, and for at least one in four of them this second pregnancy will occur within two years. Fewer than one in three of the births to unwed teenagers is intended, but 96 percent of the mothers elect to keep their child (Alan Guttmacher Institute, 1981).

Plight of the unwed mother and child.   Severe physical, economic, and social consequences for both mother and child are associated with teenage pregnancy. The mother's physical immaturity, her failure in most instances to receive prenatal care, and her tendency to have poor nutritional habits all contribute to serious health risks to herself and her child. These risks are reflected in a maternal mortality rate for adolescents under fifteen that is more than 100 percent higher than that of women in their early twenties and in a mortality rate for those aged fifteen to nineteen that is more than 10 percent higher than that of older females (Alan Guttmacher Institute, 1981; Green & Poteteiger, 1978). Teen pregnancies are also marked by a higher incidence of health complications such as urinary tract infections, iron-deficiency anemia, toxemia, uterine dysfunction, and prolonged labor.

Infants born to teenagers also fare poorly. Their risk of death is nearly twice that of children born to women in their twenties, and because many of them are born prematurely or with low birth weight (less than 5.5 pounds), they suffer more physical, emotional, and intellectual handicaps. They have a significantly higher rate of birth defects such as epilepsy, spinal deformities, mental retardation, cerebral palsy, clubfoot, and respiratory problems. They score significantly lower in IQ and achievement tests. They are more likely to be reading below the standard level in the primary grades, perform more poorly on cognitive tests in the secondary grades, and in general embrace lower educational aspirations and life goals. It is little wonder that the chances are greater that these children will follow the example of their parents and become teenage parents themselves as the cycle thus continues (Alan Guttmacher Institute, 1981; Green & Poteteiger, 1978; Hendrixson, 1979; Phipps-Yonas, 1980).

Teenage pregnancies have equally adverse effects on the options in the young mother's life. Campbell (1968) poignantly details the consequences:

> The girl who has an illegitimate child at the age of 16 suddenly has 90 percent of her life's script written for her. She will probably drop out of school: even if someone else in the family takes care of the baby she will probably not be able to find a steady job that pays enough to provide for herself and her child; she may feel impelled to marry someone she might not otherwise have chosen. Her life choices are few, and most of them are bad. (p. 238)

The majority of teen mothers leave school, never obtain a high school diploma, and are unable to take advantage of further educational opportunities. If and when child-rearing responsibilities permit, they enter the job market without career preparation, training, or experience. Lacking the qualifications to compete successfully for the more challenging, high-paying jobs, they must accept monotonous, low-status employment that pays marginal wages and is frequently seasonal. If they seek financial support and security by marrying the putative fathers of their children, they are three times more likely to separate or divorce than women who begin childbearing after age twenty. Thus families headed by teen mothers tend to be "economically disadvantaged in terms of occupation, income and assets" (Green & Poteteiger, 1978, p. 11) and are more likely to be poor; one in four are dependent on AFDC payments (Alan Guttmacher Institute, 1981).

Any discussion of existing and potential programs designed to meet the problem of the unwed sexually active teenager must focus on these facts and must recognize that the problem has two critical social dimensions. First the problem is universal in nature. The teenagers involved are not confined to any one social, ethnic, or economic group but rather are from city and farm, from poor and affluent families, from all racial groups, and from all religious denominations. Second the problem is continuous in nature. It is not an aberration that has suddenly been created by unusual social circumstances and will soon fade away. Rather it is a problem that has gradually evolved out of some rather predictable social factors and will remain as "a continuing problem which will fluctuate with the size of the population at-risk, the amount of sexual activity, and the utilization of contraceptives and abortions" (Klerman, 1980, p. 777).

Needs of unwed sexually active teenagers.   The needs of unwed sexually active teenagers evolve from their struggle to find "love and acceptance" (Rivers, 1982), "to be loved and part of a family" (Shriver, 1981), and to understand and come to grips with sex—"at once a great discovery, a great mess, a great pleasure, a great frustration, and an all around great muddle" (Alan Guttmacher Institute, 1976, p. 57). The needs of those unwed teenagers who also become pregnant or parents develop from their decisions either to abort or to carry their children to term, to keep or to place their children for adoption, to remain single or to marry, to complete schooling or to enter the job market prematurely, and to establish households or to remain in their parents' homes.

The type of help these teenagers require ranges from psychological counseling and preventive health services to health care services for mother and child. These services include programs that create "communities of caring" (Shriver, 1981), telephone hot lines to provide information and referral service, sex education courses, birth control services, and individual and family counseling. For teenagers who also become pregnant or parents, additional services include pregnancy testing; counseling; referral services; abortion services; maternity and adoption services; prenatal, delivery, and postnatal care; education on sexuality, family life, and family planning; day care programs; vocational and educational services; and financial assistance, as well as social services such as foster care, legal assistance, outreach, and programs on the prevention of child abuse.

Families' response.   The response of families to the needs of their unwed sexually active teenagers has had little impact on the shaping of human services programs. Most of what adults believe about and want for these adolescents has been ignored by policy-makers or shouted down by vocal minorities. Although seven of ten Americans believe that sex education courses that include information about contraceptives should be taught in the schools, in the early 1980s only three states (Kentucky, Maryland, and New Jersey) required such courses, while forty states either had no policy or left the issue to the discretion of each local school district (Alan Guttmacher Institute, 1981). Similarly, although a majority of both Catholic and Protestant adults favor establishing family planning clinics and making contraceptives available to adolescents (Alan Guttmacher Institute, 1981), many large cities and most rural areas lack such services, and it is estimated that "313,000 pregnancies might have been avoided" if teenagers had had access to and "consistently used, effective contraceptives" (Kadushin, 1980, p. 418; Phipps-Yonas, 1980). In general in the late 1970s and in the 1980s congressional legislation relating to such clinics that do exist has been designed so that "the push has been to reduce public funding available for contraceptive services and abortion" and to direct funding to the "assistance of those [unwed teenagers] already pregnant" (Phipps-Yonas, 1980, p. 425). Finally, although research has shown that the unwed teenage mother living with her parents receives invaluable support services that increase her likelihood of becoming more effective at child rearing, completing her education, and obtaining a job (Furstenberg, 1976; Furstenberg & Crawford, 1978), welfare programs fail to offer incentives to the family for providing such assistance; instead the unwed mother is denied financial aid unless she abandons the family and establishes an independent household (Alan Guttmacher Institute, 1981; Phipps-Yonas, 1980).

Government response: protective services. The response of government to the needs of unwed sexually active teenagers has been divided between providing two types of services—protective services for those who are pregnant or who are in risk of becoming pregnant and supportive services for those who are pregnant or who have given birth. Protective services include family planning, contraceptive services and research, and abortion. By the early 1980s they were provided by some five thousand public and private facilities such as hospitals, Planned Parenthood affiliates, health departments, neighborhood health clinics, and women's health centers. These organized facilities annually provided family planning and contraceptive services to about 1.5 million sexually active teenagers (Alan Guttmacher Institute, 1981). They also provided abortion services to almost .5 million teenagers yearly, or the nearly two in five females aged fifteen to nineteen and more than one in two younger than fifteen who elected to terminate their pregnancies by abortion (Alan Guttmacher Institute, 1981). These facilities have been supported by fees for services, private contributions, and public funding through Title X of the Public Health Services Act, sections of the Social Security Act, the Social Services section of Title XX, and the Maternal and Child Health sections of Title V.

Government response: supportive services. Supportive services offered by the government include financial assistance; housing; medical care; and educational, vocational, and child care services. The basic source of financial assistance is AFDC payments, and teen mothers comprise nearly two-thirds of the women on welfare and absorb close to half of the AFDC funding available (Phipps-Yonas, 1980). Most teen mothers elect to remain in their parents' homes while carrying their babies to term, but for those who do not government has offered two other housing options. There are a limited number of public and private maternity homes that provide shelter and care, as well as foster or "wage" homes that exchange room and board for babysitting and light housework. Most teen mothers have not been employed prior to their pregnancies and are not covered by any health insurance policy. Consequently the medical costs for the prenatal and obstetrical medical care they require are financed through Medicaid. The government has also sought to provide educational, vocational, and child care services for a limited number of teen mothers and their children on a selective and experimental basis, and multiservice, comprehensive, interdisciplinary programs have been provided at places such as the Webster School in the District of Columbia, the Interagency Cyesis program in Oakland, California (Kadushin, 1980), and the Parents Too Soon program in Illinois (Colby, 1984).

Summary. In general programs for the unwed sexually active teenager in America have been built on recognition that the failure of large numbers of teenagers to anticipate and cope with potentially negative consequences of sexual activity is a universal and continuous problem. The mission of these programs, many of which have been sponsored by government, has been largely to provide protective and supportive services.

Origins and History

The frequent incidence of premarital sex in American society is not confined to the twentieth century. It existed during the 1750s in New England, when a third of the women married conceived their first child out of wedlock, and it continues today, when more than a fourth of the first children born are conceived prior to marriage. Since the 1880s premarital sexual permissiveness has increased steadily, with periods of exceptional growth between 1915 and 1925 and again between 1965 and 1975 (Reiss, 1980). Much of this second period of growth has been fueled by the increased sexual activity of teenagers.

Impact of socioeconomic changes. Since around 1960 adolescent sexual behavior has been influenced by major social and economic changes that have resulted in what may be termed a gradual shrinking of childhood and a premature push into early adulthood. The so-called sexual revolution has occurred, certainly a distinct shift in American attitudes accompanied by a freer and more open sexual climate and a dramatic increase in premarital intercourse by teenagers. There also has been a breakdown in family structure marked by a sharp rise in the divorce rate and an increasing experimentation with alternative life styles. There has been a media revolution in programing and merchandising that has inundated the teenage audience with sex; violence; corruption; a glorification of the cheap, shoddy, and trivial; and an appeal to immediate gratification. There has been conspicuous moral bankruptcy, with national leaders being assassinated, national laws and policies being openly resisted and evaded, corrup-

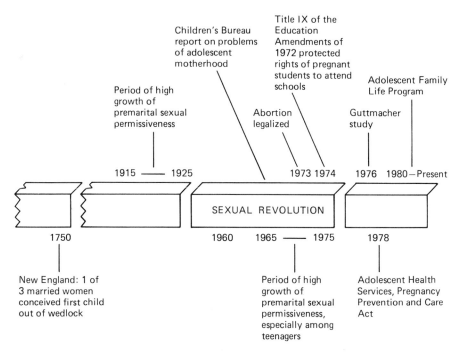

FIGURE 3–4. Timeline tracing the growth of premarital sexual permissiveness from colonial times to the present. Key legislation, programs, judicial actions, and research that have shaped the personal social services approach to adolescent sexual behavior and motherhood are identified.

tion tainting the highest offices, and use of drugs and alcohol increasing among adults and teenagers. There has been a massive movement of mothers into the work force with a growing number of children left unsupervised. Finally there has been a growing feminist movement that has redefined the place of women in society and has led to greater equality in sexual behavior. Although in the past there have been major social and economic changes in America that have influenced adolescent behavior, the magnitude, intensity, and rapidity of these changes since 1960 may be unprecedented.

Federal government intervention. As teenage sexual activity increased in the 1960s, its by-products—unwanted pregnancies and out-of-wedlock births—became more visible to the public. By 1965 extensive research by the federal Children's Bureau sounded an alarm warning the public of the health, educational, and social problems faced by adolescent mothers. In 1973 a Supreme Court decision gave women an absolute right to have an abortion during the first three months of pregnancy. The Court ruling also placed severe limitations on government intervention into this right through the sixth month of pregnancy. This right was upheld and expanded by the Court in a 1983 ruling. By 1974 sections added to Title IX of the Education Amendments of 1972 specifically protected the rights of pregnant students to attend school and encouraged them to complete their education. Under this federal legislation pregnant students could not be expelled from schools nor required to attend a special school or take special courses nor barred from any program. In 1976 the Alan Guttmacher Institute study *11 Million Teenagers: What Can Be Done about the Epidemic of Adolescent Pregnancies in the United States,* which provided a wealth of data that clearly established the magnitude of the problem, was read by a large national audience. In 1978 the federal government sought directly to address and reduce the consequences of teenage pregnancy through the Adolescent Health Services, Pregnancy Prevention and Care Act. Although this act was not funded at the levels originally intended by Congress, it established throughout the country a number of working models of community-based programs for adolescent pregnancy that provide the core services of "pregnancy testing; maternity and adoption counseling; prenatal and postpartum care; nutrition information; and sexuality, family life, and family planning education" (Hendrixson, 1979, p. 664). During the 1980s, under the Reagan administration, the thrust of this act was altered through the establishment of the Adolescent Family Life Program, which focused on discouraging teenage sexual activity. Under this program federal funding was extended only to those demonstration and research projects that were designed to "promote self-discipline and other prudent approaches to the problem of adolescent premarital sexual relations" (Isikoff, 1983, p. A-1). Those who received such funding were also restricted from providing information about various birth control methods, prohibited from mentioning abortion, and required to encourage pregnant teens to carry their babies to term and place them up for adoption.

Conservative and Liberal Perspectives: Social Norms

Role of government.   In their approaches to the unwed sexually active teenager conservatives and liberals embrace similar social norms but differ sharply on their meaning. They agree that government has an obligation to assist the helpless and the weak but disagree as to what the nature and extent of this assistance should be. Conservatives are eager to preserve the privacy and independence of the family and, although acknowledging the concept of *parens patriae,* they seek to limit government intervention to those instances in which the family environment threatens the lives or safety of unwed sexually active teenagers and their children. Public responsibility is necessary and mandated in cases of abuse and severe neglect, but

EXHIBIT 3–2   *ANTI-ABORTION MESSAGE IGNORED*

   Opponents of abortion have discovered that their viewpoint not only does not reflect that of the general public but also that it is frequently ignored by the very segments of the population who should be most receptive to it. Rhode Island is a case in point. Residents of that state provide an excellent example of a populace that should yield to pressures from opponents of abortion but that choose instead to ignore them. Rhode Island's population is more than 60 percent Roman Catholic, and it supports one of the most extensive parochial school systems in the nation. Catholic church leaders have mounted repeated drives against abortion in which parishioners have been asked to write letters to their congresspersons and to sign cards at Mass condemning abortion and calling for legislative action or constitutional amendments to end abortions. The state's General Assembly has passed laws attempting to restrict abortions, and the state lost hundreds of thousands of dollars in legal fees when this legislation was successfully challenged by the American Civil Liberties Union and struck down by the courts.

   How has the general public in Rhode Island responded to this anti-abortion activity? Three of the four congresspersons elected by Rhode Islanders are sympathetic to the prochoice position, and all were elected by large majorities. After the legalization of abortion in 1973 the rate of abortions in Rhode Island has grown each year and increased more than 700 percent over twelve years. By the mid-1980s U.S. Census Bureau statistics showed that Rhode Island's 13.1 live births per 1,000 residents gave it the second lowest birth rate in the country, while its 590 abortions for every 1,000 live births gave it the sixth highest abortion rate nationally (R.I. births 2d lowest, abortions 6th highest, 1985).

---

it becomes an unwarranted trespass and a blatant violation of the privilege and sanctity of the family when it is extended into areas of family planning, sex education, and contraceptive and abortion services. Conservatives would limit assistance to placing pregnant teens in maternity or foster ("wage") homes and to providing teen mothers with pre- and postnatal care, adoption counseling, and child placement services. On the other hand liberals are eager to protect the rights and promote the welfare of the individual, and they view government intervention as the necessary vehicle to achieve this end. They seek to broaden public responsibility and assistance to provide universal services to all unwed sexually active teenagers in the form of family planning, sex education, and contraceptive and abortion services. Liberals would also expand public assistance to all unwed pregnant or parent teenagers and their children through universal services that include pregnancy counseling; prenatal, delivery, and postnatal care; adoption counseling and child placement services; and housing and income maintenance programs.

Role of the marketplace.   Conservatives and liberals agree that private decisions and the forces of the marketplace should be allowed to operate in approaches to the unwed sexually active teenagers, but they differ sharply as to the degree of freedom of expression the forces should have. Conservatives seek to allow them maximum expression by reserving to the family all decisions and arrangements relating to the welfare of unwed sexually active teenagers and their children. The family, as the foremost social institution of nurturing and support, should select, negotiate, and contract with other private parties and agencies (doctors, counselors, lawyers, teachers, pharmacists, hospitals, clinics) for whatever services (family planning, contraceptive services, abortion, pre- and postnatal care, adoption counseling, and the like) that it determines necessary for its unwed sexually active teen members and their children. Conservatives believe that the most effective solutions to the problems of these teenagers will be found more frequently through private decisions than through governmental attempts to curtail and control marketplace forces. Only on those few occasions when private decision-making breaks down should government intervene and share in the decision-making. Liberals would also advocate the private party or marketplace decision-making process, but they would limit and control its expression by juxtaposing with it a system of government-financed universal services (family planning, contraceptive services, abortion, child care, income maintenance, and the like) that would provide the unwed sexually active teenager with options from which to select. Thus liberals would delimit family and private-party decision-making by subjecting it to the competition from government-financed, -operated, and -controlled services that would be readily available to unwed sexually active teenagers and could be freely chosen.

The Conservative Perspective Examined

Parental rights.   The conservative beliefs in order, structure, and control through established institutions and in persons as children of God who are tainted by original sin and therefore imperfect, capricious, and often foolish in matters of importance unless guided by tradition, lead conservatives to reserve to the family the basic responsibility for curbing the potential ill will of its teen members and for imbuing them with traditional values, mores, habits, and attitudes. Central to this view of the role of the family is the underlying conservative concept of parental rights that holds that fundamental to the concern and involvement of parents in the development and socialization of children is their "right and responsibility to form the character of their children" according to the traditional mores and religious and ethical values they embrace. These rights remain primary and cannot be ignored or removed by government "unless, by the standards of common law, parents have been shown unfit to discharge their parental duties" (Rice, 1980, p. 4).

Parents exercise these rights through a wide range of child-rearing functions from providing for the child's physical health and safety to extending counsel and advice. However these rights become jeopardized and are violated when government provides the child with options in family planning such as sex education and contraceptive and abortion services without the knowledge and consent of the parents. Conservatives view these government programs as driving a wedge between members of the family by tempting the child with options that may be diametrically opposed to the values and choices of the parent. These options are also condemned as being retrogressive because they undermine premarital chastity, give community sanction to premarital sex, and destroy family authority by licensing sexual activity. Thus conservatives remain adamantly opposed to all such forms of government intervention and vocally support parental rights and the privacy and independence of the family.

The private model.   To ensure the primacy of parental rights and the sanctity of the family conservatives adopt a private model in their approach to the needs of the unwed sexually active teenager. Under this model parents would have the exclusive right to educate their children according to the philosophy of their choice without government interference. Parents' compelling interest in what is happening to their children would assign to them primary responsibility for all areas of child rearing. Their handling of the sexual activity of their children would be purely a private affair. It would not be the business of government to promote sex education, provide contraceptive and abortion services, or offer income maintenance, housing, and other supportive services to the unwed teen mother, for this would only condone and facilitate teenage sexual activity, pregnancy, and out-of-wedlock births. Rather the private model assumes that only when parental authority and private-party decision-making shape the child's sexual rearing would sexuality and love remain equated and marriage and the family continue as normative in American society.

Conservatives recognize that not all parents would be willing or able to exercise effective parental authority and that private-party decision-making would sometimes break down. When this occurs the welfare of the child would supersede the right to privacy of the parents and family, and the government would be expected to intervene. As with care for the dependent elderly this intervention would be residual in approach. All benefits would be targeted at the specific individual with the problem, in this case the sexually active teenager. There would be no attempt to provide for the needs of the parents and the family or to strengthen their capacity to support the teen member with the problem. The teen member would be required to meet various eligibility criteria; for instance an unwed mother would have to establish that she is without support from either the putative father or her family and that she is unable to meet her needs through the normal mechanism of the market.

Summary.   Again, as with the reactive model for caring for the dependent elderly, the private model reflects basic conservative tenets. Its emphasis on a residual approach reflects the conservative position that state intervention must remain marginal at best if individual initiative is to be allowed to operate freely; if the primacy, independence, and self-determination of the family is to be assured; and if parents are to exercise their rights and responsibilities by providing for the health and welfare of their children.

The Liberal Perspective Examined

The emphasis liberals place on experience and an experimental attitude toward social institutions and their belief that the person is a child of nature with morally neutral needs, interests, and desires lead them to question the effectiveness of parents and the family in the sexual upbringing of children and to call for increased government intervention to correct the deficiencies inherent in older approaches to this critical part of child rearing. Liberals point to the appalling statistics documenting the consequences of the upsurge in teenage sexual activity as evidence that adolescents are not adequately prepared for the sexual revolution that engulfs them. The failure of parents and family to provide their children with contraceptive information and services combined with other socioeconomic forces such as poor family relationships, poverty, racism, and low levels of educational achievement explain the dramatic increase of teenage pregnancies and out-of-wedlock births. Liberals view conservative attempts to explain this epidemic in terms of the supposed ill will and capricious and foolish nature of the child as being simplistic at best. Therefore, although liberals do not seek to have government usurp the traditional role of parents and family in the sexual upbringing of their children, they do expect government to share in and supplement this role through policies encouraging a wide range of services—from sex education to public assistance, from housing to postnatal care—that will allow teenagers to make responsible decisions about their sexual activity.

The public model.   Toward this end liberals adopt a public model in which government intervenes at three different levels of the teenager's sexual life: before and if the teen becomes sexually active, if the teen becomes pregnant, and if the teen becomes a parent.

Government intervention: first level.   Under the public model government programs would provide sex education and contraceptive services on a universal basis at the first level of the teenager's sexual life. Sex education would be subsidized by the government and taught as a required subject from grammar school through high school. The sex education curriculum would be nonjudgmental. It would provide realistic and scientific knowledge about topics such as human relationships and sexuality; fertility, reproduction, and birth control; sexually transmitted diseases; child development; and parenting. Contraceptive services would be available free to all teenagers at family planning clinics supported by government funds. These clinics would offer contraceptive counseling designed to make the male assume responsibility for his sexual activities and to make the female aware of the efficacy and safety of the various contraceptive methods. They would also dispense contraceptives such as condoms to males and medically prescribed devices to females. The objective of these services would be to reduce the number of unwanted pregnancies and to halt the spread of venereal disease by improving the consistency and quality of use of contraceptives by sexually active teenagers.

Government intervention: second level.   At the second level of the teenager's sexual life government programs would provide both abortion and adoption services on a universal basis. The public model would adhere to the Supreme Court decision of 1973 legalizing abortion, and it would allow every pregnant teenager the option of abortion. The public model would view the provision of this procedure by government-funded clinics as neither an endorsement of abortion nor an argument for the virtue of abortion over contraception. Rather clinics would fulfill the requirements of the law when they offered the pregnant teen the choice to terminate an unwanted pregnancy. Similarly the clinics would support the principles of voluntarism and informed consent by explaining to the pregnant teen all the risks, benefits, and consequences of either abortion or maternity and by acquainting her with the various abortion or prenatal and maternity services that are available. For the teen who elected maternity, clinics would provide counseling that offered an even-handed, objective analysis of the social, emotional, and economic advantages and disadvantages of either giving the child up for adoption or accepting the responsibility for care of the child in a single-parent family. For the teen who elected to place her child up for adoption, clinics would provide counseling to aid her adjustment and social and legal services to ensure proper placement of the child.

Government intervention: third level.   At the third level of the teenager's sexual life government programs would provide health, social, and financial services on a universal basis for the teen mother who decided to raise her child. Under the public model government funds would support clinics and hospitals providing prenatal, delivery, and postpartum care to teens carrying pregnancies to term. In addition to securing the physical and emotional health of mother and infant at birth the public model would provide services that would help the new mother to complete her education or vocational training and to become gainfully employed. These services would include day care to permit the mother to attend school or work; psychological counseling to aid her adjustment to a role as head of a single-parent family; contraception to avoid subsequent unplanned pregnancies; and housing and financial assistance to permit her to live independently of her parents. Although the public model would guarantee that supportive services are available to the unwed teen mother and her child independent of the actions of parents or family, it would attempt to encourage the continuation of parental and family love, care, and nurturance for the teen mother and her child. Consequently, whenever possible the public model would adjust programs to build on the strengths inherent in the family by offering incentives to parents and family that would enable them to assist and support the teen mother as she struggled to cope with the problems of raising her child.

Summary.   Again, as with the constructive model for caring for the dependent elderly, the public model reflects basic liberal tenets. Its emphasis on a universal approach to government intervention into the sexual upbringing of the teen members of the family, an area that has traditionally enjoyed considerable independence and privacy, fits well with liberal beliefs that social institutions and socially accepted ideals must be subjected to regular scrutiny and when necessary altered to serve human welfare effectively.

Opposing Views of Unwed Sexually Active Teenager Models: The Conservative Position

First argument.   Conservatives offer the following arguments in defense of their approach to the unwed sexually active teenager. The first argument is that the private model remains the last barrier before the acceptance of a new morality implicit in government policy that seeks to promote and support the sexual revolution. Conservatives view this new morality as teaching teenagers that sexual activity is inevitable and acceptable as long as it does not result in pregnancy. It is a morality in which the government provides teenagers with contraceptives and, when unwanted pregnancies occur, either the funds for abortions or subsidies for the unwed teen mothers to use in establishing their own households. The private model opposes and constrains this new morality by calling for a return to what conservatives view as the tried, tested, and true morality and innocence of the past. This conservative morality reflects a religious framework and calls on the teenager to practice discipline and restraint in abstaining from sexual activities before marriage. Under this morality the family fulfills its natural function of nurturing caring relationships among parents, children, and other members of the extended family. When the sexual concerns of teen members are approached by parents, the emphasis is on sexuality as that part of love and marriage that strengthens and deepens commitment to one person. Teen members are encouraged to reject transitory, adolescent notions of sexuality and to adopt the more timeless commitments and values of love, marriage, and the creation of an enduring family.

Second argument. A corollary of this first argument is the conservative position that government intervention destroys the family's natural function of nurturing and its role as the foremost social institution of human support. This destruction occurs because government intervention promotes the notion that bureaucrats or human services workers rather than parents know what is best for the sexual upbringing of their children. Further such intervention encourages illegitimacy and strips away parental authority and family control because its social support programs of medical and public assistance, day care, and continuing education ensure teenagers with out-of-wedlock children the viable option of independent living without parental interference.

Third argument. The private model places the responsibility for the sexual upbringing of children squarely on the parents and the family, and it encourages their support when teenage childbearing occurs. Studies (Alan Guttmacher Institute, 1981; Furstenberg & Crawford, 1978) have shown that teen mothers who remain at home and receive food, clothing, shelter, child care, emotional support, advice, and child-rearing assistance from the family are more likely to complete their education, become gainfully employed, and make the adjustments required by single parenthood.

Opposing Views of Unwed Sexually Active Teenager Models: The Liberal Position

First argument. In response to conservatives liberals advance the following arguments in defense of their approach to providing for the needs of the unwed sexually active teenager. The first argument is that the public model responds to these teenagers' needs for information and contraceptive services and reduces the physical, emotional, social, and economic consequences of venereal disease, pregnancy, out-of-wedlock children, and undereducated and unemployable teen parents. It is a realistic, responsible, ordered, preventive approach to a problem that cannot be wished away. The public model recognizes that sex is a natural part of life that cannot be hidden from children and that each generation works or blunders its way to its own sexual ethic. It views the present society as being saturated by movies, television, and publications containing an image of sex that is exploitative, deromanticized, stripped of depth and mystery, cheapened, and made banal. The public model seeks to counteract this attitude about sex and the concomitant sexual ignorance, experimentation, and recklessness of irresponsible, sexually active teenagers with information and contraceptive services that teach them about their bodies and that promote personal and social responsibility toward sex. In support of the effectiveness of these services, liberals cite studies (Alan Guttmacher Institute, 1981; Green & Poteteiger, 1978; Phipps-Yonas, 1980) that document dramatic decreases in teen pregnancies, out-of-wedlock births, and venereal disease whenever such information and contraceptive services are available.

Second argument. A corollary of this first argument is the liberal position that, contrary to conservative claims, rapidly increasing teenage sexual activity has not been accelerated by government-funded information, contraceptive, or abortion services. Liberals note that teenagers were sexually active long before family planning clinics appeared in the 1970s and that most teenage girls are sexually active at least one year before they seek birth control help in a clinic (Alan Guttmacher Institute, 1981). Similarly, pregnant teens have sought abortion long before government-funded clinics were available, even if it meant submitting to the butchery of illegal abortionists. Thus liberals view their public model as the most effective possible response to teenage sexual activity for it tempers and controls the negative consequences of that activity. They point as evidence to studies (Alan Guttmacher Institute, 1981; Green & Poteteiger, 1978) that estimate that the number of teen pregnancies doubles when information and contraceptive services are not accessible and that the number of children born to teens is reduced by one-third when adequate abortion services are made available.

Third argument. A third liberal argument condemns the private model for its judgmental and residual approach and its almost exclusive reliance on parents and family to support the teen mother and child. Liberals fear that such support is not always fully extended and that both mother and child suffer deprivation when no other source of assistance is available.

In contrast the liberals argue that the public model is nonjudgmental in its universal approach and seeks to support and promote the dignity, self-sufficiency, health, and welfare of every unwed teen mother and her child. It recognizes her lack of knowledge about infants and parenting, her social alienation and lack of self-esteem, her limited educational and vocational preparation, and her typically low socioeconomic status. Consequently, as this model continues to encourage the family to support the unwed teen mother, it moves beyond the family by offering a wide range of supportive services that provide structure and meaning to her life and enable her to become an effective mother and a productive member of society.

Future Directions

Future directions in programs for the unwed sexually active teenager will have to reflect the continuous unfolding of the sexual revolution and of other social and economic changes in America. General trends seem to indicate that both conservative and liberal beliefs will be reflected in these programs but that the public model advocated by liberals will predominate. Although these programs will involve government in areas of child rearing that have traditionally been the sole responsibility of parents and families, they will also seek to preserve parental and family authority and integrity by working closely and cooperatively with them in providing teenagers with effective, responsible, and informed approaches to sexual activity. These programs then will blend liberal and conservative beliefs as they combine the more pragmatic and immediate objectives of a government policy based on facts and successful results with the more interpersonal and emotional concerns of parents and family based on ideological grounds.

Government intervention: a multifaceted role.   Possible future government programs will be flexible, innovative, and universal in their approach to the unwed sexually active teenager. These programs will include government-funded sex education, which will be taught through schools, youth agencies, churches, and the media; provide instruction in sexuality, reproduction, and birth control; and be designed to involve parents. Other government-funded programs will be directed at providing parents with accurate information on sexuality and training them to better understand the changing norms in teen sexual behavior and to talk more effectively to their children about sex. There will also be government-funded family planning programs directed specifically at the sexually active teenage male and designed to encourage him to be more responsible and informed in his sexual behavior and to be more concerned and committed toward his partner. These programs will also seek to develop an attitude of shared concern by involving the putative teen father in decisions regarding the pregnancy of his partner and the care and support of their child. Other government-funded family planning services, available at no cost at public clinics and at low cost at private clinics, will meet adolescent needs ranging from contraceptive services to child care and adoption services. Although abortions have become highly controversial during the 1980s, they will probably continue to be provided. All these services, which include education, counseling, referral, and medical services, will be available after school hours and at easily accessible locations. Unless there is a repeal or major reinterpretation of the Supreme Court abortion decision of 1973, these services will respect the confidentiality of the teen client and will be provided without the requirement of parental consent. Finally government will fund research for the development of more effective contraceptive methods. Technologies for contraception will be improved to provide a simple, efficient method tailored to the needs of adolescents who intermittently engage in sex. In the foreseeable future a postcoital or once-a-month method will likely be developed, tested, and available at family planning clinics.

The development of such programs is predicated on government adopting a number of policies with far-reaching social, economic, and political implications, particularly policies that will strengthen the capacity of parents and families to provide for their teen members. Government policies must include providing jobs and adequate income maintenance that will reduce poverty, child care for working parents, broad health coverage that will ensure quality care for all, social and psychological support services to parents and families that will promote and improve family communication and counsel parents on child-rearing practices, improved job and wage opportunities for women that will allow female-headed single-parent families an adequate income, and school programs that will challenge and develop the abilities of disadvantaged children. Arguments against such policies themselves will be made on ideological grounds; however a more severe threat to the wide-scale implementation of these policies is the reluctance of government to absorb the costs these programs entail. This reluctance likely will be overcome as the American public comes increasingly to believe that both the social and financial costs of *not* implementing such policies and programs considerably exceed their strictly financial cost. As these policies and programs are gradually implemented in the future, they will promote the nurturing, caring, and loving functions of parents and families, which in turn will prevent or ameliorate many social problems related to adolescent sexual activity and childbearing.

STUDY QUESTIONS AND ACTIVITIES

1. Why did the personal social services system develop later than other systems? Does this imply that personal social services are less important than other services? Why do many personal social services lend themselves to a one-to-one relationship between client and worker? List examples. Does it matter whether programs are meant to aid individual clients or to solve major social problems such as child abuse and neglect? For each primary service listed on p. 62, cite and explain several examples of their specific services to clients. What do all these services have in common? How do they differ?

2. Why are personal social services in modern America becoming less selective and more universal? Why are these services potentially controversial? Explain the ethical issues at stake. What effect have changes in family life had on personal social services? What new needs have been created by such changes and others in American society? Account for the ambivalence in the United States toward personal social services. What relationships exist between federal, state, and local governments and private agencies in providing these services? What new personal social services may develop as American society continues to change?

3. Why is it difficult to document the extent of child abuse and neglect? Of the eight kinds of child abuse and neglect listed by Kadushin, are some more serious than others? Why? What are the negative effects of each on children? Why, although incidents of neglect are reported more frequently than incidents of abuse, does abuse receive greater public attention? Why would people who suffered abuse as children tend to become abusive parents? List examples of programs of protective services and programs of supportive and supplementary services; explain the differences between the two types of programs. What are the usual goals of protective services workers in dealing with child abuse and neglect? Explain *parens patriae.*

4. How do the social and medical-legal approaches to the problem of abuse and neglect differ? What assumptions about human nature and society underlie each approach? On what social norms and specific goals do both conservatives and liberals agree in treating the problem? Why, however, do conservatives look more to human nature and liberals more to the socioeconomic system in explaining the problem and developing their own programs of treatment? Outline in detail the specific programs advocated by conservatives and liberals, explaining such basic differences as why one program includes a residual approach and the other a universal approach, how each program treats the family, and the basic arguments for and against each program. How can likely future programs specifically combine both conservative and liberal approaches?

5. Outline and account for the most basic demographic data that explain and set the conditions for the national problem of providing care for the dependent elderly. How will likely future demographic changes influence this problem and its potential solutions? Why do families provide more care for the elderly than do institutions? In what ways can institutional care be considered superior and in what ways inferior to home care? Under what circumstances should home care be terminated and institutional care begin? In what ways do the attitudes of the elderly coincide with those of the people who may care for them? What kinds of aid do children often provide for their dependent parents? Why do some kinds of aid occur more frequently in families with low incomes than in families with high incomes, and why is the reverse sometimes true? List and explain types of tangible and intangible care and aid. What needs do these different types meet? List some of the specific responses of government to the needs of the dependent elderly. What has been the basic mission of government programs?

6. What approaches to care for the elderly predominated during colonial times? Which of these carried over into the nineteenth and twentieth centuries? In what ways have the elderly become both more and less potentially dependent since colonial times? Why has financial support for the elderly become increasingly assumed by government? In what specific ways do conservative and liberal approaches to the dependent elderly embrace the same social norms? In what specific ways do these approaches differ? How can programs of support for the dependent elderly weaken family life? How can they strengthen it? Contrast the reactive and constructive models and substitutive and supportive forms of care. Outline and explain the financial, social, and personal arguments both for and against the conservative and liberal models of care. In what ways can future programs of care for the dependent elderly combine conservative and liberal ideas?

7. In what ways can decisions to engage in sexual activity be justified as purely personal? Why can the consequences of sexual activity be both potentially positive and negative? Under what circumstances do the consequences of sexual activity become public concerns? Why are teenagers less likely than adults to anticipate and cope with potentially negative consequences of sexual activity? List and describe as fully as possible the negative consequences of teenage pregnancy. Why do the children of teenage parents tend to become teenage parents themselves? In what ways can teenage sexual activity be considered a problem? In what ways can this problem be considered universal and continuous? List and explain the types of help needed by unwed sexually active teenagers. On what needs are these types of help based? How have families traditionally responded to such needs? Explain and give examples of the protective and the supportive services that government has provided in response to these needs.

8. Have social and economic conditions influencing sexual behavior since 1960 been substantially different from those conditons before 1960? In what sense have conditions since 1960 represented a diminution of childhood? On what social norms do conservatives and liberals agree in approaching the problem of the unwed sexually active teenager? How do they differ in interpreting these norms? How do they differ in defining the proper role for parents and families and for government? Contrast the private and public models for providing programs for the unwed sexually active teenager, explaining the specific programs each supports and why one incorporates a residual and the other a universal approach. List and explain the basic arguments for and against each approach. What evidence supports these arguments? What seem to be the major social trends in the United States that will influence the future directions of programs for the unwed sexually active teenager? Explain the basic ideological points of view that make abortion highly controversial. Why will future programs be likely to include both conservative and liberal beliefs but with liberal approaches predominating? Describe and evaluate likely future programs. To what extent can such programs eliminate or ameliorate the problems of the unwed sexually active teenager? Weigh the social and the financial costs of both providing and not providing such programs.

REFERENCES

Advisory Committee on Child Development. (1976). *Toward a national policy for children and families* (pp. 84–91). Washington, DC: National Academy of Sciences.

Alan Guttmacher Institute. (1976). *11 million teenagers: What can be done about the epidemic of adolescent pregnancies in the United States.* New York: Author.

Alan Guttmacher Institute. (1981). *Teenage pregnancy: The problem that hasn't gone away.* New York: Author.

Antler, S. (1978). Child abuse: An emerging social priority. *Social Work, 23,* 58–61.

Barbour, J. (1982, April 16). Growing old ain't what it used to be. *The Providence Journal/Bulletin,* p. B-9.

Berkeley Planning Associates. (1978). *Evaluation of child abuse and neglect demonstration projects, 1974–1977* (pp. 105–117). Washington, DC: National Center for Health Services Research.

Broder, D. (1985, January 24). Our changing views of the very old. *The Providence Journal/Bulletin,* p. A-12.

Callahan, J. J., Jr., Diamond, L. D., Giele, J. Z., & Morris, R. (1980, Winter). Responsibility of families for their severely disabled elders. *Health Care Financing Review,* pp. 29–48.

Campbell, A. A. (1968). The role of family planning in the reduction of poverty. *Journal of Marriage and the Family, 30,* 238.

Colby, T. (1984, April 25). Teen mothers. *The Providence Journal/Bulletin,* p. A-1.

Congressional Budget Office. (1977). *Long term care: Actuarial cost estimates.* Washington, DC: U.S. Government Printing Office.

DeSilva, B. (1981, October 4). Myths of the American family. *The Providence Sunday Journal,* p. A-14.

Furstenberg, F. F. (1976). The social consequences of teenage parenthood. *Family Planning Perspectives, 8,* 150–164.

Furstenberg, F. F. & Crawford, A. G. (1978). Family support: Helping teenage mothers to cope. *Family Planning Perspectives, 10,* 322–333.

Gaylen, W., et al. (1978). *Doing good: The limits of benevolence* (pp. 3–35). New York: Pantheon Books.

Gelles, R. J. (1978). "Violence toward children in the United States. *American Journal of Orthopsychiatry, 48,* 580.

Gill, D. G. (1971). *Violence against children.* Cambridge, MA: Harvard University Press.

Green, C. P., & Poteteiger, K. (1978, May–June). Teenage pregnancy: A major problem for minors. *Society,* pp. 8–13.

Gurland, B., Dean, L., Cook, D., & Gurland, R. (1978). *Personal time dependency in the elderly of New York City: Findings from the U.S.–U.K. Cross-National Geriatric Community Study.* New York: Community Council of Greater New York.

Hendrixson, L. L. (1979, May). Pregnant children: A socio-educational challenge. *Phi Delta Kappan,* pp. 663–666.

Hobbs, M. A. (1982, June 1). Child abuse: A nation's dirty linen. *The Providence Journal/Bulletin,* pp. 1, 11.

Isikoff, M. (1983, April 25). U.S. bolsters campaign to curb teen sex. *The Providence Journal/Bulletin,* pp. A-1, A-8.

Kadushin, A. (1980). *Child welfare services* (pp. 151–234, 413–463). New York: Macmillan.

Kamerman, S. B., & Kahn, A. J. (1977). *Social services in international perspective* (pp. 1–6). Washington, DC: U.S. Government Printing Office.

Kamerman, S. B., & Kahn, A. J. (Eds.). (1978). *Family policy: Government and families in fourteen countries* (pp. 452–458). New York: Columbia University Press.

Kempe, C., & Helfer, R. (Eds.). (1972). *Helping the battered child and his family.* Philadelphia: J. B. Lippincott.

Keniston, K., & the Carnegie Council on Children. (1978). *All our children* (pp. 2–12). New York: Harcourt Brace Jovanovich.

Kett, J. (1978). *The American family, 1978: Human values and public policy* (pp. 9–12). Philadelphia: Saint Joseph's College Press.

Klerman, L. V. (1980). Adolescent pregnancy: A new look at a continuing problem. *American Journal of Public Health, 70,* 776–778.

Lebed, H. (1984, January 21). Who will take care of the children? *The Providence Journal/Bulletin,* p. A-20.

Louis Harris & Associates. (1975). *The myth and reality of aging in America* (p. 223). Washington, DC: National Council on Aging.

Markham, B. (1980). Child abuse intervention: Conflict in current practice and legal theory. *Pediatrics, 65* (1), 180–185.

Moroney, R. M. (1978). *The family and the state: Considerations for social policy* (pp. 34–62, 116–140). New York: Longman.

Morris, R. (1979). *Social policy of the American welfare state* (pp. 120–126). New York: Harper & Row.

Newberger, E. H., & Bourne, R. (1980). The medicalization and legalization of child abuse. In A. Skolnick & J. H. Skolnick (Eds.), *Family in transition* (pp. 411–426). Boston: Little, Brown.

Newberger, E. H., & Hyde, J. N., Jr. (1975). Principles and implications of current pediatric practice. *Pediatric Clinics of North America, 22,* 695.

Norton, A. J., & Glick, P. C. (1976, May–June). Changes in American family life. *Children Today,* pp. 35–37.

Parachini, A. (1982, December 12). Out-of-wedlock births showing marked increase. *The Providence Sunday Journal,* p. B-18.

Phipps-Yonas, S. (1980). Teenage pregnancy and motherhood: A review of the literature. *American Journal of Orthopsychiatry, 50* (3), 403–431.

Reiss, I. L. (1980). *Family systems in America* (pp. 87–112, 166–192). New York: Holt, Rinehart, & Winston.

R.I. births 2d lowest, abortions 6th highest. (1985, March 1). *Providence Journal/Bulletin,* pp. A-1, A-2.

Rice, R. M. (1980, January 3). The New Right: The White House Conference on Families and Family Service Agencies (pp. 1–7). Memo sent to Executives and Directors of Accredited and Provisional Member Agencies, State Action Officials, Family Service Association of America (FSAA) Board of Directors, FSAA Staff. New York: Family Services of America.

Rivers, C. (1982, January 2). Confidence, self-esteem and teenage pregnancies. *The Providence Journal/Bulletin,* p. A-19.

Sager, A. (1977). Estimating the costs of diverting patients from nursing care to home care services. Waltham, MA: Levinson Policy Institute, Brandeis University.

Schorr, A. L. (1961). *Filial responsibility in the modern American family.* Washington, DC: Social Security Administration, Division of Program Research.

Schorr, A. L. (1980). "... *thy father and thy mother ...": A second look at filial responsibility and family policy* (pp. 1–39). Washington, DC: U.S. Department of Health and Human Services.

Schorr, A. L., & Moen, P. (1979, March–April). The single parent and public policy. *Social Policy, 9* (5), 15–21.

Shanas, E., & Hauser, P. M. (1974). Zero population growth and the family life of old people. *The Journal of Social Issues, 30* (4), 79–92.

Shriver, E. (1981, March 7). Sexuality and the "community of caring." *The Providence Journal/Bulletin,* p. A-17.

Sussman, M. B. (1985). The family life of old people. In R. H. Binstock and E. Shanas (Eds.), *Handbook of aging and the social sciences* (pp. 415–449). New York: Van Nostrand.

Sussman, M. B. (1979, January). *Social and economic supports and family environments for the elderly* (Final Report to the Administration on Aging). Washington, DC.

U.S. Department of Health, Education, and Welfare. (1978). *1978 HEW Task Force Report on Long Term Care.* Washington, DC: Office of the Secretary.

4

HEALTH SERVICES

SCOPE OF THE SYSTEM

The health services system that has developed in the United States provides a myriad of services from family counseling to biomedical research. Central to this system are selective programs directed at specific segments of the population. These programs include a federal program providing health insurance for the aged and disabled who are eligible for Social Security benefits (Medicare); a federal-state program financing health care services for the needy who are blind, aged, disabled, or members of a family with dependent children headed by a single parent or in which one parent is incapacitated (Medicaid); a federal program delivering health services to American Indians; and a federal program offering health services to veterans through a network of over 170 Veterans Administration hospitals. In each of these programs the individual beneficiaries of the services receive medical coverage that is episodic and limited to a specific illness, disability, or related need.

Unlike England the United States does not have a single, all-encompassing, national health program that attempts to reach every segment of the population. There is no federal- or state-subsidized health insurance program that provides all citizens with universal coverage for services purchased from the private sector nor is there a federal- or state-administered health program that delivers services to all citizens through public clinics. Rather the health services system in the United States comprises a mosaic of federal, state, and local programs that involve private, public, and voluntary organizations, agencies, and personnel and that are financed by public funds, private contributions, and individual private-party payments. It is a system predicated on societal norms that promote the operation of the marketplace and leave health services primarily in the hands of privately organized providers who are typically engaged in solo, independent, fee-for-service practice. Consequently two concepts held sacred in the United States dominate the system: First, the patient must have freedom of choice in selecting a physician; and second, the physician must have autonomy in selecting a treatment.

Development of Health Services

Early history.   The basic belief that medical care is a private good to be financed by private funds in a marketplace that is largely unregulated has been a critical factor in shaping the development of the health services throughout the history of the United States. Prior to the twentieth century individuals and families shouldered responsibility for their own health care, either providing it themselves or purchasing services in the private sector. When this responsibility could not be met, as in the case of the poor, private charities or cities and counties usually provided some sort of assistance. Some major cities maintained public hospitals that provided medical care for the poor and long-term treatment for those with infectious diseases. In certain localities municipal homes, poor farms, and hospitals were established to care for the needy and those with chronic diseases such as tuberculosis and mental illness. The federal government was not involved in these efforts but rather confined its health services role to the control of diseases at ports of entry and the provision of medical care to specified groups such as American Indians, merchant seamen, veterans, and dependents of members of the armed forces (Morris, 1979).

Federal intervention.   During the twentieth century the federal government has altered its role of minimal involvement in the health services system and become a major force in the development of programs and provision of funding. Federal intervention was precipitated in the early 1900s by a report from the newly established Children's Bureau on the causes of infant and maternal mortality that established that most infants died from remediable conditions existing before birth. In response Congress passed the Sheppard-Towner Act in 1921, which extended federal aid to the states for health services designed to promote the welfare and hygiene of mothers and infants. Although the act lapsed within eight years,

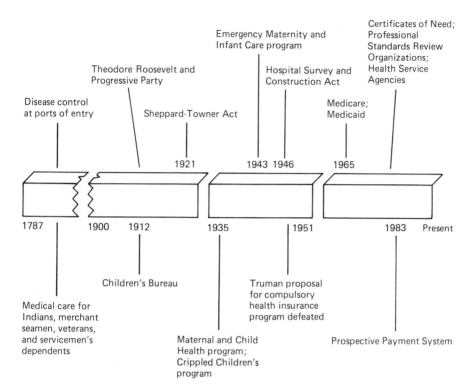

FIGURE 4–1.   Timeline tracing the role of the federal government in the health services from the founding of the country to the present. Key programs, legislation, institutions, and individuals that have shaped the development of health services are identified.

it set the precedent for future federal-state relationships and prepared the foundations for a nationwide system of state-administered maternal and child health programs. Under the Social Security Act of 1935 the federal government again became involved in child health services and provided grants-in-aid to the states for two comprehensive programs. The Maternal and Child Health program of 1935 provided a potpourri of activities, services, and facilities ranging from child health conferences and poison control centers to immunizations and services for abused children and pregnant teenagers. The Crippled Children's program of the same year provided research and diagnostic and preventive services directed at the early detection and treatment of handicapping conditions in children.

Increased federal funding.   In 1943 the demand for pregnancy care for servicemen's wives led the federal government to shift the focus of its intervention from preventive health care to involvement in the direct delivery of medical care. Under the Emergency Maternity and Infant Care program federal funds were channeled to state health departments for the hospitalization and maternity care of wives and babies of men in the four lowest grades of the armed forces. At the end of World War II this program was discontinued and federal intervention shifted to the promotion of increased availability of medical care. The Hospital Survey and Construction Act of 1946 and its later amendments provided federal funds in the form of grants, loans, and loan guarantees for the modernization and construction of a variety of public and private hospitals and public health care centers. Federal funds exceeding $4 billion were spent in the fifteen years from 1946 to 1951 to increase significantly the number of beds relative to population in rural areas and other regions with no hospitals or unaccredited facilities (Steiner, 1976; O'Connor, 1978). In 1965 the federal government's role in health services expanded dramatically with the enactment of Medicare and Medicaid. These programs were designed to remove financial barriers preventing access by the elderly, handicapped, and needy to America's fee-for-service medical care system, and they sharply increased federal expenditures in the health services system. Within ten years of their enactment federal outlays amounted to $33 billion and continued to rise rapidly (Gibson & Mueller, 1977, p. 11).

Increased federal controls.   As federal investment and involvement in the health services increased so did federal regulations and restrictions directed at the quality, availability, and cost of medical care. Federal concern throughout the 1970s and to the present has focused on monitoring the development of health services and controlling their costs. Several key laws have been directed toward these ends. States have been required to adopt Certificate of Need legislation, which subjects proposals for hospital construction and substantive changes in services by medical providers to the approval of a public body. Professional Standards Review Organizations comprising physicians, other providers, and members of state rate-setting boards have been created to set criteria determining the average method of treatment for major health conditions and the average length of hospital stays for Medicare and Medicaid patients. Health Service Agencies have been established to oversee the development and reconstruction of health delivery systems in areas throughout the country.

Thus during the twentieth century local and state activities providing health services were first supplemented and then dominated by the federal government. Under this influence the system of health services in the United States has expanded to include a comprehensive network of programs directed at the various dimensions of health care. It now provides a multiplicity of services to meet the diverse health concerns of an increasing number of Americans of all ages and from all walks of life. In accordance with American beliefs primary care is still provided largely by the fee-for-service physicians in the private marketplace, but the role of the federal government has been to expand both the kinds and the quality of care available to many Americans, and therefore the marketplace is no longer entirely private because it has come to be both subsidized and regulated by the federal government.

Health services listed.   Any inventory of goods and services provided by the health services system must remain open-ended since the boundaries of the system are frequently redefined and new services continually develop. Nonetheless the following is a reasonably inclusive listing of the primary services provided by the health services system in the United States as supplements to or subsidies for the specific treatments patients receive directly from physicians in the private, fee-for-service marketplace:

1. Hospital insurance and supplementary medical insurance for the aged and disabled
2. Health care payments for eligible poor families
3. Tax deductions for part of medical costs and health insurance premiums
4. Health services for American Indians
5. Monitoring of hospital utilization and quality of inpatient care for Medicare and Medicaid recipients
6. Subsidies for the modernization and construction of hospitals and health centers in areas without adequate facilities
7. Preventive health programs for mothers and children
8. Programs for the treatment and rehabilitation of the disabled and injured
9. Support of the National Institutes of Health and a broad program of biomedical research
10. Veterans Administration hospitals for former members of the armed services
11. Subsidies for medical education.

General aim of health services.   This listing reflects the general aim of the American health services system, namely a more equitable distribution of health care services to ensure equal access by vulnerable segments of the population such as the elderly, mothers and infants, the handicapped, the poor, and residents of rural and poor urban areas without adequate medical facilities. Fundamental to this aim is the recognition that universally available, adequate health care can reduce the debilitating effects of ill health that prevent the afflicted from realizing their full potential and enjoying meaningful and productive lives. The list includes services that are both hard and soft, and although they are usually provided to help the recipient directly, they can also be justified as alleviating health problems with broader consequences for society in general and therefore can be classified as both indirect and direct. These services are provided selectively, that is, only to the vulnerable segments of society who presumably cannot afford nor obtain adequate health care services in a totally private

EXHIBIT 4–1   *DOCTOR SURPLUS: CURSE OR BLESSING?*

Federal policy of the late 1960s and early 1970s sought to eradicate a shortage of physicians by providing aid to enlarge the classes of existing medical schools or to establish new ones. A major consequence of this policy is that medical schools in the United States will find themselves producing a surplus of doctors by the end of the century. The ratio of doctors to population has risen each year and is expected to increase from 200 physicians per 100,000 people in the mid-1980s to 250 per 100,000 by 1990. The total pool of doctors will grow from 450,000 to 600,000, and it is predicted that a surplus of between 35,000 and 85,000 doctors will develop.

Is this surplus a curse or a blessing? Those who oppose a doctor glut call for government action that will encourage medical schools to reduce the size of their classes. They argue that a surplus of doctors will not mean lower health costs because the law of supply and demand does not work in the field of physician care. The doctor as supplier almost totally controls demand; once the patient comes for an examination, the doctor determines how much care and treatment the patient will receive. Further, doctors do not lower fees to attract patients because few people shop for a doctor on the basis of cost. Opponents of a doctor glut also fear that a surplus of doctors will mean that more physicians will try to maintain their incomes with fewer patients. This will lead some doctors to preserve their standard of living by providing treatment that is either unnecessary or marginally necessary at best.

Those who favor a surplus of doctors call for government to continue to fund larger classes in the medical schools. They argue that the competition generated by a doctor glut will prove advantageous to the patient and result in better patient care. Among the benefits they foresee are physicians setting up specialized practices in smaller towns, establishing practices in ghettos and rural areas, making house calls, maintaining early morning and late evening office hours for the convenience of patients, and establishing conveniently located, walk-in clinics. Supporters of this surplus also reject the argument that overpopulation will turn doctors into predators and result in a proliferation of questionable services. Rather they point to Medicare's system of flat fees for specific ailments as an effective way for insurers to control the fees charged and the treatment provided by physicians.

The cause of the projected oversupply of physicians can be traced to the political level. Political leaders created the surplus when they provided the funds for the expansion of medical classes. They were responding not only to the medical needs of the nation but also to pressure from parents who wanted more opportunities for their children to become doctors. At the time medical schools needed the funds and reluctantly admitted more students. These schools remain committed to graduating large classes and can no longer survive without continued government funding. Thus political leaders must ultimately determine the course of action to be taken in reference to the doctor glut; they will have to answer the question of whether the surplus is a curse or a blessing.

marketplace. However, as more and more Americans have come to believe that services such as these are essential to all citizens and therefore have become a basic right, the demand for universally provided health services has grown.

Controversy Surrounding Health Services

Good health as a basic human right. The development of the health services system has not been without disagreements and misgivings. Although all will agree that good health is desirable, a sharp division has developed between those who emphasize protecting the right to good health and those who stress safeguarding the right to private-party decision-making. On the one hand there is the demand that access to medical care be viewed as a basic human right on the grounds that good health is a necessary condition for realizing the fundamental right to life. Government thus should intervene to ensure that everyone has full access to health services. On the other hand there is the demand to maintain societal norms that uphold the operation of the private marketplace and the freedom of individual choice. These norms are viewed as reflecting deeply entrenched American values that define health care as either a privilege to be dispensed in exchange for a fee or a deliberate act of charity. Government should not attempt to alter these norms by imposing regulations that determine access to health services, for such actions would violate the right of private medical practitioners to operate as independent professionals and encroach on the doctor-patient relationship. Thus although no one questions that good health is a basic human right, there is considerable controversy over the right of access to medical care.

Access to health care as a basic human right. The issue of access to medical care has been complicated by demographic changes in the American population during the twentieth century as people have become older, more affluent, and better educated. At the same time there has been a growth in both the demand that more health care be made available and the expectation that this care should be of the highest quality and involve the most advanced technologies. The population over sixty-five years of age has almost tripled from 4 percent of the total population in 1900 to over 11.7 percent in the 1980s. It comprises nearly one-third of the low-income population and suffers a higher incidence of illness. These elderly demand that the health services system provide health care programs designed specifically for the chronic and degenerative illnesses that afflict them (Gibson & Mueller, 1977; Schmid, 1985). The affluent and better educated segment of the population has also grown, and more than half of the present population has completed at least one year of college. More health conscious and aware of the role of modern medicine in improved

EXHIBIT 4–2   *WORKERS' HEALTH BENEFITS SHRINKING*

The rising cost of health care has become a major concern of industries that provide health benefits for their employees. Corporate health plans have been subject to annual increases of 9 to 20 percent, and their cost has contributed to the higher prices of the companies' products. For example, General Motors estimates that it spends more each year on health benefits than on all the steel it uses. Similarly Ford Motor Company expects health benefits to add more than five hundred dollars to the costs of each car it produces.

In an effort to contain health benefit costs industries have initiated a series of changes in their programs that will ultimately lead to the evolution of a new health care delivery system. Although not all companies have accepted these modifications or adopted them to the same degree, four basic trends are developing. First, employees are being encouraged to assume responsibility for managing their own medical affairs. They are being offered incentives to shop for less expensive care that range from precertification programs, which require company approval before elective surgery or hospital admission, to programs that pay 100 percent of the costs for procedures such as tubal ligations, hemorrhoidectomies, and tonsillectomies if the employee will elect outpatient rather than inpatient surgery. Second, workers are being required to pay a larger share of their health bill. They are expected to pay a deductible, or an initial portion of the bill, an amount that increases each year. They are also expected to pay a percentage of the cost of hospitalization after the deductible. Third, employees are being enrolled in health maintenance organizations (HMOs) and must engage the services of participating physicians and hospitals. Fourth, workers are being encouraged to participate in company-sponsored health promotion schemes that range from health screening to weight lifting and include facilities such as fitness centers and jogging trails. The emphasis is on stress management, weight reduction, smoking cessation, and physical fitness.

Employees can no longer ignore rising health care costs simply because companies have always paid for them. New company policies have clearly established that employees will share in paying for health care and that unless they become involved in decisions relating to it, their share will only increase.

health, this group demands that the health services system provide universally available health care programs involving high-cost medical technology (for example Computerized Axial Tomography [CAT] scans, cardiac-bypass surgery, renal dialysis, organ transplants, and pacemakers) that allow the patients to resume a productive life and avoid a premature death.

High costs of health care.   These growing demands that the health services system provide a larger segment of the population with a higher quality of health care have been paralleled by the skyrocketing costs of such services, by a drain on the limited resources of personnel and facilities, and by a mounting apprehension over the nation's ability to pay its health bill. By the 1980s the national health bill exceeded $355 billion, or 10.8 percent of the gross national product, and federal, state, and local governments subsidized more than 43 percent of this expenditure with public funds (Gibson & Waldo, 1981; "Health care economics," 1984). As the need to confine health care programs to manageable proportions and to control their costs has become increasingly obvious, the central issue concerning the health services in the United States has focused on establishing priorities for the distribution of health care by determining who shall have access to what health services.

Purpose of the Chapter

In this chapter we shall analyze a representative area of the health services system to show how conservatives and liberals have addressed the issue of the distribution of care. The area selected involves programs that provide access to health care for the vulnerable segments of the population: the aged and the disabled (through Medicare) and the eligible poor (through Medicaid). We shall define the mission and role of this area of health services, trace its origins and history, analyze its programs and policies from conservative and liberal perspectives, and explore its future directions.

IN NEED OF HEALTH CARE: THE AGED, DISABLED, AND ELIGIBLE POOR

Mission and Role of Health Services

Plight of the vulnerable.   The attempt to provide access to health care to vulnerable citizens such as the aged, disabled, and eligible poor is complicated by their growing numbers and increasing needs for costly services. As shown in Chapter Three, the elderly are one of the fastest growing segments of the American population and place some of the heaviest demands on the human services systems. The number of people sixty-five and older is expected to grow by 2 percent a year throughout most of the remainder of the twentieth century. The aged will be admitted to hospitals more often than younger people, will more frequently have more serious illnesses that result in more costly care, and will require more long-term home or institutional care for chronic and degenerative illnesses; furthermore before they die at least one-fifth of them will find themselves alone in nursing homes forced to look to the government for support (Rogers, Blendon, & Moloney, 1982).

Similarly the poor with their more than 20 million children are a sizeable segment of the population. Their health needs range from maternal and infant care, adequate nutrition, and immunization to clean, standard housing; safe jobs; and relief from the stress that comes with the struggle to survive. For the most part these needs are not met. It is estimated that more than 18 million children of all races, or one in three American children, have never seen a dentist, while 10 million children, or one in seven American children, have no access to regular health care. The poor also suffer more from hunger; low-income families are unable to provide adequate nutrition for one in four American children, and 30 percent of all children have iron-deficiency anemia (Advisory Committee on Child Development, 1976; Edelman, 1981).

The poor also remain disproportionately nonwhite. By the outset of the 1980s a staggering 22.7 percent of all blacks fell into this category even after all nonmedical benefits were counted as money income. This means that one in four black children were poor and that, counting only income, "a Black child born today faces a nearly one-in-two chance of being born poor" (Edelman, 1981, p. 61). Although all who are born in poverty and lack access to health services suffer serious physical and emotional consequences, the toll on the nonwhite population is particularly oppressive. The poor have the highest rate of infant mortality; the rate for blacks is almost 1,000 percent greater than for whites. The poor also have shortened lives with much avoidable suffering; poor black children under age five die at twice the rate of white children, while nonwhites in general suffer a higher risk of stroke, cancer, diabetes, and heart failure and have an average lifespan that is six years shorter than that of whites (Geiger, 1981).

Shortcomings in providing health services.   The response of government to the demands of these vulnerable groups for health care reflects some commitment to pay for needed services. It also clearly indicates government's failure to assume responsibility for programs that would provide family-oriented services and care and comprehensive coverage of health needs for all members of vulnerable groups. Rather, programs are categorical and are based on factors such as age, disease, handicapping condition, and income. Programs have brought needed benefits to the vulnerable but have also resulted in sharp contradictions and gross inequities. Medicare for example has allowed the elderly greater access to quality health care, but a combination of inflation, the increasing kinds and complexity of medical care, and the requirement that the patient pay part of the bill has led to rapidly increasing out-of-pocket costs that elderly on fixed incomes can seldom afford. Medicaid has paid for medical care for many people, but state-determined eligibility standards and benefits vary sharply from state to state, and almost half the nation's poor are not covered by Medicaid. Even for those who are eligible, certain states refuse coverage for important services such as home care and prenatal care for women pregnant the first time. Also, despite Medicare and Medicaid, approximately 11 percent of the American population, most of whom are the working poor with incomes barely above the survival level, remain without any kind of medical coverage (Medicaid/Medicare Management Institute, 1979; Muse & Sawyer, 1982).

Problems in distributing health care.   Although government programs have sought to extend medical care to people of all ages who are in need and who have previously been ignored, the distribution of health benefits has favored the aged at the expense of the young. By the 1980s more than half of the 47 billion federal dollars spent annually on health care went to those over sixty-five, a group that comprised only 11 percent of the total population! Those under nineteen who comprised 31 percent of the population received less than one-sixth of the federal dollars spent. Also, an inordinate amount of the money was spent on the last weeks of life, with approximately 31 percent of the $47 billion outlay spent on the 6 percent of the recipients who died within a year (Haney, 1982).

Summary.   In general the mission of government programs for the aged, disabled, and eligible poor has been to achieve an equitable distribution of health care that will allow them to enjoy the fullest range of medical services available. To enhance the purchasing power of the vulnerable for medical care, federal and state governments have provided funding for medical insurance and direct payment of medical fees. Federal and state governments have also imposed regulations and provided funding to encourage the development and reconstruction of those health delivery systems that provide the resources and manpower for responding to the health needs of the vulnerable. The intent is to ensure that the neediest segments of the population achieve the good health so crucial for healthy and productive lives and so essential if they are to contribute to the economic, political, and social well-being of society. Thus, although programs for the aged, disabled, and eligible poor have increased in scope and government funding has grown significantly, they still remain only partially successful in fulfilling their mission.

Origins and History

Prior to 1966, when Medicare and Medicaid became operational, the aged and eligible poor were severely limited in their access to quality health care. Because few elderly had comprehensive insurance coverage, most basically depended on their meager savings, and when these were exhausted they relied on the generosity of their children and the charity of physicians and hospitals. For some elderly even these sources were not available, and they were forced to fall back on the charity of society and its state and local programs that provided help but at the cost of a large measure of their dignity. The plight of the eligible poor was no better than that of the elderly. They received substantially less medical care than the rest of the population because state welfare systems forced them to rely on understaffed hospital outpatient and emergency departments, health department clinics, the crowded health care facilities of municipal hospitals, and whatever free care busy physicians in private practice would volunteer.

Early health insurance.   The roots of national health programs such as Medicare and Medicaid can be traced to the early years of the twentieth century when the platform of Theodore Roosevelt and his Progressive Party called for the "protection of home life against the hazards of sickness, irregular employment and old age through adoption of a system of social insurance adapted to American use" (Porter & Johnson, 1956, p. 177). This call was followed in 1913 by the first American conference on social insurance, which was initiated by the American Association for Labor Legislation, an organization of labor and civic leaders, social workers, and academicians. The conference drew up a health insurance bill that was designed to pay hospital and medical benefits for workers and their dependents; it also protected the operation of the marketplace and the privacy of individuals and providers. For the next several years the Association lobbied various state legislators to incorporate the bill in their states' public welfare programs but met with little success. In 1927 a new citizens' group, the Committee on the Cost of Medical Care, proposed a program of group payment for medical care supported by taxation and/or private insurance. This proposal received some national attention but little legislative support (Rimlinger, 1971; Morris, 1979).

Voluntary health insurance.   Among the opponents of these various health insurance proposals was the organized medical profession, which was particularly eager to keep the relationship between doctor and patient free from intrusion by third parties. Physicians tended to define medical care as a privilege and sought to preserve their autonomy as professionals by supporting the operations of a marketplace that was based on a fee-for-service system and reflected a laissez-faire philosophy of government toward medical care. In 1932 organized medicine threw its support behind voluntary health insurance as the vehicle to provide payments for hospital care that would "preserve personal relationships and the free choice of physician and hospital" (Anderson, 1972, p. 69). In the same year the American Hospital Association helped to organize the Blue Cross system of voluntary hospital insurance in which Blue Cross acts as an agent or third party between patient and health service provider for the payment of fees. Blue Shield, which covers in-hospital surgical and medical care, was added a short time later.

Medicare and Medicaid. Proposals to include some form of public health insurance in the Social Security Act of 1935 were dropped because of fear that it would generate opposition that would endanger the entire Social Security legislation. But in the following years the Roosevelt administration continued to advocate the removal of economic barriers to access to medical care, and the Truman administration unsuccessfully attempted to attain compulsory health insurance without means-testing. During the 1950s the Social Security Administration, which had become alarmed by the inability of the elderly to meet the high cost of health care, proposed that those covered by Social Security be provided with some form of health insurance. At the same time Congress had also become increasingly concerned over the growing health needs of the American people. This concern grew out of the data supplied by the newly established U.S. National Health Survey, which provided comprehensive reports on the health conditions of the general population. Throughout the late 1950s and the first half of the 1960s proposals for health insurance for all Social Security recipients were initiated by the executive branch but were countered by proposals by groups within Congress that sought to limit aid to those who were highly disadvantaged and on the verge of indigency. In 1965 these executive proposals became the basis for Title XVIII of the Social Security Act, the legislation establishing Medicare, while the congressional proposals, after some modification that expanded medical payments to include the very low income persons of all ages, became the basis for Title XIX of the Social Security Act, the legislation establishing Medicaid.

Medicare defined. Together Medicare and Medicaid have provided a growing number of vulnerable elderly, disabled, and poor with access to the medical care system. Medicare is the largest of all public-sector health programs, and it offers persons sixty-five and over two types of insurance. The first type is federally administered, and it provides coverage for hospital and related care to all persons who have paid a mandatory employer-employee payroll tax. The second type is a voluntary system of supplemental insurance that is financed by a combination of monthly contributions from retired persons and matching federal funds drawn from general revenues; it provides coverage for physicians' fees.

Medicaid defined. Medicaid is the second largest of all public-sector health programs. It is a joint federal-state program with the federal government paying from 50 to 80 percent of the costs and with the states, within broad federal guidelines, determining eligibility, type of assistance, length of time assistance is given, and costs of assistance. Medicaid is actually three distinct health care programs servicing three very different groups of recipients. One program is directed at the elderly who become poor during their retirement years. Since Medicare does not include long-

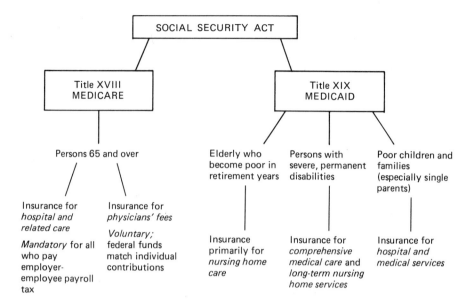

FIGURE 4–2.   Chart outlining the programs provided by the Medicare and Medicaid components of the Social Security Act.

term, open-ended, nursing home coverage, this program provides primarily for nursing home care for these elderly poor. A second program is directed at those with severe, permanent disabilities such as the blind, the severely mentally retarded, and the physically disabled. It seeks to meet their above-average needs for health services by providing comprehensive medical care and long-term nursing home services. The third program is directed at poor children, particularly from single-parent families, and their parents, and it provides them with hospital and medical services (Byrd, 1978; Slayton, 1980).

Summary.   By the 1980s government funding of almost $65 billion to Medicare and Medicaid allowed these programs to pay for most of the health care of one in five Americans—all of whom were members of the needy poor and vulnerable segments of the population. This included "25 million elderly persons, 5 million disabled persons, 9 million poor children, and 4 million unmarried, low-income parents" (Rogers et al., 1982, p. 14).

Conservative and Liberal Perspectives: Social Norms

Role of government.   In their approaches to providing access to health care to the aged, disabled, and eligible poor, the conservative and liberal perspectives embrace the same social norms but differ sharply on their meaning. Both agree that government has an obligation to assist the helpless and the weak attain health services, but they disagree as to who comprises these vulnerable segments of the population and as to what the nature of the assistance should be. Conservatives advocate a more selective or residual approach. They would use means-tested programs to restrict the distribution of health services to those members of society who lack support from the family and who, through no fault of their own, are unable to attain access to proper medical care. Specifically eligible persons would include victims of natural circumstances (for example, the blind, retarded, disabled, and elderly with chronic and degenerative illnesses) or of crises within their families (for example, the loss or underemployment of the family provider). Liberals advocate a more universal approach that would ensure the distribution of health services not only to the victims of natural circumstances and crises but also to anyone denied access to adequate health care because of economic barriers. Families would receive help in their efforts to obtain health services, and the health needs of all members of society would be ensured by programs based on the belief that every American has a right to health care.

Role of science and technology.   The conservative and liberal perspectives agree that there will be progress in health care through the resolution of problems by science and technology, but they disagree as to the nature of progress possible and the investment of resources that should be made. Conservatives have reservations about the progress achieved by a science and technology that frequently require society to invest heavily in resources for the development of techniques that produce the very opposite results of what they were designed to do. They point to the iatrogenic nature of life-sustaining machines and surgical procedures that often reduce the patient to a vegetablelike existence while creating emotional and economic burdens that undermine the social and financial structure of the patient's family. Liberals acknowledge that not all the onrushing medical technology is perfect, but they believe that science and technology have produced a medical revolution in which physicians have been given an unprecedented ability to detect and treat disease. They point to wizardlike techniques built on electronics and molecular biology, to wonder drugs and tranquilizers, to brain scanners and heart-lung machines, to orthopedic surgery and open-heart surgery, and to intensive care units as examples of the dramatic progress made possible by science and technology in relieving suffering and prolonging life. Liberals thus retain a steadfast faith that science and technology can resolve most health care problems and will allow the human race to enjoy a progressively healthier and more productive existence.

Role of the marketplace.   The conservative and liberal perspectives also agree that private-party and marketplace decision-making are essential for the privacy and independence of the patient in choosing a physician and for the integrity and autonomy of the physician in selecting a treatment, but they disagree as to how freely these marketplace forces should be allowed to operate. Conservatives are eager to avoid increased intrusion by the federal government into the health care sector, and they seek to minimize such intervention by leaving health care chiefly to market forces—the mechanisms by which most goods and services are allocated in American society. They recognize that a portion of the population lacks access to health services, but they are confident that these disparities will be corrected in time by the market, private charity, health insurance, and existing efforts by local and state governments. Liberals on the other hand believe increased federal intervention is necessary if everyone is to have access to an adequate level of health care. They condemn existent disparities in this access as a failure of the market that the federal government has the responsibility to correct. Also, although they would have each individual or their families pay a fair share of their own health costs and take responsibility for obtaining such care, they expect the federal government to assist when these costs and responsibility become an excessive burden.

The Conservative Perspective Examined

Conservatives believe in individual initiative as reflected in capitalism and private enterprise, and in tradition, established institutions, and the viability of an existing social order built on the sacrifices of past generations as reflected in the family and private charity. These beliefs lead conservatives to approach the problem of providing health services to the vulnerable by focusing on the role of the private sector and by sharply limiting the role of government. Conservatives see several sources of assistance for the vulnerable within the private sector. They believe the competitive forces of the marketplace will make health services more readily available and facilitate their distribution among the vulnerable by reducing their costs and increasing their efficiency. Conservatives expect the family to fulfill its nurturing function and to provide its vulnerable members with home care as well as emotional and financial support. They view private hospitals and physicians as having a professional obligation to their community to volunteer some of their facilities and services to the vulnerable. They expect the altruistic nature of human beings to provide a continuous flow of contributions of time, effort, and money to private charities directed at assisting the vulnerable.

Conservatives seek to confine the role of government in the health services to those state and local efforts that assist those among the vulnerable who somehow fall outside the purview of the above elements of the private sector. At best government should act as a balance wheel in the normal marketplace distribution of health benefits. It should become involved only in those situations in which the private sector is unable to assist the vulnerable, but its intervention should be consistent with the American tradition of private medical care and should preserve the position of the patient as a consumer in a pluralistic, competitive industry.

The competitive model.   To attain this end conservatives adopt a competitive model that views medicine more as a commodity to be bought in the marketplace than as a social service guaranteed by government. Under this model with its fee-for-service systems, physicians and hospitals would have a tangible good to sell, such as a blood test or an operation, and the patient would have freedom of choice in making the purchase and the concomitant responsibility of paying for it. For those among the vulnerable who are not assisted by the private sector and who are unable to pay for health services, the competitive model would offer assistance through government intervention at three levels.

First level of assistance.   On the first level of assistance government would provide health insurance or direct payment for health care through highly selective, means-tested programs to the hard-core, indigent sick who are without any visible means of family support. Unlike Medicare such programs would not be available to the broad, inclusive category of people, both affluent and poor, who comprise the aging segment of the population. Rather these programs would be restricted to those most vulnerable persons of any age who fit a defined category of low income and disability.

FIGURE 4–3.   Chart mapping the different roles that government would play under the conservatives' *competitive model* and the liberals' *control model.*

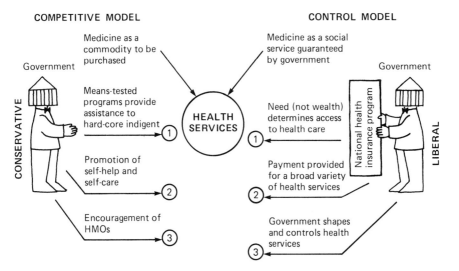

Second level of assistance.   On the second level of assistance government would support programs designed to reduce illness and to promote health by shifting the focus from a costly approach that would purchase treatment to a more economical approach that would teach the vulnerable to maintain their own health. Through education and subsidies government would promote programs that involve patients in self-care and self-help groups designed to encourage health-promoting and disease-preventing activities. These activities would include consultations with doctors and would range from complete care for minor, episodic, illnesses and injuries to continuing care for chronic diseases such as heart disease, stroke, cancer, arthritis, emphysema, diabetes, hypertension, and mental illness (Gartner, 1982). The competitive model views these programs as the major hope for substantial improvements in the health of the poor and for substantial reductions in unnecessary and costly professional care.

Third level of assistance.   On the third level of assistance government would support the establishment of health maintenance organizations (HMOs) by enrolling the eligible vulnerable in them through health insurance or direct payment plans. HMOs would be expected to encourage competition in the delivery of health services and in turn to restrain cost increases. HMOs operate as single units that provide comprehensive health services to enrollees for a fixed monthly payment. There are two types of HMOs: prepaid group practice associations that provide services at a central facility with physicians paid on a salaried or per capita basis, and independent practice associations that provide services at private physicians' offices with doctors paid on a fee-for-service basis. Conservatives expect HMOs to focus on preventive care as opposed to costly institutionalization and to establish controls over hospital admissions and length of hospital stays that will result in lower hospitalization rates. To control hospitalization use and reduce costs HMOs would be expected to use outpatient surgery whenever possible, to review and approve in advance nonemergency hospital admissions, and to monitor closely length of hospital stays. They would also be expected to provide home health care and nursing in lieu of hospital care, to provide whenever feasible preliminary diagnostic tests such as laboratory tests and X-rays on an outpatient basis prior to hospitalization, and to use financial incentives to encourage participating physicians to reduce unnecessary use of hospitals. The competitive model views HMOs as an effective and promising approach to health services because they would allow marketplace forces to operate freely while at the same time ensuring quality health care with minimum government intervention at the least cost in tax dollars.

Summary.   This competitive model reflects basic conservative tenets; it is built on a residual approach and a free enterprise framework. Its emphasis on government intervention to assist only those vulnerable who are not helped by the private sector and its commitment to a fee-for-service system of independently operating private health services providers reflect the conservative position that government involvement must remain minimal and that the health care system must allow full play to the competitive forces of the marketplace. Similarly its emphasis on a health services approach that is built on the involvement of the private sector, that encourages patients to practice self-help and self-care, and that allows them freedom of choice in selecting their physicians reflects the conservative belief in individual initiative and in the traditional rights and responsibilities of the family and the community to provide for the health needs of its vulnerable members.

The Liberal Perspective Examined

The emphasis liberals place on experience and an experimental attitude toward social institutions and their belief that truth and values are at best tentative and subject to individual verification within changing social contexts lead them to reject the prevailing American approach to health care and to propose one that they view as more responsive to the emergent needs of society. This liberal position is advanced as follows. There should be a dramatic increase in government involvement to ensure access to health care for the millions of Americans who remain without such access under the traditional approach of leaving health care solely to market forces. The poor, aged, and minorities continue to receive inadequate health care through the private sector, and liberals believe health care can be more equitably developed and delivered only if there is massive intervention by government. Health needs are too complex, their origins too diverse, and their manifestations too severe to deny health care based on the belief that individuals must be held responsible for their own health. Therefore government should become the dominant partner in its relationship with the private sector and establish programs to redistribute health benefits. Through subsidies and controls, it should establish a level of adequate care below which no one should fall. This level would ensure the right to good health care—a right that all are entitled to because it literally can make the difference between life and death.

The control model.   Liberals seek to realize this right to good health care by adopting a control model. Under this model government would impose cost controls on the entire health care system, public and private; government, primarily federal, would also provide health care for the millions who cannot afford insurance. This universal approach to access to health care would take the form of a national health insurance program with three basic features. First, the system would be based on the tenet that necessary medical care is not a commodity to be bought and sold on the open market with quality care going only to those who can pay for it; rather need and not wealth is to determine access to medical care. Second, the system would pay for a broad variety of medical and health-related services. These would be offered by both the public and private sectors; would involve a wide range of health service workers from homemakers to psychiatrists; and would be delivered in mental health centers, hospitals, physicians' private offices, clinics, nursing homes, community health centers, and the patients' homes. Coverage would include the full spectrum of services: skilled nursing and other therapeutic services; diagnostic services to continually monitor the health of children; outpatient psychiatric services; and home health services such as special therapy, medical social services, and physical and occupational therapy. Third, the system would focus on centralized planning with government retaining significant control over the objects, purposes, and directions of medical purchases; in effect government would shape the types of health services developed and the volume and fashion in which they are delivered. While government would share some decision-making with the private sector, it would limit the operations of marketplace forces by regulating hospital rates and the day-to-day medical practices of physicians. Specifically it would hold physicians accountable for the way they practice medicine because although their fees account for only 20 percent of the nation's medical bill ($45 billion in 1980), their decisions on behalf of patients affect over 70 percent of health dollar expenditures ($155 billion in 1980) (National Commission on Social Security, 1981).

The control model would seek to remove costs as a barrier to medical care. It would attempt to end the inequities and discontinuities that result from public health care coverage being neither universal nor uniform by spending whatever amount of public dollars required to assure necessary medical attention and hospital care for all. It would oppose placing limits on the percentage of the gross national product devoted to health care because it does not believe the United States has reached the point in public health expenditures where it cannot afford the medical care it provides its citizens. Rather the control model views such attempts at economizing as actually denying available medical care to the needy poor and vulnerable segments of the population.

Summary. The control model adheres closely to liberal beliefs in its emphasis on a universal approach and on government intervention in private-party decision-making. Its assertion that government should ensure that everyone has access to health care and its commitment to government involvement in the ways in which the individual and family provide for medical care, an area that has always enjoyed considerable independence and privacy, reflect the basic liberal position that social institutions and socially accepted ideals must be subjected to regular scrutiny and when necessary altered to serve human welfare more effectively.

Opposing Views of Health Services Models:
The Conservative Position

First argument.   Conservatives offer various major arguments in defense of their approach to providing the vulnerable with access to health care. Their first argument is that by controlling costs the competitive model ensures the most effective use of health care resources. It maximizes the role of the private sector and the marketplace and in so doing unleashes conventional market forces that temper costs through competition among providers of care. Its focus on patient self-help and self-care promotes the most efficient utilization of health services because individuals are thus informed, responsible for, and actively involved in the day-to-day struggle to prevent illness and maintain their own health and well-being. By minimizing government intervention this model also seeks to avoid government-subsidized, open-ended, cost-reimbursement systems that tend to become extremely expensive. For example Medicare grew from $3.2 billion in 1967 to over $68 billion by the middle 1980s (Greenberg, 1984; National Commission on Social Security, 1981). Conservatives condemn systems such as this because they impose a crushing burden on taxpayers and drive medical bills ever upward.

Second argument.   A corollary of this argument is the conservative position that the competitive model, by barring massive government intervention, freeing marketplace forces, and encouraging self-help and self-care activities, promotes a realistic assessment of priorities for health investment by the American people and leads to a more efficient and equitable allocation of scarce resources. There is however a recognition of the necessity to make the difficult choices that result in rational restraint in the application of therapeutic measures. Although conservatives would not deny care to the patient who can be cured or reasonably maintained, they question the heavy investment of resources to sustain the patient who is all but clinically dead. They seriously doubt the medical effectiveness, humanity, and costs of elaborate procedures and technology that place heavy demands on the limited health resources available and leave many of the supposed beneficiaries dead or just barely alive.

Opposing Views of Health Services Models:
The Liberal Position

First argument.   In response to conservatives liberals advance various major arguments in defense of their approach to providing the vulnerable with access to health care. Their first argument is that the competitive model is mistaken in its belief that reliance on marketplace forces and limited government intervention will lead to reduced costs and the more effective utilization of health services. Rather this model will force physicians and hospitals to charge privately insured patients more to make up for the loss incurred in treating the needy poor and vulnerable. If government does not pay its fair share of medical costs for the needy poor and vulnerable, the costs will be shifted to the private sector in the form of higher insurance premiums and increased out-of-pocket expenses for all citizens. Under the conservatives' model there will also be a tendency for hospitals that do not receive adequate reimbursement from the government to save money by giving the needy poor and vulnerable patients substandard treatment and releasing them too quickly. Further the best medical talent and facilities will gravitate toward serving the higher paying patients with private insurance. This will leave the needy poor and vulnerable with health services that are depersonalized and disorganized and treatment that is episodic and seldom geared to a comprehensive approach (Herman, 1972).

Second argument.   A second liberal argument in defense of their approach to health services begins by acknowledging that the control model is expensive for the taxpayer and that it requires health costs that will take an increasingly larger slice of the gross national product. However liberals note that the overall benefits realized by society are well worth the price. A redistribution of access to health services will occur in which quality medical care is made available to all who are in need regardless of their ability to pay. Government monitoring and control will establish high quality standards for health services delivered by the private and public sectors because services will have to conform to regulations accompanying government funding. Government-mandated licensing procedures will require high levels of preparation and training for the accreditation of paraprofessionals and technical staffs employed in ambulance services, outpatient speech and physical therapy programs, hospitals, home health agencies, independent laboratories, and nursing homes. Licensing also will impose demanding health and safety standards on buildings and various other facilities and equipment used by health services providers. Finally government subsidies, grants, and reimbursements for patient care help will promote and maintain university-owned teaching hospitals that are major centers for teaching and research and are frequently the only sources of highly specialized care for complex and difficult-to-treat illnesses.

Future Directions

Future directions in programs providing access to health care for the needy poor and vulnerable will have to reflect the continuing struggle between the opposing conservative and liberal approaches. The conservative approach will seek to minimize the role of government while allowing free reign to the operations of the marketplace. The liberal approach will seek to have government control the operations of the marketplace and impose a national health policy providing universal coverage through insurance or a direct payment plan. General trends seem to indicate that both conservative and liberal beliefs will influence future programs but that a modified version of the conservatives' competitive model will predominate. The demand for a national health policy by the liberals' control model will lose much of its public appeal because Medicare and Medicaid, the forerunners of such a policy, will continue to fuel mounting health costs. Under these programs massive government intervention and funding will continue to contribute to the inflating of health costs by stimulating an unprecedented expansion of services and facilities while introducing the neediest and more costly poor and elderly patients into the health care system (Bergstrand, 1982). Government funding of health expenditures, which accounted for only 4 percent of total federal expenditures in 1950 before the passage of Medicare and Medicaid legislation and which more than tripled to 12.4 percent less than fifteen years after passage, will continue to increase dramatically (Freeland & Schendler, 1981). During the 1980s Medicare and Medicaid will pay for one-fourth of the nation's health bill, and they will be expected to increase their contribution as health costs soar from the $943 paid per person in 1979 to a projected $3,000 per person in 1990 (National Commission on Social Security, 1981). This continuing upward spiral of health costs will result in disillusionment over the consequences of massive government funding of health services and foster serious doubts as to whether the nation can afford to extend full health coverage to all.

Prospective payment system. Although it may be unlikely that a uniform national health policy will be adopted in the future, government will continue to help the needy poor and vulnerable attain access to adequate health care. Government at all levels will continue to pay approximately 40 percent of personal health care expenditures (O'Connor, 1978). With this subsidy will come increased regulation in the form of planning agencies, inspection of facilities, medical audit systems, federal and state financial audits, and other control-type programs and procedures. Of particular concern to the government will be the need to contain rising costs. Toward this end government will place restrictions on its payments (third-party reimbursements) to medical providers to curb the use of unnecessary medical procedures and the duplication of expensive personnel and equipment. Future programs designed to raise the financial incentive for hospitals and physicians to operate efficiently will be similar to the prospective payment system enacted in late 1983. Under this program Medicare patients are placed in diagnoses-related groups (tonsillectomy, heart attack, hypertension, kidney transplant, and the like), and the government pays uniform prices for the treatment of people within a specific group. A hospital can keep all the money it saves by holding its costs below the price fixed by the government; it loses every dollar it spends on a Medicare patient in excess of the amount set by the government.

HMOs and self-help and self-care programs. Future programs of health care directed at the needy poor and vulnerable will also include highly successful and innovative approaches such as HMOs and self-help and self-care activities. The needy poor and vulnerable will be enrolled in HMOs similar to organizations in California, Oregon, and Hawaii that deliver continuous, comprehensive services stressing preventive medicine and primary care. Government will pay a fixed annual fee that will ensure the needy poor and vulnerable access to specialists as well as general practitioners and cover health needs ranging from hospital and home care to diagnostic laboratory procedures and prescribed drugs. Government will promote the self-help and self-care approach by subsidizing organized self-care education covering aspects of health promotion, disease prevention, self-medication, illness management, and use of the professional system. The needy poor and vulnerable will learn to manage their upper respiratory infections, take throat and urine cultures, use over-the-counter medicines, measure blood pressure, and provide themselves or others with the services that meet the everyday concerns of coping with a chronic disease or disability. The needy poor and vulnerable will also be encouraged to form or join mutual aid groups in which they can share their self-help skills and enjoy the support of others with common problems.

A number of other approaches will also be adopted in the future to provide the needy poor and vulnerable with high-quality health care while using substantially fewer resources. There will be greater utilization of skilled nursing facilities or home health agencies rather than extended hospital stays for convalescent care. There will be increased use of ambulatory surgical centers, outpatient psychiatric services, and other facilities in which patients receive institutional care during the day and return home at night. A new breed of health service providers such as physicians' assistants and nurse practitioners will be trained to collaborate with doctors in delivering general medical care. They will provide the needy poor and vulnerable with greater access to common health services such as routine examinations, care for the chronically ill, treatment of minor illnesses, inoculations, counseling, and patient education.

The establishment of the above programs for the needy poor and vulnerable depends on two key developments. First, government and the health community must bury their differences and forge a partnership in which they work together effectively. This means a compromise must be reached that supports medicine's assumptions of pluralism and private enterprise while at the same time allowing government to intervene by assuring the unimpaired access of the needy poor and vulnerable to the health care system. Second, government policy-makers and health services providers must increase their awareness of self-care resources and stop defining health care as virtually synonymous with professional care. Professional resources must be adapted to support the layperson, who as the primary care giver can draw on doctors to supplement self-care. A massive educational effort must be directed at the needy poor and vulnerable that will increase their competence for self-care and lead to changes in their smoking, eating, and exercise habits. To the extent that these two key developments occur, the probability of the establishment in the United States of long-term, effective programs of quality health care for the needy poor and vulnerable increases proportionately.

STUDY QUESTIONS AND ACTIVITIES

1. Investigate the differences between the American health services system and those of Canada and England. What two concepts dominate the American system? How did a basic faith in the largely unregulated operations of the marketplace shape the development of health services in the United States prior to the twentieth century?

2. Why did the federal government become involved in the health services system after 1900? Was this intervention necessary? Was it gradual? Why has increased government involvement been accompanied by increased government controls? Are such controls necessary? For each of the primary health services listed (p. 117) indicate whether federal controls and funding should be expanded, retained, or removed.

3. What is the general aim of health services? Why has the belief in good health as a basic human right been in conflict with societal norms? What factors have complicated the issue of access to health care? List the priorities used to determine what health services should be available and who should receive them. What points of view and assumptions seem to be reflected in your list?

4. What evidence shows that the aged and the poor are in need of health services? What are the shortcomings of Medicare and Medicaid? What group has benefited most from government programs distributing health benefits? Why do political leaders hesitate to redress the imbalance of benefits provided to different age groups? Predict the future consequences in the United States if this imbalance is not redressed.

5. Why has the medical profession opposed programs for national health insurance but supported those for voluntary health insurance? Discuss the differences between Medicare and Medicaid in terms of eligibility, types of assistance, and financing of programs. What other options exist for a program of national health insurance?

6. On what social norms and specific goals relating to providing health services to the vulnerable do both conservatives and liberals agree? How do they

differ in regard to these same social norms and goals? How are these disagreements expressed?

7. What assumptions about human nature and society underlie the conservative
    and liberal approaches to the problem of providing health services to the
    vulnerable? Outline in as much detail as possible the specific programs advo-
    cated by conservatives (competitive model) and liberals (control model), ex-
    plaining basic differences such as why one program includes a residual ap-
    proach and the other a universal approach, how each program treats the
    eligible vulnerable, and the basic arguments for and against each program.
    How can likely programs in the future specifically combine both conservative
    and liberal approaches?

REFERENCES

Advisory Committee on Child Development. (1976). *Toward a national policy for children and families* (pp. 55–64). Washington, DC: National Academy of Sciences.
Anderson, O. W. (1972). *Health care: Can there be equity?* (p. 69). New York: John Wiley & Sons.
Bergstrand, C. R. (1982). Big profit in private hospitals. *Social Policy, 13* (2), 49–54.
Byrd, B. S. (1978). Medicare counts successes on HEW's 25th anniversary. *Health Care Financing Administration Forum, 2* (2), 39–40.
Edelman, M. W. (1981). Funds for children. *Social Policy, 12* (2), 60–63.
Freeland, M. S. & Schendler, C. E. (1981). National health expenditures: Short-term outlook and long-term projections. *Health Care Financing Review, 2,* 97–126.
Gartner, A. (1982). Self-help/self-care: A cost-effective health strategy. *Social Policy, 12* (4), 64.
Geiger, H. J. (1981, March 22). Why do the poor and minorities have poor health? *The Providence Sunday Journal,* p. B-16.
Gibson, R. M., & Mueller, M. S. (1977). National health expenditures, fiscal year 1976. *Social Security Bulletin, 40* (4) 3–22.
Gibson, R. M., & Waldo, D. R. (1981). National health expenditures, 1980. *Health Care Financing Review, 2,* 1–54.
Greenberg, D. (1984, January 16). Health costs: Laying it all on Medicare. *The Providence Journal/Bulletin,* p. A-21.
Haney, D. G. (1982, December 5). The marvels and anguish of bio-engineering. *The Providence Sunday Journal,* pp. E-1, E-21.
Health care economics are beginning to work. (1984, October 12). *The Providence Journal/Bulletin,* p. A-16.
Herman, M. (1974, January). The poor, their medical needs, and the health services available to them. *The Annals of the American Academy of Political and Social Science,* p. 21.
Medicaid/Medicare Management Institute. (1979). *Data on the Medicaid program: Eligibility, services, expenditures* (DHEW Publication No. HCFA 79–20005). Baltimore: U.S. Department of Health, Education, and Welfare.
Morris, R. (1979). *Social policy of the American welfare state* (pp. 71–97). New York: Harper & Row.
Muse, D. N. & Sawyer, D. (1982). *The Medicare and Medicaid data book, 1981.* Baltimore: Health Care Financing Administration.
National Commission on Social Security. (1981). Medicare and Medicaid in America's future. *Health Care Financing Administration Forum, 5* (2), 29–35.
O'Connor, J. T. (1978). The radically new medical care industry: Implications for decision making. *The Journal of Applied Behavioral Science. 14* (3), 266–282.
Porter, K. H., & Johnson, D. B. (Eds.). (1956). *National party platforms* (p. 179). Urbana: University of Illinois.
Rimlinger, G. V. (1971). *Welfare policy and industrialization in Europe, America, and Russia* (pp. 62–71, 239–243). New York: John Wiley & Sons.

Rogers, D. E., Blendon, R. J., & Moloney, T. W. (1982). Who needs Medicaid? *The New England Journal of Medicine, 307* (1), 13–18.

Schmid, R. E. (1985, February 17). The aging of America. *The Providence Sunday Journal,* p. B-1.

Slayton, A. (1980). State treasury bare, some Medicaid programs find. *Health Care Financing Administration Forum, 4* (2), 23–24.

Steiner, G. Y. (1976). *The children's cause* (pp. 206–239). Washington, DC: The Brookings Institute.

5

EDUCATION SERVICES

THE NATURE OF EDUCATION

Education is a universal human activity, for all human beings must go through a prolonged period of infancy and childhood during which they are dependent on others initially for survival itself and later for acquiring the skills, knowledge, attitudes, and values that permit them to function as adults in society. Their initial needs for survival and rudimentary education are usually met by parents and families, but as children grow older families are less able informally to provide the variety of activities and resources necessary to transmit adequately the culture of the extended society. This limitation is true not only in complex modern societies but in primitive societies as well. Thus virtually every known society has devised formal means for transmitting the culture from one generation to the next. Formal education typically includes selecting portions of the culture for transmission, determining methods of instruction, assessing progress of students, and the like.

However, education does not exist only for children nor does education serve only to transmit culture. For a wide variety of reasons many adults undertake formal courses of study, and life itself can be considered a series of new lessons. Walton suggests that a subtle and often paradoxical relationship exists between school and society (1971, esp. pp. 14–19). This relationship is not widely understood. Formal educational systems exist as part of the societies that support them yet the very nature of academic institutions makes them partly independent of society. Particularly as societies grow more complex formal education becomes the principal means to transmit and change culture. Hence any educational institution has simultaneously a conservative function (transmitting culture) and a liberal one (changing culture), which may exist in an easy or uneasy tension.

An educational institution may begin by being dependent on the society that supports it and committed to transmitting the prevailing culture; however in all but the rarest of circumstances education takes on an independence. Because the institution cannot practically transmit all of the culture, it must select what it will transmit. Because what is not transmitted is indirectly deemphasized, the culture may be changed. Furthermore as teachers and students carry out their tasks they may develop new knowledge that was not previously part of the culture. Students may become more autonomous and hence increasingly able to question and improve society and its culture. Moreover the institution may find itself deliberately making recommendations for improvement that may or may not correspond to the prevailing values in society. Although society may find utilitarian uses for academic institutions (for instance, asking a university to compile statistics about traffic accidents in order to design safer highways), both teachers and students often find personal satisfactions in learning itself and do not abandon this pursuit, even outside the institution. Thus although education's conservative function of transmitting culture may be the better understood and seemingly more compelling, especially where the young are concerned, the liberal function of changing the culture also inevitably intrudes. Society may entirely support educational activities but it cannot entirely control them. Such activities may at first be pursued because they are supported and because society may realize immense utilitarian benefits from them, but because of the intrinsic satisfactions such activities provide and the personal development inherent in them education is sought for its own sake, and both individuals and culture change as a result.

This chapter on education as one of the basic human services in the United States should be viewed with these ideas in mind. We will confine our discussion to the formal system of schooling deliberately designed both to transmit and change American culture, but all of society also educates—through families, churches, community organizations, political groups, businesses, the mass media, the armed forces—sometimes intentionally, often incidentally and informally. The formal educational system supported by society serves a wide variety of utilitarian ends (such as developing technical knowledge, increasing the general level of wealth, and reducing the incidence of crime), but it is increasingly pursued for its own sake as it contributes to individual development by fulfilling a wide range of intellectual, aesthetic, social, and emotional needs (Walton, 1971, pp. 110–124). Thus because of its paradoxical nature education is unique among the six basic human services systems in America. It, like the other systems, meets fundamental human needs, but it also creates new needs that only more education can fulfill. In so doing education preserves and transforms both society and the individuals who comprise it.

THE FORMAL SYSTEM OF EDUCATION

The formal system of education that has developed in the United States is characterized by its universality and diversity. It represents the largest and most sustained effort by any society in human history to provide extensive educational services to all its members, yet there remain wide differences of opinion about its basic purposes. In contrast to the formal systems of education in most developed nations—particularly in Europe—the American system is not centrally controlled by the federal government, yet by the time of World War I every state had passed laws requiring all children of certain ages to attend school. Despite placing high value on education as a means of solving social and personal problems, Americans have frequently criticized their schools. Given the extensiveness of formal schooling in American society, the variety of purposes schools serve, the lack of central control over the nation's schools, and the extremely high expectations Americans have traditionally held for their schools, Graham (1984, pp. 10, 17) has perceptively referred to the American system of education as unsystematic, as "an organizational nightmare but a functional triumph" subject to certain forms of dissatisfaction that remain endemic despite whatever successes schools achieve.

In general the services offered by the American educational system range from preschool to higher education, from academic education to vocational. They are delivered by both public and private institutions and are directed to every member of American society. Their purposes include the personal development of individuals intellectually, physically, and emotionally; the maintenance of national security through technical training programs; and the transformation of American society by giving all citizens the means to raise their socioeconomic status. They are supported financially by federal, state, and local governments, with most of these services delivered at the local level but legally controlled by the states. Because they are directed at all members of society and are usually intended to promote their development rather than providing immediate, tangible benefits, education services can be classified as universal and soft. We will now consider the American educational system more specifically in terms of its variety of purposes, its organization and control, and some of its major problems.

Purposes

The purposes of formal schooling were simple and straightforward during the colonial period and into the early decades of the American republic. Relatively few children attended school and those that did learned rudimentary reading, writing, and mathematics primarily as an aid to their religious training. Being able to read the Bible was important to several religious groups that settled colonial America, and in the colonies of Massachusetts and Connecticut where this belief predominated laws were passed requiring local towns to establish public schools. Nonetheless the pattern varied from colony to colony, with private schools or no schools at all being the norm. Most children received no formal education and only a few received more than several years of elementary schooling. Children of extremely wealthy families were usually taught by tutors. Secondary and higher education were devoted almost exclusively to the study of Latin, Greek, and Hebrew in order to be able to read the Scriptures in their original languages. In a predominantly frontier and agrarian society formal education was unimportant for the masses, and practical skills were passed on through apprenticeships and home training.

The nineteenth century was a period of transition from the simple purposes that had characterized early American schools to the complex, multiple, and conflicting purposes that characterize American education in the twentieth century. In the first half of the nineteenth century changes in American society began to expand the role of schooling. As villages began to grow into towns and towns into cities as new commercial ventures developed, a greater proportion of the population needed basic skills of reading and arithmetic. Practical knowledge of applied fields such as surveying or newly developing fields such as chemistry gradually began to obtrude into the curricula of secondary schools and colleges. Perhaps most important the new nation increasingly recognized that democracy required intelligent participation by its citizens and that mass education was therefore a means of ensuring freedom and improving self-government. Pre–Civil War advocates of universal schooling such as Horace Mann (1796–1859) optimistically argued that education could make all humans equal, eliminate rancorous divisions in society, create immense wealth, eliminate poverty, diminish crime, and generally aid in the pursuit of happiness promised by the Constitution (Cremin, 1961, pp. 8–9). New schools sprang up to fulfill this vision, and when in 1852 Massachusetts became the first state to pass a compulsory school attendance law the quest for universal education began in earnest. Because of the diversity of religious groups in the country the character training that in earlier days had been provided as part of the influence of specific religions on education became more secularized in the so-called common schools that attempted to instill what were believed to be common American values. By the end of the nineteenth century schools were working not only to provide academic, civic, and moral education on a large scale but also were beginning to cope with a host of social, vocational, and even health-related problems that had arisen in a society newly urbanized, industrialized, and open to massive immigration. Whereas in the first half of the century the prevailing American belief seemed to be that everybody needed some education but only a few people needed a lot, by the end of the nineteenth century the goal was to provide as much education as possible for all (Butts, 1984, p. 30). This multiplicity of purposes for American schools was confirmed in 1918 when a committee of the National Education Association issued the most famous and widely cited report in the history of American education, *The Seven Cardinal Principles of Secondary Education,* which advocated that all secondary schools teach health, command of fundamental processes, worthy home membership, vocational preparation, citizenship, leisure-time activities, and ethical character.

During the twentieth century American education has attempted to be virtually all things to all people, so much so that Tesconi (1984) has stated that "the public school has become a combined educational *and* social services agency" (p. 7 [emphasis in the original]). Citing the work of Goodlad (1979), Tesconi lists some of the diverse and conflicting demands now placed on schools in the United States:

> Teach reading, writing, arithmetic, the humanities and the arts and sciences.
> Enhance certain kinds of cognitive functioning—mathematical reasoning, scientific reasoning characteristic of the "hard" sciences, and reasoning appropriate to the social sciences.
> Train carpenters, auto mechanics, tool and die makers, secretaries, computer programmers, a host of diverse clerical workers, athletes, homemakers, marriage and sexual partners, and parents.
> Teach children and youth how to handle stress and its consequences.
> Teach young people how to live as bachelors.
> Americanize immigrants.
> Instill certain values and moral codes.
> Perpetuate particular beliefs and myths.
> Instill patriotism and good citizenship behavior.
> Delay the entry of youth into the labor market, and serve as custodians of children and youth during certain hours of the day.
> Help students become wise consumers of society's goodies.
> Teach children and youth to be industrious, conscientious, reliable, alert, self-controlled, open-minded, competitive, cooperative, efficient, and attentive.
> Help to desegregate society.
> Eliminate our traditional habit of isolating the handicapped and the elderly.
> Battle drug abuse.
> Eliminate poor health and nutritional habits.
> Instruct about the dangers of nuclear armament and the horrors of nuclear war.

Provide hot breakfasts, hot lunches, playgrounds, recreation, psychological testing and counseling, and all kinds of other services aimed at the welfare of youth and the amelioration or elimination of social problems. (p. 6)

Tesconi's thesis is that American schools are not as good as they should be because of confusion about their purposes. They respond to demands placed on them not by redefining their purposes and delivering appropriate services but by adding new programs while seldom eliminating outmoded or even conflicting ones. More specifically he asserts:

The purposes currently served by the public school are unarticulated and exist ad hoc, a function of additive reforms occasioned by periodic shifts in public preferences.

The inarticulation of purpose fragments direction, resources, and curricula, and provides little or no basis for determining what roles and functions the schools should assume.

The inherent difficulty of dealing with purpose is compounded by this fragmentation and accounts, at least in part, for the general disdain for dealing with purpose and the bumper sticker slogans and sentimental bromides which so typically issue from some well-intentioned efforts in these regards.

The ad hoc character of purpose makes judgments of school performance tenuous at best, spurious at worst.

Serious public attention to purpose demands a massive campaign to educate the American public about the nature and function of the school. (p. 2)

Some demands placed on schools are reasonable. Schools may or may not respond to these. However, unreasonable demands are exemplified in the famous report *A Nation at Risk: The Imperative for Educational Reform* (National Commission on Excellence in Education, 1983). Issued in April 1983, this report claimed that American schools are sufficiently weak, especially compared to foreign schools, as to threaten "our very future as a Nation and a people" (p. 5) and that the weaknesses will not be corrected until the schools widely adopt reforms requiring more students to spend more time studying basic academic subjects. The two reasons why the report is unreasonable have nothing to do with the merits of the academic curriculum it promotes. First, as Tesconi (1984, pp. 4–5) incisively pointed out, in justifying its claim that schools have failed the report both distorts and omits critical evidence, perhaps deliberately. Second, the report was so uncritically heralded in the mass media and so uncritically supported by influential politicians from the moment of its issue that public opinion could not be intelligently formed; instead the reception of the report stands as an example of how "hyperbole, backed by spectacular symbols of failure, can manipulate and shape public opinion" (Tesconi, 1984, p. 4). Schools can resist such unreasonable demands only with great difficulty, even when they are charged with fulfilling other compelling purposes.

Whether schools should strive to fulfill the wide variety of purposes described above, during the twentieth century they have attempted to do so in part because of public demand. Education still centers on those services directly related to academic instruction, but because of the variety of purposes American schools serve considerable overlap exists between those education services provided within the formal system of schooling and human services such as psychological counseling typically associated with and provided by other human services systems.

Organization and Control

Despite their importance neither education nor its governance is mentioned by the Constitution of the United States. The Tenth Amendment does state that "the powers not delegated to the United States by the Constitution, nor prohibited by it to the States, are reserved to the States respectively, or to the people." Therefore control of education is not a federal matter. Most state constitutions do mention education, explicitly reserving legal control of schools to the states within which they exist, and all states have established a body of laws to regulate both public and private schools. Perhaps because local schools in America antedate the states and their constitutions, all states but one (Hawaii, which operates a single state-wide school district) have legally created local school districts empowered to administer many of the details of running public schools. These districts exist to carry out a state function, they are largely independent of ordinary municipal governments (although often dependent on such governments for funds), and their boundaries may not correspond to municipal boundaries. For instance, two or more towns may be joined in a central school district, and local wrangling about tax rates, location of school facilities, and other policies may ensue. In 1900 there were probably about 200,000 local school districts in the United States, many operating as little more than a one-room schoolhouse. However during the twentieth century many changes promoted consolidation, particularly in rural areas, and by 1932, the year in which the U.S. Office of Education began keeping records, the number of districts had declined to 125,000. In 1950 there were 85,000 districts, and in 1970 the decline had continued to just under 18,000 (Clifford, 1975, p. 7). In the 1980s there are slightly more than 15,000 districts, and nearly 30 percent of the nation's public school pupils are enrolled in the largest 1 percent of these districts.

State control.   States are legally empowered to run public schools, and state laws create local school districts to carry out this function. These laws may be changed to reorganize or abolish local districts, and both public and private schools operate within the framework of such laws. In general these laws apply more restrictively to public than to private schools. For instance states may require all schools to teach basic subjects such as reading and mathematics, but states may not forbid private schools from teaching other subjects such as religion, nor may states prohibit students from attending private schools. These rights of private schools were clearly established by two U.S. Supreme Court decisions, *Meyer v. Nebraska* (1923) and *Pierce v. Society of Sisters* (1925), which asserted that parents' rights to make reasonable decisions about the education of their children include the rights to include certain subjects in the curriculum and to choose the type of school attended. Nonetheless states may license private schools and make reasonable regulations for all schools within their boundaries, although many laws concerning curricula, selection of textbooks, licensing of teachers, and a host of other matters may apply solely or more restrictively to public schools.

The controlling framework of state laws is of course created and exercised by the general state government, including its executive, legislative, and judicial branches. Specifically to oversee education states have set up state boards of education and state departments of education that report to the boards. State departments of education are staffed by professional educators and charged with determining that state laws are being followed by local schools and with otherwise administering education, collecting and disseminating information, and aiding the improvement of local schools. This last function may range from providing schools with field services to suggesting new laws or policies for education. Heading the state department of education is the chief school officer of the state, usually called the state superintendent of schools or the commissioner of education. This person is the liaison between the state department of education and the state board and may have considerable influence over education in the state. It is the state board, however, that sets educational policies. In most states this board is a group of lay citizens appointed to their positions, but in a few states they are elected directly by the people. Ostensibly this board controls education in the state, although in reality most boards work closely—but not always harmoniously—with the state government on matters such as the preparation of budgets and the creation of new laws and policies for education.

As well as making laws and policies for schools, states also provide funds to local school districts. Table 5-1 indicates that the percentage of funding from state sources for public elementary and secondary schools has risen during the last half-century. In 1979–80 state funding of public schools exceeded local funding for the first time. This trend probably reflects a growing authority of state governments over local school districts and a corresponding decline in the autonomy of local school officials. Although some state funds are provided to local districts simply on the basis of the number of pupils the districts enroll, other state funds are provided for special purposes. For instance states provide relatively greater funds to

TABLE 5-1   **Percentage of Revenue Receipts for Public Elementary and Secondary Schools from Federal, State, and Local Sources, 1919–20 to 1979–80**

SCHOOL YEAR	PERCENTAGE DISTRIBUTION		
	FEDERAL	STATE	LOCAL
1919–20	0.3	16.5	83.2
1929–30	0.4	16.9	82.7
1939–40	1.8	30.3	68.0
1949–50	2.9	39.8	57.3
1959–60	4.4	39.1	56.5
1969–70	8.0	39.9	52.1
1979–80	9.8	46.8	43.4

Source: National Center for Education Statistics, 1982, p. 75.

poor rather than rich districts in an effort to equalize the number of dollars spent per pupil per year. Still other state funds are made available for special purposes only and therefore are not provided to districts that do not comply with these purposes. Most federal funds also are designated for special purposes only and are not spent at the discretion of local officials. Readers should note, however, that Table 5-1 presents national averages, which do not necessarily reflect the distribution of funding in any specific district. For example, in New Hampshire, a state with a long history of providing little state support, approximately 85 percent of local school expenditures are provided by local sources; in Hawaii, with its single state-wide school district, almost no revenues are provided by local governments, with more than 90 percent of school expenditures coming from the state.

Local districts. Local school districts exist within the framework of state laws governing education and are thus subject to control by the regular state government, the state board of education, and the state department of education. In recent decades local districts have become increasingly dependent on funds from both state and federal governments. Traditionally they have been largely autonomous in terms of many of their day-to-day activities, but this historic autonomy has rapidly eroded during the twentieth century. Local school officials are also subject to a wide variety of pressures at the local level, including those from the local government, special interest groups, teacher organizations, parents, and students. In many communities school politics takes on a life of its own.

Local districts are administered by groups of lay citizens usually known as boards of education or school committees. Approximately 85 percent of the local districts in the United States choose their school committees through popular elections, and candidates may or may not campaign as affiliated with conventional political parties. Within the frame-

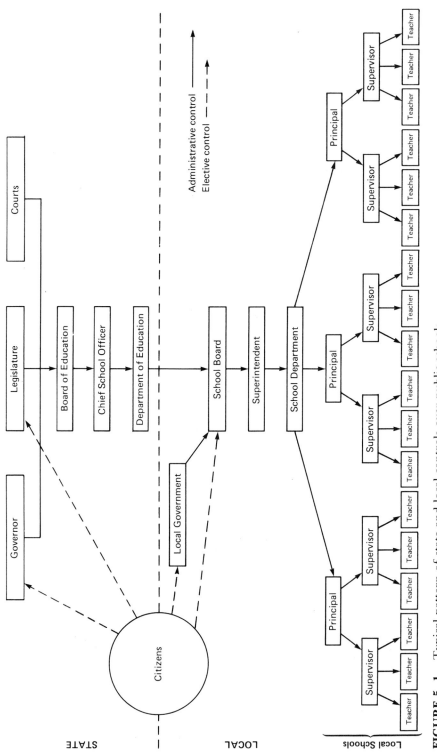

FIGURE 5–1. Typical pattern of state and local controls over public schools.

149

work of state laws and policies, local school committees administer their own districts, setting their own policies on matters such as homework and disciplinary procedures; determining programs and curricula; and dealing with business matters such as hiring teachers, establishing budgets, and creating community support for schools. School committees also hire the chief educational professional for their districts, usually titled the superintendent of schools. The superintendent is responsible to the school committee but may in fact do much of the actual administration, business management, and public relations for the district. The superintendent heads the district's school department, which includes educational professionals directly concerned with instruction (such as principals, supervisors, and teachers) and other workers who provide a variety of closely connected human services (such as guidance counselors, nurses, and dieticians) and support services (such as clerks, custodians, and bus drivers). Teachers are in some districts well respected, well trained, well paid, and largely free to make professional decisions about curriculum content and instructional methods; in other districts entirely the opposite conditions prevail.

Although the percentage of public school expenditures derived from local funds has been declining during the twentieth century, local districts are still highly dependent on local revenues. They may have little discretion over how such money is actually spent, however, because local revenues usually do not even meet the minimum cost of those education services required by state laws. The principal means through which local communities raise revenues is the property tax. Most communities designate a certain portion of their property tax revenues to support their schools. Some communities are able to provide far better support through this tax than are other communities because the amount and value of taxable property varies considerably from district to district. In fact districts with the lowest tax rates may sometimes raise the greatest amounts of money (and vice versa) because of these variations. Also, especially during the financial stringencies imposed in the 1970s and 1980s, property taxes have become a convenient target for local citizens intent on reducing taxes. Thus in recent years struggles over the financing of schools have increasingly become part of the politics of education in local districts, even as the historic autonomy of local districts has been eroded by state and federal governments. Nonetheless much of the texture and quality of basic education services offered in the United States is still determined in local districts, especially by teachers.

Federal influences.   Although for constitutional reasons the federal government has no direct authority over that part of the formal system of education operated by the states, it has itself operated a portion of the overall system and has otherwise considerably influenced education within the jurisdiction of the states. Historically the federal government has been responsible for the operation of the public schools in the District of Columbia and U.S. territories, schools on Indian reservations and certain military bases, and the U.S. service academies. In addition education within the jurisdiction of the states has specifically been shaped by federal court decisions, laws, policies, and financial aid. These specific influences have themselves been often directed by the general bent of the federal government, particularly the executive branch. As an example Clifford (1975, p. 11) cites President Lyndon Johnson's determination to be remembered as the "education president." President Johnson, a former teacher, saw opportunities for the federal government to help improve the quality of American education in general and the education of disadvantaged children in particular. As a result, according to Clifford, during his administration the executive branch

> sponsored a varied program of federal legislation, actively lobbied Congress, and sent staff from the Executive Office and the cabinet departments to Congress as expert witnesses. The White House created an environment for federal court activism in school civil rights cases, prosecuted federal enforcement of existing laws, . . . escalated the budget and staff of the United States Office of Education, and generally encouraged a public mentality favoring quickened educational expansion. (p. 11)

Other presidents of course have exerted much different influences over education.

Decisions of the U.S. Supreme Court have shaped American education considerably. In addition to the two cases cited in the above section on state control that protected the rights of private schools the Court has developed the "child benefit theory" (*Cochran v. Louisiana State Board of Education,* 1930), which permits public funds to be used in private education as long as their expenditure benefits the individual child and not the private institution. Originally applied only to the purchase of textbooks, the child benefit theory has been extended by other decisions into areas such as the transportation of children to private schools (*Everson v. Board of Education,* 1947). The Court has also protected the rights of students to freedom of personal conscience and expression, specifically to their right not to salute the flag because of religious beliefs (*State Board of Education v. Barnette,* 1943), their right not to be subject to school-sponsored prayer (*Engle v. Vitale,* 1962), and their right to express dissenting political beliefs peacefully (*Tinker v. Des Moines Independent School District,* 1969). In one of the most significant decisions in its history the Court declared racially segregated education to be unconstitutional (*Brown v. Board of Education of Topeka,* 1954), thereby overturning the legality in all walks of American life of the separate but equal doctrine of segregation that the Court had affirmed in an earlier decision (*Plessy v. Ferguson,* 1896).

Federal laws that deal with the rights of citizens may also have specific application to education services and their delivery throughout the system. An example is the Education for All Handicapped Children Act of 1975 (known as Public Law 94-142). This law requires that all handicapped children be educated in the "least restrictive environment" (that is, the conventional classroom) whenever possible. The effect of this law has been to curtail sharply the previously common practice of educating handicapped children apart from the nonhandicapped in special classrooms staffed by teachers trained specifically for this purpose. Since 1975 teachers have had to learn to cope with the special educational problems of handicapped children "mainstreamed" into conventional classrooms and to educate simultaneously both the handicapped and nonhandicapped. For each handicapped child Public Law 94-142 also requires the development of an individualized educational program agreed to by the school and the child's parent or guardian. The federal government may set policies for the enforcement of such laws. Therefore the federal government exercises considerable discretion over the general educational laws it will pass and over the interpretation and application of these laws.

Perhaps the greatest influence of the federal government on the formal system of education in the United States is financial. The federal government has a long history of financial support for education. It has passed such legislation as the Morrill Act of 1862, establishing land-grant colleges and bringing practical subjects into their curricula; the Smith-Hughes Act of 1917, supporting programs in agriculture and home economics in secondary schools; the Servicemen's Readjustment Act of 1944 (known as the GI Bill of Rights), providing financial aid to veterans attending institutions of higher education; and the National Defense Education Act of 1958, supporting education in science, mathematics, and other areas deemed to represent national interests. The most important federal act shaping education in recent decades has clearly been the Elementary and Secondary Education Act (ESEA) of 1965. This act provided generous funding for a wide variety of purposes such as basic skills improvement, consumer education, bilingual education, and acquisition of instructional materials and equipment. However by far the most generous funding was committed to aiding educationally deprived and disadvantaged children, with approximately five-sixths of all ESEA funds allocated for this purpose (Ravitch, 1983, p. 159). ESEA helped propel the nation into an era of "compensatory education." The idea behind compensatory education is that many children do not do well in school because of deficiencies in their early environments and that these deficiencies can be overcome by providing educationally enriched environments that compensate for this disadvantage. ESEA also set certain precedents making it possible for local school districts to receive directly from the federal government large amounts of money to be used for federally designated purposes.

Since 1965 ESEA has been revised and extended. It has become the model for dispersing most federal aid to the nation's schools. Although local schools are under no obligation to apply for or accept such aid, they have in fact become increasingly dependent on it in the last two decades to maintain those programs so encouraged by the federal government. For better or for worse the federal government has exercised considerable influence over American education through this means and occasionally has threatened to withdraw all federal funds from school districts or institutions of higher education that it feels have failed to comply with federal regulations and guidelines on any of a host of matters. This coercive influence can be used wisely or foolishly. The reader should note too that Table 5-1 indicates that the proportion of funds for public schools supplied by federal sources jumped dramatically during the 1960s and rose to a high of 9.8 percent in 1979–80; however during the 1980s the federal share of support subsequently declined to less than 7 percent by the middle of the decade. Some commentators suggest that this decline represents a beneficial decrease in federal control over public schools; still others, that it represents merely a weakening of federal support for public education.

Problems

Most problems that the typical American associates with education focus on teaching: how best to organize and present material while at the same time creating a classroom climate conducive to both academic learning and personal development for the different and sometimes unmotivated pupils in the class. Such problems are indeed fundamental to education and the delivery of education services. In Chapter Two we discussed such problems in explaining how education services can represent either conservative or liberal theory and practice and how analogous roles apply to human services professionals in other systems. In this chapter we will consider some of the more general problems of function of the formal system of education in American society. These general problems of course set the conditions under which teachers work and all education services are delivered.

General problems concern both the tangible characteristics of the system and its functions and the expectations that Americans hold for it. One hundred years ago most Americans would have regarded the prospect of 10 percent of the population obtaining higher education as a lofty but unreachable and unnecessary goal; today most Americans would regard such a prospect as an unmitigated disaster. Thus even as American education has changed and improved historically, these changes have seldom been able to keep up with rising American expectations for the schools. We have attempted to demonstrate this point in several ways throughout this chapter, particularly in our discussion of the multiple purposes schools serve and the decentralized system of formal education that has evolved. Schools can neither serve overly simplified purposes in American society nor be all things to all people. Expectations that they function in either of these ways all too readily become translated into unreasonable demands that cause considerable grinding within the system and inhibit the delivery of high-quality education services.

Consider for example the issues of universality and quality in American education. What have Americans expected of their schools in these regards? How well have schools performed? In 1879–80 less than two-thirds of the school-age population attended elementary or secondary schools, the average length of the school term was 130 days, and the average pupil attended for just 81 days; by 1979–80 more than 96 percent of the school-age population attended, the average length of the term was 179 days, and the average pupil attended for 161 days (National Center for Education Statistics, 1982, p. 35). The availability of schooling and the sheer quantity of schooling obtained by Americans has thus significantly increased. Table 5-2 illustrates the dramatic increase in both absolute numbers of students and the proportion of potential students attending American secondary schools. At the turn of the century secondary education was essentially an elite enterprise serving a small portion of the population. During the twentieth century it has for all practical purposes become universally available. No doubt Americans have supported the expansion and come to expect the universal availability of formal education.

During the twentieth century most Americans have also probably come to believe that universal education and quality education are compatible, that is that virtually all children can be educated well. But is this belief

TABLE 5-2   Enrollment in Grades 9–12 in Public and Private Schools Compared with Population 14–17 Years of Age, 1889–90 to 1979–80

SCHOOL YEAR	ENROLLMENT, GRADES 9–12			POPULATION 14–17 YEARS OF AGE	PERCENTAGE OF POPULATION 14–17 ENROLLED
	ALL SCHOOLS	PUBLIC SCHOOLS	PRIVATE SCHOOLS		
1889–90	359,949	202,963*	94,931*	5,354,653	6.7
1899–1900	699,403	519,251*	110,797*	6,152,231	11.4
1909–10	1,115,398	915,061*	117,400*	7,220,298	15.4
1919–20	2,500,176	2,200,389*	213,920*	7,735,841	32.3
1929–30	4,804,255	4,399,422*	341,158*	9,341,221	51.4
1939–40	7,123,009	6,635,337	487,672	9,720,419	73.3
1949–50	6,453,009	5,757,810	695,199	8,404,768	76.8
1959–60	9,599,810	8,531,454	1,068,356	11,154,879	86.1
1969–70†	14,418,301	13,084,301	1,334,000	15,550,000	92.7
1979–80†	15,191,000	13,756,000	1,435,000	16,275,000	93.3

*Excludes enrollment in subcollegiate departments of institutions of higher education and in residential schools for exceptional children.
†Some data for these years are estimated.
Source: National Center for Education Statistics, 1982, p. 44.

actually justified? How well have American schools provided high-quality education to an expanding proportion of the population? In the long historical view there is absolutely no doubt that quality has gradually risen even in the face of massive expansion. Literacy rates have risen and more and more well educated Americans have helped create and are prepared to take their places in the coming twenty-first century society with its projected emphasis on quality of life, leisure activities, intellectual skills, and a white collar, service-oriented work force. Still, it is difficult to obtain data documenting increasing quality in schooling and, as might be expected in an educational system of tremendous size and diversity, the overall picture is invariably mixed. Furthermore negative examples such as the decline in average Scholastic Aptitude Test scores during the 1970s and sensationalized critiques such as *A Nation at Risk* often are well publicized. In fact education has been one of the nation's highest and most successful priorities, yet improving on such success is extremely difficult although the perpetually rising expectations of Americans insist on improvement. Compounding this problem is the fact that certain ill-considered attempts at improvement may be counterproductive and actually exacerbate whatever problems do indeed exist. This may be the case today, for certain reforms of recent decades may have created a depressed system of education in the United States. If this is true we should not abandon belief in the success of the American education but rather expect further success to be gradual and painstaking, the result of increasing professionalism and honest intellectualism instead of panaceas. All children can probably be educated well but to date this has not occurred. Thus America's experiment with universal and quality education is incomplete. In recent decades much of this experiment has been carried out by attempting to provide equality of educational opportunity, which has become a catchall phrase and general goal for American schools. It encompasses a wide variety of specific programs and practices including Project Head Start, school busing, and minimum competency testing that have changed the very face of the American educational system and the services it provides. In the remainder of this chapter we will explore but not attempt to answer the basic question of whether the search for equal educational opportunity has tended to improve or to depress the quality of American education.

EQUALITY OF EDUCATIONAL OPPORTUNITY

We suspect that very few Americans would object to equality of educational opportunity as a general goal to be used in guiding the delivery of education services in the United States. The three principal words in the phrase are deeply embedded in the nation's psyche and carry favorable connotations. Equality of individuals and their rights is a fundamental principle on which the nation was founded. The American people have traditionally valued education and used it to solve their problems and enrich their personal lives, and the Constitution of the United States contains an implicit bias in favor of educational purposes. Opportunity is consistent with American beliefs in the virtue of work and self-initiative and the rewards to be obtained through them. We suspect, however, that very few Americans hold a clear conception of what the phrase equality of educational opportunity means, for it is prone to widely differing interpretations.

Definitions of Equality of Educational Opportunity

Smith and Orlosky (1975) identify four meanings of equality, which they represent by the following statements:

1. Any child is worth neither more nor less than any other child as an object of development.
2. The rules that apply to any child apply to all others alike.
3. Any child has just as good an opportunity to learn as any other child.
4. Any child acquires as much knowledge and skill as any other child. (pp. 78–79)

The first meaning they define as "moral equality." It expresses a desirable state of affairs and acts as a general guide but has no specific directive value for what education services are to be provided or how. The second they define as "rules of equality." It too does not specifically direct particular education services but does demand a uniformity in their application by suggesting that everyone should be treated in the same way. The third they define as "equality of opportunity." It suggests that everyone does not have to be treated identically but rather fittingly or appropriately. Education services should be individualized to maximize the potentials of individuals to take advantage of available services. The fourth they define as "substantive equality." It suggests that neither rules nor treatments need be the same for each person but that the results of education services should be equalized for each, with no one individual receiving greater benefits than any other.

Three distinct and different ways of providing education services are consistent with these last three definitions of equality because all three are arguably plausible ways of implementing the first definition, moral equality. Under the first way of providing services, rules of equality, students are to be treated the same. Historically this has meant providing schools for all children and increasing school attendance. Indeed until well into the twentieth century a major struggle in American education was simply to make schools, teachers, and materials available to the entire population so that all individuals could benefit in their own ways from the equal accessibility. In this conception schooling is equally available to everyone, but it is up to the individual to take advantage of this opportunity, and different individuals will benefit differentially. Under the next way of providing services, equality of opportunity, not only must education services be available to all but educators must also individualize services to fit the different needs of students. Only when educators have made services equally appropriate do all students enjoy equal opportunities to learn. In this conception educators take professional initiatives, students may actively assist in the process, and both share in the responsibility for the individual benefits that accrue. Under the final way of providing services, substantive equality, the availability of services or their appropriateness is unimportant. Equality is determined only by the equality of resulting benefits to individual students. In this conception educators take complete responsibility for the results of their services. Equity demands that they produce the same benefits for each student. According to one commentator the goal of making schools equally available prevailed in the United States until about 1920, the goal of providing individually appropriate services prevailed from about 1920 to 1960, and the goal of providing equal results has prevailed since about 1960 (Jarolimek, 1981, pp. 144–145). Hence over time the operational definition of how schools equitably provide education services has changed, even before the phrase equality of educational opportunity was coined or reached the status of a slogan.

Mission and Role of Education Services

The mission and role of programs or services intended to provide equality of educational opportunity depend therefore on the conception held by the provider. Although different conceptions, goals, or meanings have prevailed at different times, there is little consensus today on this matter. Throughout the nineteenth century much of the energy of educators went into the struggle to make schooling universally available (in that sense to treat everybody the same). Throughout much of the twentieth century, as educators came increasingly to understand differences among learners, they began as a matter of course to account more for individual differences (in that sense to treat everybody appropriately). When appropriate education of reasonable quality is routinely available to all, lack of consensus about equity seldom becomes a burning issue. However the concept of equality of educational opportunity became problematic especially in the 1960s as policies of the federal government drew national attention to the third meaning of equality—equality of results. At the same time well-publicized evidence cast doubts on the efficacy and costs of American education, doubts that were heightened by the financial stringencies of the 1970s and other changes in national life that placed considerable strain on local schools. Under such circumstances lack of consensus about the meaning of equity can leave—and often has left—national policy on education a shambles, teachers bewildered about the value of the basic services they provide, and the public frustrated and confused.

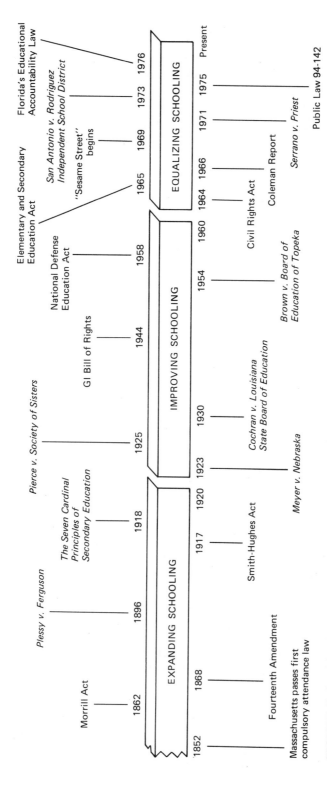

FIGURE 5–2. Timeline tracing the three principal eras in the development of equality of educational opportunity in America. Key legislation, publications, and judicial actions are identified.

The programs and services that emerged during the 1960s when the concept of equality of results prevailed were originally intended to fulfill federal policies. Despite the current lack of consensus a mission and role for these and similar initiatives consistent with the goal of equality of results probably still prevail. Many of these specific programs (which we will discuss more comprehensively in the next section) are devoted to what has become known as compensatory education. The general idea behind compensatory education is that some children do not do well in school because of deficiencies in their environments. These deficiencies include the lack of proper nutrition or intellectual stimulation, and often are found in children from impoverished homes. Therefore for identifiable segments of the population actions can be taken to overcome and correct these deficiencies so that such children will be able to perform well in school. For instance school breakfast and lunch programs have been directed at overcoming lack of proper nutrition and early childhood education programs at overcoming lack of intellectual stimulation. The basic mission for compensatory education seems to be to help those children most in need of help to be able to learn as much as any other children. Presumably the success of such programs can be measured by how well the children who receive compensatory services actually learn as compared with other children, at least insofar as the concept of equality of results prevails.

The well known children's television program "Sesame Street" can serve as an example of how the same compensatory education service can be considered as having different missions and roles depending on which of the three conceptions of equality of educational opportunity is applied. Begun in 1969, federally funded, and carried by the Public Broadcasting System, "Sesame Street" is directed primarily at preschool children. It emphasizes skills basic to school learning: understanding spatial and chronological relationships, recognizing the names and shapes of letters, counting, and so on. Because preschool children from impoverished homes often are deficient in such skills, "Sesame Street" seems especially useful for them as a compensatory service that fulfills the mission and role of equalizing the results of school learning for all children. However "Sesame Street" is viewed by children from all kinds of environments; those who do not need compensation may also benefit from it, perhaps even more so than children from impoverished homes. Therefore it may fulfill the mission and role of raising the general level of school learning in the nation simply by being universally available and may not tend to equalize results at all. Further compounding the difficulty of designating an unequivocal mission and role for "Sesame Street" is the fact that in actuality it is not universally available and may not be equally appropriate for all children to whom it is available. For instance in 1969 when "Sesame Street" was first broadcast in the Baltimore, Maryland, metropolitan area, it was received by a greater proportion of affluent suburban families than impoverished inner-city families. The state of Maryland had only just begun operating a public broadcasting station, which was a low-power, ultrahigh-frequency (UHF) station with a suburban transmitter. Its signal simply did not reach much of the inner city where in any case many families who did have television sets owned older models not equipped to receive UHF signals. Eventually "Sesame Street" became available to much of its targeted audience in inner-city Baltimore when the power of the station was increased, additional transmitters were constructed, and the federal law requiring all new televisions to be equipped to receive UHF signals caused a gradual phasing out of the older models. Furthermore there are simply no assurances that "Sesame Street" is viewed by children in the targeted population or that it is equally appropriate for all such children. Some may profit from viewing, others by entirely different activities. If the mission and role of "Sesame Street" is to provide appropriate services for even a well-defined and well-targeted audience, it may do so for many children in this group but cannot do so for all it reaches. Presumably additional, more appropriate services should be available if all children are to have their needs met under the individualized and appropriate conception of equality of educational opportunity.

There are therefore three different missions and roles for education services intended to provide equality of educational opportunity: (1) providing equality of treatment for all, (2) providing individualized and appropriate treatment for all, and (3) providing equality of results for all. Many worthwhile, basic education services can be justified in all three ways, thereby creating disputes having little to do with the intrinsic value of the services. Even compensatory education, which by its usual definition is directed at students requiring special help and is therefore ordinarily seen as fulfilling the second or third mission and role, can be conceived as helping *all* students compensate for whatever deficiencies exist in their own environments. These three different missions and roles for equality of educational opportunity can thus be considered three basic models for the delivery of any education service. Later in this chapter we will explain why for ideological reasons conservatives tend to argue for the equality of treatment model and liberals for the equality of results model, but for practical reasons both conservatives and liberals are far more favorably disposed toward the individualized and appropriate model than their ideological disputes would make them appear.

Origins and History

Programs and specific services typically associated with equality of educational opportunity are diverse and their origins are many. In this section we will describe five general types of programs and services dealing with (1) constitutional rights and race, (2) compensatory education, (3) local school financing, (4) handicapped students, and (5) minimum competency testing and required learning.

EXHIBIT 5-1 *LATCHKEY CHILDREN*

Approximately three out of five of all school children in the United States now have mothers in the labor force, and approximately one out of five now lives in a single-parent home. As a result more than one-third (or roughly 10 million) of all elementary school students are latchkey children using their own keys to let themselves into empty homes when they return from school each day.

Although being a latchkey child can help develop responsibility (for instance, in doing chores or caring for brothers and sisters) in some individuals, few latchkey children are entirely happy with their status. Few say that they would be willing to allow their own children to go home alone after school. Two characteristics typical of latchkey children are loneliness and fearfulness. These children would prefer to stay after school and talk with friends and teachers but must often hurry home to call or be called by parents. When at home they are usually forbidden to entertain friends and are admonished to lock the door. Many report difficulty with homework because no one is home to help them, while others doubt their ability to handle emergencies that may arise when they are alone.

Only relatively recently have school districts begun to recognize the problems of latchkey children and to establish programs to cope with these problems.

"Separate but equal" and its legacy.   The Fourteenth Amendment to the Constitution, adopted in 1868, contains two clauses that have gradually attained sweeping significance in determining how equity is provided in all phases of American life. The amendment requires states to provide due process of law and equal protection of the laws to all citizens. (In Chapter Eight we discuss the due process clause in relation to juvenile justice in the United States.) Both clauses have come to be legal safeguards for the individual rights guaranteed by the Constitution. In 1896, however, neither clause was applied by courts nearly so extensively as they are today, for in that year the U.S. Supreme Court rendered the *Plessy v. Ferguson* decision, which had an extraordinary impact on racial relations. In this decision the Court upheld the constitutionality of a Louisiana law that segregated the races on public conveyances, and in so doing developed the so-called "separate but equal" doctrine: segregation by race is lawful as long as the separate facilities for each race are equal. The Court in making this decision considered the fact that at the time Congress itself was running a segregated school system in the District of Columbia and suggested that equality could be defined in terms of physical facilities as opposed to the attitudes that different groups held toward enforced separation.

Plessy v. Ferguson immediately became the legal basis for segregation in all phases of American life, including education. For many years children in the South attended legally segregated schools, and even in Northern cities many children attended all-black or all-white schools because of housing patterns, deliberate intentions of school committees, or other extralegal reasons. The separate but equal doctrine was of course a national disgrace both for moral reasons and for its role in engraining segregation in American life long after slavery had ended. Beyond this it was also a sham. Especially in Southern communities separate schools were a reality but equal school facilities were not. In almost every discernible way, including expenditures, physical plant, availability of books, and training of teachers, black schools were kept decidedly inferior to white. Under the separate but equal doctrine black citizens were legally excluded from the mainstream of American society for more than half a century, and thus were stigmatized, and suffered unmeasurable harm because of the inferior education services made available to them.

The end of the separate but equal doctrine as the legal basis for segregation came in 1954 when the Supreme Court rendered the *Brown v. Board of Education of Topeka* decision. After World War II the Court had become increasingly concerned about whether separate could ever be equal in fact, even if the tangible characteristics of educational facilities and services were equalized. In deliberating in the *Brown* case the Court considered the historical record of segregated education, the available social scientific evidence on the harmful effects of segregation, and the requirements of the Constitution, especially of the Fourteenth Amendment. It declared that education had become perhaps the most important function of state and local governments, that the stigma attached to segregation harms black children, that segregation deprives black children of equal educational opportunities, and that segregation is therefore unconstitutional because it deprives black children of the equal protection of the laws guaranteed by the Fourteenth Amendment.

As unequivocally as the *Brown* decision denounced segregation, it still left the nation with two closely related problems: how to identify segregation and how to end it. In a second *Brown* decision of 1955 the Court provided some instruction on the second problem. It did not order segregation ended virtually overnight but instead permitted segregated school districts to draw up and implement their own plans for integration "with all deliberate speed." In the South, where segregated schools had existed as a matter of law and were thus easily identified, progress toward integration proceeded slowly.

> By 1962, substantial progress had been achieved in the border states of Oklahoma, Missouri, Kentucky, West Virginia, Maryland, and Delaware, where 25 to 60 percent of black students attended biracial schools. But in eight southern states (Texas, Georgia, Virginia, North Carolina, Arkansas, Louisiana, Tennessee, and Florida), where about 2 percent or less of black students were in biracial schools, strategies of "tokenism" had been used to admit only a few black to white schools. And in Mississippi, Alabama, and South Carolina, not a single black attended school with a white. (Ravitch, 1983, p. 138)

Given the original *Brown* decision, any means that ended segregation was of course a means of providing equality of educational opportunity. Progress in this direction quickened under the administration of President Lyndon Johnson. In 1964 the Civil Rights Act, originally proposed by President John Kennedy, was passed. This act prohibited various forms of discrimination, gave the federal government increased leverage in enforcing progress toward integration, and ordered the U.S. Commissioner of Education to conduct a survey on the availability of equal educational opportunity. The passage of the Elementary and Secondary Education Act in 1965 gave the federal government still further leverage over school districts, for when the federal government began supplying massive amounts of aid to local schools it could also withdraw aid from districts that did not comply with federal directives. By the middle 1960s the stage was set for the federal government to identify segregation and demand progress toward ending it through its policies on equality of educational opportunity.

The Coleman Report.   Prior to 1966 progress toward integration was defined primarily in terms of having black and white children attend the same schools (equality of treatment); however in that year a major social-scientific study of schooling helped shift federal policy toward promoting equality of results. As a follow-up to the directive in the Civil Rights Act, James S. Coleman of the Johns Hopkins University in Baltimore, Maryland, was commissioned to lead a team of sociologists to study progress toward equal educational opportunity. During the 1965–66 school year the team surveyed some four thousand schools and six hundred forty-five thousand students from all parts of the country in what can be described as an input-output study. The team surveyed the socioeconomic and racial characteristics of students and a large number of characteristics of schools (such as facilities, curricula, availability of books, and experience of teachers) often associated with the quality of education. It attempted to correlate these "inputs" with the school "outputs" it had measured—the scores of students on achievement tests. The study, officially titled *Equality of Educational Opportunity* but widely referred to as simply the Coleman Report, was released in 1966 and contained some surprising findings. It suggested that the differences in physical facilities between black and white schools was not as great as previously believed, that the academic achievement of whites exceeded that of blacks, and that this achievement did not seem to be related to the characteristics of schools themselves but to the family background of students and the socioeconomic and racial composition of the student populations of individual schools. If equality of results is desirable, the Coleman Report suggested that

> if a white pupil from a home that is strongly and effectively supportive of education is put in a school where most pupils do not come from such homes,

his achievement will be little different than if he were in a school composed of others like himself. But if a minority pupil from a home without much educational strength is put with schoolmates with strong educational backgrounds, his achievement is likely to increase. (Coleman et al., 1966, p. 22)

The Coleman Report was widely interpreted as indicating that schools "don't make a difference," thus damaging efforts to support both good, basic education itself and new programs of compensatory education that had sprung up after the passage of ESEA, and as providing a rationale for busing as a means of ending segregation and improving the achievement of black children. This latter interpretation also corresponded with new policies in the Department of Health, Education, and Welfare (HEW) to promote racial balancing of individual schools and with the new willingness of courts to enforce numerical quotas for racial mixing as means of progressing toward integration. Districts could integrate their schools through any number of voluntary means, but when they failed to do so courts were increasingly prone to order busing as a way of ending segregation. The impetus from HEW and the courts was effective. Whereas in 1964 only about 2 percent of black students in the South attended schools with whites, by 1968 the proportion had grown to 32 percent and by 1972 to 91 percent (Ravitch, 1983, pp. 164–167). The social-scientific evidence provided by the Coleman Report supported the idea that busing—whether voluntary or court ordered—and other direct means of racially mixing schools would promote both integration itself and equality of educational opportunity newly conceived by Coleman and others to mean equality of results. On its surface this idea seemed consistent with the original *Brown* decision.

Ironically, however, although the evidence supplied by the Coleman Report and its rationale for busing were used to help end the segregation that the *Brown* decision had declared unconstitutional, the Coleman rationale leaves a racist residue quite inconsistent with *Brown*. Whereas the *Brown* decision used social-scientific evidence to assess the damage to black children caused by schools legally segregated under the separate but equal doctrine, it provides a much different rationale for busing or whatever means become necessary to end segregation. The *Brown* decision was not based primarily on social-scientific evidence but on moral principles contained in the Constitution, especially on the equal protection of the laws clause of the Fourteenth Amendment. Under *Brown* busing may be necessary because the Constitution makes segregation morally unacceptable. *Brown* therefore provides a rationale for busing based on the concept of equality of treatment. Accordingly all children regardless of race should be provided the same opportunity to attend the same schools. In contrast the Coleman Report provides a rationale for busing based on the concept of equality of results, particularly on the racist premise that mixing black and white children in schools is necessary to help black children learn, but not white children. Interestingly the Coleman Report found sections of the country where achievement for black children was higher in all-black schools than in integrated schools, thereby negating the racist premise, but the report could not reconcile such inconsistent evidence with the generalizations it suggested.

The Coleman Report was fundamentally flawed for several reasons. Its specifics and generalizations were sometimes inconsistent and the popular interpretation that schools "don't make a difference" contradicts the far more compelling evidence offered by the life of virtually every American who has ever attended school, but, most important, in considering only what was easily measured, the report missed what is most important about schooling and painted a grossly distorted and oversimplified picture of education itself. It is not the only social-scientific study to have done this but it was certainly the most influential, especially during the educationally pivotal decade of the 1960s. Its influence has been both good and bad. It hastened the pace of integration but reinforced racist beliefs. It focused equality of educational opportunity on the benefits children were actually obtaining from schools but set up unreasonable expectations about both the difficulty and ease of helping all children achieve the same results. Because of the Coleman Report's influence on busing by the early 1970s de jure segregation in the South was largely ended but de facto segregation in the North may have increased due to "white flight" from cities where busing was employed. By the 1980s beneficial effects of integration seemed to have occurred and at least the most virulent attitudes remaining from the era of the separate but equal doctrine seemed to have subsided. American schools appeared to have refocused on the task of providing equality of educational opportunity through improving the quality of education for all instead of solely through further progress in integrating schools.

Compensatory programs and their cost.   The *Brown* decision and the national commitment of the 1960s seem to indicate that progress toward equality of educational opportunity cannot take place in the presence of segregation; however progress toward high-quality education for all cannot occur without direct improvements in the immediate education services offered. In a fundamental sense compensatory education and high-quality education are the same thing. The theory of compensation suggests that certain children need to be exposed to enriched environments to overcome environmental deficiencies and to help them do well in school, yet high-quality education can be considered the enriching of all students' environments in order to help them realize their full potentials. Schools exist to do things for students that would not ordinarily or incidentally be done outside the school environment.

Questions that inevitably arise when compensatory education is distinguished from ordinary, high quality education are: Who should receive compensation and on what basis? Is failure to do well in school attributable solely to deficiencies in students' environments or also to deficiencies in students themselves? Can compensatory programs actually make the performances of students in schools more nearly equal? With the national commitment of the 1960s and federal policies encouraging equality of results the federal government attempted to answer these questions by putting large amounts of money into newly developed compensatory programs directed at what ESEA described as "culturally deprived" children and intended to help them do as well in school as nondeprived children. Because the early years of childhood were seen as being the most critical in determining the long-range results of schooling, most programs focused on the preschool and early elementary years. Project Head Start, perhaps the best known of these programs, began in 1965 and was directed toward providing intellectually stimulating activities for three and four year olds; it was quickly followed by Follow Through, a program intended to continue the environmental enrichment of Head Start into the elementary grades. Other programs were developed that included still older children, notably the More Effective Schools (MES) project, which begun in slum schools in New York City but rapidly spread to other cities. MES attempted to reduce class size and provide special services such as psychologists, psychiatrists, social workers, breakfasts, and remedial reading classes (Clifford, 1975, p. 120). Other compensatory education programs included the Neighborhood Youth Corps, Upward Bound, Educational Talent Search, and Career Opportunity Program (Jarolimek, 1981, p. 150). Also sometimes considered as compensatory education were programs of bilingual instruction and the Job Corps, which was intended to provide vocational training for impoverished school dropouts between sixteen and twenty-one years old. Although compensatory education was provided to youths of all racial groups, it was in fact directed to high proportions of blacks and other minorities and therefore by no means escaped being perceived by large segments of the nation as being based on a racist premise consistent with the rationale for busing suggested by the Coleman Report.

When compensatory education is perceived simply as the good education that is necessary for all, it can easily be justified in terms of the individualized and appropriate concept of equality of educational opportunity. Yet given certain perceptions and the pejorative tone of the phrase "culturally deprived," it is difficult to justify in terms of the equal treatment concept. However, compensatory education was in fact justified by the federal government during the 1960s in terms of the equal results concept, and the government wanted to know what it was getting for the many millions of dollars it was pouring into compensatory programs through ESEA and other sources. Research on the results of compensatory programs was not encouraging. The first evaluations seemed to show that the academic effects of programs like Head Start were limited and transitory, and that despite some initial gains Head Start children eventually fell just as far behind nondeprived children during elementary schooling as did other culturally deprived children who had not received compensatory services. What such evaluations did not show was that many of the specific compensatory programs had been hastily slapped together, were ill managed, and were staffed by ill-trained teachers. In its haste to produce and demonstrate discernible results the federal government did not sufficiently examine differences in the quality of the newly minted programs nor sufficiently anticipate the formidable difficulties of even attempting to equalize educational results for all children. Thus the principal results of these actions were to produce considerable skepticism by the late 1960s about the efficacy of compensatory education and to restrict the flow of funding. Yet the federal tap by no means ran dry, and many compensatory services are still routinely offered in school districts as part of their regular programs; however few of the original programs of the 1960s now exist. Head Start has survived into the middle 1980s as a reasonably modest federal program concentrating on in-home visits by specially trained teachers. These teachers visit impoverished families to provide intellectually stimulating activities for young children and show their parents how to maintain an enriched environment. Ironically recent evaluations of Head Start and other compensatory programs show far more optimistic results than did the original evaluations and appear to indicate that well-conceived and well-organized compensatory practices can achieve some tangible long-range gains in the school performance of impoverished children.

Local school financing. National attention has also focused on whether students can enjoy equality of educational opportunity if the amounts spent on education services vary widely depending on the wealth of the districts in which they live. Historically local school districts have depended heavily on their own funds to finance their schools, and nearly half the financial support for public schools in the United States is still derived from local taxes, usually the property tax. Because wealthy districts contain far more valuable property than do poor districts, richer districts are able to spend far more money on their schools, despite state efforts to provide so-called equalization funds to poor districts to help overcome their relative financial disadvantages. Opponents of the prevailing system of local school financing have argued that the quality of children's education and even their chances for success in life depend largely on the amounts of money spent on their schooling. Encouraged in the 1960s by the national attention to equity, such opponents initiated a school financial reform movement to agitate for equal expenditures.

Two court cases have been extremely influential in shaping the issue of local financing. In 1971 the California State Supreme Court considered the equity of a neighboring school district's being able to spend less than half the money per pupil per year than the affluent Beverly Hills district in spite of a tax rate twenty-three times higher than that in Beverly Hills. In the resulting decision, *Serrano v. Priest* (1971), the Court held that under the California state constitution the system of financing schools based on the property tax was illegal because it discriminated against children in poor districts. This decision stimulated challenges in several other states to the prevailing method of financing schools; however the school financial reform movement was dealt a significant blow in 1973 when the U.S. Supreme Court issued its ruling in *San Antonio Independent School District v. Rodriguez.* This case was similar to the case in California two years before, but the U.S. Supreme Court in a five-to-four decision held that the U.S. Constitution does not define education as a fundamental right and therefore provides no basis for striking down the use of the property tax to finance schools in every state. The effect of this decision was that there would be no national uniformity on the use or nonuse of the property tax as the principal means of financing local schools, nor would there be national uniformity of expenditures. The matter of local expenditures was to be decided by each state in light of the requirements of its state constitution. In some states, like New Jersey and Connecticut, reliance on the property tax was struck down. In other states, like New York, it was not. However by 1981 twenty-eight states had responded to demands for equity in expenditures by revising their systems of financing public education (Ravitch, 1983, p. 313).

The movement to reform the financing of local schools is based at least in part on a national interpretation of equality of educational opportunity as the concept of equality of results, namely that the benefits one child receives from schooling should be received as well by all other children. But if all children are receiving basic education services, why worry about equalizing expenditures unless benefits depend on them? Therefore by tending to equate expenditures with benefits the school financial reform movement also partly interpreted equality of educational opportunity as the concept of equality of treatment. The movement of course simply happened. It never represented national policy, for it in fact ran contrary to certain ideas about equity on which federal policies on integration and compensatory education were based in the 1960s. By incorporating two different interpretations of equality of educational opportunity, the reform movement also ran contrary to itself in some ways. To the extent it was self-contradictory, it no doubt added to public confusion about equity and made more difficult the task of advocates of the concept of individualized and appropriate treatment, who in the case of compensatory education, for instance, argued that good, basic education might require the expenditure of more money on impoverished or deprived students than on other students without the expectation that all students would achieve the same results. In this sense attention to the principle of equity in school financing has had a great deal to do with conflicting public beliefs about the purposes of schools and with the texture of the education services provided there.

Educating handicapped students.   The passage of Public Law 94-142 in 1975 culminated a long battle fought in the name of equity by one of the best-organized and most-effective special interest groups in the history of American education, the parents of handicapped students. Seizing upon growing national attention to equality of educational opportunity in the 1960s, parents dissatisfied with the education their handicapped children were receiving organized on a national scale and convinced Congress to pass a law that dramatically changed the conditions under which public schools offer education services. Because the federal government has no direct legal authority over public schools, Public Law 94-142 was passed to protect certain constitutional rights (particularly due process) of handicapped students; it also included extremely detailed and costly regulations for public schools.

Prior to 1975 students with physical or mental handicaps that significantly impaired their ability to learn in conventional classrooms were usually taught in separate special education classrooms by teachers trained specifically for this task. The ability of these classrooms to meet the differing needs of variously handicapped students was uneven. Some of these students dropped out of school prematurely; others were never offered special services at all. Public Law 94-142 was intended to assure that all handicapped students received "free appropriate public education" to meet "their unique needs." Services were to be provided in regular classrooms whenever feasible, in special classrooms when necessary. A written, individualized plan was to be developed for each student that listed (1) the present level of educational performance, (2) the annual and short-term goals, (3) the special and regular education services to be provided, (4) the projected dates of such services, and (5) the procedures to be used in evaluating educational progress. Parents had the right to approve or disapprove plans for their children, and the federal government was to pay a substantial portion of the added costs to school districts. Although Public Law 94-142 succeeded in focusing detailed attention on education for handicapped children, it also made such education controversial. The federal government paid much less of the substantial extra costs than originally anticipated, which eventually resulted in reduced services to nonhandicapped children in many financially pressed districts. Confusion resulted in many classrooms where regular teachers inexperienced in educating handicapped students struggled to meet the new demands placed on them (Ravitch, 1983, pp. 308–310). However since 1975 the standard education services offered in the regular classrooms of public schools across the nation have by law included services appropriate to the special needs of the handicapped.

Since the passage of Public Law 94-142 the availability and quality of education for the handicapped has doubtlessly improved, especially as districts have eventually absorbed the initial costs and learned to implement programs and as teachers have received training and gained experience in instructing handicapped children. However the national emphasis on educating the handicapped that culminated in Public Law 94-142 is still justified in terms of all three concepts of equality of educational opportunity, thereby causing both confusion and controversy to linger. First, Public Law 94-142 was ostensibly passed to protect for the handicapped the constitutional rights that all Americans enjoy. In fact it does protect the handicapped from a form of discrimination in receiving education services: separation from the mainstream classroom. In this sense it is based on the first concept of equality of educational opportunity, treating everyone the same. Second, the law also requires that handicapped students receive special services appropriate to their unique needs. This requirement is consistent with the second concept of equality, treating everyone individually and appropriately. When nonhandicapped students are also treated individually and appropriately there should be no controversy, but in fact many nonhandicapped are not treated appropriately, they do not have the force of law behind their claims, the appropriate services offered to the handicapped are often conspicuous and costly, and these special services have sometimes been offered at the expense of reducing even the regular services offered to the nonhandicapped. Third, claims have been advanced that handicapped students require the services mandated by Public Law 94-142 if they are to learn to their fullest potential. This was part of the strategy used by the parents' organization in lobbying Congress for passage of the law. Such claims are reasonable enough, but they were often easily exaggerated into claims consistent with the third concept of equality of educational opportunity, namely that results for everyone should be the same, which after all seemed to be the prevailing national norm at the time. But if handicapped students can learn as much as the nonhandicapped, in what sense are they educationally handicapped? If through special services they can learn as much as the nonhandicapped can through regular services, could the nonhandicapped not learn still more through special services of their own? Answers to such questions are by no means clear. Indeed, justified in terms of equality of results, education for the handicapped came to be suspected by many Americans as being a way of reducing what other children actually learn. One result of the passage of Public Law 94-142 in 1975 has been to create countermovements in the 1980s to improve education services for gifted and normal students who are seen as relatively neglected by the schools.

Minimum competency testing and required learning. The related topics of minimum competency testing and required learning are treated in detail by Wise (1979, esp. pp. 1–46). In many ways they are logical outcomes of America's emphasis on equality of educational opportunity as equality of results, for they both are completely consistent with this concept. It is but a small step from holding the goal that everyone should learn the same things to attempting to devise ways to ensure that everyone will learn the same things. Taking this step was consistent with the growing interest of the federal and state governments in educational equity during the 1960s and 1970s. Providing equal protection under the laws, promoting integration, helping disadvantaged and deprived children, equalizing school expenditures, and educating the handicapped were left less and less to the vagaries of individual school districts. When governments are skeptical about the effectiveness of school programs, as the Coleman Report led them to be, and about the efficiency of school expenditures, as the high costs and modest results of compensatory education also led them to be, they are prone to attempt education reforms intended to guarantee desired results. The optimism of the middle 1960s dissipated into a kind of desperation by the 1970s. If conventional school practices do little to provide equity, it was argued, then why not devise and require the use of new methods that will?

Governments cannot actually guarantee results but they can pass laws requiring schools to adopt procedures believed capable of producing them. During the 1970s one state after another passed such laws. For a variety of reasons these laws were based on highly rationalistic and bureaucratized notions of education and required schools to adopt procedures such as management-by-objectives, systems analysis, zero-based budgeting, competency-based education, behavioral objectives, and criterion-referenced testing. As states quickly discovered, however, such procedures did not increase either the quality or quantity of learning. Thus the stage was set for the final step: the passage of laws that required students to meet minimum competency standards, although procedures that states had used in attempting to achieve such standards had not proved effective.

Florida's Educational Accountability Act of 1976 is an example of a law requiring that students reach a certain level of achievement. The act set forth elaborate procedures to be followed by schools in planning, diagnosing, evaluating, and placing students and in filing reports, but in case these procedures did not work the act also specified minimum learning standards for every student and contingencies to be followed with students who failed to attain these standards (Wise, 1979, pp. 25–26). Although the act required schools to follow elaborate procedures, it ultimately held individual students responsible for acquiring the minimum learning levels whether mandated procedures were useful or not. Other states passed such

EXHIBIT 5-2   *THE FIRST EDUCATIONAL MALPRACTICE SUIT*

In 1972 the first educational malpractice suit was filed against a local school district. The student, known as Peter Doe, charged that he had graduated from high school in the San Francisco public school system but remained for all practical purposes a functional illiterate. Because of his inability to read and write above a fifth-grade level, he was qualified only for low-paying employment and as a result suffered mental pain and distress. He alleged that his illiteracy was due to the negligence of his instructors and sought damages from San Francisco in excess of $500,000.

Records showed that Peter Doe was of average intelligence, had attended San Francisco schools regularly for thirteen years, had received average grades, and had never been involved in a serious disciplinary action. Throughout his attendance his parents had repeatedly tried to obtain information about his educational progress but had always been told by school officials that he was performing at or near grade level and required no compensatory instruction.

Among his specific allegations was that the school district, through its employees, had "negligently and carelessly permitted [the] plaintiff to graduate from high school although he was unable to read above the eighth-grade level, as required by [California] Education Code Section 8573, . . . thereby depriving him of additional instruction in reading and other academic skills."

Peter Doe lost his suit, as have subsequent plaintiffs in other educational malpractice cases. However, Section 8573 of the California Education Code, which had been in force at the time of Doe's graduation and which in fact had required all California high school graduates to demonstrate reading competency at the eighth-grade level or to have taken a remedial reading course, was amended shortly after Doe brought suit so that demonstrated competency in reading was no longer mandatory.

laws, usually replete with procedures for testing whether students had attained the minimum competencies that the laws specified. Usually graduation from high school was the final stake or, more immediately, at least promotion to the next grade. By mid-1978 thirty-three states had laws requiring minimum competency testing for advancement in or graduation from public schools (Wise, 1979, p. 2).

Such laws reduced the latitude both teachers and students had traditionally enjoyed in determining the course of study and methods for pursuing it. For instance teachers might have reason for believing that a certain method of instruction would be particularly effective in their own classrooms and that both teachers and students would enjoy its use. However the law requiring that different procedures be followed and demanding that students be prepared for competency tests might make its selection a practical impossibility. Furthermore for obvious political reasons states quickly learned to set minimum competency standards low enough so that most students could pass. For this reason alone laws that required specific learning and minimum competency testing, although almost always justified as ways of boosting academic achievement, actually served the prevailing norm of equality of educational opportunity as equalizing results by focusing teaching procedures and expectations on uniformly low levels of achievement. Interestingly there is no compelling evidence to suggest that the rationalistic and bureaucratic procedures such laws mandated are any more educationally or cost effective than the variety of traditional procedures of providing education services that they have supplanted. Although intended to promote equity by raising educational accomplishment to uniformly high levels, they have instead focused it at low levels. In practice the uniformity of procedures that they have required has substantially eroded the ability of teachers and local school districts to treat students individually and appropriately or even to treat all students the same according to judgments made at the local level. The passage of laws requiring learning and minimum competency testing has been intended to promote equality of results but has more surely removed professional educational judgments from educators themselves and placed them in the hands of legislators.

Conservative and Liberal Perspectives

In Chapter Two we used education services to exemplify both the conservative and liberal perspectives on human services. Those discussions focused on the roles of teachers and students, with conservatives favoring a hierarchical relationship in which teachers impart time-tested truths to help students become useful, functioning adults in an orderly society, and liberals favoring a colleagial relationship in which teachers and students share in the pursuit of truth to change society intelligently. These same conservative and liberal views of teachers and students hold for the ways in which any education service is specifically provided. In this chapter we have focused on national beliefs about equality of educational opportunity and described some of the general programs and practices that have most influenced and been most influenced by the belief that became predominant in the 1960s. The discussion of conservative and liberal perspectives that follows deals primarily with differing conservative and liberal views about equality of educational opportunity and the relationship between these views and the delivery of education services. However the general conditions described in this discussion set the tone and shape the texture for the ways in which all educational professionals specifically provide services, whatever their ideological bent and whether they be administrators struggling with the problems of equitably financing school programs, school psychologists working to improve the conditions for mental health in students, or teachers attempting to make small gains in the developmental levels of handicapped children.

The conservative perspective examined.   In the United States debates about education frequently take on a decidedly ideological tone. This has been true about longstanding debates between conservatives and liberals over the proper purposes of education and the definition of good teaching. It has been particularly true of more recent debates about equality of educational opportunity after the policies of the federal government in the 1960s focused national attention on this topic. Perhaps in part in reaction to the federal government's favoring of the decidedly liberal ideology of equality of educational opportunity as equality of results in the 1960s, conservatives have debated in terms of their own preferred ideology, the same treatment for all, which we call the equal treatment model. However under many circumstances conservatives are also favorably disposed to programs and practices that actually operate consistently with the remaining ideological position for which neither conservatives nor liberals have strenuously argued in recent decades—individual and appropriate treatment.

Conservatives generally believe in equality of treatment because of their philosophical and social ideology. They believe that truth is the same for everyone and that human nature is the same everywhere. Human nature is imperfect but many specific defects in individuals can be avoided or corrected by inculcating them with fixed truth. In this sense education is developmental; it consists of services that develop knowledge, character, and skills essential to conserving and maximizing human potential. There is thus little reason for believing that the same basic treatment of people will not produce the same basic development for all. The overriding purpose of education should be, therefore, to provide the same essential services to everyone. Teachers should attempt to teach as effectively as possible, but it is still up to students to take advantage of these opportunities for development that are placed equally before them. The development of individual citizens is critical to preserving society, for society represents the best traditions of the past that can only be transmitted by proper education. Development may help individuals attain self-sufficiency, but self-sufficiency must be harmonious with the good social order. Individual interests are relatively unimportant compared with preserving the best of society.

Conservatives believe that because all human beings require development, education is both necessary and universal. This accounts for the fact that conservatives hold some preferences for education services that differ from their ordinary preferences for other human services. They believe, for example, that basic education services must be universal, not selective, and that these services are necessary, not contingent. Because basic services do not provide material goods but aim at long-range development, they are more properly classified as soft than hard. These elements of the conservatives' approach to education also help account for conservatives' belief in equality of treatment.

Despite this difference between the conservatives' approach to education services and their approach to other human services, certain preferences conservatives hold for education services are consistent with their preferences in other human services areas. They believe, for instance, that the aim of education is more to control the student than to promote understanding. This preference reflects the conservative emphasis on the importance of the prevailing society and the teacher's superior wisdom in deciding what the student needs to know to function in the social order. Proper control may indeed lead to understanding, but control by teachers is the necessary starting point. Additionally conservatives prefer that education services be provided by voluntary agencies and private schools to a great extent, although in practice they temper this preference by reference to the sheer magnitude of the task of formally educating each member of society for many years and to the schisms about truth as reflected by different private schools. Therefore only a small number of the most extreme conservatives oppose mandatory education laws or public schools, although virtually all conservatives are hostile to proposals that would move the American system of formal education toward being solely public.

For such reasons conservatives have favored equality of educational opportunity under the equal treatment model. Schools have traditionally functioned well under this ideology. The historical problems of schooling have been due to practical shortcomings such as poorly trained teachers and not to the ideology itself. Countless students have been educated well and have taken advantage of their opportunities to become functioning members of society. Those who have not are the unfortunate but inevitable residue of a system that still needs practical improvements and must deal with the imperfectability of human nature. For such reasons conservatives have argued against the liberal ideology that favors equality of results. Equalizing results, they assert, is unworkable in practice, tends to reduce achievement to a uniformly low level, and removes those initiatives and responsibilities that properly belong to the student. Rather equity is served by making the same opportunities available to all students, not by insisting that all students be educated to the same degree.

Although conservatives have argued in favor of the equal treatment model, they have also generally recognized that it too can be pushed to ridiculous extremes by those who refuse to make any concessions to genuine differences among students. Just as not all students speak the same language, not all students have precisely the same needs, learn in precisely the same ways, nor function at precisely the same developmental levels. Therefore conservatives make practical accommodations to the individual and appropriate treatment of students as long as such treatment represents the fine-tuning of specific practices consistent with the general and overriding goal of making the same services available to all. Naturally disagreements arise among conservatives over when individual treatment represents a distinct break with conservative ideology about equity. For example, presenting different mathematics lessons to second and tenth graders poses no difficulties under the equal treatment model, but allowing students to choose whether they will learn mathematics at all or not presenting mathematics lessons to certain second graders poses great difficulties.

Given their ideological beliefs tempered by practical considerations, conservatives have clearly seen that under the equal treatment model there is no place in American society for segregated schools, even if the historical record of inferior treatment of separate black schools had not existed. Those not swayed by other considerations have joined with most liberals in opposing segregation, although they have generally been more reticent than liberals to embrace direct means of enforcing integration (such as required busing or numerical quotas), preferring instead voluntary and cooperative means whenever possible. Conservatives have likewise favored some forms of compensatory education but have had grave reservations about others. When compensatory programs have in practice been reasonable ways of enabling children to function successfully in regular classes—and where costs have been under control—conservatives have readily supported them; however they have not supported other programs that seemed overly ambitious, ineffective, and too costly. The equal treatment model has lead some conservatives to support efforts to equalize school expenditures, while others have preferred to let school districts finance their programs as they have traditionally done as long as those schools continued to provide the basic services consistent with conservative beliefs. Programs for educating handicapped students have also been supported by many conservatives for the same reasons that they have supported compensatory programs, but Public Law 94-142 and some practices required by it have usually been viewed skeptically under conservative ideology, especially when conservatives have believed the limits of permissible individualized treatment have been stretched into impermissible preferences, even for the handicapped. Nonetheless some conservatives of a libertarian bent have supported Public Law 94-142 on the grounds that it has wrested authority from states and restored certain personal freedoms to handicapped students and their parents. Finally, under the equal treatment model some conservatives have supported required learning and minimum competency testing as a means of treating all students alike, while other conservatives have found such practices highly destructive of basic educational purposes and traditional educational practices consistent with conservative philosophical and social beliefs.

These conservative stands on the major programs associated with equality of educational opportunity have also been bolstered by several American social norms, which collectively suggest that education services should be universally available but that students should take individual initiative for learning. In general conservatives hold that the American belief in government of shared responsibility promotes individual initiative, skepticism of excessive governmental controls, and a traditional view of the authority of society. Conservatives' belief in private-party decision-making does much the same thing, and their belief that government has an obligation to assist the helpless and the weak justifies individualized treatment for those students (such as the culturally deprived and handicapped) who might not be able to profit fully from their educational opportunities through no fault of their own. Otherwise all students should be treated the same.

In sum, as the above discussion has shown, the equal treatment model advocated by conservatives has been sufficiently modified by practical considerations so that no precise boundaries exist between it and many programs making available different degrees of individual and appropriate treatment of students.

The liberal perspective examined. Just as conservative ideology seems clear whereas conservative stands on programs concerned with equality of educational opportunity appear muddied by practical considerations, so too is the case with liberal ideology and practice.

Whether more a cause or result of federal policies in the 1960s, liberal ideology has advocated what we call the equal results model of equality of educational opportunity. Despite defending this model in debates with conservatives and attacking the equal treatment model as inadequate in light of modern educational knowledge and as all too consistent with a separate but equal rationale, most liberals, like many conservatives, are favorably disposed to programs and practices that operate consistently with the individual and appropriate conception of equality of educational opportunity.

Some of the reasons for the liberals' defense of the equal results model stem from their philosophical and social beliefs. For liberals the essence of being human is to use one's intelligence to promote the healthy growth of one's self and the society in which one lives. Truth is not fixed, nor is knowledge an end in itself. Instead knowledge is encountered and verified through experience within one's changing environment and is a means to the ends of personal and social development. Education, according to liberals, thus develops individual human potential to help people intelligently direct their own lives and improve society. In this sense education helps individuals to pursue simultaneously their own goals and the common good of society. Furthermore one's ability to pursue fruitfully both personal and social ends depends on the entire society. In a still deeper sense, then, how far and how well one develops depends on how far and how well all others develop. According to liberals education should be devoted to maximizing the development of everyone, although everyone needs certain degrees of freedom to exercise individual intelligence in the most beneficial ways. Education services should therefore provide both general conditions conducive to the healthy development of all people toward the same general ends and specific conditions that permit each person to develop in individual ways through the most appropriate individual means. These beliefs leave liberals with something of a dilemma about education: whether to emphasize the common ends or the individual means.

Liberals, like conservatives, believe that because all humans require development education is universally necessary. Basic education services must thus be universal, not selective, and necessary, not contingent. Developmental services do not provide material goods, so they are properly classified as soft, not hard. Unlike conservatives, however, liberals prefer that education be aimed at developing the student's intelligence, not at controlling the student. In fact liberals believe that too much direct control can constrain development of intelligence and that with a well-developed intelligence a student can exercise self-control. Teachers therefore should appropriately guide students toward the development of intelligent self-control. Additionally liberals prefer that education services be available through public schools, for only in this way can a mass society be sure that appropriate services are universally available. However only a small number of the most extreme liberals are hostile to private schools and education provided by private agencies, because liberal theory recognizes that education is an ongoing process that takes place at all times and in a variety of ways that serve the same general developmental ends.

Most liberals assume that given proper conditions for development virtually all individuals will fulfill their human potentials. Such people will not be identical in all details, but because they will be sufficiently alike liberals can support the equal results model of equality of educational opportunity. Liberals argue that when schools treat everyone alike, an approach conservatives tend to prefer, not everyone will equally benefit. Some students may be educated well but others will fall by the wayside. Thus conservative ideology is belied by practical results. Liberals believe that students who do poorly in school are not the inevitable result of imperfections in human nature nor of their own failures to take advantage of their opportunities. Instead responsibility falls on the school to ensure that all students benefit from appropriate schooling. When schools focus on equal results, not equal treatment, practical improvements accrue and students learn to take advantage of their opportunities more surely than when schools treat them the same but hold them responsible for the results. Liberals also argue that the equal results model is preferable to the equal treatment model for moral reasons, since it helps the most disadvantaged members of society to realize their full potentials as completely as the most advantaged members. Equity is thus served for both individuals and the collective society by equalizing the beneficial results of schooling, not be treating all students the same and then holding some responsible for not achieving the ends that good schooling can and should produce.

The equal results model explicitly recognizes that in practice different persons require individual and appropriate treatment to realize the same beneficial results of schooling as others. Therefore liberals advocate individual and appropriate treatment of students but usually insist that such treatment is not an end in itself but rather a means to the greater goal of maximizing human potential for all students and thus equalizing results. Naturally disagreements arise among liberals about the relative value of means and ends. Following the philosophy of John Dewey many liberals argue that means and ends cannot be separated and that value derives from both; however, especially since the 1960s still others have argued that the value of the means is derived from its contribution to desirable ends. It is this latter group of liberals who have argued most vociferously for the equal results model. They do not deny that students may enjoy educational activities and derive all kinds of intrinsic values from them, but they insist that such activities should still serve the more important purpose of equalizing the results of schooling. Given the fact that liberal ideology explicitly recognizes the need for individual and appropriate treatment, liberals have been sympathetic to programs and practices that provide such treatment, even when there is little or no evidence that these programs and practices actually contribute to equalizing the benefits of schooling for all students.

Liberals have used the equal results model to condemn the separate but equal doctrine and segregated schooling. Although they have also opposed segregation on moral grounds, they have pointed to social-scientific evidence that indicates that segregation has a harmful effect on the academic achievement of some segregated students, and thus have argued persuasively that integration is a necessary step toward equalizing the results of schooling. Using the same kind of evidence liberals have generally been far more ready than conservatives to support directly interventionist means toward integration (such as court-ordered busing and federally mandated racial balancing) instead of relying on voluntary efforts. Under the equal results model liberals have also strongly supported programs of compensatory education and education for the handicapped, although they, like conservatives, have worried about excessive costs. Both types of programs, which are quite consistent with liberal ideology, also extend individual and appropriate treatment to clearly identifiable groups who would not otherwise receive it and can be justified in terms of bringing academic achievement among these groups closer to the norms of the general population. For similar reasons liberals have generally supported the school financial reform movement, accepting the assumption that the benefits children receive from their educations may be roughly equivalent to the amount of money spent. Equalizing school expenditures for each child tends to equalize results, although liberals have also argued that bringing the academic achievement of culturally deprived and handicapped children closer to national norms usually requires greater expenditures for such children. Finally, under the equal results model some liberals have supported required learning and minimum competency testing on the grounds that they improve the achievement of weak students. Other liberals hold that such practices hurt the academic achievement of most students, are destructive of the intrinsic values of learning and the cooperative relationships that should exist between teachers and students, have increased the dropout rate, and have introduced an unnecessary and costly level of excessively bureaucratic procedures into American schooling.

Several American social norms have heavily influenced liberal stands on the major programs and practices associated with equality of educational opportunity. Belief in governmental obligation to assist the helpless and weak underlies the equal results model itself, for the helpless and weak surely require special treatment if the benefits they obtain from school are to be equal to the benefits derived by other children. This norm is a basis for liberal support for programs of compensatory education and education for the handicapped, and especially for integration, which most liberals have seen as a means of ending the systematic suppression of minority groups caused by segregation. Belief in progress through science and technology has made credible to many Americans the use by liberals of social-scientific evidence to support educational programs and practices that purportedly tend to equalize results, although confusion has resulted when such evidence has been counterintuitive or contradictory. The belief in government of shared responsibility is consistent with the most basic liberal ideology advocating conditions for all Americans conducive to maximizing their abilities to participate intelligently and cooperatively in improving society.

In sum, as this discussion has shown, the equal results model advocated by liberals makes both theoretical and practical accommodations for many programs providing individual and appropriate treatment of students.

Future Directions

As we have indicated, both the equal treatment model advocated by conservatives and the equal results model advocated by liberals leave considerable room for individual and appropriate treatment of students. Conservatives recognize that the practice of good, modern education necessarily takes into account individual differences among children and attempts to treat different children appropriately through the use of different grade levels, reading materials, instructional techniques, and a host of other practices within the system of modern education services. These practices would not vanish even if conservatives were able to defeat liberals in debate. Literally treating all students identically is patently absurd and simply unfair to students for whom such treatment is inappropriate. The equal treatment model can thus be defended, but only when it is modified to include treating all students equally appropriately. Liberals recognize within their theory the necessity of accounting for individual differences in attempting to equalize the results of schooling for all children. Even if liberals were able to defeat conservatives in debate, few new practices dealing with individual differences could be added to those now in use in the schools. Yet such practices have not literally equalized results and in reality many have served to underscore the fact that different people profit differentially from good education. The equal results model can thus also be defended, but only when it is modified to include treating all students appropriately so that they equally can achieve the same result of maximizing their own unique potentials. When both models are modified to make them defensible, they look suspiciously alike.

We think such basic points have often been missing from debates and discussions about equality of educational opportunity in the United States. We do not mean to obscure the very real differences between conservatives and liberals on educational theory and practice, but we think lack of attention to the basic points we have attempted to identify in this chapter has contributed to confusion about purposes in modern American education and to lack of direction and ineffectiveness in some education services now provided. Yet on some reflection most people find that the points are quite obvious and commonsensical.

Although national attention in the 1960s and to a lesser extent in subsequent decades focused on the meaning of equality of educational opportunity, the issue at stake has really been good education itself. There is no doubt that extreme positions were drawn in the 1960s because of the separate but equal doctrine and its legacy. For many years when separate but equal was the law of the land, segregation was excused as providing equal treatment. When separate but equal was overturned, a lot of its damage needed to be repaired and extravagant claims about equalizing results seemed plausible. These claims, tested on a wide scale especially during the Johnson administration, invited equally extravagant counter claims as the nation struggled to make sense of the idea of equality of educational opportunity and, as a practical matter, defined good education in terms emphasized by these debates.

Years have intervened, and the policies of the Johnson administration have more than been tempered by the policies of the Reagan administration. No doubt basic programs and practices associated with equality of educational opportunity such as integration, compensatory education, education for the handicapped, and the like will continue. They have become too thoroughly ingrained in American education to be ended altogether. Whether they continue in the future as matters of law and policy and whether they are financially supported are other matters that depend on the ideological bent of future administrations and of the American people. Given the similarities of the modified conservative and liberal models of equality of educational opportunity, however, in the future the nation will probably talk about equity less in terms of equal treatment or equal results and more in terms of the kinds of individual and appropriate treatment that constitute good education. If this becomes the direction taken, America's attention will less likely focus on the ideological debates themselves, and the nation will be in a stronger position to pursue intelligently the task of deciding how to equitably provide high-quality education services for all.

STUDY QUESTIONS AND ACTIVITIES

1. Explain why education is a universal human activity. Why can families not provide all the education that their children need? What education should be provided by families and what by other institutions? Explain why any educational institution has simultaneously both a conservative and a liberal function. List as fully as possible the different educational activities that take place in American society and the institutions that provide them. Which of these activities are formal? Which are informal? Which transmit culture? Which change culture?

2. What changes in American society during the nineteenth century caused schools to expand their purposes? In what specific ways did the schools change? Prioritize the items on Tesconi's list of what American schools are expected to provide (pp. 144–145). Is the basic problem that some items conflict with others or that schools simply have neither the time nor the resources to provide them all? Does the holding of multiple purposes always indicate confusion about purposes? List the human services offered in American schools that are typically provided in other human services systems.

3. Why are public schools in the United States legally controlled by states and not by the federal government? In what ways do state laws apply more restrictively to public than to private schools? Investigate and discuss the different kinds of control of schools exercised by different branches of state government. In what ways have local school districts been autonomous? How has their autonomy been eroded by states and by the federal government?

4. Describe the government of local school districts. Attend the meetings of a local school board or school committee. In what ways are teachers professionally autonomous? In what ways are they not? Explain the property tax and its use to support local schools. In what ways has the federal government influenced education in the states? Although the federal government provides a smaller percentage of support to local schools than do state or local governments, why is federal support more powerful than state or local support in shaping school programs? What problems do schools encounter in attempting to keep up with public expectations about the kinds and quality of services they should provide?

5. Why is the goal of moral equality (a belief that each person is of the same worth) difficult to translate into practice? Thoroughly differentiate and discuss the meanings of rules of equality (treating each person the same), equality of opportunity (treating each person individually and appropriately), and substantive equality (providing the same results for each person) and how they apply to education services. How can the same service be justified in all three ways?

6. Explain the separate but equal doctrine. Investigate its historical influence on education and other areas of American life. In what ways can separate facilities be equal? In what ways can they not? Explain the differences between de jure and de facto segregation. In addition to busing, how can schools be integrated? What are the differences between the moral reasons for integration and the educational reasons? In what sense were the educational reasons for integration suggested by the Coleman Report consistent with racist beliefs? Enumerate the ways in which schools do in fact make powerful differences in the lives of many Americans. In what ways can and cannot schools overcome the socioeconomic backgrounds of their students? How might national policies and public attitudes toward education have differed if the Coleman Report had not defined equality of educational opportunity as equality of results?

7. Define compensatory education. How are compensatory education and high-quality education the same? Can compensatory education actually make all students more alike, or will it inevitably make them different? Explain cultural deprivation. Why are the early years of childhood critical in determining the long-range results of schooling? Explain the pros and cons of attempting to justify compensatory education according to different conceptions of equality of educational opportunity.

8. In what ways is the quality of a child's education dependent on the amount of money spent on that education? In what ways is that quality independent of the money spent? Should the U.S. Constitution be amended to define education as a fundamental right of all citizens? Explain the *San Antonio Independent School District v. Rodriguez* decision and its implications. How did the school financial reform movement incorporate two different concepts of equality of educational opportunity?

9. List and explain the basic differences between the special education offered to handicapped students prior to 1975 and the kind of education offered to them after the passage of Public Law 94-142. Interview experienced teachers about the new demands placed on them by this law and the ways in which they learned to cope with these demands. How have changes in the education of the handicapped opened and expanded roles in schools for human services workers such as psychologists, social workers, teacher aides, and others? Explain why education for the handicapped has become controversial.

10. Identify the assumptions about education on which minimum competency testing and required learning are based. Which assumptions seem warranted? Which seem unwarranted? Why? Why should governments pass and maintain laws requiring school districts to use certain specific procedures to assure minimum competency standards even after such procedures have proved

ineffective? Why does the ineffectiveness of such procedures place teachers in the position of being blamed for the ineffectiveness? How can students be blamed for such ineffectiveness? Why have states set minimum competency standards low enough so most students can pass? In what ways can individual districts, schools, and teachers make better decisions about how to treat students than can educational "experts" from state or federal governments?

11. Identify and explain the most important philosophical and social beliefs of conservatives that are consistent with the equal treatment model of equality of educational opportunity. What responsibilities does this model place on teachers? On students? What conservative preferences for education services differ from the conservative preferences for the ways in which other human services are provided? Analyze and discuss the specific stands of conservatives on the educational issues and programs described in this chapter. How has the conservative belief in the equal treatment model been tempered by practical considerations?

12. Identify and explain the most important philosophical and social beliefs of liberals that are consistent with the equal results model of equality of educational opportunity. What responsibilities does this model place on teachers? On students? Why are liberal preferences for education services generally consistent with liberal preferences for the ways in which other human services are provided? Analyze and discuss the specific stands of liberals on the educational issues and programs described in this chapter. How has the liberal belief in the equal results model been tempered by practical considerations?

13. Describe and critically analyze any basic similarities or differences between the idea of treating all students equally appropriately and the idea of treating all students appropriately so that they can equally maximize their unique potentials. How do either or both ideas compare with your own notion of good education? Explain. In what ways must good education be defined before it can be put into practice?

REFERENCES

Butts, R. F. (1984). Search for freedom: The story of American education. In F. X. Russo & G. H. Willis (Eds.), *Exploring American education* (pp. 18–40). Lexington, MA: Ginn.

Clifford, G. J. (1975). *The shape of American education* (pp. 2–32, 75–128). Englewood Cliffs, NJ: Prentice-Hall.

Coleman, J. S., et al. (1966). *Equality of educational opportunity.* Washington, DC: U.S. Government Printing Office.

Cremin, L. A. (1961). *The transformation of the school: Progressivism in American education, 1876–1957* (pp. 3–22). New York: Vintage Books.

Goodlad, J. (1979). *What schools are for.* Indianapolis, IN: Phi Delta Kappa Educational Foundation.

Graham, P. A. (1984). America's unsystematic education system. In F. X. Russo & G. H. Willis (Eds.), *Exploring American education* (pp. 10–17). Lexington, MA: Ginn.

Jarolimek, J. (1981). *The schools in contemporary society: An analysis of social currents, issues, and forces* (pp. 137–163). New York: Macmillan.

National Center for Education Statistics. (1982). *Digest of education statistics, 1982.* Washington, DC: U.S. Government Printing Office.

National Commission on Excellence in Education. (1983). *A nation at risk: The imperative for educational reform.* Washington, DC: U.S. Government Printing Office.

Ravitch, D. (1983). *The troubled crusade: American education, 1945–1980* (pp. 114–181, 267–320). New York: Basic Books.

Smith, B. O. & Orlosky, D. E. (1975). *Socialization and schooling: The basics of reform.* (pp. 59–86). Bloomington, IN: Phi Delta Kappa.

Tesconi, C. A., Jr. (1984). Additive reform and the retreat from purpose. *Educational Studies, 15,* 1–10.

Walton, J. (1971). *Introduction to education: A substantive discipline* (pp. 12–25, 110–124). Waltham, MA: Xerox College Publishing.

Wise, A. E. (1979). *Legislated learning: The bureaucratization of the American classroom* (pp. 1–46). Berkeley, CA: University of California Press.

6

HOUSING AND URBAN ENVIRONMENT SERVICES

SCOPE OF THE SYSTEM

The boundaries of the six basic human services systems in the United States are difficult to define with precision. This difficulty is due primarily to two realities that we attempt to point out throughout this book. First, the services provided by any system overlap with those provided by other systems. Second, the services provided formally by any system, whether through public or private initiatives, tend to blend into the informal and incidental forms of helping that individuals receive in their personal lives, especially from their families and communities. Particularly in the system of housing and urban environment services, however, this difficulty is compounded by a third reality: Defined sufficiently broadly this system encompasses the other five basic systems and becomes unwieldy, yet defined sufficiently narrowly the system is not comprehensive enough to be considered a human services system at all.

Defined broadly the housing and urban environment services system is concerned with the impact of people's environments on their lives, and the quality of life for most Americans is determined largely by the quality of the personal social services, health services, education services, and justice and public safety services available in their environments. Providing such services has been a traditional concern of local and city governments. Income transfer services, although increasingly a federal concern in the United States, determine the kind and quality of housing affordable by many Americans. The coordination of all these services systems and their impact on people's environments and lives could therefore be considered a function of the housing and urban environment services system itself. Defined narrowly, as it has often been in the United States, the system is concerned not with the impact of the entire environment on people's lives but of housing only, which is usually limited to concern for physical standards and the number of housing units available. Traditionally the construction of housing has been left to private initiative, with builders regulated by state and local building codes and zoning rules. The irony of this historical pattern is that although the physical units produced by the housing industry have been highly regulated by such codes and rules, the industry itself has been so unregulated that it has never become part of a comprehensive system devoted to the coordinated improvement of the physical and social environments in which people live but rather remains a hodgepodge of diverse practices. Perhaps, then, the fundamental problem in the development of a modern housing and urban environment services system in the United States is the extent to which the marketplace initiatives of the largely private housing industry, even when shaped and regulated by government policies, can be coordinated with more comprehensive human services activities to improve the overall quality of individual lives. In this chapter we will examine America's search for an ideal program of housing and urban environment services, one that best balances the need for physically adequate and affordable dwelling units with other human needs.

Interpreting "A Suitable Living Environment"

The modern system of housing and urban environment services that has developed in the United States has struck an uneasy and at times shifting balance between attempting to meet America's physical need for housing and trying to satisfy the personal and social needs that arise from the ways in which people are housed. The modern system has been built on the foundation of the private housing construction industry that developed on a large scale during the nineteenth century. The primary focus of this system has been on encouraging construction to provide physically adequate housing for Americans. However, because the Federal Housing Act of 1949 articulated the somewhat broader goal of providing "a decent home and a suitable living environment for every American family," all succeeding federal administrations have in some ways honored this goal, with sometimes reluctant administrations ultimately forced to consider the social consequences of their housing policies. The specific balance struck at any time has therefore depended on the particular mix of programs maintained or emphasized by each administration, in effect, on how each administration has interpreted the phrase "a suitable living environment."

Encouraging homeownership. The greatest single constant in the policies of all post–World War II administrations has been the active stimulation of housing construction by the private market. The federal income tax deductions that homeowners have received for mortgage interest payments and for property taxes have been the most effective means for the federal government to stimulate private homeownership and private construction because they have made owning a home affordable for a greater proportion of the population than would otherwise be the case and have encouraged even relatively affluent families to purchase more elaborate dwellings. Although upper and middle class families have received far greater benefits from this tax advantage than have lower class families, this mechanism has well served the basic purpose of making homeownership

FIGURE 6–1.   Timeline tracing the programs and policies relating to housing and urban development from colonial times to the present. Key legislation that has shaped the development of housing and urban environment services is identified.

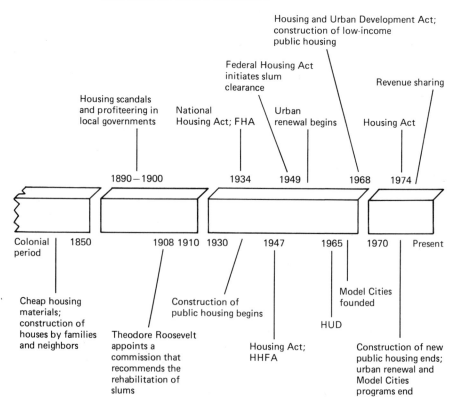

accessible to a broad segment of the population. A second mechanism used by the federal government has been to make money available for mortgage financing and mortgage insurance and loan guarantee programs, especially for low- and middle-income groups but also for other specifically designated groups such as veterans. These two federal mechanisms have been imitated by states, many of which have permitted state tax deductions for mortgage interest payments and property taxes and have established their own state mortgage corporations to make still more money available for homeownership. Both of these mechanisms assume that individuals, when financially able, will choose for themselves what they consider suitable living environments. Both mechanisms also encourage the private market to meet this demand, and both have become thoroughly engrained in the beliefs and practices of modern America.

Physical adequacy vs. social concerns. Apart from the constant represented by these mechanisms, the housing policies of different administrations have taken various forms. Most notable among these variations are the degrees of emphasis given to housing for the poor and to the determinants of individuals' environments aside from housing itself. For instance federal programs that have encouraged only homeownership through the private market have meant that poor families could obtain better dwellings only by occupying those dwellings no longer wanted by more affluent families who had moved into newer homes; in contrast different programs could provide construction of new dwelling units especially for the poor or other special groups such as the elderly or handicapped. Still other programs could encourage the development of local businesses, recreational facilities, open spaces, the aesthetic qualities of poor neighborhoods, or even the ability of neighborhoods to organize their own community groups to deal with their collective problems. In general the federal government has in recent decades slowly taken on a variety of new programs devoted to all the above concerns, but the kinds of programs in housing and urban environment services that any administration has emphasized have reflected the specific bent of that administration.

Although the federal government initiates major nationwide programs, these programs may be targeted at longstanding concerns of state and local governments that have dealt with the problems of creating adequate housing and livable environments for many years prior to the in-earnest entry of the federal government into the struggle during the twentieth century. Aside from federally sponsored programs themselves, much of what happens from day to day in any locality may still be shaped more by state and local laws and practices than by the federal government. City officials hear about crumbling plaster, deteriorating streets, crime, litter-strewn parks, and poor sanitation services far sooner than do federal bureaucrats in Washington. Federal policies therefore tend to view problems at a macro-level and at least in theory are meant to provide and supplement financial support for existing micro-level state and local initiatives in providing housing and urban services that coordinate with the services offered by the other human services systems. What is now considered as the modern system of housing and urban environment services, however, has in practice been shaped by the programs of the federal government, and federal preoccupations have substantially influenced the kinds of services state and local governments have been encouraged to provide. Therefore the specific balance struck by the programs emphasized by any administration has heavily influenced the comparative emphases on physical housing or social problems reflected in the mix of services provided at the state and local levels. In general, as the modern system has evolved, federal preoccupation with physically adequate housing has predominated.

Federal agencies.   Regardless of specific administration, federal policies and programs have themselves been shaped by the activities of the bureaucratic agencies established by the federal government. The Federal Housing Administration (FHA) was created in 1934, and its principal activity of insuring market-rate loans for mortgages for qualified families became the dominant housing program of the federal government for at least two decades. The FHA has insured more than 11 million mortgages worth nearly $200 billion; popularized the long-term, low-down-payment, fully amortizing mortgage; and made possible the suburbanization of the United States in the late 1940s and the 1950s (Egan, Carr, Mott, & Roos, 1981, p. 12). In the 1950s the activities of the Urban Renewal Authority came into prominence. The Federal Housing Act of 1949 and follow-up legislation in 1954 made possible what was first known as "slum clearance," then "urban redevelopment," and finally "urban renewal." As interpreted by the Urban Renewal Authority, federal activities focused on clearing and rebuilding slum areas of cities. Both the FHA and the Urban Renewal Authority were constituent branches of the Housing and Home Finance Agency (HHFA), which had been created in 1947 to administer federal programs of housing and community development, but both acted with considerable independence. Because of a growing accumulation of independent federal programs and some major scandals in the early 1960s over the misuse of urban renewal money, the HHFA was superseded in 1965 by a "super" federal agency created at the executive department level, the Department of Housing and Urban Development (HUD), headed by its secretary, a new presidential cabinet position. The creation of HUD was probably intended to unify federal policy on housing, and the emphasis on urban areas probably reflected a collective belief in the United States that reversing the perceived decay of its major cities was a national priority. Whatever the original intent, the primary activities of HUD focus on the construction of housing as the principal means of improving the physical environments of urban areas and now dominate the activities of the larger system of housing and urban environment services to which HUD has lent its name in only slightly modified form.

Limited but irreversible steps. Despite preoccupation by federal agencies with physically adequate housing and cities, the general evolution of federal policies has still been gradually toward considering the broader social consequences of its housing programs, including the nonmaterial determinants of a livable environment. For instance the federal government has sponsored a large number of programs intended to create housing explicitly for low-income families and on a smaller scale has experimented with programs designed to create comprehensive living environments, alter population densities, and stimulate the resettlement of inner city neighborhoods. However limited such federal efforts to improve the overall living conditions of all segments of the American population have been, they have become engrained within the federal bureaucracy to the extent that Morris (1979) suggests they now represent an irreversible trend:

> The extensiveness and breadth of federal involvement has now become sufficiently great for it to be difficult to visualize any retreat. The goal of social policy concerning the poor is still concentrated on improving the physical environmental conditions, but supplementary efforts to support beautification, to improve air and water standards, and to alter densities are all moves in the direction of wider social responsibility by federal action. The worst that can be said of the nominal steps taken thus far is that they are just that: they represent tentative probes and experiments with continuity, but limited financial support. Nonetheless, they represent steps in a clear direction. (p. 111)

Summary. As reflected in the activities of HUD and other federal agencies, the policies and programs that now define the modern system of housing and urban environment services in America can be summarized in the following way. The federal government is concerned with creating a suitable living environment for all its citizens, and this concern extends to considering both the material and the nonmaterial determinants of the environment as well as the social consequences of government actions. Nonetheless government prefers to allow individual citizens to make their own decisions about what constitutes suitability in housing by encouraging them to own homes that are constructed privately in a free market regulated only by minimum housing standards, building codes, and zoning requirements. The two principal means by which the federal and state governments encourage homeownership are tax deductions for mortgage interest payments and property taxes and programs that make funds available for home loans and mortgages and lower mortgage interest payments. The federal government works jointly with state and local governments in providing programs of low-rent public housing and rent subsidies for citizens who are not fully able to exercise their own choices about suitability, such as the poor, elderly, and handicapped. Federal, state, and local governments also combine with the private sector in a wide variety of programs of slum clearance and urban renewal, and the federal government in particular has encouraged clean air and water standards and provided funds for water and sewer projects, highway construction, recreational facilities, open spaces and general beautification, and community development. As it has slowly evolved the overall system has gradually become cognizant of the human dimensions of housing construction and urban development, such as the sociological impact of housing projects on neighborhoods, and of the possibilities of coordinating the many hard goods and services it has traditionally provided with the often less tangible soft goods and services provided by other systems of human services.

SOCIAL CONSEQUENCES OF AMERICA'S APPROACH TO HOUSING

Origins of the Housing Problem

During the colonial period of America and the early decades of the United States, housing for most people was a simple necessity of life and not a social problem. In what was originally a sparsely populated wilderness building materials were cheap or, especially along the frontiers, free for the taking. Most able-bodied people could construct homes that were adequate by the standards of the times, and they often did so in cooperation with their neighbors. In a nation energetically clearing vast areas of land, wood was not only the principal building material but also was readily available to heat virtually every home. Indeed one of the principal attractions of America to early immigrants was the easy availability of land and the kind of housing it made possible. Prior to the development of indoor plumbing, central heating, and electricity, the homes of the most well-to-do Americans might contain more living space than those of their neighbors and be more elegantly finished and elaborately furnished, but they were unlikely to offer substantially better shelter, heating, or access to clean water. Only where populations began to concentrate in towns and cities did a rudimentary housing industry begin to emerge.

During the nineteenth century the United States gradually became less agrarian and more urbanized. The development of industries requiring large numbers of workers and the arrival of massive numbers of immigrants rapidly enlarged the populations of big cities to unprecedented levels and created major housing shortages. Hastily and poorly constructed tenements superficially met the most immediate demands for new housing in large cities, but these buildings also served further to concentrate urban populations into ethnic and cultural ghettos where inadequate, overcrowded, and unsanitary housing was the norm. Regulations concerning construction of physically adequate housing, practices of landlords, and standards for safety and sanitation were slow to emerge. A diminishing proportion of families owned their own homes. By the end of the nineteenth century America had developed a large-scale, free-market housing industry, but it had also developed large-scale slums and a growing consciousness of housing as a social problem.

Early reform movements.   Increasing awareness of the deplorable living conditions in the slums of major cities gave rise to demands for solutions, and the civic reform movements these demands generated often created conflicts with those local politicians and builders who were profiting handsomely from slum housing. Although the reformers were generally concerned with the human problems of slum dwellers, their solutions took the form of regulation of the private construction industry. Such regulation was seen as preferable to efforts by government to construct and administer public housing, for during the 1890s the corruption of local governments had become a widely publicized national concern. The reformers assumed that tough regulation of the physical standards of housing would remove the profit motive responsible for slums, which would in turn improve both the physical environment and social conditions of slum dwellers (Morris, 1979, p. 99). During this era state and local governments enacted building and housing codes. There were neither federal policies nor programs on housing, although a commission appointed in 1908 by President Theodore Roosevelt recommended that the federal government acquire and rehabilitate the worst of the nation's slums.

Federal Involvement in Housing

Direct federal involvement in housing did not begin until the Great Depression. State and local regulations had temporarily alleviated the most glaring inadequacies of slum housing, but President Franklin Roosevelt called national attention to the ongoing nature of the problem by describing one-third of the population of the United States as ill housed. Furthermore the problem of physically inadequate housing was soon compounded by an acute housing shortage caused when the national financial crisis of the 1930s and the national war effort of the early 1940s substantially reduced the construction of new housing units. Although a few public housing projects were constructed in the mid-1930s under programs directed by the Works Progress Administration, the basic response of the federal government was to stimulate the private housing industry. The National Housing Act of 1934 created the FHA and its system of mortgage guarantees for private homeownership as the cornerstone of federal housing policy. From 1931 to 1945 construction of new housing still lagged far behind America's need, and the population continued to migrate into urban areas, crowding many people into small dwelling units created by subdividing previously larger apartments and homes. However, beginning in 1946 FHA stimulation of the private housing industry launched the nation into an era of unprecedented massive construction of new homes. Abetted by federally supported highway construction, FHA encouragement of new housing construction rather than rehabilitation of old but still sound units in cities created a mass movement of urban families to the burgeoning suburbs during the 1950s and 1960s. The problems created for cities by the rapid loss of population and the deterioration of inner-city housing were addressed during this era by other federal programs. The Housing Act of 1947 initiated major construction of low-rent public housing intended originally for working-class families. Administered through local housing agencies, nearly 2 million units of public housing have been constructed. This effort to supply Americans with physically adequate housing is small compared with the 11 million mortgages underwritten by the FHA, and public housing has not been available in many small towns and rural areas because the necessary local agencies were never created. Ironically the principal difficulties encountered by public housing projects have been caused by efforts to increase their scale. As large high-rise buildings were constructed in major cities, they were occupied by fewer working families and by more very poor families, often dependent on public welfare payments, thus exacerbating a variety of social problems among the tenants of such public housing projects. After 1968 construction of public housing focused on small-scale projects scattered throughout metropolitan areas. The Federal Housing Act of 1949 initiated other federal programs for dealing with urban housing. Eventually known collectively as urban renewal, these programs provided financial assistance to local authorities to clear slum areas to make way for private development. Although such programs did contribute to the rebuilding of the downtown areas of some cities, they did not by themselves contribute to alleviating the national housing shortage, since urban renewal has cleared far more units of substandard housing (four hundred twenty-five thousand) than it has replaced (one hundred twenty-five thousand), and replacement units have usually been too expensive for the original occupants, thus dispersing slum dwellers to other slum areas of the same cities.

Shaped by federal involvement, the post–World War II boom in housing construction lasted nearly three decades and changed the character of housing in the United States. As a result the number of housing units increased from 46.1 million in 1950 to 76 million units in 1973. During this time 42.5 million new units (including mobile homes) were constructed, or the equivalent of 92.2 percent of the existing housing stock at the beginning of the period. Deducting older units that had been demolished or abandoned, the net gain of 29.9 million units represented an increase of 65 percent. During the same time the number of American households increased by 56.7 percent and the total population by 38.2 percent. More than half the net gain in units came from construction in suburban areas, which increased the number of suburban units by 16 million, from 11 million units in 1950 to 27 million units in 1973, an increase of 145 percent (Downs, 1978, p. 171).

Federal involvement in housing, then, which began during the Great Depression, has been directed primarily at stimulating and shaping the private housing industry through financial incentives. A major result has been to shift a substantial proportion of the national population to suburban areas. A secondary activity of the federal government has been to design and encourage local authorities to carry out programs intended to improve housing in urban areas. These policies and programs of the federal government form the core of the modern system of housing and urban environment services and have been intended to increase the availability of adequate housing to Americans. In some ways this system has been remarkably successful; in other ways it has been unsuccessful.

Successes and Failures of Approaches to the Housing Problem

From shortage to surplus.   The major success has been to eliminate the shortage of housing units that had developed prior to 1946. Between 1946 and 1973 the FHA-stimulated private housing building boom created a surplus of dwelling units. Furthermore the occupancy of dwelling units that met or exceeded minimum standards also dramatically increased. As a result housing units over thirty years old comprised 45.7 percent of those units occupied in 1950, 46.5 percent in 1960, but only 40.6 percent in 1970; housing units lacking complete plumbing decreased from 35.4 percent in 1950 to 16.8 percent in 1960 to 6.9 percent in 1970; housing units classified as overcrowded decreased from 15.8 percent in 1950 to 11.5 percent in 1960 to 8.2 percent in 1970; and housing units classified as dilapidated decreased from 9.8 percent in 1950 to 5.0 percent in 1960 to 4.5 percent in 1970 (U.S. Department of Housing and Urban Development, 1973, pp. 6–9). Recent estimates suggest this trend has continued into the 1980s at a reduced pace, even though new construction has more or less been balanced with demand since 1973.

Housing deprivation.   The success of federal policies and programs in eliminating the shortage of housing in the United States must be tempered by other considerations. A thorough definition of what has come to be known as housing deprivation takes into account four criteria:

1.   the physical adequacy of the house and its equipment,
2.   the space available in relation to the number of occupants,

3. the ability of low-income families to pay the cost of decent housing,
4. the adequacy of the surrounding environment and its neighborhood services. (Frieden, 1977, p. 640)

According to this definition the actions of the federal government in eliminating the housing shortage have been successful in reducing deprivation as measured by the first two criteria but much less successful in terms of criteria three and four. Much success of course can be attributed to the increasing wealth throughout the nation as a whole for more than two decades following World War II. Increased wealth thus made good housing accessible to a larger segment of the population regardless of federal actions. However, during the 1970s and into 1980s the nation experienced an era of economic stagnation as indicated by several recessions and periods of high inflation. Between 1979 and 1983 more than 9 million Americans were pushed below officially designated poverty levels, raising the proportion of Americans that the federal government classified as poor from 11.7 percent to 15.2 percent of the total population (Klutznick, 1985, pp. 9–10). Without further increases in the general level of wealth further success in terms of the first two criteria cannot be continued indefinitely. In terms of the third criterion evidence suggests that even before the 1970s, although the overall level of wealth in the nation was still increasing, poor families were finding it more difficult to afford decent housing. Between 1960 and 1970 the number of American households classified as housing deprived declined from 15.3 million to 13.1 million, but during the same decade the percentage of families paying excessive costs for housing (defined as costs exceeding a fixed percentage of family income) rose from 24 percent in 1960 to 42 percent in 1970 (Frieden, 1977, p. 644).

Impact on families.   During the 1970s and 1980s not only low-income families but also middle-income families have found it increasingly difficult to afford physically adequate housing. Since 1970 an increasing proportion of the disposable income of such families has been spent on housing costs, in part because of rising mortgage interest rates, especially for those not eligible for government subsidization. One result of this has been that in an increasing proportion of American families both spouses work outside the home, although many other influences contribute to this trend. Another trend is for families to be smaller than in the past, with a substantial proportion of married couples now choosing to remain childless. Increasing proportions of households in the United States are now single-person households or households headed by single parents. All these trends are indicative of some of the major influences of housing policies on American families since World War II. Although most families have benefitted from the improved physical standards of housing, its increased availability, and the reduction of overcrowding in homes, the shift from a housing shortage to a housing surplus initially encouraged larger, extended families to break up into smaller, nuclear families. More recent social and economic strains, including the increased costs of housing, have contributed to the breakup of the nuclear family itself. Downs, in his analysis of housing policies and family life (1978, p. 170), suggests that living in separate dwellings reduces contact between family members and has probably contributed to the decline in importance of family ties throughout American society. For instance families tend to seek help and services for things such as housing repairs and babysitting from outsiders more now than in the past. Middle-income households with two working parents or with a single parent who works outside the home can afford to hire babysitters, but low-income households often cannot. Thus in part because of their need to meet housing costs, low-income families tend to leave young children unattended or to use low-cost (and often low-quality) day care facilities. Some parents forsake job opportunities that might raise their incomes. These alternatives either reinforce their poverty immediately or reduce the chances of their children's being able to escape poverty after they have grown up.

Neighborhood environments.   In terms of the fourth criterion of housing deprivation, the adequacy of the surrounding environment and its neighborhood services, debates rage about whether many places in the United States, particularly its largest cities, are better places to live than they were in the past. Evidence is mixed. Certainly the mass migration from central cities to suburbs following World War II both improved the surroundings of many such migrants and precipitated urban deterioration. Whether central cities have been sufficiently rebuilt so that they are now physically better environments than they were before migrations to the suburbs is highly speculative. In light of conflicting evidence, whether basic services such as police, fire, education, health, transportation, and sanitation have improved or declined is also an open question. Compounding the problem is still another question on which little tangible evidence is available: whether displaced human supports that were supplied incidentally and informally in previous decades on a personal level by family, neighborhood, and community contacts have been adequately replaced by the formal systems of human services that have developed over time in the United States. Finally, even when it is possible to obtain tangible measurements of public services, population density, access to parks and playgrounds, local taxes, adequacy of street repairs, condition of dwelling units, air quality, and a host of other objective conditions, such measurements do not necessarily determine the subjective, personal satisfactions experienced by residents of any locale. Campbell, Converse, and Rodgers (1976, pp. 236–237) have developed a conceptual model that compares the objective environmental attributes of a community with the quality of life residents experience. According to their studies, objective attributes are important determinants of the quality of life, but highly idiosyncratic personal perceptions of conditions such as friendliness of neighbors, levels of traffic and noise, and general attractiveness of neighborhoods are also important subjective determinants of satisfaction. In general the level of expressed satisfaction of residents of different American communities varies inversely with the size of the community. At best the results of long-range federal policies and programs in terms of their improvement of the adequacy of the surrounding environments and neighborhood services experienced by Americans seem mixed. Progress has been slow in developing these kinds of human services as part of a comprehensive system of housing and urban environment services because of the longstanding American assumptions that improving the physical adequacy of housing necessarily improves social conditions and improving the physical adequacy of housing is best left to the private housing industry.

The Trickle-Down Process of Housing Redistribution

Trading one set of problems for another. The social consequences of America's housing policies and programs warrant thorough examination. A complete examination is beyond the scope of this chapter, but in foregoing sections we have attempted to identify a few of these consequences such as the impact on families. Perhaps the most significant social consequences, however, are also the result of another longstanding American assumption. In eliminating the shortage of dwelling units between 1946 and 1973 and in improving the physical standards of housing by stimulating and regulating the private housing industry, American government has improved both the housing and the social conditions of a majority of citizens. Unfortunately the gains of the majority have come at the expense of a minority who have found their problems of affording adequate housing within a decent living environment to have been exacerbated by federal policies and programs. The reason for the improvement in living conditions for the majority coupled with the decline in conditions for the minority lies in the nature of the so-called trickle-down process by which dwelling units have been distributed throughout the population.

The trickle-down process derives its name from the fact that as housing units age they tend to pass from the hands of comparatively affluent families into the hands of poorer and poorer families. Because of the relatively high cost of meeting standards set by local building codes and zoning regulations, "less than half of all American households can afford to occupy newly built housing without ever receiving a direct subsidy or spending over 25 percent of their incomes on housing. Hence, only households in the upper half of the income distribution normally live in new housing" (Downs, 1978, p. 171). Americans have assumed, however, that this process serves the interests of the poor, because as affluent families move into newly constructed homes the quality of older homes available for occupancy by less affluent families also improves. Although many poor families have improved their housing through this process, the assumption has not proved true for the poorest families in the United States.

Creating slums.   Following World War II the migration from cities to suburbs was made up primarily of families able to afford new housing, and their urban homes were purchased by less affluent families. As this process has continued, inner-city housing has either been abandoned altogether or has been occupied by the poorest families in the general population. For a number of reasons not all neighborhoods decline, but once a neighborhood is occupied by a sufficient proportion of families who cannot afford the costs of maintaining or rehabilitating their homes (or the costs of rents sufficiently high to provide landlords with sufficient incentives to maintain or rehabilitate rental buildings), housing deteriorates precipitously and a slum ensues, further throwing together high concentrations of people suffering not only from the ravages of poverty itself but also from a variety of associated difficulties such as psychological and marital instability and antisocial behavior. "Such neighborhoods become dominated by high crime rates, vandalism, unemployment, drug addiction, broken homes, gang warfare, and other conditions universally regarded as

FIGURE 6–2.   How a neighborhood becomes a slum.

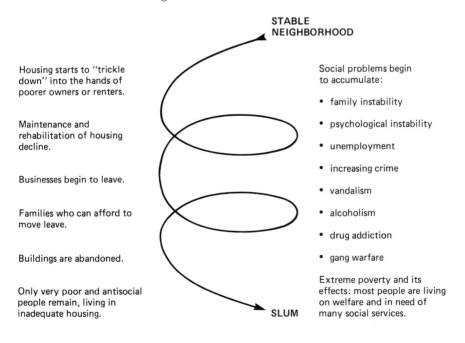

STABLE
NEIGHBORHOOD

Housing starts to "trickle down" into the hands of poorer owners or renters.

Maintenance and rehabilitation of housing decline.

Businesses begin to leave.

Families who can afford to move leave.

Buildings are abandoned.

Only very poor and antisocial people remain, living in inadequate housing.

SLUM

Social problems begin to accumulate:

- family instability
- psychological instability
- unemployment
- increasing crime
- vandalism
- alcoholism
- drug addiction
- gang warfare

Extreme poverty and its effects: most people are living on welfare and in need of many social services.

undesirable. Most households with incomes high enough to have a choice move somewhere else; so do many employers and retailers" (Downs, 1978, p. 174). In such neighborhoods the quality of housing and other determinants of a decent living environment spiral downward together. The effect of the trickle-down process thus is to concentrate in slums the worst elements of the general population with other people who are simply too poor to escape from this environment and who are victimized by their antisocial neighbors. While the poor are thus victimized, slums benefit more affluent citizens by isolating poverty and social problems in neighborhoods that the more affluent do not frequent. The trickle-down process of housing redistribution in the United States therefore graphically illustrates the connections between housing and the social problems associated with urban environments.

Alternative Federal Strategies on Housing

The federal policies and programs on housing pursued since the Great Depression have intertwined with a multitude of laws, regulations, and actions of state and local governments to form the modern system of housing and urban environment services that has developed in the United States. Ironically national preoccupation with physically adequate housing and success in providing it to increasing proportions of the population have helped to create or at the very least to exacerbate the social problems now associated with urban environments, as illustrated by the trickle-down process. Formal services directed at the human costs of these social problems have been slow to develop within the housing and urban environment services system itself and usually have been provided through the existing mechanisms of other human services systems. The boundaries between urban environment services and other human services systems are still unclear. In practice, however, the working definition of urban environment services that has evolved as part of a larger human services system dominated by housing has been—not surprisingly—one that is directed more at improving the physical and material conditions in urban environments than at improving the social and personal conditions of urban dwellers. The American belief that improving physical conditions will necessarily improve social conditions, the same belief that animated the housing reform movements at the turn of the twentieth century, has prevailed throughout the century. Nonetheless since World War II the federal government has become increasingly cognizant of the negative impact on the lives of urban dwellers of forces such as the trickle-down process of housing redistribution and since the 1950s has engaged in a series of alternative strategies intended to fulfill its general policy of ameliorating this impact. Programs consistent with different strategies have been tried out at various times. Although some programs have continued to focus on improving the physical environment of urban areas, others have deliberately attempted to confront the social problems of urban dwellers. In the following section of this chapter we analyze several programs intended to improve housing for the urban poor. Each program is based on an alternative strategy pursued by the federal government since the 1950s. These programs illustrate America's search for the program of housing and urban environment services that best balances the need for physically adequate housing with other human needs.

HOUSING THE URBAN POOR

Aside from doing nothing at all about the problems of housing and urban environments in the United States, the federal government has six basic strategies open to it. The first is to continue to stimulate the private housing construction industry, much as it has done since the Great Depression. Because such activities are the core of the modern system of housing and urban environment services in the United States and have improved the housing of a majority of American citizens, the federal government will continue to provide them despite the fact that they have also helped to create slums and exacerbate urban social problems. The last strategy is to encourage the development of what have come to be known as "mediating structures." This strategy has not yet been widely applied, and we will discuss it in the final section of this chapter, devoted to exploring future directions. The remaining four strategies have been tried through different federal programs, although with varying degrees of thoroughness. These four strategies are (1) constructing publicly subsidized housing for the urban poor, (2) providing a comprehensive and integrated social approach to the problems of housing in urban neighborhoods, (3) sharing federal revenues for housing with state and local governments, and (4) providing monetary housing allowances to needy families. Different administrations have variously supported or condemned these strategies. In practice programs and strategies have overlapped considerably and none of the four strategies has been totally discontinued. In the future each might be reemphasized separately or in various combinations along with continued federal stimulation of the private housing construction industry.

Mission and Role of Housing and
Urban Environment Services

Each of the four strategies has intended to fulfill the general federal policy of providing a suitable living environment for the urban poor. More affluent citizens have been helped by federal programs providing incentives for private construction and homeownership. Such citizens can afford physically adequate housing and have been able to buy their way out of deteriorating neighborhoods and slum environments. The rural poor have also been faced with the hardships of physically inadequate housing but not, for the most part, with the same intensity of grinding social conditions caused by heavy concentrations of poor people in the nation's worst urban slums.

America's central cities have been in decline at least since the late 1940s, when both population and financial resources began to shift to suburban areas. City dwellers now have less income and fewer job opportunities than before. They live in older housing than suburbanites and receive poorer quality human services such as health care and education. They are more often the victims of crime. Cities contain heavy concentrations of minority groups, the elderly, the unemployed, and families whose incomes fall below the officially established poverty line. Concentrated into slums, many of the nation's poorest urban dwellers live in overcrowded and physically inadequate housing, find their neighborhoods crime-ridden and unsanitary, experience social problems such as the breakup of families and drug addiction, and have their personal lives blighted by feelings of hopelessness and despair. The mission of the housing and urban environment services system in dealing with the urban poor focuses on providing affordable, physically adequate housing and improving the material conditions of surrounding neighborhood environments, but it also includes, in conjunction with other human services systems, improving the level of community services available to the poor and ameliorating the social and personal problems associated with poverty.

Origins and History

Public housing and urban renewal.   Public housing and urban renewal are not identical. In practice, however, they are overlapping programs that illustrate the same federal strategy toward the problem of housing the urban poor: the construction in urban areas of publicly subsidized housing units for low-income families. The basic difference between public housing and urban renewal is that in the former programs housing is publicly financed and operated, whereas in the latter programs housing is financed through federal supports but privately developed and operated in accordance with community plans. We have briefly described both programs and their principal shortcomings in a preceding section.

Public housing began on a very small scale during the 1930s and became a major federal housing program only after the Housing Act of 1947. Intended more to help eliminate the general post–World War II housing shortage than to house the urban poor, public housing increasingly assumed the latter function during the 1950s and 1960s as fewer and fewer options for low-cost housing remained available in American cities.

Although many of the older public housing projects were well designed and served to integrate their residents into the surrounding neighborhoods, the large high-rise projects emphasized in the late 1950s particularly served to isolate their increasingly impoverished residents into what became little more than publicly maintained slums. Despite this mixed but generally negative record and the deemphasis begun by the Nixon administration in 1973, public housing still represents the largest federal initiative yet undertaken to provide affordable, physically adequate housing directly to low-income citizens. Nearly three thousand local housing authorities now administer 1.9 million units of public housing, which house 3.4 million Americans.

Urban renewal is another means of carrying out the same general federal strategy of subsidizing the construction of housing units for low-

EXHIBIT 6-1   *SCREENING TENANTS FOR LOW-INCOME HOUSING*

Regulations of HUD require local public housing authorities to develop criteria for screening tenants for low-income housing projects. These criteria focus on the previous behavior of applicants and are intended to exclude potential tenants who would be likely to harm the health, safety, or welfare of other tenants or to damage the physical environment of the project.

As an experiment in developing such criteria, the Housing Authority of Baltimore City (HABC) studied the feasibility of using the prior criminal histories of applicants as a basis for screening out undesirable tenants. The findings of the study included the following:

Of the 407 adults studied, 375 had no criminal record either before or after moving into public housing. Only 21 had criminal records after moving in.

Of the 15 adults with prior criminal records, only 4 engaged in criminal activity after moving in. However this rate of 26.3 percent was six times greater than the rate of 4.4 percent (17 of 392) for adults with no criminal record before moving in.

Using prior criminal records as a criterion would have screened out approximately one of every four adults who committed a crime while residing in public housing but also approximately three of every four adults who did not commit a crime after moving in.

For juveniles the rate of delinquency after moving in was twenty-two times greater (70 percent to 3.4 percent) for those with a previous record of delinquency (7 of 10) than for those without a previous record (5 of 145).

After considering this study HABC decided not to use previous criminal records as a criterion for screening out tenants because the low reliability of this method would likely result in frequent legal challenges by applicants who were denied housing.

income families. Its original purpose, however, was broadened to include the construction of civic, commercial, and industrial properties as well as housing in order to revitalize urban areas. Initiated as "slum clearance" by the Federal Housing Act of 1949 and known briefly in the early 1950s as "urban redevelopment," programs of urban renewal have been financed largely by federal loans and grants made to local public agencies empowered under state laws of eminent domain to take slum properties from their owners to make way for new development. Compensation has been provided to owners for their property and to tenants to help with relocation. Financial incentives such as reduced prices for sites and tax preferences have been provided to private contractors for development in accordance with community plans. Communities also have invested in public facilities that are part of these sites (Schussheim, 1974, p. 113).

Although urban renewal programs have succeeded in rebuilding portions of hundreds of American cities, they have been controversial. Early projects not only displaced slum residents from their homes but the housing that was rebuilt was often designated for middle- or upper-income families. Even so, by 1954 progress on construction was so slow that Congress reorganized these programs under the new name of "urban renewal" and initiated reforms that emphasized rehabilitation of old but sound housing stock, thorough community planning in consultation with citizens affected by such projects, and increased federal supports for mortgages. Urban renewal was further emphasized by the Kennedy administration in the early 1960s but by the end of that decade had run afoul of civic disorders, especially by low-income citizens displaced by urban renewal projects but untouched by any economic revitalization their cities might have experienced, and of the inability of numerous cities to find developers for condemned sites. The Housing and Urban Development Act of 1968 initiated still further reforms by stipulating that a majority of housing units constructed on urban development land must be for low- and moderate-income families, a stipulation that urban renewal projects then lived up to until the Housing Act of 1974 effectively ended urban renewal as a federal strategy to provide housing for the urban poor. Nonetheless, perhaps because of the controversies surrounding it, urban renewal had called national attention to certain problems of providing affordable housing for the poor and had left a legacy in the form of state and local initiatives directed at these problems. For instance some state and local laws calling for rent controls or "fair share" housing (the requirement that a community provide some housing units for low-income residents) are traceable to the influence of urban renewal.

The one greatest failure of urban renewal, however, was that between 1949 and 1974 it destroyed more than three times as many housing units as it replaced. Thus as a practical matter it never actually achieved its intended impact as a federal strategy for providing low-cost housing to the urban poor, permitting at least one critic to describe it with considerable justification as a "de-housing" program and to summarize it harshly:

> [Urban renewal] was taken over at the local level by those who wished to reclaim urban land occupied by the poor for commercial, industrial, civic, and upper-income residential uses. . . . Over half a million households, two-thirds of them nonwhite and virtually all in the lower income categories, have been forcibly uprooted. A substantial percentage of these persons were moved to substandard and overcrowded conditions and into areas scheduled for future clearance, at a cost of considerable personal and social disruption. There have been widespread increases in housing costs, often irrespective of improvements in housing conditions or the family's ability to absorb these added costs. The program has clearly exacerbated the shortage of decent low- and moderate-rent housing. (Hartman, 1975, p. 107)

Taken together public housing and urban renewal failed as a strategy for making an appreciable impact on the problem of providing affordable, physically adequate housing for the urban poor, a problem created in part by the far greater federal housing strategy of stimulating the private construction industry. In fact the history of urban renewal may illustrate how the smaller strategy was overrun by interests unleashed by the larger one. Both public housing and urban renewal embodied the strategy for housing the urban poor that dominated federal thinking for a quarter of a century. During that period federal policy-makers learned much about the connections between housing and the social and personal problems of urban dwellers; however throughout the period the dominant federal strategy for housing the urban poor remained one that emphasized construction of physically adequate housing, often at the expense of social and personal concerns.

Model Cities. On November 3, 1966, President Lyndon Johnson signed into law the Demonstration Cities and Metropolitan Development Act, which formally initiated what became known as the Model Cities program. Model Cities was to be a test of still another federal strategy for providing housing for the urban poor. Although short-lived, beset by political problems from its inception until its demise, and extremely small-scale compared to federal efforts in·public housing and urban renewal, Model Cities has left behind a very interesting legacy.

The strategy on which Model Cities was based can be described as an integrated social approach to the problems of American cities, including housing for the urban poor. Rather than concentrate only on the physical determinants of a livable urban environment, Model Cities was to concentrate and coordinate diverse federal programs and to focus on a few of America's poorest neighborhoods. It was meant to stimulate innovative approaches to improving the quality of life, particularly by increasing the ability of local governments to mesh construction programs with social programs in areas such as health, education, public safety, employment, and economic development. Perhaps most important Model Cities was meant to give residents of targeted neighborhoods the opportunity to participate in planning and carrying out programs for improving their neighborhoods, thereby developing their capacities to improve their own lives. Under the program housing for the urban poor would be part of a comprehensive effort to improve social and material conditions throughout urban neighborhoods. The federal government would supply grants to local governments to supplement a variety of existing programs and to create new ones. Additionally the federal government would supply support services in the form of modern management methods and technology, such as systems analysis and low-cost construction methods, that would help specific programs more efficiently meet their goals. All in all Model Cities was very much part of the general approach to winning the War on Poverty and building the Great Society advocated by the Johnson administration. It shared many of the assumptions and procedures of other Great Society programs and suffered from similar shortcomings.

Despite its own broad and lofty goals Model Cities encountered a series of difficulties that changed its form and greatly blunted its practical impact, so much so that as America's only major attempt to provide a comprehensive series of housing and urban environment services coordinated with other human services, it remains an incomplete experiment.

Following the urban riots of 1964 and 1965 President Johnson appointed a Task Force on Urban Problems that developed the original form for Model Cities. The program was to be an experiment running for five years and limited to approximately sixty-six cities of varying sizes. It was to be a modestly funded demonstration of new methods of aiding slum dwellers. Even so, to secure passage by Congress the original form had to be modified. What emerged was no longer a modest demonstration program but a much more ambitious effort to create through a system of federal grants a series of programs that collectively would solve all of America's basic urban problems (Frieden & Kaplan, 1975, pp. 35–66).

The overall Model Cities program that emerged was beset with both conceptual and practical difficulties. The original proposal had called for a federal coordinator for each city who was to make sure that both existing and new federal programs would work harmoniously. Congress, however, deleted this provision and placed extraordinary authority in the hands of mayors. The result was often to politicize the program at the local level, with mayors sometimes dispersing Model Cities grants for use in nonslum neighborhoods and carrying on power struggles with both independent boards in their own cities and federal bureaucrats in the Model Cities Administration in HUD. HUD officials in turn carried on power struggles with officials in the Department of Health, Education, and Welfare, which also dispersed federal monies for social programs in urban areas. Often neighborhood groups that should have participated in local planning for the program were excluded because of the elaborate planning process required by the federal government (Haar, 1975, pp. 156–159). Ironically the greatest problem of Model Cities was that despite the increased scope that Congress had insisted upon, it was still far too small to change the direction of existing federal programs in cities. Urban renewal, for instance, remained autonomous and largely unchanged. Existing federal programs received fifteen to twenty times the financial resources that Model Cities did; hence Model Cities had no practical chance of coordinating such programs into a comprehensive attack on urban problems consistent with its own goals. Given congressional wishes, Model Cities was not to be a small-scale demonstration program, but Congress granted it neither the resources nor the authority to solve the major urban problems that Congress insisted it should be able to solve.

Model Cities was deemphasized by executive policy of the Nixon administration in 1973 and effectively terminated by the Housing Act of 1974, which shifted federal resources into still another strategy for coping with the problems of housing the urban poor. During its existence Model Cities had received over $2.3 billion in federal appropriations and 152 cities had participated, including every city in the United States with a population of one-half million or more. Twenty percent of Model Cities funds went to education services, 17 percent to environmental protection and development, 16 percent to housing, and 11 percent to health programs. Smaller allocations went to manpower and job development, social services, economic development, recreational and cultural programs, and prevention of juvenile delinquency and other crime. About 60 percent of all money was spent on programs devoted to improving social conditions in urban areas and about 40 percent on improving material conditions (Schussheim, 1974, p. 128).

Before being terminated Model Cities had made very little impact on improving the physical housing of the urban poor, and it had certainly failed to reach the unreachable goal of solving the nation's urban problems that Congress had forced on it. It had also failed in the potentially more manageable task of coordinating federally initiated social programs into a coherent attack on those problems. It was unpopular both with Congress and with many of the local governments it was intended to help. Because of the changes Congress had made in its original form, the program never had a chance to succeed nor to be a valid experiment of the viability of the federal strategy it was supposed to embody, yet even before its termination that strategy had become discredited in the minds of many Americans. Despite these difficulties, thoughtful critics of Model Cities have been able to identify some positive lessons to be learned from its record. Haar (1975) suggests that "the undifferentiated imposition of a single set of national priorities on the widely differing situations in hundreds of cities" was a mistake, but that some national goals need to be maintained, including commitment to improving the plight of the urban poor (pp. 272–277). Frieden and Kaplan (1975) echo these sentiments, suggesting that future urban planners "avoid grand schemes for massive, concerted federal action" (p. 238), but also that Model Cities demonstrated a national willingness to redistribute resources to the urban poor and that those programs that Model Cities was able to create in urban neighborhoods, while not capable of solving all urban problems, did make modest improvements in the lives of the urban poor (pp. 192–193).

Model Cities, then, did not demonstrate that the specific federal strategy it was supposed to embody was wrong, but only that it was unworkable in the form in which Congress had cast it. A comprehensive and integrated social approach to the problems of American cities might still make conspicuous improvement in the quality of urban living if it were combined with better federal coordination or greater local variations and initiatives. When the Model Cities Program was terminated it had not lasted long enough to make an appreciable impact on housing for the urban poor; however it had demonstrated some national commitment to the urban poor, and many of the small-scale programs it set in motion—both federal and local—have continued.

New Federalism and revenue sharing.   Executive actions of the Nixon administration in 1973 and the passage of the Housing Act of 1974 effectively terminated federal programs such as public housing, urban renewal, and Model Cities and the policies on housing and urban environment services they embodied. Federal policies on all phases of American life moved in the direction President Richard Nixon dubbed the "New Federalism," a direction in which the nation has generally continued during the 1980s. Essentially the New Federalism is an effort to reduce the size and cost of the federal government and its intrusiveness in all areas of American life. It is based on the assumptions that state and local governments can better provide many services that have gradually been assumed by the federal government during the twentieth century and that the operation of these services should be returned to them. In practice the New Federalism is a vast conglomeration of policies and programs consistent with these assumptions.

A principal means of pursuing the New Federalism is revenue sharing, the practice of the federal government returning to state and local governments a portion of the money it has raised. This money comes from the federal government with few or no strings attached. Whereas before the New Federalism virtually all federal aid was in the form of categorical grants to be used only in specifically designated ways, or "categories," under revenue sharing much federal aid has been in the form of general or block grants to be used in ways the state or local governments determine.

Since the second term of the Nixon administration, revenue sharing has been a principal strategy of the federal government for coping with the problems of housing the urban poor, although in fact under the Reagan administration federal outlays for revenue sharing declined.

Although revenue sharing represents a federal strategy, it hardly comprises a program directed specifically at improving urban housing because in its pure form it is the antithesis of a consistent, coherent program. As a practical matter, however, most federal revenue-sharing funds have not been totally unrestricted. They have instead been designated by Congress for use in certain general areas such as community development, and formulas have been adopted that direct more funds to economically depressed communities than to well-to-do ones. These general restrictions notwithstanding, local communities have used revenue-sharing funds for a wide variety of purposes. Some have continued construction programs like public housing and urban renewal. Others have maintained or developed comprehensive social programs similar to Model Cities. Still others have used federal funds for projects that were in no way intended to improve either the physical housing or the social conditions of the urban poor. After well over a decade of federal experience with the strategy of revenue sharing, there is little clear-cut evidence to demonstrate whether the housing needs of the urban poor have been better or more poorly served by revenue sharing than they would have been by a continuation of the two federal strategies that it supplanted. One of the longstanding criticisms of revenue sharing, however, has been that it is a means of reducing the federal commitment to the poor developed under previous strategies and of providing less money for their needs in a more politically expedient form.

Housing allowances.   Another strategy open to the federal government is that of providing direct housing subsidies to the poor. This money could be in the form of direct cash payments for rents and mortgages or vouchers or certificates redeemable in cash by landlords and mortgage institutions. These subsidies could be determined by a formula that would include a family's size, income, and the local cost of housing. The primary assumption behind housing allowances is that once subsidized the poor could solve their own problems on the open housing market by becoming discerning consumers. Secondary assumptions are that housing allowances for poor consumers would permit the free market to flourish, thereby increasing the supply of physically adequate housing available to the poor, and that allowances are therefore preferable to direct attempts to subsidize housing construction for the poor and manage their allocation using bureaucratic mechanisms that might stifle the market and reduce the range of personal choices for consumers.

The essential question about housing allowances is whether the poor would be better served by the free market than they have been in the past. To be sure the poor would have more money to spend on housing, but the net effect might simply be to inflate the cost of housing available to them, leaving their material conditions largely unchanged but creating huge profits for private housing entrepreneurs. Proponents of housing allowances argue that this result would be no more likely for the urban poor than it was for the nation as a whole in ending the post–World War II housing shortage through federal stimulation of the private housing construction industry. Opponents point out that the same history illustrates numerous defects in the free market that have left many poor people as a kind of permanent underclass in American society, perpetually ill housed and suffering from other social problems. Government intervention is needed, they argue, to correct these defects, especially to create an adequate supply of affordable housing throughout urban areas, prevent excessive profiteering from shoddy construction and inadequate maintenance, and eliminate various forms of discrimination against the poor. However, the strategy of providing housing allowances without stringent governmental controls on the providers of housing seems to ignore the history in the United States of "persuasive housing discrimination with respect to acceptance of tenants, eviction, and rents charged—on the basis of race, welfare status, number of children, family composition, age, and life style" (Hartman, 1975, p. 156). Housing allowances alone will not necessarily make the poor into intelligent consumers, especially where their choices remain limited. Greater education and experience may also be required. Finally, housing allowances may serve to stigmatize their recipients and concentrate them in ghettos, much as welfare payments have served their recipients, despite the intents of either program.

The idea of housing allowances is not new in the United States. It originated in the 1930s and 1940s when the U.S. Chamber of Commerce and conservative real estate interests advocated such programs as a means of undercutting "socialistic" public housing programs that had begun under the New Deal policies of the Roosevelt administration, and since 1968 the federal government has carried out several experimental housing allowance programs (Hartman, 1975, p. 154). In programs in which a portion of the general welfare payments to poor families has been designated as a housing allowance, results seem negative. In a ten-year experimental program of housing allowances in more pure form, a major social-scientific evaluation sponsored by HUD has indicated mixed results (Friedman & Weinberg, 1983). Still another, smaller-scale study has suggested that allowances are more effective than subsidized construction in reducing the burden of rentals on the poor (Sa-Aadu, 1984). Despite much talk about housing allowances the Nixon administration did little to implement them, and little happened under the Ford and Carter administrations. In the early 1980s housing allowances became an officially endorsed policy of the

Reagan administration for improving housing for the urban poor; however, despite its endorsement of such programs the Reagan administration did little to implement them because of its emphases first on reducing the size of the federal budget and then on reducing the size of the federal deficit. As a federal strategy for dealing with America's problems of housing the urban poor, housing allowances have therefore generated much talk but little action.

Conservative and Liberal Perspectives

The problems of housing the urban poor are so complex and the strategies pursued by the federal government so practically and ideologically intertwined that completely different and clear-cut models embodying conservative and liberal perspectives have not emerged within the system of housing and urban environment services in the United States. Nonetheless conservatives tend to view problems in terms of the physical adequacy of housing and seek solutions through the private housing industry, although they favor federal actions to stimulate private housing construction. Liberals tend to view housing problems in terms that include both physical and social conditions and seek solutions through a variety of direct federal actions, including stimulation of private housing construction. Despite such overlap between conservative and liberal perspectives on the problems of housing the urban poor, we will designate the conservative approach as the free market model and the liberal approach as the comprehensive model.

The conservative perspective examined.   In general conservatives prefer to view problems of providing housing for the urban poor as part of the larger problem of providing housing for the overall population. They point out that during the twentieth century this problem has been substantially ameliorated first by the development of laws and codes regulating the private housing industry and second by the actions of the federal government in stimulating private housing construction. The result has been substantially to eliminate the shortage of affordable housing and markedly to improve the quality of that housing. Conservatives see little reason for changing a system that has worked so well for so many people. Because some urban poor are still ill housed does not mean that the system created that condition. In fact there is considerable reason to believe that as the system continues to operate over an extended period of time further gains will accrue in the quality of American housing and the proportion of the population remaining ill housed will continue to diminish. For these reasons conservatives wish to preserve the basic federal strategy of stimulating private housing construction in a free marketplace, since this strategy has come to represent a normal state of affairs in American society, and, they believe, is the best system yet devised for dealing with the problem of providing physically adequate housing. They argue that it admirably balances individual interest pursued in the marketplace with creation of the common good and illustrates how the free marketplace has come to be a traditional social arrangement that acts as a check on the imperfections of human nature by helping individuals achieve the solution to certain contingent problems within the prevailing social order. This strategy is consistent with the conservative emphasis on the American social norms stressing the virtue of hard work, private-party decision-making, and government of shared responsibility because both the producers and the consumers of housing take individual initiative as they work hard to construct or achieve the means to purchase housing under a system in which government intervention is minimized. Finally this strategy illustrates conservative preferences for selective rather than universal services, the delivery of hard rather than soft services, and the delivery of services through voluntary and private means rather than through public agencies because it provides hard economic incentives to that portion of the population in need of them on a temporary, contingent basis. In the future even these services will no longer be necessary if and when society attains a sufficiently high level of general wealth to enable all Americans to be well housed through the workings of an unaided private marketplace.

Conservatives are much less enthusiastic about several other strategies the federal government has pursued to provide housing for the urban poor, primarily because these strategies tend to run counter to conservative preferences and to alter the basic system that has generally worked well. Nonetheless conservatives can justify these strategies in terms of the American social belief that government has an obligation to assist the helpless and the weak. On these grounds conservatives can support public housing, urban renewal, and housing allowances, programs embodied within strategies intended to provide housing directly to the urban poor; however conservatives have traditionally remained skeptical of such strategies because of a suspicion that not all poor people are helpless or weak through no fault of their own but instead through personal deficiencies such as a failure to work. Conservatives would therefore prefer such services to be delivered on a highly selective basis and only until deserving recipients could be restored to effective functioning within the free market model. One reason why conservatives have not widely supported housing allowances, despite endorsements by the Nixon and Reagan administrations, is that such allowances would have to be granted universally to all poor people regardless of personal deserts, thereby stifling individual initiative and creating dependence among the undeserving poor, people who have the capacity but lack the will to provide adequate housing for themselves within the free market. For all these reasons conservatives have also been opposed to the federal strategy embodied by Model Cities. However, opposition to an integrated social approach to the problems of housing the urban poor based on the ideological preferences of conservatives does not necessarily make them opposed to the development of a modern, comprehensive system of human services. Some conservatives suggest simply that the system of housing and urban environment services should confine itself to providing physically adequate housing, leaving other problems of the urban poor to other, more appropriate human services systems. Integration of the overall system of human services would then become an incidental outcome of each of its various subsystems working effectively, rather than a centrally planned result.

Conservatives have widely supported the final federal strategy toward housing problems, revenue sharing, because it does not interfere with the basic federal strategy of stimulating the private market, it shifts funds and authority from the federal government to state and local governments, and it is consistent with conservative ideological preferences, particularly the skepticism of governmental controls. In fact many conservatives have supported revenue sharing precisely because it has drained funds away from other federal strategies favored by liberals.

The liberal perspective examined. In dealing with the problems of providing housing for the urban poor, liberals are not opposed to continuing the federal strategy of stimulating private housing construction, which, in any case, is consistent with the social norm of private-party decision-making; however they quickly point out that despite its obvious benefits for a majority of Americans, the strategy has consigned many poor people to living conditions that are deplorably low by the prevailing standards in the United States. These conditions include physically inadequate housing, rundown and dangerous neighborhoods, and poor social environments. Furthermore, as the trickle-down process of housing redistribution clearly indicates, many poor people are not responsible for these conditions and have no way to escape from them unless the federal government pursues additional strategies. In light of these circumstances liberals tend to support a variety of federal strategies intended directly to ameliorate all such conditions. They are far less likely than conservatives to assume that improving the physical adequacy of urban housing will improve the social conditions of the urban poor. In fact they assert that poor social conditions usually exacerbate the deterioration of housing. Consequently in adopting a variety of strategies liberals adopt the comprehensive model.

To liberals poor conditions do not represent a normal state of affairs, for individual intelligence can be used to improve the social order. In pursuing the common good individuals may also be pursuing their own best interests. Many of the urban poor are victims of illness, poverty, or an economic system that does not provide jobs for everyone who would like to work or adequate housing for all Americans. The social norm emphasizing governmental obligation to assist the helpless and the weak demands a comprehensive effort to create conditions conducive to the maximal development of every American. For these reasons liberals prefer the universal delivery of both hard and soft goods and services carefully coordinated and provided by public agencies. Yet however successful a comprehensive approach might be in ameliorating the problems of the urban poor, these problems are still not likely to disappear. Thus liberals view a comprehensive approach as part of a necessary rather than a contingent system of housing and urban environment services.

Because of these preferences liberals tend to support most of the strategies pursued by the federal government in addition to the strategy of stimulating the private market, although they have reservations about the ways in which certain strategies have been carried out, especially the strategy of revenue sharing. Public housing and urban renewal are direct attempts to provide decent housing to those to whom it has not been provided by the private market. As such this strategy is in the forefront of the comprehensive approach advocated by liberals. Their reservations are not with the strategy itself but with how certain public housing projects were mismanaged into slums and how urban renewal displaced poor residents and destroyed more units of housing than it created. Liberals are particularly supportive of the strategy embodied by Model Cities, for an integrated social approach that treats problems of the physical and social environments as interconnected is virtually synonymous with their comprehensive model. Their disappointment lies in the distortion of Model Cities by Congress and its subsequent incomplete implementation. Using Model Cities to improve all of American society would have been consistent with the social norm emphasizing progress through the resolution of problems by science and technology, in this case including modern methods of management and construction. In the eyes of liberals the failure of the federal government to carry out Model Cities appropriately and fully does not invalidate the basic strategy of developing an integrated social approach to the problems of the urban poor, and since the demise of Model Cities liberals have continued to support a variety of individual programs that, taken together, represent an approximation of this strategy. Liberals also tend to support the strategy of providing housing allowances for the poor. Their support of such programs stems in part from their optimistic view of human nature: Individuals are capable, once granted the right conditions, of using their intelligence critically to improve both themselves and society. Housing allowances are a direct step toward creating optimal conditions for individuals who in fact have been deprived of decent housing by the workings of the American marketplace. Liberal support also stems from the generally egalitarian thrust of their social belief that the common good in society is maintained only when all citizens individually partake of the good. The major reservation of liberals about how housing allowances have been used is that the allowances have easily become an excuse for abandoning other more comprehensive efforts to ameliorate the problems of the physical and social environments of the urban poor.

Although in some ways favorably disposed to the strategy of revenue sharing in theory, liberals have had extreme reservations about revenue sharing in practice, particularly as it is a part of the New Federalism. Revenue sharing is consistent with the American social norm of government of shared responsibility. In so far as revenue sharing thus tends to make state and local governments equal partners with the federal government in setting the social agenda of the nation and encourages participatory democracy right down to the grass roots level, it is consistent with liberal beliefs in intelligence, democracy, and governmental actions to maximize individual freedom. However in practice liberals have often opposed revenue sharing and the New Federalism, seeing them as a means by which the federal government has eschewed its commitment to the urban poor. Revenue sharing by itself does not guarantee that local communities will use funding equitably or wisely. Although a few communities have used these funds to develop worthwhile approaches to the problems of housing the urban poor, the creation of programs throughout the nation that will attain the universality and breadth demanded by the comprehensive model favored by liberals may require central coordination by the federal government.

Future Directions

As we have indicated efforts by the federal government to improve the quality of housing for a majority of Americans have been a success. In contrast efforts to provide high-quality housing and urban environment services for the urban poor present a dismal picture. The basic federal strategy of stimulating private housing construction has improved the lives of a majority of Americans but often at the expense of the poor. Alternative strategies intended to improve housing for the urban poor directly have been pursued by the federal government since the late 1940s. These strategies either have been unsuccessful or have only replaced one set of problems with another. Public housing projects have become slums. Urban renewal bulldozed slums but created few new housing units for displaced residents. Model Cities was both inflated and eviscerated before it even began. Housing allowances prove too costly to be provided to all who need them. Revenue sharing abandons the national commitment to the urban poor and tosses the problem of housing them into the laps of often ill prepared local communities. Thus prospects are not bright for solving the problem of housing the urban poor during the remainder of the twentieth century, whether conservatives are correct and the free market approach will eventually melt the problem away or liberals are correct and a comprehensive approach will eventually be fully implemented. Barring dramatic political or social shifts in the United States during the remainder of the century, the problem of housing the urban poor will continue to be addressed in the same way: Federal stimulation of private housing construction will continue and a variety of other federal strategies—some conservative, some liberal, but none completely new—will alternatively be tried. Attention to the physical adequacy of housing will continue to predominate over social concerns. The system of housing and urban environment services will continue to evolve toward comprehensiveness, but at a painfully slow rate.

Although this not entirely promising direction is the most likely direction of the future given current realities in the United States, there is open to the federal government still another strategy that is perhaps the most promising of all. It is in some ways consistent with both conservative and liberal ideologies, but for several reasons it may prove unacceptable to both conservatives and liberals as organized political groups and is therefore not likely to be actively pursued in the immediate future as a formal policy of the federal government. The strategy is one of encouraging what have become known as "mediating structures." We describe it as a possible future direction because of its great promise as a new and untried federal strategy, not because of any great likelihood that the federal government will actually pursue it vigorously.

Mediating structures.   Mediating structures are those institutions that stand between the personal lives of individuals and the megastructures of American society such as big government, big labor, and big corporations. The principal mediating structures are family, neighborhood, church, and voluntary associations, precisely those institutions that in former times either incidentally or intentionally provided many of the services that have since been assumed by the modern system of human services that has developed in the United States. The idea behind encouraging mediating structures is not that the human services now provided by the so-called welfare state should be discontinued but that the ways in which they are provided on a mass scale often represent unwarranted intrusions into personal lives. In contrast mediating structures tend to empower persons individually and collectively to define and meet their own needs in accordance with their own value systems. By personalizing decisions and actions mediating structures help meet the legitimate goals of both individuals and government better than is possible through the actions of impersonal bureaucracies; therefore human services systems should involve mediating structures in the process of designing and delivering services (Egan et al., 1981, pp. viii, ix, 6).

One might not ordinarily think of a neighborhood, for example, as either an institution or a structure within American society, but a functional definition may indeed point out how neighborhoods can be classified as such. A national conference on the status of families in the United States has defined a neighborhood as a support system for family living, noting that although a neighborhood is tied to geographic proximity, it is more accurately identified in terms of "lay activities," the informal aid and support services exchanged among its residents. As such a neighborhood can act as a helping network with the capacity to define and cope with problems on its own terms. Said one conference participant about his neighborhood, "I like to think of it as one of the levels of systems in this society that I turn to for help, one of the primary sources of help for me and my family." The neighborhood support system can act as a buffer between individuals and families and the formal systems of human services that exist in the extended society, making the latter more responsive to the needs of the former (Kinch, 1979, p. 8).

Neighborhood support systems, therefore, are not limited to providing informal and personal supports. Neighborhood groups may be organized for community development or advocacy, with agendas that include projects such as gardening, preventing illness, controlling crime, creating jobs, conserving energy, and rehabilitating housing. Citing an increase from five hundred thousand to nine hundred thousand in the number of incorporated nonprofit organizations (most of which are community groups) in the United States between 1975 and 1980, Boyte (1982) believes such groups represent a major social trend of the 1980s and suggests that "their main thrust as they have evolved has been . . . positive, a revival of the old American traditions of community involvement and self-help once embodied in such practices as barn raising and quilting bees" (pp. 4–5). Although some of these groups have worked directly to improve the physical adequacy of housing in urban neighborhoods through means such as construction, rehabilitation, and tenant advocacy, they have also illustrated how their efforts can be linked with attempts to improve the larger physical and social environments of neighborhood residents. They also show how mediating structures such as voluntary neighborhood associations can improve the lives of individual urban residents by working cooperatively with the formal, governmentally sponsored systems of human services that exist in the United States.

It is possible, therefore, for the federal government to pursue policies that strengthen the mediating structures of family, neighborhood, church, and voluntary associations and encourage their working toward the solution of a wide variety of problems that fall within the purviews of all six of the basic systems of human services in America. Egan et al. (1981, pp. 96–97, 101–114) believe that the first step in addressing the specific problems of housing in the United States is to eliminate general federal policies that have worked against mediating structures. These policies involve general issues of taxation, family policy, and welfare. The next step they suggest is for the government to adopt policies that minimize the amount of disruptive change introduced into neighborhoods. These policies focus on transportation, relocation, and zoning. Finally they suggest a series of steps intended directly to create better housing and social climates in urban neighborhoods by working with mediating structures. These proposals include, among others, means for redistributing resources to low- and middle-income neighborhoods, facilitating private funding, supporting neighborhood housing services, providing information and technical assistance, managing public housing, reclaiming abandoned buildings, creating tax credits for volunteer work, instituting a modified housing allowance program, and enforcing civil rights laws. Taken together these suggestions illustrate how the federal government could pursue the strategy of encouraging mediating structures to solve the problems of housing the urban poor.

The encouragement of mediating structures is consistent with certain basic tenets of conservative ideology, for conservatives see family and church especially as repositories of traditional social values, and likewise favor encouraging individual initiative and hard work and limiting intrusive government intervention into private lives. This strategy can also be pursued by the federal government simultaneously with the strategy traditionally favored by conservatives, stimulating private housing construction. Encouraging mediating structures is also consistent with certain basic ten-

EXHIBIT 6-2 *ENCOURAGING URBAN HOMESTEADING*

In Philadelphia in the mid-1970s squatters began moving into abandoned and vacant buildings. Rather than forcibly evicting them and allowing neighborhoods to further deteriorate as buildings remained empty, the city has developed a comprehensive plan for promoting what has become known as urban homesteading, the turning over of abandoned properties for little or no charge to people who want to refurbish and live in them. The Philadelphia plan includes four specific programs:

1. The Gift Property Program, which transfers ownership of abandoned property from the city (which is prohibited by its charter from giving away property) to the city's Redevelopment Authority, which can legally give the property to homesteaders.

2. The Real Estate Non-Utilization Tax, which permits the city to tax vacant or abandoned property 10 percent of its value yearly in addition to its regular property tax, thereby encouraging owners to put their properties to use or relinquish ownership.

3. The Donor–Taker Legislation, which simplifies the process by which owners can legally give away their vacant properties and the city can accept such donations.

4. The Nuisance Abatement Legislation, which allows the city to take possession of any abandoned or vacant property that it has declared to be a public nuisance.

ets of liberal ideology, for liberals favor limited government actions that encourage individual initiative and development, particularly actions that improve the individual's ability to think intelligently and participate in improving society. This strategy is also consistent with the liberal theory that clients of human services systems should be helped to take charge of their own lives instead of being directed by human services workers, and it can be pursued as part of the comprehensive approach to human services favored by liberals. Finally, in so far as this strategy harks back to many traditional American values such as the pioneering spirit in which neighbor helped neighbor to construct frontier homes, it can be supported by conservatives and liberals alike.

The major obstacle standing in the way of conservative political support for this new and potentially useful federal strategy for providing housing for the urban poor is that conservative politicians have grown accustomed to viewing the private construction industry itself as representing the American status quo that should be preserved. Hence they are mistrustful of any means that might encourage individuals to upset the status quo or to work outside the norms that the private marketplace represents. In the future conservative political support for the strategy of encouraging mediating structures is likely to grow if conservatives recognize their own best traditions and reemphasize the importance of the social repositories of American values instead of merely the bare economic megastructures of American society.

The major obstacle standing in the way of liberal political support for this strategy is that liberal politicians have grown accustomed to viewing the solution to the problems of America in terms of massive programs administered by the federal government. Hence they are mistrustful of any means that might encourage individuals to pursue their own solutions apart from the comprehensive and coordinated programs that federal managers have planned. In the future liberal political support for the strategy of encouraging mediating structures is likely to grow if liberals recognize their own best traditions and reemphasize the role of individual intelligence in solving American social problems, instead of merely the bare organizational megastructures of American society.

In the absence of such changes in how both conservatives and liberals perceive the problem of providing housing for the urban poor, the strategy of encouraging mediating structures is likely to continue to receive support at the grass-roots level throughout the United States, but not to become a major policy of the federal government.

STUDY QUESTIONS AND ACTIVITIES

1. Why does the system of housing and urban environment services, when defined very broadly, encompass the other five human services systems? Why does it, when defined very narrowly, not constitute a human services system

at all? In what ways has the housing industry in the United States been regulated? In what ways has it been unregulated? Explain the relationship between housing and other human needs.

2. List what you believe to be the most basic determinants of a suitable living environment. Do tangible or intangible determinants predominate? Investigate the ways in which federal tax laws have stimulated housing construction. List and investigate the kinds of programs and institutions through which federal and state governments have made money available for mortgages. Have tax laws and mortgage programs more greatly benefited affluent or low-income families? Why?

3. Explain the relationship between federal programs of housing and urban environment services and the kinds of human services state and local governments provide. Obtain an up-to-date listing from HUD of its programs and activities. Which of these are directed solely at housing? Which at urban environments? Which at social problems? Do HUD programs and activities seem to represent an irreversible trend?

4. During the colonial era, why was housing for the poor nearly as adequate as housing for the rich? Explain the social changes that occurred during the nineteenth century that helped create the housing industry. Explain the social conditions of the 1930s and 1940s that exacerbated the shortage of housing in the United States. Why did large cities lose population and suburban areas gain population during the late 1940s and 1950s? Describe the extent of federal involvement in housing during each of these periods.

5. Which of the four criteria in Frieden's list for housing deprivation (pp. 195–196) seem most important? Which seem least important? Explain. Investigate whether the relative costs of housing have declined or risen during the last decade. Is the answer the same for all segments of the population? Explain how family life, work, and housing influence each other in contemporary American society. Are America's major cities better or worse places to live than they were in the past?

6. Explain the trickle-down process of housing redistribution. Why do the poorest families not improve their housing through this process? Identify the basic changes that turn a neighborhood into a slum. Why do some poor neighborhoods become slums while others do not? How do slums benefit affluent citizens?

7. Explain and justify what you consider to be a proper balance between providing adequate housing and meeting other human needs. Why will the federal government continue to stimulate the private housing construction industry? Why are social conditions usually worse for the urban poor than for the rural poor?

8. Explain the differences between public housing and urban renewal. What common goal has public housing come much closer to meeting than has urban renewal? List the specific problems encountered by urban renewal. Which of these are related to the political and economic climates of cities? How?

9. What was the goal of Model Cities? Why could it not reach this goal? What

features of Model Cities were supported by liberals? What features were supported by conservatives? What positive lessons could be learned from Model Cities?

10. Define revenue sharing. Explain its relationship to the New Federalism of the Nixon administration. What features of the New Federalism are pursued by the current administration? Obtain statistics on the types and amounts of federal aid to states and localities since 1972. What trends are evident? In what ways can revenue sharing improve housing for the urban poor? In what ways might it not help them at all?

11. Explain the basic controversies that surround housing allowances. Which arguments seem to be strongest? Why? Why have housing allowances generated much talk but little action?

12. Explain the free market model for providing housing for the urban poor. How is this model consistent with the basic conservative preferences for hard goods and services delivered selectively by private means? In what ways can this model fit with a comprehensive system of human services? Explain the comprehensive model and the basic liberal beliefs that support it. How does this model reflect liberal preferences for hard and soft goods and services delivered universally by public agencies? What basic similarities exist between the free market and the comprehensive models? What are the most irreconcilable differences?

13. Define mediating structures. List as fully as possible the mediating structures that exist in any society and those that exist in the contemporary United States. Why is encouraging mediating structures a potentially fruitful strategy for attempting to solve urban housing problems but one the federal government is not likely to pursue vigorously? List and comment on specific actions that the federal government might take to encourage mediating structures to help solve housing problems. What changes have to take place for conservatives and liberals to support this strategy?

REFERENCES

Boyte, H. C. (1982). Reagan vs. the neighborhoods. *Social Policy, 12* (4), 3–8.
Campbell, A., Converse, P. E., & Rodgers, W. L. (1976). *The quality of American life: Perceptions, evaluations, and satisfactions* (pp. 217–266). New York: Russell Sage Foundation.
Downs, A. (1978). The impact of housing policies on family life in the United States since World War II. In A. S. Rossi, J. Kagan, & T. K. Hareven (Eds.), *The family* (pp. 163–180). New York: W. W. Norton.
Egan, J. J., Carr, J., Mott, A., & Roos, J. (1981). *Housing and public policy: A role for mediating structures.* Cambridge, MA: Ballinger.
Frieden, B. J. (1977). Housing. In *Encyclopedia of social work*, 17th issue, vol. 1 (pp. 639–652). New York: National Association of Social Workers.
Frieden, B. J., & Kaplan, M. (1975). *The politics of neglect: Urban aid from Model Cities to revenue sharing.* Cambridge, MA: The MIT Press.
Friedman, J., & Weinberg, D. H. (1983). *The great housing experiment.* Beverly Hills, CA: Sage Publications.
Haar, C. M. (1975). *Between the idea and the reality: A study in the origin, fate and legacy of the Model Cities program.* Boston: Little, Brown.

Hartman, C. W. (1975). *Housing and social policy.* Englewood Cliffs, NJ: Prentice-Hall.

Kinch, R. (Ed.). (1979). *A wingspread report.* Racine, WI: The Johnson Foundation.

Klutznick, P. M. (1985). Poverty and politics: The challenge of public housing. *Journal of Housing, 42,* 9–10, 12.

Morris, R. (1979). *Social policy of the American welfare state.* New York: Harper & Row.

Sa-Aadu, J. (1984). Another look at the economics of demand-side versus supply-side strategies of low-income housing. *Journal of the American Real Estate and Urban Economics Association, 12,* 427–460.

Schussheim, M. J. (1974). *The modest commitment to cities.* Lexington, MA: D. C. Heath.

U.S. Department of Housing and Urban Development. (1973). *Housing in the seventies* (pp. 6–9). Washington, DC: U.S. Government Printing Office.

7

INCOME TRANSFER
SERVICES

SCOPE OF THE SYSTEM

The income transfer services system that has evolved in the United States consists of a complex variety of programs that seek to assure that no member of society is without the minimum requirements for survival. It does this through direct monetary payments by the federal and state governments to the individuals in need so that they may purchase the essentials of food, shelter, clothing, and other necessary goods and services. It also does this through government funding of public, private, and voluntary agencies that purchase these items on behalf of the individuals in need.

Central to the income transfer services system is the government's role in income redistribution by taxing the income and gifts of some of its citizens and transferring part of this revenue to others through social insurance and welfare or assistance programs. This redistribution occurs between generations, between the healthy and the sick, between the single and the large families, between the employed and the unemployed, between families large and small, and between families with and without children. In this process of income transfer government does not tamper with income distribution inside the market; rather it is only after the market has distributed income that government attempts to lessen some of the

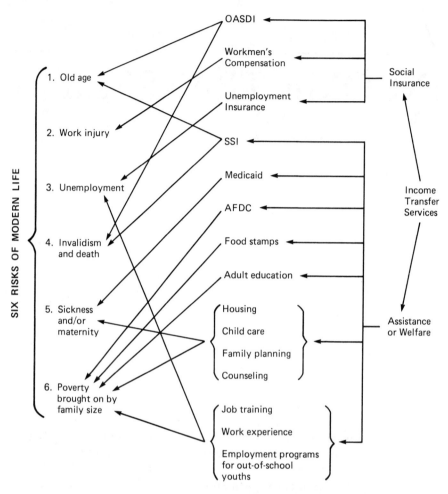

FIGURE 7–1. Chart mapping the key goods and services directed at the six risks of modern life by the social insurance and assistance components of the income transfer services system.

inequality that exists between those in and those outside the labor market and that exists among those who are employed.

Income transfer services seek to insure the general public against the six risks of modern life: old age, unemployment, work injury, invalidism and death, sickness and/or maternity, and poverty brought on by increased family size. Toward this end the system has developed the two broad program areas of social insurance and assistance or welfare. Within these programs aid is given either in the form of direct cash payments or of benefits in kind such as food, health care, housing, and education. With direct cash payments the recipient retains the freedom and responsibility to select and purchase the goods and services with public funds. With benefits in kind the recipient's freedom and responsibility is sharply curtailed, and the recipient must spend publicly provided resources only on those specific goods and services that the programs define as worthy and essential. Special groups with vested interests have often been in the vanguard of those promoting this latter type of aid, and much of the political support for these programs has come from the farmers, doctors, educators, and homebuilders who supply the benefits required by them.

Social insurance. Social insurance includes Old Age, Survivors, and Disability Insurance (OASDI); workmen's compensation; and unemployment insurance. These programs are directed at recipients whose eligibility is determined by labor-force attachment and a specific status or history of being unemployed, disabled, orphaned, or widowed. Participants are required to make mandatory contributions from their salaries, and on the basis of these deductions from their work-related earnings they become entitled to benefits that they view and expect as a right. Each of these programs replaces lost earnings to the wage earner or to those primary relatives for whom the wage earner is legally responsible. OASDI does so when there is retirement, disability, or death (payment to survivors); workmen's compensation when there is a job-related disability; and unemployment insurance when there is involuntary and temporary unemployment.

Assistance or welfare. Assistance or welfare includes Aid to Families with Dependent Children (AFDC), Supplementary Security Income (SSI), food stamps, Medicaid, adult education, and programs providing for housing, child care, counseling, family planning, job training, work-experience opportunities, and employment programs for out-of-school youths. These are means-tested programs, and eligibility is determined by categories of need such as low income, inability to earn regular wages, living arrangements, and a specific status or history of loss of support of parent, or of being disabled, orphaned, or widowed. Participants must establish that they have been reduced to a condition of "deservedness," that is, that they "deserve" assistance because they fall within the above categories of need. For instance they may have little income, may not be employable, or may lack sufficient work-force participation to be eligible for social insurance. Under this concept of deservedness benefits distributed by welfare programs and paid with public revenue are viewed as a "privilege" bestowed on the recipient at the expense and discretion of the taxpayer. Each of the programs involved contributes specific goods and services that ensure a minimum level of subsistence that the recipients are unable to provide for themselves. AFDC cash payments provide some measure of economic security to families with children who have lost support of a parent through incapacity, absence, or death. SSI provides cash assistance to the aged, blind, and disabled. Specific programs such as food stamps, Special Supplemental Food Program for Women, Infants, and Children (WIC), and Medicaid and other programs of adult education, housing, child care, and family planning supplement cash assistance by providing benefits in kind such as food vouchers, health care, education, public housing, rent and purchase subsidies, day care payments, counseling, and family support services. Finally, job-training, work-experience, and special employment programs provide unemployed adults and disadvantaged youths with limited cash payments and extensive vocational and on-the-job training in marketable skills.

In the above programs social insurance is founded on a strong commitment to individualism and the marketplace, whereas assistance or welfare relies on the assumption that government will intervene to provide for those who are unable to help themselves. This faith in individual achievement, self-help, and the marketplace coupled with this expectation that local and federal governments will assist the helpless have been critical factors in shaping the development of income transfer services throughout the history of the United States.

Development of Income Transfer Services

Poverty as character deficiency.   Prior to the twentieth century the American attitude toward poverty reflected the thinking of the early settlers. The colonists brought with them from Europe the belief that poverty was basically the result of character deficiency and should be dealt with on an individual basis. As their European forefathers had done since the Middle Ages, the colonists distinguished between two types of poor people. The worthy or morally respectable poor were primarily widows and orphans with legitimate needs, and they were considered to be deserving of relief. The unworthy poor were able-bodied paupers who were viewed as having failed to apply themselves, work hard, and save. Poverty was the evidence of their immorality—an immorality that was frequently expressed in the vices of drunkenness, sloth, and mendacity. Consequently they were considered to be undeserving of relief. To offer some relief to those worthy of assistance, the colonists adopted measures similar to the Elizabethan Poor Laws (see Chapter One), and thus very early in the nation's history the principle of government responsibility to assist the helpless was established.

Throughout the nineteenth century the poor laws became the last refuge for those whose resources were exhausted, and the almshouse remained the "fundamental institution in American poor relief" (Bruno, 1957, p. 74). Efforts by local and state governments to aid the needy were supplemented by voluntary charity groups that imported the organization-society approach used in England. The federal government did not become involved in these early local assistance efforts, but rather restricted its role to providing some income support to veterans of the armed forces.

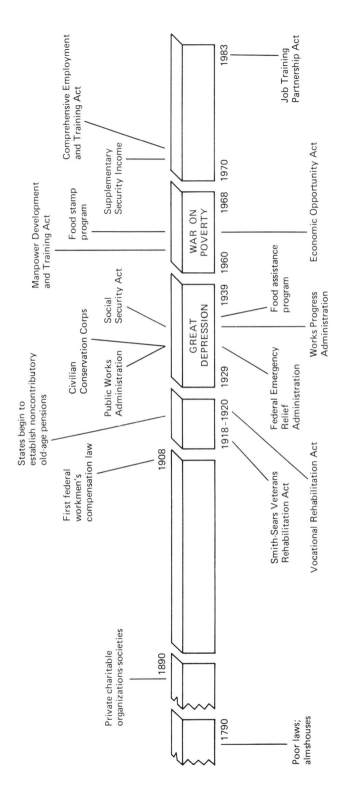

FIGURE 7–2. Timeline tracing the evolution of income transfer services from the birth of the United States to the present. Key programs and legislation that constitute the heart of the income transfer services system are identified.

A product of economic and social forces.   In the late nineteenth and early twentieth centuries a new theory of poverty, which had nothing to do with morality, emerged. The closing of the frontier and the rapidly industrializing and ever-expanding economy resulted in a society in which big business and financial manipulators enjoyed concentrations of economic power and control while many farmers and craftsmen became permanent industrial workers reduced to misery and poverty by low wages, inadequate housing, and the absence of safeguards relating to safety, health, and security. For these newly emergent workers trapped on the bottom of the economic ladder by this rapid economic change, poverty was not, as their forefathers living in an agrarian society had assumed, a matter of character deficiency that could be remedied by a spirit of individualistic self-help. Rather they were victims of a poverty that was the product of an array of economic, demographic, and social forces that were beyond their individual control and that in an industrialized society could be dealt with effectively only through cooperative action. Furthermore they viewed the state as the only social institution with the necessary resources to cope effectively with the economic and social forces that create poverty.

Early social insurance legislation.   During the first three decades of the twentieth century growing popular pressure led federal, state, and local governments to initiate programs responsive to the needs of workers and the poor. In 1908 demonstrations against widespread incidents of industrial accidents and work-connected disease moved the federal government to act on behalf of workers, and Congress passed the first workmen's compensation law. Within seven years of its passage thirty state governments had enacted similar compensation laws, and today all states have such legislation. The growth of workmen's compensation programs brought high costs for caring for those disabled through injury or work-connected disease and convinced employers and insurance companies of the need for programs to train the disabled to become self-supporting. Consequently employers supported a national movement for rehabilitation, which also received considerable popular backing during and after World War I because of national concern for disabled veterans. The federal government responded to the pressure of this movement by passing legislation (Smith-Sears Veterans Rehabilitation Act of 1918, Vocational Rehabilitation Act of 1920) that provided some federal funds and stimulated states to establish rehabilitation programs for both civilians and veterans. Rehabilitation services continued to expand over the next sixty years, and today the federal government provides states with funding to support the construction of facilities, research, and programs supplied by public and private organizations that utilize the most recent medical rehabilitation procedures and technology. Parallel to these movements for compensation and rehabilitation was a growing popular demand for an adequate form of security for the increasing number of destitute aged being maintained in almshouses and county poor farms. Again government was moved to respond, and by 1931 the territory of Alaska and seventeen states had established non-contributory old-age pension systems that provided assistance for needy aged persons who were not in institutions.

The Great Depression and government intervention.   By 1930, in the early years of the Great Depression, income transfer services as reflected in social insurance and assistance for the workers and the poor were primarily the responsibility of state and local governments and private charitable organizations. The federal government was not involved in welfare programs and had refused to aid the unemployed during the recessions of 1893, 1914, and 1921. With the onslaught of the Depression unemployment rose to 15 million (or one-third of the work force), wages fell by one-third, farm income dropped more than two-thirds, families depleted their savings and exhausted their credit, and mortgages were foreclosed on homes and farms (Piven & Cloward, 1971). State and local welfare organizations and private charities were suddenly confronted with mass unemployment and destitution and found themselves pushed beyond their capacity to respond. In 1932 fewer than one-quarter of the unemployed were being assisted, and as each year passed it became increasingly obvious that the limited resources of state and local relief organizations were simply unable to cope with the unprecedented demands of an ever increasing army of the jobless, dispossessed, and hungry poor. By 1935 widespread distress fueled growing popular discontent, agitation, and disorder, and the federal government was forced to act. Recognizing that state and local public and private relief agencies were unable to provide the necessary long-term assistance to the indigent, dependent, and incapacitated, Congress passed the Social Security Act in that year to encourage states to establish and administer—with the aid of local governments—public welfare programs. This act also committed the federal government to participate in providing assistance to the aged, blind, and dependent children living with responsible relatives.

With the passage of this act the federal government's role in income transfer services expanded dramatically, and federal programs were established to maintain employment, secure income, and promote the economic security of the worker and the family. During the Depression these programs included emergency measures such as the Federal Emergency Relief Administration, which provided cash assistance to the widowed, orphaned, and unemployed; the Works Progress Administration; the Public Works Administration; and the Civilian Conservation Corps, which provided employment for able-bodied workers on public projects ranging from construction of roads, bridges, and buildings to the drainage of swamps and the restoration of parks. Efforts were also directed at reducing the immediate danger of hunger and malnutrition that confronted the poor family, and by 1939 a food assistance program had distributed government-purchased surplus agricultural commodities to some 13 million people (Slater, 1981).

Eliminating the causes of poverty.   By the close of the 1950s most of the emergency relief efforts had ended as the economic conditions that spawned them abated. However the federal government remained concerned about the unemployed able-bodied worker and the needy family without economic security. Throughout the 1960s it became heavily involved in income transfer services as it sought to promote full employment and abolish poverty. This period became known as the era of the Great Society with its War on Poverty. (See Chapter Five for a discussion of the influence of the Great Society on education services.) It was marked by a significant shift in federal policy from the earlier approach that had attempted to provide a minimum subsistence level that ameliorated the immediate needs of the poor and needy to a new approach that would attempt to prevent poverty by eliminating its causes. Central to this new approach was the strategy of combining several different goods and services—income maintenance, education, job training, and job creation—under single, all-encompassing programs such as the Manpower Development and Training Act (MDTA) of 1962 and its later amendments and the Economic Opportunity Act (EOA) of 1964. MDTA retrained and paid allowances to experienced but unemployed workers, low-income farm workers, and unemployed young persons aged seventeen to twenty-one. EOA established programs at three different levels that were directed at unemployed youth. They included a work-study program that created part-time employment for college students from low-income families; a Job Corps with residential centers that provided room, board, and living allowances along with education and training for youths aged sixteen to twenty-one; and a Neighborhood Youth Corps that provided unemployed out-of-school youths or potential dropouts with training and work experience. Another critical dimension of this new approach was the attempt to reduce the number of families in poverty through federally financed "remedial medical and nutritional services, family planning, [and] various child-care programs designed to relieve parents and to start children on constructive careers" (Morris, 1979, p. 51).

Ameliorating immediate needs of the poor.   By the close of the 1960s the War on Poverty had become bogged down in controversy over the nature of the problems poverty presented and the most effective way to solve these problems. As optimism about and commitment toward eliminating the causes of poverty waned, the federal government turned again to programs that were designed to ameliorate the immediate needs of the poor and needy. Throughout the 1970s and early 1980s federal intervention focused on providing food assistance to the hungry poor, maintaining the economic security of those dependent needy outside the labor force, and providing job training for the able-bodied unemployed. In the area of food assistance programs, which included the food stamp program enacted in 1964, federal spending increased from $1 billion in 1969 to $8 billion in 1979 and the number of such programs doubled (Slater, 1981). In the area of providing for the economic security of those needy unable to work, a federalized public assistance program that ensured a guaranteed income for the blind, permanently and totally disabled, and elderly not on Social Security was established in 1972 with the enactment of the Supplemental Security Income (SSI) program. In the area of providing job training, the

EXHIBIT 7-1   *WAS CETA A FAILURE?*

Congressional tampering has undermined the purpose, and led to the termination, of enacted programs that had considerable promise. The Comprehensive Employment and Training Act (CETA) is a case in point. CETA was enacted in 1973 as a relatively small program directed at preparing the chronically unemployed for unsubsidized jobs in the private sector. However, the severe recession of 1974 eliminated the very jobs CETA trainees were seeking. It also added millions of workers to the jobless rolls and placed considerable pressure on Congress to provide relief for the unemployed. Congress responded by requiring CETA to serve as an employment agency for temporary public service jobs. CETA was given a greatly expanded budget but received virtually no guidelines for its new role. From 1974 to 1979 it became one of the government's largest agencies and provided hundreds of thousands of Public Service Employment (PSE) jobs for the unemployed. These were subsidized jobs that did not require training; many of them were with state and local governments or various social agencies, all of which were suffering under budget constraints because of the recession and welcomed the funding. CETA spent $55 billion during the eight years of its operation and became one of the first victims of President Reagan's budget cutting.

Was CETA a failure? There are two basic criticisms of CETA. First, it had obviously failed to make a permanent difference for almost two-thirds of those 6 million unemployed workers who received PSE jobs but who were unable to land jobs after their subsidized positions were terminated. Second, it had obviously become a taxpayer's nightmare and a questionable expenditure of the national treasury; its costs totaled roughly $24 billion for the wages of the 6 million employed in PSE jobs. But both of these criticisms are directed at the role that was foisted on CETA by Congress and that had absolutely nothing to do with CETA's original purpose—job training. How did CETA perform in terms of job training? With roughly $24 billion, or the other half of its total expenditures, CETA became one of the more successful job-preparing efforts and trained over 18 million workers!

Comprehensive Employment and Training Act (CETA) was passed in 1973 to train the chronically unemployed for unsubsidized jobs in the private sector. This act was succeeded in 1983 by the Job Training Partnership Act, which sought to retrain experienced but unemployed adult workers and to train disadvantaged youths in marketable skills.

Income transfer services listed.   Thus during the past fifty years state and local roles in income transfer services have been both supplemented and dominated by the federal government. The income transfer services system has become deeply involved in ensuring the economic security of an ever expanding segment of the American population. Through its social insurance and welfare programs it has provided an increasing number of costly goods and services. As with goods and services provided by other human services systems, any inventory must remain open-ended because the boundaries of the income transfer services system are frequently redefined and new services continually develop. Nonetheless the following is a reasonably inclusive listing of the primary services currently provided by this system in the United States:

1. Insurance for workers against industrial accidents and diseases
2. Programs to encourage full employment through the training of the unemployed and the matching of workers and jobs
3. Rehabilitation and vocational rehabilitation services to restore and develop the ability of the mentally and physically disabled to work or meet the demands of daily living
4. Laws to promote the economic security of workers through the establishment of minimum wages
5. Insurance to replace wages lost through involuntary unemployment
6. Insurance to replace earnings lost through old age or retirement
7. Cash benefits for dependent survivors of deceased workers
8. Assistance to the blind, permanently and totally disabled, and elderly not on Social Security
9. Cash payments to families with children who have lost support of a parent through incapacity, absence, or death
10. Programs that supplement direct cash payments to the eligible and dependent needy by providing benefits in kind such as food vouchers, health benefits, education, public housing, rent and purchase subsidies, day care payments, counseling, and family support services.

General aim of income transfer services.   This listing reflects the general aim of the income transfer services system to maintain a level of income for the vulnerable segments of the population that will ensure them some measure of economic security and enable them to subsist at a minimum level of health and decency. Fundamental to the realization of this aim is the assumption held by many Americans that all government efforts to transfer income, from cash payment programs to benefits in kind, should promote individualism and supplement the basic marketplace economy. The list includes services that are both hard (from cash payments to food vouchers) and soft (from counseling to job training and placement). The services are provided to help the recipient directly, but they can also be justified as alleviating related poverty problems with broader social, economic, and political consequences for society in general; therefore they can be classified as indirect as well as direct. With the exception of certain components of the Social Security system these services are provided selectively, that is, only to the vulnerable segments of society. Although more Americans have become concerned with the problems of economic security and maintaining a minimum level of subsistence, they continue neither to expect nor to demand that all income transfer services be provided on a universal basis.

Controversy Surrounding Income Transfer Services

"Man in the house" rule. The development of the income transfer system has not been without controversy and misgivings. AFDC, which is the largest of the means-tested public assistance programs, has been criticized for excluding any family from benefits if there is the presence of an able-bodied father in the household ("man in the house" rule). This has encouraged divorce, separation, and desertion by unemployed able-bodied fathers eager to have their families receive AFDC benefits. Despite federal efforts to curtail this practice by further subsidizing those states that would provide benefits to families with unemployed fathers, more than half the states continue to refuse to extend such aid.

Eligibility criteria too restrictive. Welfare and income transfer programs have also been criticized for their extremely narrow definitions of who may be considered a member of a family unit receiving assistance and what the criteria are for determining a family's eligibility for assistance. In determining who may receive assistance, these programs fail to acknowledge the existence and in turn the needs of the unemployed or low-income adults who may also be part of the family, and thus they do not extend benefits to them. In establishing the criteria for determining a family's eligibility for assistance, these programs have denied benefits to the working poor and ignored the hardships they suffer as a neglected segment of the vulnerable population. Prior to 1981 the eligibility criteria for these programs, although not totally excluding the poor but stable and intact family of the working poor, allowed them only the most minimal levels of assistance in Medicaid, food stamps, and AFDC payments. With the passage of the Omnibus Budget Reconciliation Act of 1981, the keystone of President Reagan's effort to reform social policy, eligibility criteria were further tightened and the working poor lost even these minimal benefits. Under this act, which was designed to reduce welfare caseloads and to save money, two hundred thousand families of the working poor were stripped from the welfare roles and denied the food stamps and small public assistance payments, often from Medicaid, they needed to subsist. Although the working poor were thus placed in a position in which they would be financially better off if they quit their jobs and applied for welfare, less than 15 percent of those purged from the welfare roles had returned to welfare by 1983. In 1984 the General Accounting Office reported the "significant hardships" suffered by those who continued to work. They included problems of hunger, unpaid rent, and loss of private or public health insurance with the consequent denial of medical and dental care because of inability to pay ("GAO," 1984, Joe & Meyer, 1983; "Poor," 1983).

Failures of federal-state cooperation.   Charges of inefficiency, inconsistency, and inequality have also been leveled against welfare and income transfer programs because of inherent weaknesses in attempts by federal and state governments to administer and fund them jointly. In the federal government's attempt to work closely with the states, that is, to establish a pluralistic, federal-state cooperative system, Congress allowed individual states considerable discretion in determining the social rights of their residents. With the exception of the Old Age Insurance component of the Social Security Act of 1935 by which Congress created a uniform, national program administered solely by the federal government, Congress has limited the federal role in welfare and income transfer programs to offering financial inducements to the states and to establishing minimum standards that state laws must meet for states to be eligible for federal subsidies. Federal legislation establishing these programs makes the needs of the person in the state who is applying for assistance the condition for benefit receipt. But Congress does not attempt to define needs, instead leaving it to each state to define needs and devise the measures to establish their existence. The approach of the individual states has been one of massive intervention into the personal lives of recipients. Each state has established specific regulations governing benefit levels and eligibility requirements in terms of financial need, residency, age, citizenship, responsibility of relatives, recoveries, and liens. These regulations and benefit levels vary considerably from state to state; consequently equally poor families of similar structure are treated differently depending on where they live. For example blind, disabled, and aged recipients of SSI benefits in Massachusetts receive almost twice the amount paid to recipients in Indiana. Similarly recipients of SSI in half the states receive smaller payments because their states refuse to supplement the national minimum floor of income funded by the federal government. Again, recipients of AFDC in Wisconsin enjoy benefits several times greater than recipients of AFDC in Mississippi. These variations in programs contain incentives that encourage families to break up, discourage recipients from seeking work, and induce families to migrate from low- to high-benefit regions (Edelman, 1981; Muller, 1983).

The high cost of income transfer services. Although Americans have embraced the social norm of government's responsibility to assist the helpless and the weak, they have also been concerned about the high costs of such assistance and the need to preserve work incentives. Further, their basic commitment to individualism and the free operation of the marketplace has always served to dampen their enthusiasm for any form of income distribution no matter how limited and how necessary it may be. Yet the income transfer services have grown appreciably each year since the mid-1970s, when they distributed more than $160 billion annually and commanded over 13 percent of the gross national product (Kamerman & Kahn, 1978). Since the onset of the 1980s a rising payroll tax to support expanded benefits for a growing army of retirees coupled with an increasing drain on state and federal budgets to maintain welfare rolls that swelled dramatically during the 1970s has posed serious questions about the nation's ability to define and support its income transfer commitments. As the need to contain social insurance and welfare programs and control their costs has become increasingly obvious, the central issues confronting the income transfer services system have focused on determining who shall receive benefits, what the nature of these benefits shall be, and how these benefits shall be financed.

Purpose of the Chapter

In this chapter we shall analyze a representative area of the income transfer services system to show how conservatives and liberals have addressed the above issues. The area selected involves programs in social insurance (OASDI) that provide benefits to the retired elderly. We shall define the mission and role of income transfer services in this area, trace its origins and history, analyze its programs and policies from conservative and liberal perspectives, and explore its future directions.

THE RETIRED ELDERLY IN NEED OF ECONOMIC SECURITY

Mission and Role of Income Transfer Services

The struggle to develop a fiscally sound, effective social insurance program for the elderly that will provide them with economic security in their retirement years has been complicated by dramatically shifting demographic patterns that project a surge in the number of retirees receiving benefits and an equally sharp drop in the number of future workers paying taxes to support these benefits. Since the onset of the 1980s the group of Americans over sixty-five has increased by sixteen hundred persons each day. It is expected to grow from 11.3 percent of the population (26 million people) in 1981 to 12.2 percent (31.8 million people) in 2000 and 17.2 percent (50.9 million people) in 2025. In less than a century (1960–2040) the percentage of the population sixty-five and older is expected to double. During this period the productive working population will rapidly shrink. This will occur because the postwar baby-boom population (born 1946–66), with a birth rate that averaged more than 3.5 children per couple, will retire between 2010 and 2030, while the generation of economic recessions and birth control pills (born late 1960s–early 1980s), with a birth rate that averaged slightly more than two children per couple, will replace it in the work force. Within the forty year period from 1980 to 2020, the ratio of workers who contribute to retirees will change from three to one to two to one. This greatly reduced pool of workers will be required to increase their contributions by 50 percent to support the expanding population of re-tirees (Joint Economic Committee, 1982; Shulins, 1981b).

Social Security as an intergenerational contract.   The response of gov-ernment to the economic needs of these elderly reflects a growing recogni-tion and concern that some measure of economic security must be ensured them in their retirement years. With the passage of the Social Security Act in 1935 the federal government became actively involved in the redistribu-tion of income through transfer payments. Under the OAI component of this act the federal government assumed sole responsibility for the estab-lishment and administration of a public retirement fund, henceforth re-ferred to as Social Security. Employer and worker were required to con-tribute to this fund during the worker's active years, and the worker became entitled to receive cash payments from the fund during retirement years. Social Security is based on an intergenerational contract and oper-ates on a cyclical basis. Each generation of younger workers, during their period of economic activity, agrees to contribute to support older workers during their retirement, and in turn expects each new generation of younger workers to contribute to support them when they become elderly and are no longer economically active.

Shortcomings of Social Security.   The purpose of Social Security is to provide partial replacement of income lost to old age. It was originally designed as one part of a threefold approach to retirement security. Per-sonal savings and investments and the employer's pension plan were the other two parts. However, when personal savings were lost to inflation and when only half the working force participated in employers' pension plans,

Congress sharply expanded the mission of Social Security by increasing the benefits it provided. But although Congress voted to increase the average Social Security retirement benefit from about $40 per month in 1950 to more than $380 in 1980, it did not vote adequate funds to pay for these increases. Congress also failed to revise Social Security policy so that it would be more responsive to today's norms and values and would not in turn penalize elderly women for societal changes in marital customs and patterns of work. Rather Congress allowed Social Security to continue policies and practices—highly disadvantageous to several groups within the elderly population—that were grounded in the economic and social conditions of the Depression era in which they were first conceived.

The result has been that although Social Security is welcomed by many among the elderly as an effective means of providing an adequate measure of economic security, it is also questioned by others who have not been able to share in its benefits and who raise claims of inconsistency and inequity against it. For example, during the 1970s Social Security payments helped to reduce the number of aged poor by more than a million and a half, but this reduction in poverty was spread very unevenly among the different groups of the aged. Disadvantages of race, sex, and family status were reflected in the slower pace of improvement for minorities, females, and persons outside of families. By the outset of the 1980s one in four elderly Hispanics and one in three elderly blacks remained poor, while two out of five nonmarried elderly women and three out of five elderly black women living outside the family were poor. Of the 6.7 million women who lived alone or with unrelated adults, over 2 million were poor. Although they were only 42 percent of all women over the age of sixty-five, they constituted 85 percent of all the people over sixty-five who lived alone and were officially designated as "poor" (Bureau of the Census, 1977a, 1977b, 1978; Forman, 1983).

Social Security's method of determining eligibility, which is based on legal relationship and not on living arrangement, has also worked considerable hardship on specific groups within the elderly population. This legalistic bias channels the wage earner's pension to primary relatives even though he or she may have never lived with them or supported them. The focus is on the initial legal marriage, and subsequent nonsupport, divorce, or desertion is ignored. But even legal marriage does not immediately ensure the nonworking wife of her share of her husband's benefits. There is no recognition of her contribution as homemaker and mother, and she becomes vested with pension rights only after the first ten years of her marriage. The legalistic bias also creates problems for widowed persons. Often they will find they cannot remarry without suffering a loss in their survivors' benefits, and they will reluctantly choose to cohabitate rather than lose part of their economic security.

Finally, the basis for determining Social Security's survivor-dependency benefits remains tied to Depression-era assumptions about the family and family roles. There is no recognition of the expanded role of married women in the labor market, and the taxes they pay during their working years frequently make little difference in the benefits they receive at retirement. Thus the one-earner family of the 1930s has been replaced by the two-earner family of the 1980s; more than 55 percent of today's families have two working adults, and more than 43 percent of married women with children under six are working (Muller, 1983). But the working wife, who must pay Social Security taxes, does not receive additional retirement benefits unless her salary is high enough to guarantee her benefits larger than what she would receive as a nonworking dependent spouse of a retired worker, that is, one-half her husband's entitlement. Because women generally receive lower salaries than men, and because the years they stay home to raise their children are averaged into their earnings history as zero, few women find that the benefits they would receive based on their earnings would be higher than their benefits as a dependent wife.

Summary.   In general the mission of the social insurance program for the retired elderly has been to provide a floor of economic protection or adequacy that will ensure them a minimum level of health and decency, one that raises them above bare subsistence and the poverty level. To attain this end the federal government has established Social Security as a system of national retirement insurance that covers over 90 percent of all paid employment and from which more than three-fifths of the elderly derive more than 50 percent of their income (Joint Economic Committee, 1982). As the largest and most inclusive retirement program in the nation, Social Security has effected both a modest income distribution on a national scale and a "substantial redistribution [of income] from the whole society to the aged" (Kutza, 1981, p. 39). It has secured minimum federal standards for the elderly while providing adequate income support for a majority of the retired. It has also sought to address the incidence of poverty among the aged, and amendments to its program have broadened its coverage and increased its level of support. But despite all of these achievements, Social Security has been only partially successful in realizing its objectives. Its mission remains unfulfilled as "the incomes of the elderly remain lower, and continue to be more unequally distributed, than those of the rest of the population" (Kutza, 1981, p. 39) and as the number of aged poor has held relatively constant over the past decade (Joint Economic Committee, 1982).

Origins and History

Noncontributory old-age pensions.   Nearly a century before the economic and social crises generated by the Depression proved to be the watershed in the struggle for successful passage of Social Security legislation, other critical demographic, economic, and social factors were building pressure for some form of old-age protection. Primary among these was the aging of the American population. Between 1860 and 1930 the percentage of the population over age sixty-five rose from 2.7 percent to 5.4 percent, and within the first thirty years of the twentieth century the number of elderly more than doubled from 3,089,000 to 6,634,000 (Rimlinger, 1971). Americans were living longer, and more of them required and requested economic assistance in their old age. Parallel to this early phase of the graying of America was a rapid expansion of urbanization and industrialization focusing on mass production that combined to exclude older workers from gainful employment and increase dependency among the aged. There emerged a growing number of unemployed, dependent elderly who were forced to take refuge in almshouses or poorhouses, the only form of public assistance available. As more of the destitute aged sought relief, the cost of maintaining them in these institutions increased, which led to a search for a less expensive approach to providing assistance. Noncontributory old-age pensions that had rigorous eligibility requirements and were based on individual needs were found to be cheaper than almshouses. Consequently taxpayers, led by business interests, joined the movement to pressure state governments to enact noncontributory old-age pension laws. By the outset of the Depression more than one-third of the states had such laws, and with this growing acceptance by state government of its responsibility for providing pensions to the destitute elderly, the stage was set for greater federal involvement in the movement to establish old-age insurance.

Early social insurance movements.   During the 1920s and early 1930s several influential writers led movements that sought to organize popular support for some form of retirement protection that required federal intervention. In 1927 Abraham Epstein founded the American Association for Old Age Security, and it quickly received wide popular support when it called for the prompt enactment of a social insurance program. In a September 30, 1933, letter to the *Long Beach* (California) *Press Telegram* Dr. Francis E. Townsend proposed a pension scheme, to be financed by a sales tax, in which all persons sixty and over were to receive $150 a month from the federal government providing they quit work and spent the money immediately. Townsend's plan sought to provide economic security for the elderly and at the same time to revive the economy with the money the pensioners would be pumping into it. The Townsend scheme had instant popular appeal. Within two years after its proposal, 4,450 Townsend Clubs with more than 2 million members had been formed throughout the nation, and a series of bills based on the Townsend scheme had been introduced into the House of Representatives. Although all of these bills ultimately failed, Congress became increasingly aware that it must respond to the growing mass movement, triggered by the Townsend scheme, demanding some form of social protection for the elderly. While the Townsend movement was at its height of popularity, Ernest Lundeen, a farmer-laborite from Minnesota, organized a rival social protection movement. Through this movement, which was far more radical than any of its predecessors, Lundeen proposed a comprehensive social insurance program. First introduced as a bill in Congress in 1934, this scheme provided universal coverage of unemployment, disability, maternity, and old age for all workers, and it paid benefits that were the same as average local wages. The bill did not contain a revenue clause, but it did specify that workers were not to be required to contribute to its funding in any way. Again, as in the case of the Townsend bills, the Lundeen bill did not pass, but it added to the pressure on Congress to enact social insurance legislation (Rimlinger, 1971; Schottland, 1967).

Social Security Act of 1935.   Prior to the Depression government and private industry were not concerned with retirement programs, and as late as 1929 less than 15 percent of the labor force received pensions (Joint Economic Committee, 1982). But once the Depression struck with a severity and for a duration that made mass unemployment and loss of savings commonplace, government could no longer ignore the need for a more systematic provision of income support for the elderly. When local government and private charities were unable to provide this support, the federal government intervened and enacted the Social Security Act of 1935. This act established a Social Security system on two distinct levels. One level embodied the public assistance approach to public welfare of means-tested programs, and it included Old Age Assistance, Aid to Dependent Children, Aid to the Blind, and Aid to the Permanently and Totally Disabled. The other level embodied the social insurance approach to public welfare of wage-related contributory programs, and it included Old Age Insurance (OAI). This chapter will focus on this latter level and will be concerned with the social insurance programs providing retirement benefits for the elderly.

Old Age Insurance.   The OAI segment of the Social Security Act was strongly supported by President Franklin Roosevelt. It eventually gained acceptance in Congress where it was recognized as providing the most effective vehicle for meeting the need for socially assured income protection while at the same time protecting the individualistic values of the American society. On the one hand OAI provided the elderly with a floor of economic protection, and on the other it restricted benefits to a level that would not discourage savings and investment and private employer-employee plans. Central to the success and popularity of OAI was the requirement that workers contribute part of their wages to establish eligibility.

These taxes enabled OAI to be perceived as a right and not a handout, and as a universal entitlement and not a means-tested program for the poor. Thus OAI was appealing to two cherished American values: the age-old tradition of self-help and the belief that rewards should be related to individual effort. It fit well with the American expectation that individuals must be responsible for and prove capable and prudent in the management of their own affairs.

Under OAI the right of individuals to benefits arises from the payment of Federal Insurance Contributors Act (FICA) taxes on earned income. By earning benefits individuals establish their rights as beneficiaries on a quasicontractual basis. They have a permanent legal right to benefits that can be enforced by the courts. President Roosevelt insisted on this emphasis on contractual rights because he was eager to free individuals from dependency on the benevolence of the ruling powers. He said,

> we put those payroll contributions there so as to give the contributors a legal, moral, and political right to collect their pensions and their unemployment benefits. With those taxes in there, no damn politician can ever scrap my social security program. (quoted in Schlitz, 1970, p. 30)

As it was first enacted, the OAI program established a self-supporting, public retirement system independent of government funding and financed through contributions by employers and their employees. Membership was mandatory for workers in commerce and industry, and it provided them with a monthly cash benefit at retirement after age sixty-five. This benefit was based on a formula in which the disbursements were closely related to the amount contributed and "replacement rates were lower for higher-wage earners and higher for lower-wage earners" (Joint Economic Committee, 1982, pp. 435–436).

Survivors Insurance.   In 1939 amendments to the Social Security Act sought to provide family protection by extending benefits to dependents of retired workers receiving OAI payments. OAI now became Old Age and Survivors Insurance (OASI), and under its Survivors Insurance (SI) provision, the contributor's aged spouse, parents, and children under age eighteen became eligible for benefits. The 1939 amendments also broadened

EXHIBIT 7-2   *SMALL INVESTMENT—LARGE RETURN*

Ida Fuller of Ludlow, Vermont, received the first Social Security check, No. 00-000-001, in 1940. At that time workers and employers contributed 1 percent of the workers' pay up to a maximum of $30 a year. Ida Fuller lived to be 100, and after having paid $22 in FICA taxes into the system, she received more than $20,000 in benefits.

benefits by relating them to average covered earnings instead of accumulated contributions, and they relaxed eligibility requirements by changing the formula to quarters of coverage rather than accumulated wages. This new formula allowed workers to become eligible after eighteen months of covered employment rather than the five years required previously.

During the 1950s a series of amendments to OASI extended its coverage to the self-employed, professionals, regularly employed domestic and farm workers, nonprofit institution employees, most clergy, and some state and local government employees. This increased the percentage of covered employed workers from 64.5 percent in 1949 to 89.9 percent in 1955. Amendments in 1983 added the only remaining large block of uncovered workers by requiring that all federal employees hired on or after January 1, 1984, as well as all members of Congress, the president and vice president, federal judges, and other top level appointees, be covered by Social Security. In addition coverage became mandatory for all employees of nonprofit organizations such as hospitals and most religious institutions, and any further withdrawals from the system by state and local employees were prohibited (U.S. House of Representatives, 1983).

Disability and Health Insurance.   In 1956 and 1965 amendments to the Social Security Act dramatically expanded the risks it covered. By the 1956 amendment and subsequent additions in 1958 and 1960 OASI became Old Age, Survivors, and Disability Insurance (OASDI). Under the Disability Insurance (DI) component of the program benefits were extended to the disabled of all ages and their dependents. By the 1965 amendment OASDI became Old Age, Survivors, Disability, and Health Insurance (OASDHI). Under the Health Insurance (HI [Medicare]) provision of the program all persons aged sixty-five and over gained access to hospital, surgical, and medical care. (For a more extensive treatment of the Medicare program, see Chapter Four.)

Benefit levels increased; eligibility requirements relaxed.   Beginning in 1950 and continuing throughout the 1970s the benefit formula of the Social Security Act was regularly amended, and benefits increased as eligibility requirements were further relaxed. In 1950 amendments raised OASI benefit levels approximately 80 percent and made it easier for a person to qualify for benefits. The benefit determination date was raised to 1950, coverage was required for only one-half the calendar quarters after this date, and the minimum number of earned quarters of coverage was set at six. Amendments in 1956 lowered the retirement age to sixty-two for women and in 1961 did the same for men. Early retirement was allowed at a reduced benefit level equivalent to 80 percent of the amount that would be received at age sixty-five.

At the outset of the 1970s the failure of adjustments in benefit levels to keep pace with the increases in per capita disposable income prompted lobbying groups for the elderly to pressure Congress to provide a long-term solution to their failure to share in the rising real income and their consequent loss of purchasing power. Until this time Congress had attempted to keep pensions somewhat constant in terms of purchasing power by making continuous ad hoc adjustments to benefit levels as the need arose. But in 1972 Congress sought to free itself from this politically hazardous task of fine-tuning benefit levels by passing amendments to the Social Security Act that linked pension benefits to the cost of living. Henceforth benefit levels would respond to changing economic conditions as cost of living adjustments (COLA) automatically raised benefit levels to match increases in the consumer price index announced on the first day of July each year.

Wage replacement rates controlled. Again, in 1977, Congress acted to affect benefit levels of future retirees. It was eager to control the rapidly rising wage replacement rate, that is, the ratio of benefits to preretirement earnings. This rate had allowed only 20 percent to 32 percent of wages to be replaced by benefits during the inflation-free days from 1950 to 1972. But the congressional action of 1972, which tied benefits to COLA, coupled with the mushrooming inflation of 1973–82, caused this rate to spiral upward, and by 1981 it allowed 55 percent of wages to be replaced by benefits. To preserve the ratio of benefits to preretirement earnings at roughly constant levels through time regardless of economic conditions, Congress passed amendments to the Social Security Act that fixed the wage replacement rate at a 42 percent level beginning in 1984. Future generations of retiring elderly would now be limited to the same proportion of preretirement earnings replaced by Social Security benefits as that received by the present generation.

From its inception OAI was founded on a pay-as-you-go basis with participating employees paying half the tax and their employers paying the other half. As self-employed persons were included in the program, they were taxed at roughly one and one-half times the employee rate. This pay-as-you-go principle was extended for the funding of SI and DI and for the hospital and related care insurance provision of HI. Because OASDHI was a federally operated program, Congress was empowered to set the tax rate. This rate was imposed at the same level for both employee and employer on annual earnings up to a certain amount, and the money was deposited in separate trust funds for OASI, DI, and HI. Congress arrived at the tax rate by projecting the amount of funds that would be needed in the long-range future to pay for benefits as they fell due.

Benefits exceed taxes. In its early years OASDI accumulated large reserve funds as more taxes were taken in than benefits paid out. But during the 1970s a combination of factors reduced receipts to the trust funds, drained their surpluses, and, in the case of OASI, resulted in pen-

EXHIBIT 7-3 *AN ABUSE OF SOCIAL SECURITY*

Legal and illegal aliens who illicitly worked in the United States are placing a heavy drain on Social Security funds. In 1983 the General Accounting Office revealed that these aliens are currently living abroad and are beneficiaries of Social Security for which they worked only half as long as the average recipient in jobs covered by Social Security and contributed less FICA taxes, but had more dependents than the average beneficiary. Many of these dependents were added to the benefit rolls *after* retirement through forms of subterfuge such as the following:

One alien who is living in a foreign country retired at 62 and, in a common law marriage, has fathered two children. These two children have drawn $12,896 in dependents' benefits and will remain on the rolls until the youngest one becomes 18 in 1995.

There are 313,000 beneficiaries of Social Security living abroad today and drawing nearly $1 billion in benefits annually. "Incredibly, it is estimated that 194,000 of these people are not U.S. citizens and many of them have never, and will never, set foot on U.S. soil" ("Aliens," 1983, p. A-4).

---

sion benefits exceeding taxes legislated to pay for the benefits. These factors included the escalating costs of expanded benefits and reduced eligibility requirements established by Congress; a 39 percent increase in the number of beneficiaries as more elderly retired earlier and lived longer; inflation; the slowing of economic growth; and the repeated increases in benefits tied to COLA. Within a decade (1970–79) these factors led to a 227 percent growth of Social Security benefits in real terms, an increase in the costs of these benefits from 5.5 percent to 9 percent of payroll, and a raising of the ceilings on covered earnings from $7,800 to $22,900 (Joint Economic Committee, 1982).

Bankruptcy averted. The type of surplus Social Security enjoyed in 1970 when it collected $35 billion in taxes and paid out $32 billion in benefits was no longer possible by 1975, and in 1979 benefits of $104.3 billion exceeded contributions of $103 billion. The deficit increased in the early 1980s as economic growth continued to lag, prices increased faster than wages, and monthly pension checks rose faster on the average than workers' take-home pay. In less than six years (1975–81) Social Security benefits had actually grown 19 percent faster than private sector wages and salaries. In 1981 Social Security paid out $145 billion and collected only $140 billion, and at that time the projected deficit for OASI alone for 1982–86, assuming an improved economy, was expected to reach $60 billion (Joint Economic Council, 1982; McManus, 1982). To avoid the financial collapse of the Social Security system and ensure its solvency into the next century, Congress passed a series of amendments to the Social Security Act in 1983. These amendments postponed COLA for six months (July–December 1983); increased Medicare premiums on the optional major medical plan; taxed Social Security benefits when adjusted gross income plus tax-exempt earnings plus one-half of Social Security benefits exceeded $25,000 (for single taxpayers) or $32,000 (for married couples); increased the ceiling on income subject to withholding Social Security taxes; increased FICA for 1984, 1988, and 1989; raised the retirement age to sixty-six (effective 2009) and sixty-seven (effective 2027); and decreased future early retirement benefits levels to 70 percent the amount that would be received at age sixty-seven (U.S. House of Representatives, 1983).

Summary. By the 1980s 116 million working people paid into the Social Security program, and OASDHI paid out over $156 billion a year or about $13 billion a month in benefits to 36 million Americans. The Social Security program accounted for almost one-quarter of the federal budget. Its OASI component alone paid over $99 billion a year to provide income support to 19.3 million retired workers and their 11.6 million dependents and survivors. This figure is expected to more than double to $214 billion a year before the decade ends (Joint Economic Committee, 1982; McManus, 1982; Mulligan, 1983). OASDHI has become an umbrella program that protects more than 90 percent of the laboring force and their families against the loss or cessation of earnings because of retirement, death, or disability. The OASI segment of the Social Security system has become a system of national retirement insurance for persons of all walks of life, and it has a distributional impact that has vastly different meanings for the very different classes of Americans that are its recipients. As economist Robert Lekachman (1982) has noted,

> for low-income Americans Social Security is essential to survival, the only alternative to the stigma of welfare. Middle-class individuals and couples supplement Social Security with income from investments, private pensions and accumulated savings. For them, Social Security frequently spells the difference between maintenance of past living standards in retirement and a decline in those standards. For the affluent, Social Security is an . . . unneeded addition to income far above the national median. (p. F-13)

Conservative and Liberal Perspectives: Social Norms

Assisting the vulnerable. In their approaches to providing retirement benefits for the elderly the conservative and liberal perspectives hold certain social norms in common but differ sharply on others. Conservatives

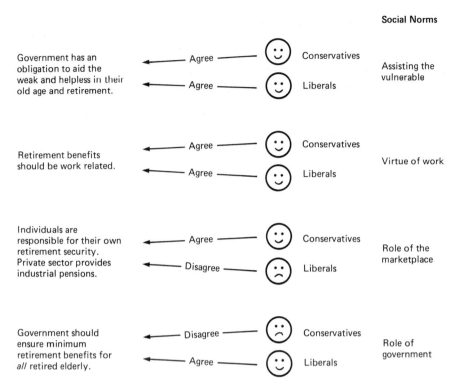

Social Norms

Government has an obligation to aid the weak and helpless in their old age and retirement.

— Agree —————— 😊 Conservatives

— Agree ————— 😊 Liberals

Assisting the vulnerable

Retirement benefits should be work related.

— Agree ————— 😊 Conservatives

— Agree —— 😊 Liberals

Virtue of work

Individuals are responsible for their own retirement security. Private sector provides industrial pensions.

— Agree ——— 😊 Conservatives

— Disagree — ☹ Liberals

Role of the marketplace

Government should ensure minimum retirement benefits for *all* retired elderly.

— Disagree — ☹ Conservatives

— Agree —— 😊 Liberals

Role of government

FIGURE 7–3.   Chart indicating the impact of social norms on conservative and liberal approaches to providing retirement benefits for the elderly.

and liberals both agree that government has an obligation to assist the weak and helpless in their old age and retirement years. They recognize that government has a responsibility to provide economic security to those vulnerable segments of the elderly population whose participation in the work force during their economically active years was limited or totally lacking because of contingencies beyond their control such as sickness, disability, and being widowed with children.

Virtue of work.   Conservatives and liberals also agree that work is virtuous and that income should not be made available to individuals who have not worked. They both have the highest praise for the worker, and they agree that individual effort through work in the open marketplace must remain one of the strongest underlying values in American society. They view the world as a work-conscious society in which persons should have as their primary goal their upward economic and social advance through hard work. Therefore, because persons receive income primarily through the exchange of their services for money, it follows that persons should earn their leisure by work; whatever income they receive during retirement years should be drawn from savings or contributions that accumulated in trust funds during their work years. But although conservatives and liberals agree that retirement benefits should be work related and earned, they disagree as to whether the private or the public sector should play the dominant role in administering and distributing these benefits.

Role of the marketplace.   Conservatives stress the role of the private sector in providing retirement benefits because of their belief in private-party or marketplace decision-making and their eagerness to avoid government intervention in the operations of the marketplace. They expect the individual to be self-reliant and responsible for initiating plans for his or her own security. Individual initiative should result in the privately accumulated financial resources needed to meet the economic contingencies of retirement and old age. Conservatives also expect employers in the private sector, acting on their own, to provide industrial pensions that will supplement the resources accumulated by their workers to be drawn upon in their retirement and old age.

Role of government.   Liberals stress the public sector's role in providing retirement benefits because they lack confidence in the willingness and ability of the private sector and marketplace forces to provide for the retirement needs of all segments of the aging population: the employed and the unemployed, the healthy and the sick, the prudent and the foolish, the economical and the profligate, the able and the disabled, and the affluent and the indigent. Liberals hold that just as the federal government has the obligation to make whatever economic arrangements are necessary to maintain full employment and a level of wages or compensation that will assure a decent standard of living to the younger and economically active segment of the population, so too has the federal government the obligation to mitigate, through the maintenance of income, the effects of unemployment on the older and no longer economically active segment of the population. Liberals are particularly concerned with the facts that wages do stop when certain contingencies, such as the aging process, occur, and that many elderly find themselves destitute for reasons over which they have lost all control. Liberals expect government, primarily at the federal level, to intervene on behalf of all retired elderly to ensure a measure of economic security that allows them to live at or above the minimum level of subsistence and decency and enjoy a degree of social and economic independence.

Although liberals accept the work ethic with its assumption of some sort of a moral base to be derived from work, they reject the more restrictive conservative view that tends to discern an immoral connotation in any distribution of income to those who do not work. For the conservatives government involvement in the provision of economic security should be limited and exclusive; toward this end they advocate a more selective or residual approach that would provide retirement benefits only to the vulnerable segments of the elderly population. For the liberals government involvement in the provision of economic security must be expansive and inclusive; toward this end they advocate a more universal approach that would require whatever level of government intervention is necessary to ensure minimum retirement benefits for all elderly regardless of their economic, social, physical, and emotional circumstances.

The Conservative Perspective Examined

The conservative beliefs in the worth and integrity of the individual, individual initiative, and the continuity of institutions, beliefs, and practices that have been developed through the sacrifices and efforts of past generations, lead conservatives to look to the efforts of each individual, to the operations of the marketplace, and to the private sector rather than to the government for the maintenance of the economic security of the retired elderly. In the conservative view the primary duty and responsibility of each person is to accumulate, through whatever personal effort, sacrifice, and hard work is necessary, the financial resources required for his or her own welfare and future economic security. Conservatives expect the traditional American assumptions of self-help, self-denial, and individual responsibility to prevail.

Economic individualism.   A logical outgrowth of this view is the conservatives' support of economic individualism as it is manifested in private-party and marketplace decision-making. The doctrines of economic individualism emerge from the requirements of the industrial system for "some competition for occupational position on the basis of criteria relevant to the performance of the role, as well as some system of special reward for the development of scarce talents and skills" (Wilensky, 1975, p. 32). These requirements find expression in success and mobility ideologies, where they serve as the incentives for everyone to work hard to get ahead and for those with specific talents to use their skills and abilities and prepare themselves for the most complex jobs. Conservatives reflect their commitment to economic individualism by embracing the ideologies of success and mobility and asserting that "everyone has an equal opportunity to achieve a better job, that everyone has the moral duty to make the most of his talents, to try to get ahead, [and] that if a person fails it is at least partly his own fault" (Wilensky, 1975, p. 32). Conservatives also assume that economic individualism and civil liberties are interdependent and that democratic liberties will thrive only when there are lively free markets in services, goods, and labor. They seek to limit government intervention for they fear that if "everyone becomes a dependent client of the bureaucratic state, the virtues of self-reliance, as well as the independence of mind and spirit, erode, inevitably giving way to an oppressive collectivism" (Wilensky, 1975, p. 115).

The individual model. On the basis of this insistence that each individual be responsible for his or her own economic security, this embracing of economic individualism, and this emphasis on private property, the free market, and minimum government, conservatives adopt what is best described as the individual model in their approach to the maintenance of economic security for the retired elderly. Under this model Social Security as it currently exists would be phased out and replaced by two programs. The first program would provide income maintenance only for those elderly who are defined as poor on the basis of need. The second program would provide tax incentives that would allow economically active persons of all income levels to select individually and to contract for voluntarily private retirement plans. By eliminating Social Security and the provision of social insurance on a universal basis defined by the category of age, the individual model would seek to avoid the inefficiencies of paying benefits to both those who need them and those who do not. Rather it would provide social insurance to those who are vulnerable among the elderly on a selective basis defined by the category of need, that is, low income and disability. This concern with need instead of age arises because conservatives do not view age as a good indicator of an individual's circumstances. They reject the use of chronological age as a basis for distributing public benefits and maintain that

> age is simply not a useful indicator of changes within a person. Since any changes occurring with an individual occur at a place that is unique to him or her, a more useful way to understand the needs and attributes of individuals is to examine their development on other dimensions of time—social time, biological time, and historical time—the dimensions along which the events of their lives have been patterned. (Kutza, 1981, p. 40)

In phasing out Social Security the individual model would allow a period of thirty to fifty years to elapse to ensure that total benefit levels would be maintained for all current pensioners and those nearing retirement. General revenues would be used to finance continuing benefit obligations during the transitional period in which the Social Security payroll tax would be abolished and individual retirement accounts would be established. As Social Security ceased to exist, the task of providing welfare benefits and a minimum income maintenance to those elderly who fall below the poverty line would be turned over to a means-tested system such as SSI. Benefits and pensions would be granted only on the basis of proven need, and the amount given would be directly related to the degree of need. The focus would be on offering a small number of vital services to some 30 percent of the elderly who are destitute and in greatest need.

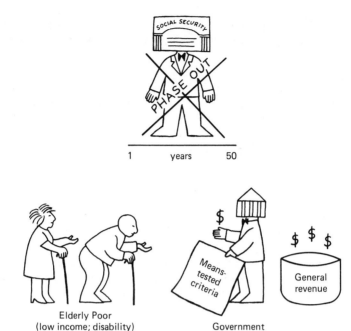

ECONOMIC SECURITY

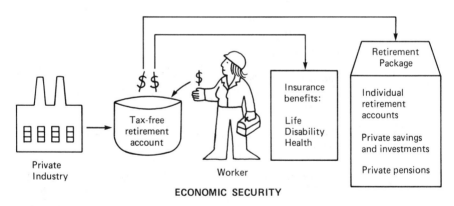

ECONOMIC SECURITY

FIGURE 7–4. Chart mapping the two programs of the conservatives' *individual model* that would replace Social Security as it currently exists.

To promote voluntary private retirement insurance plans, all workers would be allowed to invest in tax-free retirement accounts the money that they and their employers currently pay in Social Security taxes. Workers would also be allowed to purchase through their accounts benefits similar to those provided under Social Security such as life, disability, and health insurance. Conservatives believe that the general benefits individuals would receive through these accounts would be much greater than those available under the present Social Security system. Individual retirement accounts would realize a greater return on workers' investments because they would have larger amounts to invest and would be free to invest them in stocks on the private market that yield high interest rates. In contrast Social Security, which operates on a pay-as-you-go basis, has less funds to invest and restricts its investments to U.S. Treasury bonds that yield low interest rates to avoid general fund costs (Ferrara, 1982; Kutza, 1981).

Under the individual model the individual retirement accounts would be one part of the conservatives' three-part retirement package; private savings and investments accumulated during working years and private pensions earned at the place of employment would be the other two. Conservatives are particularly eager to promote the expansion of retirement income plans in the private sector. Not only must private pension benefits remain at their present level where they provide 20 percent to 25 percent of an individual's preretirement benefits, but they would also be expected to expand significantly and include far more than the 30 million persons currently covered and the 7.5 million retirees receiving benefits (Joint Economic Committee, 1982).

Summary. This individual model reflects basic conservative tenets. Its emphasis on a residual approach to social insurance, with Social Security being turned over to the private sector and government intervention being restricted to providing tax incentives and assisting only the most needy elderly, reflects the conservative position that government intervention in the income transfer services system must be limited primarily to supplementing or complementing the operations of the marketplace. The model's support of economic individualism, with incentives for each person to achieve economic security through application of abilities and hard work, also reflects the conservative position that marketplace forces must be allowed to function freely and that government must limit its role in the transfer of income. Further, its emphasis on persons being responsible for their own social insurance and being allowed the freedom to save and invest in a retirement account of their own choice reflects the conservative beliefs in individual initiative and the worth and integrity of each person.

The Liberal Perspective Examined

The liberal beliefs in the power of intelligence, in experience and an experimental attitude, and in the test of consequences and an emergent truth and values lead liberals to question the effectiveness of and in turn to reject established traditional approaches to maintaining the economic security of the retired elderly such as depending on individual initiative and the operations of the marketplace. Rather liberals look to more experimental approaches that focus on increased government intervention and control. For the liberals these approaches are the products of reflective thought that grew and developed in the human experiences of the Depression era and that meet the test of consequences because they have proven more responsive to the emergent needs of society.

Central to these approaches is the Social Security system, which liberals embrace as the most successful and humane retirement income program available and as an excellent example of the effectiveness of government intervention in providing social insurance. Liberals feel that it is only because of Social Security that the bulk of retired Americans have realized a degree of income protection that has allowed them to enjoy at least a minimum level of health and decency. They maintain that Social Security has raised the vast majority of its recipients out of poverty and that it is far superior to private pension plans because of its cost-of-living protection and coverage that follows workers from job to job. Liberals praise Social Security because it promotes a principle of redistribution in which income is transferred intergenerationally from the higher paid to the lower. This occurs because the distribution of benefits is "skewed so that those who earned less during their working lives receive a higher proportion of their earnings than those who earned more" (Rosen, 1983, p. 40). Finally, because liberals do not expect families and single persons confronted with today's living expenses to be able to put money away for the future, they affirm that it is not only desirable but also absolutely necessary that government impose a forced savings plan on future retirees through Social Security.

Economic collectivism.   A logical outgrowth of this liberal endorsement of Social Security and a major expansion of the role of government is the liberals' support of economic collectivism. Under economic collectivism government is expected to be interventionist by inclination, eager to manage the capitalist economy, and seeking to provide "economic security for the overwhelming majority of the population through a large public sector" (Logue, 1979, p. 69). These doctrines, which are pro-welfare state, emerge from the requirements of the industrial system for "incentives to keep the least successful in the race or at least working." Central to these incentives is "a pension at the end of a hard life . . . [which serves as] a powerful pacifier for workers confined to the least attractive jobs" (Wilensky, 1975, p. 37). Liberals embrace economic collectivism because they view this pension and the government intervention that accompanies it as effective means for meeting their demands for family security and social justice. Liberals reflect this commitment to economic collectivism by blaming the system of private decision-making with its marketplace forces rather than the individual for loss of employment income (the principle cause of poverty), and by demanding government intervention to "protect the living standards of those forced out of employment temporarily by sickness or unemployment, or permanently by age or disability" (Logue, 1979, p. 71).

The collective model.   On the basis of this confidence in Social Security's effectiveness as a retirement income program, this embracing of economic collectivism, this emphasis on increased government intervention and control, and this criticism of the shortcomings of the system and not of the individual worker for the loss of employment income and the consequent poverty, liberals adopt what is best described as a collective model in their approach to the maintenance of income security for the retired elderly. Under this model, Social Security, as a public system in which retirement contributions and the amount of pension that accrues are both related to the individual's earnings, would be retained. However, gradually, through amendments or supplementary programs enacted by Congress, eligibility requirements would be broadened, benefits would be expanded, and government funding and control would be increased. Two basic programs would evolve: a liberalized version of the OAI component of Social Security, and a liberalized version of the SSI program.

FIGURE 7–5.   Chart mapping the amendments or supplementary programs of the liberals' *collective model* that would liberalize the OAI components of Social Security and the SSI program.

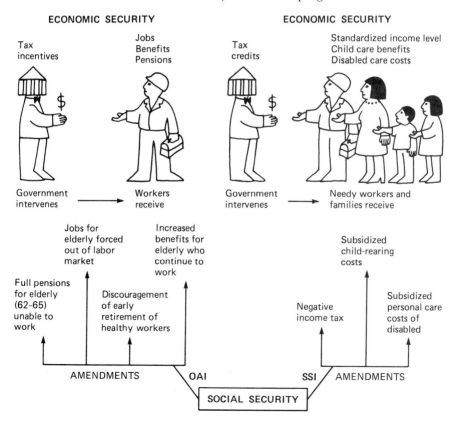

Old Age Insurance expanded. The liberalized version of OAI would remain an aged based, universal program, but it would also include four additional features that would be financed by general revenues in addition to taxes on wages (FICA). First, it would recognize that many older workers are forced out of work before age sixty-five by poor health, and it would provide them with full pension benefits as early as age sixty-two. Second, it would recognize that many older workers are prematurely forced out of the labor force because jobs are not available, and it would provide a special unemployment program for them. Toward this end the federal government would use tax incentives to encourage employers to provide flexible retirement programs and part-time employment for older workers. Third, it would encourage healthy, economically active older workers to remain on the job by allowing increased benefits for older retirees. Fourth, it would modify the tax laws to make it difficult for private employers to provide pension plans supplementing OAI that encourage healthy workers to retire early.

Supplementary Security Income expanded. The liberalized version of SSI would remain a means-tested system, but it would also include three additional key features. First, it would guarantee a person's right to relief by requiring government to provide standardized levels of income assistance to all of the needy. To achieve this end government would establish a negative income tax with standardized income levels related to family size and a sliding scale of assistance that would encourage the needy to seek employment. Second, it would extend the conditions determining eligibility for income assistance beyond those of unemployment, illness, and income loss to include the special needs of children. Government would subsidize the child-rearing costs of all families, regardless of their economic status, for each of their children from birth until the age of majority. This subsidy would be in the form of cash grants, tax credits, or Social Security entitlements. Third, it would expand benefits to those who are disabled and without families to care for them by including costs of personal care in addition to minimum income relief payments.

Liberals are confident that this collective model with its liberalized versions of OAI and SSI would transfer income from the relatively prosperous to those who are less prosperous, an intentional redistribution that would reduce the degree of income inequality in the economy. In so doing the collective model would reflect the values of equality and humanitarianism that sustain social welfare programs. For the liberals this means the collective model would successfully serve as "a major instrument for building and preserving the sense of justice and fair treatment that constitutes the heart of a social contract, basic to the cohesion of any society" (Rosen, 1983, p. 40).

Summary. The collective model reflects basic liberal tenets. Its emphasis on an age-based universal approach to OAI and a negative income tax approach to SSI, with increased government intervention that broadens benefits and eligibility requirements for the aged and needy, reflects the liberal position that government must become involved in the income transfer system to whatever extent necessary to enable it to acknowledge its responsibility to these vulnerable groups and to provide the economic security and welfare care they require.

Opposing Views of Income Transfer Models: The Conservative Position

First argument. Conservatives offer several major arguments in defense of their approach to maintaining economic security for the retired elderly. The first argument attacks the collective model, with its emphasis on Social Security and increasing government intervention, for its lack of faith and confidence in the initiative and judgment of individuals to determine their own future welfare. Conservatives view Social Security as being predicated on the assumptions that people will not display the mental fortitude to prepare for their later years by giving up some present enjoyment and that it will be better for government to do the job rather than attempting to educate people to become more responsible. Conservatives view this emphasis on government intervention as having two serious weaknesses. First, such involvement is difficult to define or control, tends to become unwieldy and overextended, and often violates the privacy of the family or denies the rights of the very individuals it is supposed to be helping. And second, such involvement places policy decision-making in the hands of Congress, where issues frequently become politicized, fall prey to special interest groups, and become the objects of programs in which bureaucracy proliferates and costs are excessive. That these weaknesses have plagued the collective model is evidenced in the following description of how Social Security evolves and makes increasing demands on the resources of the country:

> As years roll by, more of the covered persons either reach retirement age or experience disability or the death of a working spouse; the mass of citizens press for higher benefits and expanded coverage for themselves and their dependent relatives; political elites see a greater need for programs; bureaucrats entrench, cultivate budget, personnel, and clientele; while politicians, bureaucrats, and the mass alike spread information about the programs, thereby encouraging claims and reinforcing the demand for more. (Wilensky, 1975, p. 25)

In effect conservatives argue that although Social Security began as a modest insurance program supported by an adequate tax base designed to provide a safety net for the least affluent during their retirement years, over the years Congress has transformed it into a national insurance umbrella that is financed by inadequate taxes and is actuarially unsound; requires mandatory coverage for more than 90 percent of the population, including most of its more affluent members; absorbs 26 percent of the federal budget; and pays out over $160 billion in benefits ranging from welfare-type medical payments to full retirement pensions with built-in, automatic accelerators indexed to inflation. Conservatives believe that these changes were made because Congress was intimidated by the political clout of the growing elderly population that has increasingly turned to Washington for assistance. This clout has been expressed by the American Association of Retired Persons, a powerful lobby with over 16 million members whose average age is sixty-six, and by the elderly in the voting booths, who in 1980 comprised 16.8 percent of all voters with a 65.1 percent voter turnout ("Lobbyists," 1984; Pepper, 1984). In courting the elderly voter during the 1960s and 1970s Congress promised more benefits than it could deliver at a time when the bill was yet to come. As one conservative described the process, "that none of us has paid in anything like the projected outgo has been shrugged aside by members of Congress who assure us that they have finally reached the pinnacle of fiscal achievement—a federal slot-machine programmed to furnish everyone with a jackpot" (Cary, 1983, p. A-19).

Conservatives argue that the bill for Social Security is now starting to come in and that, disregarding inflation, public spending for retirement programs and tax benefits for the elderly doubled between 1969 and 1979 and then doubled again from 1979 to 1983 (Muller, 1983; Weaver, 1981). Conservatives agree that it will be necessary to honor these promises regardless of the cost and to pay the benefits in full to those who have retired or are about to retire. However, they believe that it is also time to end the politicizing of social insurance programs and correct past congressional errors in social insurance legislation. For the conservatives this will happen only after the existent Social Security system is abandoned and the individual model is adopted in its place.

Second argument.   A corollary of this first argument is the conservative position that the existent Social Security system, which remains central to the collective model, reflects the consequences of increased government intervention. In their view it is an inequitable, inefficient, "Big Brother" approach to social insurance that is financed by a regressive tax and benefits the rich at the expense of those who are most in need—the working poor and low-income families. Under this system government imposes a tax for retirement income on most workers and gives them no choice in the matter. But because the tax consists of a fixed percentage of a portion of their earnings, the advantages fall to the better paid for the higher the worker's income, the lower the effective percentage of tax paid. And because people with higher incomes generally have longer life expectancies and thus collect Social Security payments for a longer period, it follows that the higher the income, the higher the ratio of benefits received to taxes paid. Further, Social Security, unlike individual income tax, allows no exemptions and does not apply to interest, dividends, rent, or capital gains. For millions of the working poor and low-income Americans who pay little or no personal income tax because their taxable income is not sufficient, the Social Security tax consumes more than one-tenth of their earnings and represents a major reduction in their income (Miller, 1974).

Third argument.   A final conservative argument directed at the collective model, with the Social Security system as its basic component, is that it will fuel future intergenerational conflict. Conservatives predict that the implicit intergenerational compact on which Social Security is premised will break down because the younger generation will revolt against paying increasing taxes to support a system that will provide them far fewer retirement benefits than those enjoyed by the present generation of retired elderly. A combination of political, economic, and demographic factors will contribute heavily to this revolt. At the political and economic levels the generous benefit increases affecting eligibility and income that were voted by Congress since the end of World War II will allow workers currently retiring to receive from Social Security their lifetime contributions and accrued interest in 3.25 years. This means that today's sixty-five-year-old retirees who earned average wages will each have contributed $8,324 to the system but will collect $120,870 if each lives the seventeen years more that life expectancy tables predict (Brock, 1982; Shulins, 1981a). In contrast the rate of return will be proportionately smaller for the members of the younger generation. They will start their careers with a higher tax rate and make higher contributions than previous generations, will have larger taxable incomes, will pay longer into the system, and will likely have smaller families and make fewer demands of the system. Conservatives point out that in "terms of what they put in and what they take out of Social Security, today's elderly will get five times as much as their grandchildren can expect to receive. In fact, if the economy performs as poorly as it has in the past decade, this 'inequity ratio' could be a shocking 7:1" (Dunton, 1983, p. A-19).

Because Social Security operates on a pay-as-you-go basis, members of the younger generation will be taxed at disproportionately higher and higher rates to pay for that portion of a current retiree's benefits that is unearned and several times greater than the earned annuity portion. In effect they will be required to pay a maximum Social Security tax that has skyrocketed from $30 annually in 1947 to $2,791 in 1985, an increase of over 9,000 percent. More will be taken from their paycheck every two weeks than was taken in a year from a worker's paycheck during the first twenty years of Social Security from 1937 to 1956 (Boaz, 1982; "Social Security," 1984)! At the demographic level dramatically shifting population patterns as the number of retirees collecting benefits is increasing while the number of workers paying taxes is decreasing will reduce the ratio of workers paying for one recipient's benefits from ten to one (1940) to two to one (2015). This shift will force the younger generation to increase sharply their contributions to make up the difference. Conservatives believe that these political, economic, and demographic factors have contributed to a growing skepticism and resentment among the younger generation over being forced to carry such an excessive intergenerational burden. With the passage of each year, as these factors threaten to bankrupt the system, society will become even more sharply polarized with each raise in taxes or cut in benefits that will be necessary to ensure the system's solvency. Conservatives maintain that this skepticism and resentment will ultimately grow into open resistance unless Social Security is replaced by the individual model. Only then will there be a restoration of the principle of intergenerational fairness in which a proper balance is established between the needs of the younger and older generations and nondiscrimination between generations is ensured.

Opposing Views of Income Transfer Models: The Liberal Position

First argument. In response to conservatives liberals advance several major arguments for their approach to the maintaining of economic security for the retired elderly. The first argument defends the collective model for making it possible for the elderly to enjoy a considerable measure of dignity, independence, and relative comfort in their retirement years and for freeing the children and relatives of the elderly of the responsibility and financial burden of providing for their economic welfare. Liberals view the economic support provided through Social Security and SSI as bringing to the elderly person the sense of worth and self-respect that accompanies reliance on one's own income—even if it allows only partial support. The independence that comes with having their own source of income enables the elderly to establish a relationship with their children that is open, spontaneous, and warm. It frees them from the guilt of being beholden to their children who, to provide the elderly with financial assistance, must divert income from the needs of growing families. By having their own source of income the retired elderly also realize a significant expression of independence in their freedom to select their own living arrangements. Although most elderly enjoy visiting with their children, they prefer living away from them. Social Security and SSI benefits facilitate such independent living by enabling the elderly to maintain their own households and improving their capacity to move from one dwelling to another as they please. Finally, liberals credit the retirement benefits available to the elderly with relieving younger people of some of the responsibility for supporting their parents and in turn freeing their income for investment in their own occupational pursuits or in their children and families. The guarantees of retirement benefits have also freed both the elderly and middle-aged from some of the necessity of saving for the future and thus have enabled them to invest in their children and grandchildren. In sum, liberals point out that before Social Security one-third of the aged depended on their relatives or organized charity for support, but within forty-three years after the enactment of Social Security this ratio dropped to one in ten even though the aged population had tripled in size. They also estimate that without Social Security and SSI more than one-fourth of the aged would be forced to share a dwelling unit with an adult child, more than three times as many aged persons would be poor than in fact actually are now, and most middle-aged persons would be forced to divert money from investment in their families and into savings for their retirement or ill health in old age (Schorr, 1980).

Second argument. A second liberal argument defends the collective model on the grounds that its aged-based, universal, categorical programs are easy to administer, remain politically popular, and prove less stigmatizing for its recipients. Liberals view such programs as administratively simpler because benefits are distributed on the basis of age and are directed at "a group having attributed rather than demonstrated needs" (Kutza, 1981, p. 4). This approach reduces eligibility disputes, minimizes the opportunities for fraud, and eliminates the necessity for periodic screening and recertification of eligible recipients. Liberals view aged-based, universal, categorical programs as politically popular because they extend benefits to all the aged regardless of income. The public tends to be highly supportive of those programs in which the beneficiaries include an entire population within a group and Congress in turn is sensitive to the popularity of such programs and responds by enacting further legislation that allows them to thrive. Such programs contrast sharply with means-tested type of programs that are limited to one segment of the population within the group such as the poor, women, or minorities and that tend to have less popular appeal and to become embattled in Congress where politicians reflect their constituents' lack of support for such legislation (Bell, Lekachman, & Schorr, 1974). Finally, liberals view aged-based, universal, categorical programs as being less stigmatizing because beneficiaries have neither to declare nor prove themselves poor to be eligible for assistance. Means-tested programs become demeaning to recipients who in effect must acknowledge personal failure and suffer severe loss of pride to prove they are in need. Further, liberals also raise serious questions about recipients in such programs being treated as second-class citizens by human services workers who are empowered to examine in depth all facets of the recipients' personal lives—from finances to living arrangements—and to determine what levels of benefits they receive. In brief, liberals are convinced that the amount of fraud and inefficiencies accompanying aged-based, universal, categorical programs is relatively minor and represents but a small price to pay compared to the failings of the means-tested, selective approach.

Third argument.   A final liberal argument defends the Social Security component of the collective model by identifying and attacking the political and economic forces responsible for the recent fiscal problems that have plagued Social Security. Liberals view these problems as having three causes: (1) a failure of the support base of wage earners to continue to expand, (2) a prolonged period of inflation during which prices rose markedly faster than wages, and (3) a relatively high rate of unemployment in recent years. Liberals blame Congress for failing to recognize and remedy the first cause by enacting legislation that would allow general revenues to supplement taxes on wages (FICA). They blame recent presidents and Congress for contributing to the second cause by adopting policies such as massive military budgets and deficit spending that further fueled the inflationary spiral. And they blame major corporations for contributing to the third cause through policies of short-term investments and quick profits that allowed the American industrial economy to deteriorate. Thus liberals argue that

> neither the wage earners whose taxes pay the benefits nor the elderly and their dependents and survivors who received them had anything to do with these massive failures of economic leadership and policy, nor should they be held in the smallest degree responsible for the problems that Social Security faces and will continue to face. (Rosen, 1983, p. 39)

In sum, liberals do not see defects inherent in the Social Security system itself as the source of the problems confronting it. Rather they attribute these problems to the failures of politicians and management who must be held responsible for implementing policies that will resolve them and allow Social Security to thrive.

Future Directions

Future directions in programs providing retirement benefits for the elderly will have to reflect the continuing struggle between the opposing conservative and liberal approaches. The conservative effort will seek to allow the private sector to determine social insurance policy through individual initiative, voluntarism, and the marketplace. The liberal effort will seek to control the private sector and impose a national social insurance policy focusing on government-operated, universal, aged-based, cate-gorical programs. General trends seem to indicate that both conservative beliefs and liberal beliefs will influence future programs but that a modi-fied version of the liberals' collective model will predominate. The conser-vatives' position that Social Security should be turned over to the private sector will continue to have little public appeal for many Americans who will prefer to have the federal government retain control over their retire-ment system and secure for them pension benefits that they view as having been earned and to which they have a right. Therefore Social Security will likely be retained as the basic old-age insurance program available to all. However trends indicate that government will seek to encourage Ameri-cans not to rely solely on Social Security and instead to turn to other sources for economic security in retirement. Toward this end Congress will enact legislation to stabilize and contain Social Security benefit levels and tax rates. Laws will also be passed to expand and liberalize tax deduction allowances in present-day programs that encourage workers to invest in private retirement accounts and induce private industry to establish pen-sions for their employees.

Older worker as an asset.   Future programs directed at meeting the retirement needs of the elderly will also reflect and respond to demograph-ic, social, and economic changes. There will be a rethinking of prevailing attitudes toward retirement age and an abandoning of the use of age sixty-five as a dividing line between the middle-aged and elderly. These at-titudinal and policy changes will occur in response to labor shortages re-sulting from the decline in the number of young workers entering the labor force in the 1990s when the baby-boom generation is succeeded by the baby-bust generation. Such changes will also occur in response to the improved health and dramatic increase in longevity of many older Ameri-cans who will remain mentally alert, vigorous, healthy, and eager to be productive. Thus older persons, with their skills, abilities, and reliability, will be looked on more as an asset than as a liability, and Congress will modify Social Security to make it worthwhile for them to continue to be productive in the labor force rather than to opt for early retirement. Cur-rent trends indicate that among these modifications will be the following. There will be a phasing out of the retirement earnings test that imposes a 50 percent benefit reduction rate on earnings above $7,000 for persons aged sixty-five to seventy-two. This will remove a particularly burdensome tax on gainfully employed older workers and provide them with an incen-tive to remain on the job. There will also be a removal of compulsory retirement requirements. This will return the decisions about retirement to the older workers and restore their freedom and mobility in pursuing their careers. In addition there will be the allowance of increased pension amounts for those who delay retiring. This will provide an additional economic incentive for those older workers who would prefer to delay retirement.

Phased retirement.   A number of other approaches will be adopted in the future to meet the retirement needs of the elderly. Public and private business policies will be initiated that encourage older workers who prefer a reduced working schedule to remain on the job. Through innovative programs that include flexible hours, job sharing, retirement rehearsals, and part-time employment, older workers will have the option of a phased retirement that allows them to blend periods of productive work for wages with periods of retirement and pension benefits.

Improved pension benefits for women.   There will also be a major upgrading of pension coverage for women by both Social Security and private industry. Policy will be revised to be more responsive to the changing nature of the modern woman's life, particularly to changing marital customs and patterns of work. Alterations will be made in how benefits are provided, thereby allowing women to be equitably compensated and not penalized for having interrupted paid employment histories, for often not joining the labor market until after age fifty-five, and for being a mother and housewife during which years of zero salary were averaged into her records. These changes will affect vesting, portability, and the division of Social Security entitlements between husband and wife. They will affect vesting, which refers to a worker's legal right to his or her pension contribution after a specified period of employment, by limiting this period to five years. This will ensure that most working women will be vested with pension rights although they frequently spend fewer years on a job than men. It will also mean that a wife becomes vested after only five years of marriage and is entitled to a share of her husband's benefits from that period on. These changes will affect portability, which refers to a worker being able to keep vested benefits when leaving an employer, by establishing portability as a worker's right that the employer must honor. This will allow women who frequently shift jobs to take their vested benefits with them and place them in their own private individual retirement accounts. Finally, they will affect the division of Social Security benefits between husband and wife by requiring that such entitlements "be split equally throughout a marriage, whatever each spouse contributes through Social Security taxes" (Kamerman & Kahn, 1978, p. 445). If either husband or wife dies the surviving partner would inherit retirement credits earned by the deceased spouse and would count them toward his or her benefit level.

The establishment of the above programs and policies is predicated on a singular key development. Government and private industry must be in the vanguard of those who recognize that age sixty-five has become an anachronism as a basis of employment and social insurance policy, that the image of old as useless is contradicted by the increased vigor and longevity of older Americans, and that the early retirement of seasoned workers is a colossal waste of human talent. This fundamental attitudinal change must be accompanied by a commitment to initiate employment and pension policies that reflect a societal expectation that older workers will remain productive and continue to be contributing and fully involved members of the community. To the extent that this development occurs, the probability of the United States establishing effective programs providing retirement benefits for the elderly increases proportionately.

STUDY QUESTIONS AND ACTIVITIES

1. How do income transfer services affect income redistribution? Against what risks of modern life are income transfer services directed? Define benefits in kind and list arguments for and against this type of assistance.

2. Compare social insurance with assistance or welfare in terms of eligibility, types of assistance provided, and program financing. Compare the social insurance approach to benefits as an earned right or entitlement with the assistance or welfare approach to benefits as a privilege determined by deservedness. Explain why you agree or disagree with the respective approaches.

3. How did the early settlers' view of poverty differ from that which developed in the early twentieth century? Why did this change occur? List the early social legislation enacted to deal with poverty, and explain why government became involved in these programs. Why did the government's role in income transfer services expand during the Depression? What emergency relief programs did the government establish? How did the War on Poverty mark a major shift in government policy toward the poor and needy? Explain why you would support or oppose government policy to eliminate poverty rather than a policy to ameliorate immediate needs of the poor?

4. For each of the primary income transfer services listed (p. 232), indicate whether federal controls and funding should be expanded, retained, or removed. What is the general aim of income transfer services? What are the criticisms directed at income transfer programs? Respond to these criticisms, and suggest measures to support, eliminate, or change these programs. How have societal norms contributed toward the ambivalence of Americans to income transfer services?

5. How have shifting demographic patterns complicated efforts to provide social insurance for the retired elderly? Explain how Social Security is based on an intergenerational contract, and indicate your reaction to this approach to social insurance. List the shortcomings of Social Security, and discuss actions to support, eliminate, or change the existent program.

6. What factors between 1860 and 1930 contributed to the growing demand for some form of old-age insurance? Comment on the weaknesses and strengths of the pension schemes proposed by Townsend and Lundeen. Why did the federal government enact the Social Security Act of 1935? What were the two

levels on which this act established a Social Security system? Discuss OAI in terms of its provisions, popularity, and evolution into OASDHI. How and why did Congress increase benefits and relax eligibility requirements for OASI from the 1950s to the 1970s? Why did OASDI have financial difficulties from the 1970s to the early 1980s, and how did Congress resolve them?

7. On what social norms and specific goals do both conservatives and liberals agree in providing retirement benefits for the elderly? In reference to these same social norms and goals, where do conservatives and liberals differ and how are these disagreements expressed?

8. What assumptions about human nature and society underlie the conservative and liberal approaches to providing for the economic security of the retired elderly? Outline in as much detail as possible the specific programs advocated by conservatives (individual model) and the liberals (collective model), explaining basic differences such as why one program includes a residual approach and the other a universal approach, how each program treats the retired elderly, and the basic arguments for and against the program. How can likely programs in the future specifically combine both conservative and liberal approaches?

REFERENCES

Aliens draining Social Security Funds. (1983, February 3). *The Providence Journal/Bulletin*, p. A-4.

Bell, W., Lekachman, R., & Schorr, A. (1974). *Public policy and income distribution* (pp. 30–32). New York: Center for Studies in Income Maintenance Policy.

Boaz, D. (1982, April 15). Income tax: It's higher than ever. *The Providence Journal/Bulletin*, p. A-10.

Brock, H. (1982, August 31). Social Security: A reform spearheaded by the young? *The Providence Journal/Bulletin*, p. A-16.

Bruno, F. J. (1957). *Trends in social work 1874–1956* (pp. 25–75). New York: Columbia University Press.

Bureau of the Census. (1977a). *Current population reports: Consumer income—Characteristics of the population below the poverty level* (Series P-60, no. 119, pp. 13, 19–20). Washington, DC: Author.

Bureau of the Census. (1977b). *Current population reports: Consumer income—Characteristics of the population below the poverty level* (Series P-60, no. 129, p. 25). Washington, DC: Author.

Bureau of the Census. (1978). *Current population reports: Consumer income—Characteristics of the older population* (Series P-60, no. 129, p. 37). Washington, DC: Author.

Cary, B. (1983, May 21). Untying Social Security's Gordian knot. *The Providence Journal/Bulletin*, p. A-19.

Dunton, L. (1983, August 22). Inequality of Social Security. *The Providence Journal/Bulletin*, p. A-19.

Edelman, M. W. (1981). Funds for children. *Social Policy, 12* (2), 60–63.

Ferrara, P. (1982). *Social Security reform: The family plan*. Washington, DC: Heritage Foundation.

Forman, M. (1983). Social Security is a women's issue. *Social Policy, 14* (1), 35–38.

GAO says loss of welfare plunged many into poverty. (1984, March 31). *The Providence Journal/Bulletin*, p. A-3.

Joe, T., & Meyer, J. (1983, May 20). The lowest-income workers are severely penalized. *The Providence Journal/Bulletin*, p. A-11.

Joint Economic Committee. (1982). Social Security and pensions: Programs of equity and security. In U.S. House of Representatives, Committee on the Budget, *Impact of the Omnibus Reconciliation Act and the proposed fiscal year 1983 budget cuts on entitlements, uncontrollables, and indexing* (pp. 430–441, 448–463). Washington, DC: U.S. Government Printing Office.

Kamerman, S. B., & Kahn, A. J. (Eds.). (1978). *Family policy: Government and families in fourteen countries* (pp. 440–448). New York: Columbia University Press.

Kutza, E. A. (1981). Toward an aging policy. *Social Policy, 12* (1), 39–43.

Lekachman, R. (1982, June 13). Social Security poses some ethical questions. *The Providence Sunday Journal,* p. F-13.

Lobbyists for elderly dig in for big battle. (1984, November 22). *The Providence Journal/Bulletin,* p. A-13.

Logue, J. (1979, Fall). The welfare state: Victim of its success. *Daedalus,* pp. 69–87.

McManus, M. (1982, October 6). Social Security: The painful choices. *The Providence Journal/Bulletin,* p. A-13.

Miller, R. L. (1974, June). The cruelest tax. *Harper,* pp. 22–27.

Morris, R. (1979). *Social policy of the American welfare state* (pp. 38–70). New York: Harper & Row.

Muller, C. (1983). Income supports for older women. *Social Policy, 14* (2), 23–31.

Mulligan, J. E. (1983, January 16). Social Security: What's at stake. *The Providence Sunday Journal,* p. A-8.

Pepper, C. (1984, September 24). Elderly look hard at Reagan record. *The Providence Journal/Bulletin,* p. A-14.

Piven, F. F., & Cloward, R. A. (1971). *Regulating the poor* (pp. 43–119). New York: Random House.

Poor forced off aid rolls cling to low-pay jobs. (1983, April 28). *The Providence Evening Bulletin,* p. A-3.

Rimlinger, G. V. (1971). *Welfare policy and industrialization in Europe, America, and Russia* (pp. 62–86, 207–214, 233–239). New York: John Wiley & Sons.

Rosen, S. M. (1983). The Social Security crisis: Poor economics, dangerous politics. *Social Policy, 14* (1), 39–40.

Schiltz, M. (1970). *Public attitudes toward Social Security* (USDHEW Report No. 33, pp. 29–35). Washington, DC: Social Security Administration.

Schorr, A. L. (1980). *". . . thy father and thy mother . . .": A second look at filial responsibility and family policy* (pp. 3–4, 23–25). Washington, DC: U.S. Department of Health and Human Services.

Schottland, C. I. (1967, February). Government economic programs and family life. *Journal of Marriage and the Family,* pp. 76–79, 92–97.

Shulins, N. (1981a, October 6). The problem: Too few pay for too many. *The Providence Journal/Bulletin,* p. A-1.

Shulins, N. (1981b, October 10). Pension woes tarnish "golden years." *The Providence Journal/Bulletin,* pp. A-1, A-12.

Slater, M. D. (1981). Going hungry on food stamps. *Social Policy, 11* (4), 18–24.

Social Security benefits increase by 3.5% in 1985. (1984, October 25). *The Providence Journal/Bulletin,* p. A-7.

U.S. House of Representatives. (1983). *Social Security amendments of 1983* (House of Representatives Conference Report No. 98-47 [March 24, 1983]). Washington, DC: U.S. Government Printing Office.

Weaver, W., Jr. (1981, March 9). 35 or younger? You can forget retirement. *The Providence Journal/Bulletin,* pp. A-1, A-8.

Wilensky, H. (1975). *The welfare state and equality* (pp. 15–49, 87–119). Berkeley, CA: University of California Press.

Will, G. (1981, February 5). The elderly: A big part of the problem. *The Providence Journal/Bulletin,* p. A-17.

8

JUSTICE AND PUBLIC SAFETY SERVICES

A UNIQUE SYSTEM

The system of justice and public safety services, more than any of the other five systems of human services in the United States, is intended to benefit those citizens who do not come into direct contact with the system itself. In fact a majority of Americans live their entire lives without any direct contact (except perhaps for minor traffic offenses) with the system, yet they can perhaps more surely be considered the clients of the system than those citizens who are processed by any of the system's three component parts: police, courts, and institutions of correction. In this sense the system of justice and public safety services is unique among the six basic human services systems in America; its basic function is not to provide direct services to individual citizens based on some specific assessment of their needs, but merely to maintain what can be considered normal or optimal social conditions under which all citizens can pursue their own interests and private lives without undue interference from others. Whereas the human condition itself demands that all individuals receive basic services and resources such as counseling, health care, education, income maintenance, and housing, which are formally provided by the five other systems, only maladaptations—usually called "crime"—within the social relations that prevail within any society necessitate the existence of a system of justice and public safety services. For this reason there is considerable tension within the system over its primary responsibilities. Can it protect the rights of its real but indirect clients, the individual citizens who comprise the society at large, and still honor the rights of those clients with whom it deals directly, the citizens who have potentially or actually violated the rights of others? Should it be directed primarily at preventing crime, ameliorating the results of crime, or punishing criminals? In any case, those justice and public safety services that are directed at crime can be considered universal, indirect, and soft for the general society and selective, direct, and hard for those citizens who come directly into contact with the system.

Society and Law

As we have noted several times in our previous discussions, any human services system is shaped by the particular society in which it exists. A society is a group of people sharing a common identity, usually through their culture, comprising ideology, beliefs, values, mores, customs, and the like. Within any society there may be considerable agreement or disagreement on these matters. Actions may be consistent or inconsistent with prevailing beliefs and values, and these guides to social conduct may be either explicit or implicit, consistent or inconsistent. Different societies exhibit different degrees of tolerance for actions inconsistent with prevailing beliefs. In some societies there is considerable consensus about beliefs and actions, while in others operative beliefs and tolerated actions are hammered out only after a good deal of conflict among members.

In primitive societies prevailing beliefs, acceptable actions, and sanctions for unacceptable actions are all generally well known through patterns of customs and folkways. In such societies consensus is high, there is little reason for codifying operative beliefs into a formal body of written law, and there is little or no distinction between morality and lawfulness. However, as societies become more complex and relationships more impersonal, the consensus transmitted through customs and folkways tends to break down. What individuals recognize as moral and what society recognizes as lawful are not necessarily the same. Developed societies therefore require formally codified bodies of written law to account for their complexity and diversity and to make their operative values and rules of conduct explicit. Without such rules modern societies would not be possible, for chaos would prevail and much of the energy that individuals put into productive, creative, and cooperative pursuits would be drained away by constant efforts to defend one's property and other interests. On one hand law thus represents a collective effort by society to specify rules of behavior to protect and free personal conduct; on the other hand law represents a means by which society regulates personal conduct. The system of justice and public safety services that exists in any modern society represents the efforts of that society to extend both the potentially liberating and the potentially coercive rule of law into the lives of all its citizens.

Among the specific purposes of law are the following: protecting ownership, defining the parameters of private and public property, regulating business, raising revenue, providing redress for broken agreements, upholding social institutions, regulating relations, protecting the legal and political systems, protecting public and private interests, maintaining the status quo yet providing for needed change, and preserving order (Reid, 1982, pp. 20–21). The system of justice and public safety services serves to fulfill any of these purposes of the law. However, many of these purposes, such as defining parameters of property, regulating business, raising revenue, and providing redress for broken agreements, apply solely or in part to civil rather than criminal matters, and can be attended to by courts without the aid of the other two component parts of the system, police and institutions of correction. Civil matters involve disputes over the law's application to rights between individuals or organizations. Losers in civil cases may be required to pay monetary damages or other remunerations to winners. Criminal matters do not involve direct disputes about meanings and applications of laws and rights but instead focus on questions of guilt or innocence in cases that involve victims or threaten the general welfare. Losers in criminal cases may be placed in institutions of correction, and police may have been involved in their apprehension and arrest. Some cases involve both civil and criminal matters. Although court cases involving civil disputes fall under a broad conception of the system of justice and public safety services in America, in this chapter we will more narrowly define the system to include only criminal matters that may be dealt with directly by all three parts of the system.

Finally, in considering the relationships between society, law, and a system of justice and public safety services, we note that in using law both to protect and regulate personal conduct society is exerting a form of social control and coercion over its citizens that is enforced by police, courts, and institutions of correction. In examining this coercive power, two fundamental questions should be considered: (1) How is this coercive power legitimated?, and (2) How should it be exerted? Although different societies provide different answers to these questions, in the United States the conservative and liberal perspectives substantially agree on an answer to the first question but considerably disagree on the second question. Both perspectives accept that laws should ultimately be legitimated by the people through democratic political processes and that they should be derived from the will of the majority but written consistently with principles derived from the Declaration of Independence, the Constitution, and basic American social norms to maximize the freedoms of all citizens, including minorities and dissenters. On the question of how the coercive power of the law should be exerted, however, conservatives and liberals disagree. While both affirm that laws should be general enough to be universally applicable yet specific enough to permit the weighing of the merits of individual cases, they disagree on just how these generalizations should be specifically applied. This disagreement stems from their differing ideologies, with conservatives emphasizing the general welfare of society and the retributive function of law and liberals placing relatively greater emphasis on the rights of individuals and the rehabilitative function of law. This disagreement will be explored later in the chapter when the role of juvenile courts in American society is considered.

In light of this discussion of how society's beliefs and values codified into law overarch the system of justice and public safety services, let us now consider the three component parts of the system.

A THREE-PART SYSTEM

Police

Purpose and organization. Throughout history order has been maintained in most societies by the direct or threatened use of armed force, often military organizations, with justice meted out by whatever persons such force has maintained in positions of authority. Police organizations, however, differ from military organizations in a most important way: Their basic purpose lies in upholding law, not in upholding authority. Therefore even when police exert force they are still emphasizing the potentially liberating rule of law instead of a solely coercive rule. This distinction holds true in principle although in practice the basic purpose of police activities can be subverted or police can function as military organizations.

Because the authority for police activities derives from law and not from some central authority or source of power in the society itself, a system of police may be highly decentralized. This is the case in the United States, where a variety of police organizations share overlapping jurisdictions and responsibilities. Reid (1982) traces this decentralization to the historical development of police systems, which originated in ninth-century England when Alfred the Great (849–899) delegated groups of local families responsible for the actions of all their members. Eventually every ten such groups were consolidated under the direction of a constable, the first police officer, and still later these larger groups were further consolidated into shires (the English equivalent of counties). Each shire was directed by an officer appointed by the king and called a "shire-reeve," a term corrupted into "sheriff." In English cities and towns police systems developed out of watch systems. Watchmen at first were responsible for protecting city walls and gates but eventually became responsible for public behavior and were permitted to carry arms. Eventually local watchmen were organized into local police forces, with the first modern force established in London in 1829 by Sir Robert Peel (1788–1850); its members are still referred to as "bobbies" after their founder's first name. In the United States decentralization follows from these antecedents, with most law enforcement agencies being located in counties, cities, towns, and villages; with states maintaining their own police forces; and with no national police system, although the Federal Bureau of Investigation is authorized to enforce federal laws and assist local and state authorities in investigating nonfederal crimes (Reid, 1982, pp. 319–321). This decentralization may at times impede efficiency but it is consistent with the notion that police organizations are responsible to the law and not to a central authority.

Activities.   Aside from the law itself and whatever good will citizens maintain toward each other, police represent the front line of the system of justice and public safety. Although their primary activities are directed toward ensuring public safety, the belief that providing justice is left to the courts is by no means true, for police activities, even in times of chaos and danger, must be consistent with law and thus represent the will of the just society toward those citizens with whom police come into contact. Primary activities directed toward ensuring public safety include preventing crime, maintaining order, and enforcing law. These represent the front line of the system because the normal functioning of society would quickly break down without them, because they must be carried out prior to most activities of courts or institutions of correction, and because they often must be carried out immediately and under difficult circumstances. Furthermore, such activities may be highly visible, and many citizens hold ambivalent attitudes toward them. Finally, good police work can minimize the work of courts and institutions of correction. Secondary activities that maintain public safety include providing a wide variety of social services to individuals, often under emergency circumstances when counselors, social workers, or health care professionals are unavailable. Such activities are secondary only in the sense that they are directed not toward the general public safety but rather toward the immediate needs of individuals that under ordinary circumstances could usually be met by other human services.

In ensuring public safety most police activities are directed toward preventing crime. Activities such as informing citizens how the law will be enforced or providing visible police patrols in high crime areas may take place prior to the commission of specific crimes and be intended to reduce the occurrence of crimes. Activities such as issuing a summons for a traffic offense, investigating a robbery, or arresting a suspected criminal take place after specific crimes have been committed and are intended both to enforce the law and to prevent future crimes by the same criminal or potential criminals for whom such activities may act as a deterrent. Activities directed at maintaining order, such as preventing riots or interceding in street fights or violent family quarrels, also prevent potential crimes and may include both law enforcement and social service. For instance, in investigating a case of domestic violence a police officer may enforce laws against assault and battery or simply mediate the dispute and counsel family members. Police officers may also provide public safety at the same time they provide social services when they respond to accidents and emergencies and in many other ways assist people, maintain their well-being, and protect their property. Officers exercise considerable discretion in carrying out their duties. For example, on encountering a drunken person an officer may make an arrest or escort the person home. Officers must often make immediate decisions about whether crimes have been committed, whether arrests should be made, or whether force should be used. Because such decisions can easily be questioned and because most citizens wish both to be protected from crime but not to be investigated as potential criminals, many people hold ambivalent attitudes about police activities that contribute to the difficulties officers face in carrying out their duties. Nonetheless police activities represent the front line of the system of justice and public safety because without them conditions could not be maintained for a rule of law rather than force.

Courts

Purposes and organization. Courts also help to maintain order and prevent crime in society, but these are incidental outcomes of their primary purpose, which is interpreting and applying the law to provide justice. In criminal cases courts must decide how the law applies to specific circumstances, whether accused criminals are guilty, and, if guilty, how they should be sentenced. Although courts, therefore, are bound by the operative values of society as codified in law, they still have considerable latitude in determining the law's meaning and functions in society. In this sense justice is not something absolute; in the United States it represents the prevailing views about fairness as put into operation by the actual rulings of courts.

The system of federal courts in the United States is based on the Constitution, which establishes the judicial branch of government as part of the system of checks and balances maintained with the legislative and executive branches. State constitutions establish the same three branches of state government, including systems of state courts. Unlike the other two branches of government, however, courts do not initiate actions. Instead they act as deliberative bodies, considering and weighing evidence in light of the law and deciding on the legality of courses of action, including actions of the legislative and executive branches. For instance, the U.S. Supreme Court may rule on civil matters such as whether new laws passed by Congress or executive orders of the president are consistent with the

EXHIBIT 8-1 *ARRAIGNMENT COURT*

In New York City in a typical year there are approximately two hundred thousand arrests for crimes of various seriousness. Of these approximately ninety thousand are for felonies, which the law defines as major crimes. In New York, as in the rest of America, the "big four" felonies (robbery, assault, burglary, and grand larceny) account for about 25 percent of all cases that are prosecuted in the courts.

In New York, Arraignment Court initially processes the ninety thousand felony arrests, deciding how each should be handled by the court system. This court can be considered either a part of the system of criminal justice that keeps the entire system from breaking down or an example of how the system *is* breaking down, for on the average judges in Arraignment Court dispose of one case every four minutes. A majority of felony arrests are settled through plea bargaining, an agreement usually struck between a defendant's legal aid defense counsel and an assistant district attorney representing the city. In a typical plea bargaining case the defendant agrees to plead guilty to a lesser crime than the one he or she was arrested for (a felony is often reduced to a misdemeanor) in return for a lesser sentence, and the court can quickly ratify the agreement. Approximately 25 percent of robberies, 40 percent of assaults, and 60 percent of burglaries and grand larcenies are disposed of through plea bargaining. Approximately 40 percent of robberies but less than 10 percent of assaults, burglaries, and grand larcenies result in felony prosecutions. The rest of these cases are dismissed in Arraignment Court—usually in short order.

Constitution and existing federal laws. In criminal matters deliberations pertain to the actions of accused criminals, the courts ruling on whether certain actions constitute guilt or innocence under the law. Because the U.S. Supreme Court has the power to review, interpret, and in fact strike down as unconstitutional actions of the other two branches of the federal government, it has sometimes been criticized for "making" the law. Although this criticism is not literally true, the Supreme Court does wield tremendous influence. In deciding which cases it will hear, it often looks for cases with the broadest consequences for the United States as a whole. In ruling on cases its nine members are undoubtedly influenced by prevailing societal beliefs, their own ideologies, and their beliefs about the future social consequences of their decisions. However this power is balanced by the fact that no courts—including the Supreme Court—rule on purely hypothetical matters. All rulings are based on actual cases and the legality of real actions undertaken, so courts may not raise issues that do not come before them. Furthermore, in making decisions courts rely heavily on legal precedents, that is on similar cases that have previously been decided, and for the most part courts are extremely reluctant to reverse or modify previous judicial opinions. The reason for this reluctance is obvious. Without reliance on legal precedents the law as interpreted by the courts would have little stability. The same action that was declared legal one year might be declared illegal the next and vice versa. Chaos over the meaning and application of the law would ensue, and justice would not be served. However courts may reverse previous decisions when circumstances are sufficiently compelling, thus providing needed flexibility in the law, but the necessity for stability also balances the power of even the Supreme Court to shape society through its rulings.

The United States has what is known as a dual system of courts, because courts exist on both the federal and state levels. (Minor offenses may also be heard and ruled on by local magistrates, as authorized by state laws.) Federal courts have jurisdiction over violations of federal laws and state courts over violations of state laws; therefore violations of state laws may not be tried by federal courts and vice versa, although some crimes involving violations of both federal and state laws may result in separate federal and state trials. Both federal and state court systems include trial and appellate courts, and under some circumstances appeals concerning rulings of state courts may reach the U.S. Supreme Court. Trial courts establish facts about the actions of accused criminals and decide their guilt or innocence. Appellate courts in effect try the rulings of trial courts. A loser in a trial case may appeal the decision. An appellate court may thereupon examine procedures used by the trial court or specific points of law and either affirm or not affirm the decision of the trial court. Decisions not affirmed are often remanded to trial courts for reconsideration. The existence of both trial and appellate courts within the overall system of justice and public safety services is intended to provide safeguards for citizens accused of crimes while still protecting the general citizenry from crime.

Due process. A common reason for appeal in criminal trials is that the accused person was not provided due process of law, a phrase taken from the Fifth and Fourteenth Amendments to the Constitution. Especially since the Fourteenth Amendment was adopted in 1868, due process has come to represent a fundamental principle of American justice that essentially restricts the power of federal and state governments to conduct investigations and trials in any manner they please. In the adversarial system of trial in the United States, which has grown out of traditions in English law, both the accuser and the accused present their cases but the burden of proof falls on the accuser (in criminal trials this is usually the state as represented by a district attorney or prosecuting attorney). Suspected criminals are presumed innocent until proven guilty. This American notion of fairness seems to suggest that it is better for some guilty persons to be acquitted than for some innocent persons to be convicted. As it has historically developed in the United States, however, due process now consists of a series of specific safeguards for the rights of suspected or accused criminals that must not be violated by the police or the courts. Among these safeguards are the following: suspects shall be free from unreasonable searches; upon apprehension by police they shall immediately be notified of their rights; they shall be notified of charges against them; they shall not be required to testify against themselves; they shall receive legal counsel; they shall receive an impartial, speedy, and public trial by—if they choose—a jury of their peers; certain evidence against them obtained by illegal means shall be excluded from trials; and a final decision shall be rendered only once for each offense. Violation of any right of due process by either police or trial court may constitute grounds for an appellate court to reverse a conviction by a trial court. Questions concerning the nature of due process and whether specific individuals or even whole groups of people have received it are among the most pressing and controversial of any questions concerning the workings of the system of justice and public safety in the United States.

Sentencing.   Once tried and convicted of a crime, a criminal still faces sentencing by the court. Depending on prevailing statutes, a court may exercise considerable discretion or no discretion whatsoever over the type and severity of the sentence imposed. Sentences may include fines, restitution, work, community service, probation (that is, supervision by correctional authorities without a period of incarceration), incarceration in any

EXHIBIT 8-2   *SELECTING JURIES*

The impartiality of juries is supposed to be ensured by drawing members randomly from the community; however groups such as women and minorities have often been underrepresented on American juries, and both prosecutors and defense attorneys are ordinarily allowed to challenge and dismiss a certain number of prospective jurors they believe might be biased against their cases. During the Watergate trials, for example, several defendants allegedly escaped conviction because their attorneys strategically used challenges so that the juries empaneled fit a predetermined demographic profile believed to be sympathetic to the defendants' cases.

In 1975 a North Carolina jury found Joanne Little, a young black woman, not guilty of murdering her jailer, who she claimed had tried to assault her sexually. Her defense cost $325,000, most of it raised through a sophisticated, national, direct-mail campaign that portrayed her as a political victim. A defense team that included sociologists, psychologists, pollsters, an expert on body language, and a psychic had spent more than nine months conducting over a thousand telephone interviews to determine the personal attitudes and demographic characteristics that would predispose prospective jurors in Joanne Little's favor. This "Joanne Little Fair Trial Jury Project" culminated in ten days of questioning and challenges to 150 prospective jurors. All this was done, the defense team claimed, to assemble an impartial jury.

one of a number of kinds of institutions of correction, or, in extreme cases, capital punishment. Courts sometimes also have the power to suspend sentences. Sentences imposed may be either determinant or indeterminant. When statutes prescribe a specific sentence for all persons convicted of a certain crime, the sentence is determinant and courts must impose it; however courts may be able to exercise some discretion and still impose a determinant sentence. This is the case when statutes prescribe a range of sentences that may be imposed (for instance, incarceration for not less than one year nor more than five years) but permit the court to consider mitigating circumstances and the like in deciding the specific sentence. Sentences are indeterminant when courts impose the range of sentences specified by law but leave to the discretion of correctional authorities the specific point at which the criminal has fulfilled the sentence. Periods of incarceration that may be terminated by parole boards are examples of indeterminant sentences, although parole itself may represent a less restrictive form of supervision by correctional authorities than did incarceration and not a final release from the system. Among the most controversial issues concerning sentencing are the consistency and appropriateness of the sentences courts impose.

Institutions of Correction

The work of police in apprehending criminals may primarily serve to ensure public safety. Similarly the work of courts in trying, convicting, and sentencing criminals may primarily serve to provide justice. The work of institutions of correction in carrying out certain sentences contributes directly, in theory at least, to both public safety and justice. Nonetheless institutions of correction have been heavily criticized in American society, and, to the extent that such criticisms are justified, existing institutions of correction may in practice contribute only minimally to both public safety and justice. Although the correctional system in the United States includes probation officers, parole boards, and jails for the detention of prisoners who are awaiting arraignment or trial and who are unable to free themselves on bail, we will confine our brief discussion to prisons, those institutions of correction that exist to carry out sentences of incarceration that have been imposed by courts.

Prisons.   Prisons in modern America range from minimum to maximum security. At one extreme minimum security prisons may provide little more than sleeping, dining, and recreational facilities for their inmates. Inmates may be permitted to leave daily to work at their regular jobs, visit their families, and conduct personal business, being required only to return each evening. Extended furloughs may also be granted. Because such institutions are little more than administrative arrangements for accounting for criminals sentenced to serve time but deemed no threat to society, they are relatively inexpensive to operate and the trappings and atmosphere of other kinds of prisons may be absent. At the other extreme maximum security prisons may confine inmates for extended periods in small, dank, and overcrowded cells; some may be kept in solitary confinement. Few opportunities may exist for exercise, recreation, meaningful work, or education, and visitors from the outside world may be sharply restricted. The psychological atmosphere may be as depressing and demeaning as the physical facilities, and fear, coercion, and outright brutality may prevail among inmates and even guards. Because such institutions require heavy expenditures for the special facilities and numerous personnel required to maintain order among potentially violent and dangerous inmates, they are extremely expensive to operate. A heavily punitive atmosphere usually prevails within them.

Purposes.   Critics contend that prisons in the United States have failed to achieve their purpose, yet there is considerable debate and disagreement among the critics over what the purpose of prisons should be. In her chapter tracing the concept of punishment and the development of prisons in the United States, Reid (1982, pp. 473–517) suggests that there are four basic purposes for incarceration: deterring potential criminals, protecting society from the criminal, rehabilitating the criminal, and administering retribution against the criminal. Evidence is inconclusive about whether any form of punishment, including incarceration, actually deters crime, and although incarceration surely protects society from the criminal during the period of confinement, questions remain concerning what happens when the criminal eventually returns to the social mainstream. Therefore debate about the purposes of prisons focuses on rehabilitation versus retribution. In Europe prior to the eighteenth century most punishment was corporal, and its basic purpose was retribution. Under the spirit of humanitarianism and reason that arose during the Enlightenment, incarceration gradually became the principal means of punishment, and this development spread to America. During the nineteenth century the United States continued to exact retributive justice, but it gradually replaced corporal punishment with a penitentiary system. It also developed the beginnings of alternative forms of incarceration such as reformatories, which in principle placed far more emphasis on rehabilitation than retribution. During the twentieth century programs explicitly designed to rehabilitate criminals for normal functioning within society gradually obtruded into the mainstream of prison theory, and programs of psychological counseling, recreation, education, and vocational training became common in American prisons. Wrapped in an ethos of humanitarian concern for inmates, the idea that the public could be protected from criminals by using prisons to rehabilitate them became accepted by many Americans.

Despite general acceptance of this belief that rehabilitation of the criminal and protection of the society are the same thing, Reid notes that beginning in the early 1970s the American public has increasingly turned away from this idea because of increasing crime rates, high recidivism rates for criminals, and major problems such as riots and high costs in prisons themselves. She concludes her chapter with the assertion that of the four purposes of incarceration only retribution "makes sense":

> Rehabilitation has failed; crime rates have soared. The only justification for imprisonment that has any meaning, therefore, is . . . punishment, social retribution, the community's retaliation against the criminal for having violated its rules. . . . Many assume that this position is a "new" and progressive one, but it is clear to those who scrutinize history that it is a return to an earlier era in which the words of the classical criminologists "let the punishment fit the crime" were dominant. (p. 516)

If Reid is correct, justice honestly meted out through incarceration as a form of society's retribution against criminals may be a surer way of ensuring public safety than dishonestly and fecklessly attempting to rehabilitate inmates. Despite the humanitarian ideal conditions in many American prisons remain both physically and psychologically squalid, and prisons themselves continue to be incubators for future crime. This situation does not necessarily justify the "get tough" attitude toward crime that seems to have prevailed in the 1980s. Harsher sentencing and less attention to conditions and problems in prisons may also be self-defeating courses of action for American society. Therefore even if the basic purpose for incarceration should be retribution, retributive justice meted out in an even-handed way may still be combined with humanitarian efforts to improve the management of prisons and make them potentially more rehabilitative for their inmates.

JUVENILE COURTS

As noted above, the system of justice and public safety in the United States has been guided by high ideals and respect for the law. Its failures are primarily practical. Some police officers, correctional authorities, attorneys, and judges may be inept, even corrupt. Efforts to provide justice on a mass scale may fall far short in individual cases. Rights may be violated, adequate facilities lacking, and the public ill served.

America's juvenile courts are a collective example of how practical realities have failed to live up to high ideals and expectations. Perhaps expectations for what juvenile courts could accomplish have been so high that they could never be fulfilled. In any case, especially since the late 1960s what juvenile courts should attempt to accomplish and how they should go about accomplishing it have become an area of major controversy and heated debate, one on which basic differences between conservative and liberal perspectives on human services have focused.

Mission and Role

Until the end of the nineteenth century the judicial system in the United States made no clear distinction between juvenile and adult offenders. However, recognizing that children often are not responsible for their actions in the same sense adults are, that a bad environment over which they have no control may all but force some children to become delinquent or commit crimes, and that few children have hardened into incorrigible criminals, American society has developed a system of courts and institutions of correction responsible for overseeing juvenile offenders. Until children reach the specific age designated by each state they generally may not be tried in the same state courts as adults. Prior to adulthood they usually fall within the jurisdiction of what are ordinarily called "juvenile courts" but sometimes "family courts" or "domestic courts."

The purpose of juvenile courts is ultimately to enforce the law and provide justice; however juvenile courts have traditionally been charged with acting in the best interests of the youthful offenders who come within their jurisdiction. In this way juvenile courts adopt the purpose of providing rehabilitative and not retributive justice.

In acting in the best interests of juveniles, juvenile courts are concerned with both criminal offenses and so-called status offenses. Criminal offenses are the same violations, such as burglary or assault, with which adults may be charged. Status offenses are not considered crimes if committed by adults but are seen as indications of delinquency when committed by juveniles. They include running away from home, truancy, unmanageable behavior, and a host of very vague offenses such as use of bad language, which may do little more than offend a community's sense of propriety. In dealing with criminal offenses juvenile courts may in effect try and convict offenders. Sentences may include assignment to some kind of institution of correction for juveniles such as schools, homes, or juvenile prisons, but not to the same institutions as adult offenders. In dealing with status offenses juvenile courts may hold hearings to determine the causes and circumstances of the offenses. The purpose of these hearings is for the court to learn as much as possible about the juveniles, their families, and their backgrounds to make a decision that will be best for each child. For instance, in determining that a juvenile is delinquent the court may simply issue a warning, counsel the juvenile and his or her parents, or place the juvenile directly under some kind of supervision that the court oversees, such as probation or placement in a training school or foster home.

The basic mission and role of juvenile courts, therefore, is to uphold the law when crimes have been committed by juveniles in such a way as to rehabilitate the offenders. This mission extends to rehabilitating status offenders, those juveniles who have not necessarily violated criminal laws but whose lives provide evidence that they may become criminals or simply unhappy, unproductive, or antisocial adults. In either case juvenile courts represent the lawful interest of the state in overseeing the upbringing of children who are not receiving their right to proper circumstances, such as education or moral guidance, necessary to their becoming productive members of society. Each year thousands of juveniles come before juvenile courts for violations of criminal laws, but thousands more are referred to these courts as status offenders by police, community organizations, schools, and families. When the ordinary guidance offered by family and community has broken down, juvenile courts may intervene on behalf of children whether or not criminal laws have been violated. In acting to rehabilitate juvenile offenders courts serve both the interests of juveniles not to commit future crimes and the interests of society to be free from future crimes.

Origins and History

Throughout most of human history children have either been subjected to virtually absolute control by their parents or treated by the state as adults. Under ancient Roman law fathers held the power of life and death over their children, and infanticide was common. In England prior to the Norman conquest of 1066 fathers could both kill their newborn children and sell children under age seven into slavery. As late as 1904 a court in the District of Columbia upheld the right of a father to confine his daughter in a reform school without providing reasons and without obtaining her consent (Bersoff, 1976, p. 10). Under English common law a child as young as seven was subject to the authority of the state and could be tried and punished as an adult. Justice in colonial America followed this English example, with children facing corporal punishment, forced labor, and incarceration along with adults. Not until the mid-nineteenth century did the judicial system in the United States begin to move toward distinguishing between children and adults by recognizing probation for children and creating separate detention facilities for children. The development of protective societies for children, such as the Society for the Prevention of Cruelty to Children, established in New York City in 1875, further served to deepen this distinction (Reid, 1982, pp. 423–424).

The juvenile court movement.   The event that provided the first clear legal distinction between adult and juvenile offenders and at the same time created the first juvenile court was the passage of the Illinois Juvenile Court Act in 1899. This act either encouraged or directly incorporated

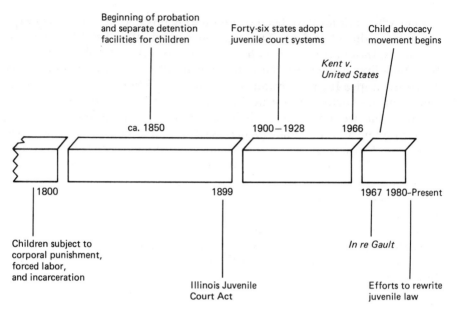

FIGURE 8–1.   Timeline tracing the programs and policies relating to juvenile justice from colonial times to the present. Major movements, legislation, and judicial actions that have shaped justice and public safety services for juvenile offenders are identified.

many of the then modern and progressive notions about individuals and society that have underlain the twentieth-century development of social science, therapy, and social casework. Under the provisions of the act delinquent children were viewed primarily as victims of circumstances beyond their control. They were not to be accused of crimes by the court but instead were to be offered individualized assistance and guidance based on the court's assessment of their specific circumstances. Court proceedings were not supposed to stigmatize them. Proceedings were informal and took place privately in comfortable rooms without the trappings of adult courts. Records were unavailable to the press or public. Judges were supposed to personalize their relationship with juvenile offenders, acting very much as doctors-therapists who diagnose children's problems and proffer solutions. The act also incorporated the doctrine of *parens patriae*, whereby the state's interest in the upbringing of children superceded the rights of parents. The Illinois act became a prototype for legislation in other states. Wisconsin (1901), New York (1901), Ohio (1902), and Colorado (1903) quickly passed their own laws establishing juvenile courts, and by 1928 only two states had not adopted the juvenile court system (Platt, 1969, pp. 137–143).

Problems.   Despite the humanitarian intentions of its early advocates and some very real improvements in how the judicial system in the United States dealt with juvenile offenders, the juvenile court movement immediately suffered from excesses and practical problems. Platt (1969) characterizes the movement in this way:

> The juvenile court movement was "anti-legal" in the sense that it encouraged minimum procedural formality and maximum dependency on extra-legal resources. The judges were authorized to investigate the character and social background of both "pre-delinquent" and "delinquent" children. They examined personal motivation as well as criminal intent, seeking to identify the moral reputation of problematic children. . . . The requirements of preventive penology and child saving further justified the courts' intervention in cases where no offense had actually been committed but where, for example, a child was posing problems for some person in authority, such as a parent or teacher or social worker. (pp. 141–142)

The creation of juvenile courts had thus created a mechanism for the state to intervene abstrusely and otherwise extralegally into the personal lives of children. Status offenses had previously been a nuisance to the state but for the most part did not constitute prosecutable violations. Now status offenses—both real and alleged—were the business of the state to investigate, correct, or punish. Although some judges exercised common sense and restraint in their new duties, the juvenile court system made it extremely easy for other judges to push the doctrine of *parens patriae* all too far, even in the interests of individual children. For instance, at the discretion of a judge children could now be separated from their parents for little more than idleness or youthful rebellion in school. Furthermore, judges varied considerably in their ability to diagnose and treat the causes of individual children's delinquency, even with the help of social workers, probation officers, the emerging tools of social science, and the creation of new forms and institutions of juvenile correction. Additionally, early expectations of unequivocal success in eradicating juvenile delinquency could hardly be realized by juvenile courts despite successes in individual cases and the general improvement in the treatment of children by the judicial system as a whole.

Despite success in some individual cases, neither the early juvenile courts nor more recent ones have been able to realize effectively even the modest expectation of simply acting in the best interests of all children who come before them. The foremost practical problem that blunts the best efforts of juvenile courts is lack of resources and facilities. Despite what the juvenile court system has done to improve juvenile justice and ensure public safety, sufficient funding has never been provided to enable the system to work as well as its early advocates had envisioned. This deficiency became apparent in the years immediately following the Illinois Juvenile Court Act. Platt (1969) notes that the act

> did little to change the quality of institutional life for delinquents, though it facilitated the means by which juvenile offenders could be "reached" and committed. Contrary to a specific provision in the act, children continued to

be imprisoned with adult criminals in county and city jails. . . . Some Chicago reformers soon realized that there was a wide difference between idealized goals and operating realities. Judge Tuthill told a national audience that the John Worthy School was a "well-equipped public school," while acknowledging to his professional colleagues at home that it was overcrowded, poorly equipped, badly situated, and more like a prison than a school. (p. 146)

In practice the same situation has held true for the juvenile court system throughout the twentieth century. Disillusionment about the workings of juvenile courts continues to be expressed (Bortner, 1982). Juvenile offenders have often been jailed with adult offenders, court procedures have often been demeaning and perfunctory, and institutions of correction for juveniles have often been overcrowded, poorly run, and anything but rehabilitative. The goal of providing treatment for and prevention of juvenile delinquency is still not being realized effectively by the system of juvenile courts, for systematic evidence indicates that delinquents apprehended by police and processed through the system "subsequently commit more delinquent acts than do those who are not apprehended" (Gold, 1977, p. 218).

Critics.   Aside from such practical deficiencies, juvenile courts in the United States have historically been criticized from two different ideological points of view. The first suggests that juvenile courts should provide retributive instead of rehabilitative justice; the second, that juvenile courts have traditionally suppressed the constitutional rights of children. Both groups of critics have influenced the functioning of juvenile courts, the latter especially since a major Supreme Court decision in 1967.

Even during the twentieth century numerous Americans have remained skeptical of the idea that rehabilitation of criminals is the proper function of the system of justice and public safety services. These citizens may object on moral grounds to the idea of society's aiding individuals who through their criminal activities have damaged the well-being of other members of society. These critics may also argue that retribution is the only morally proper way for society to express its indignation at crimes. Furthermore these citizens may argue that retribution has a stronger deterrent effect on future crimes than do efforts—usually ineffective—to rehabilitate criminals and that ironically retribution often has the effect of rehabilitating criminals more surely than do efforts to provide rehabilitation without retribution. In fact many such citizens have so argued on both moral and utilitarian grounds against the original ideology of the juvenile court movement. Although throughout the twentieth century juvenile courts have retained their basic mission of rehabilitating juvenile offenders, in practice they have been shaped by such critics to the point that their operative ideologies and activities have considerably been blurred. For example, due to their skepticism such critics have been reluctant to support funding for juvenile courts, and lacking adequate funding courts have found that activities intended to be rehabilitative have become retributive by default. Placing a juvenile in a vocational training school, for instance, may be rehabilitative if the school is well run but retributive if it is not. Gold (1977) argues that in practice the operative strategy of juvenile courts is not rehabilitation of juvenile offenders but merely containment of juvenile crimes (pp. 221–222). Although few members of this group of critics actually favor abolition of juvenile courts and a return to the earlier system of treating juvenile and adult criminals indiscriminantly, this group cites statistics showing increases in the rate and seriousness of juvenile crimes and generally favors a "get tough" policy toward juvenile offenders. Especially since the early 1970s these ideas have created pressures on the ideology and practices of juvenile courts in the United States.

Critics holding a different ideological point of view have also pointed with displeasure to the traditional practices of juvenile courts. This second group of critics does not object to the ideology of rehabilitation nor the courts' efforts to work in the best interests of juvenile offenders; however they have argued that the best interests of juveniles cannot be realized in legal proceedings that strip juveniles of the constitutional rights of due process that protect adults. The good intentions of juvenile courts are insufficient, they have contended, especially in light of the practical problems the juvenile court system has historically encountered in failing to live up to its own ideals. Whatever the intentions, traditional juvenile court proceedings have deprived children of constitutional rights, often stigmatized them as delinquent, and frequently remanded them to various forms of punishment. In the case *Kent v. United States* (1966), this kind of skepticism about juvenile courts was forcefully articulated for the nation in an often quoted opinion of U.S. Supreme Court Justice Abe Fortas: "There is evidence, in fact, that there may be grounds for concern that the child receives the worst of both worlds: that he gets neither the protections accorded to adults nor the solicitous care and regenerative treatment postulated for children." In 1967 the Supreme Court issued its first decision on the juvenile court system itself. Known as *In re Gault,* this decision turned the skepticism of such critics into a set of procedural regulations that have since bound juvenile courts and given considerable impetus to a movement now known as "child advocacy."

The *Gault* decision and child advocacy.   In the *Gault* case a fifteen-year-old boy had been sentenced by an Arizona juvenile court on the basis of informal hearings to commitment in a state institution until his twenty-first birthday. The crime for which the boy was convicted was making obscene phone calls. If found guilty of the same crime an adult would have been fined from $5 to $50 or imprisoned for a maximum of two months. In reversing the Arizona conviction the U.S. Supreme Court noted the arbitrariness of juvenile court proceedings and the necessity for procedural safeguards. It did not strike down the judicial distinction between juveniles and adults nor did it require juvenile proceedings to resemble adult proceedings in all ways (requiring, for instance, the option of trial by jury); however the Court did require juvenile proceedings to honor certain due process rights, including notification of charges, representation by legal counsel, cross-examination of witnesses, and abstention from testifying against oneself.

The *Gault* decision was of course a victory for the second group of critics, who claimed that juvenile courts had historically failed to honor the constitutional rights of children. The impact on juvenile courts was to make proceedings more formal and adversarial and to drop the pretense that courts always act in the best interests of children; hence since 1967 courts have moved closer to procedures advocated by the second group of critics and ironically closer to an ideology of retributive justice advocated by the first group of critics. Nonetheless the decision has by no means completely changed the long-prevailing ideology and intentions of juvenile courts. Since *Gault* juvenile courts have still been bound to act in the best interests of juvenile offenders and provide rehabilitative justice, but they have in practice recognized that even their best-intentioned decisions may be faulty and that even juveniles are not obligated to accept them by forfeiting their constitutionally protected rights to argue against and potentially change the decisions. The *Gault* decision has also helped expand the focus of the second group of critics from juvenile courts themselves to other social institutions and services that impinge on the lives of children, such as families, hospitals, and schools. These critics have merged with others holding similar ideological beliefs to form the child advocacy movement. Child advocates seek "to enhance the status of children and broaden their rights under the Constitution and federal and state laws" (Bersoff, 1976, p. 11). Working primarily through the judicial system of the United States, they have sought not simply to protect children from illegal encroachments by adults (such as physical abuse and violation of privacy) but also to extend children's rights to include active participation in making all decisions that affect their lives (Bronars, 1979, pp. 291–298). Since 1967 the child advocacy movement has influenced juvenile courts to seek actively and to take seriously the wishes and beliefs of juvenile offenders and thus further to reduce the arbitrariness of court deliberations.

In the future juvenile courts will continue to be shaped by the tensions generated among groups such as the child advocacy movement, critics holding the retributive theory of justice, citizens advocating a "get tough" policy with juvenile offenders, the remnants of the original juvenile court movement, and critics holding the rehabilitative theory of justice. Ryerson (1978), however, in reviewing the entire history of juvenile courts in the United States, warns advocates and critics alike not to hold unduly high expectations about what courts can accomplish, regardless of how they are shaped, for she sees disillusionment with juvenile courts as part of "a more general disappointment with modern society, and particularly with spiraling aspirations toward progress by means of science and bureaucracy" (p. 15).

Conservative and Liberal Perspectives

The conservative and liberal perspectives on the purpose and function of the juvenile courts are heavily influenced by these conflicting forces and expectations. Although neither conservatives nor liberals favor dismantling the juvenile court system that has developed in the United States, neither group is entirely happy with it. In general conservatives tend to stress the retributive purpose of juvenile justice and the welfare of the entire society. Their disagreements have been more with the traditional ideology than with the traditional practices of juvenile courts. Conservatives advocate what we will term the societal model of juvenile justice. In general liberals tend to stress the rehabilitative purpose of juvenile justice and the welfare of individual children. Their disagreements have been more with the practical problems encountered by juvenile courts than with their traditional ideology. Liberals advocate what we will term the child-centered model of juvenile justice.

The conservative perspective examined.   The societal model of juvenile justice advocated by conservatives is shaped by their general beliefs as applied to the system of justice and public safety services. Conservatives believe that there is a fixed, universal truth. Although human nature is imperfect, individual human beings can be inculcated with this truth by the best traditional wisdom handed down through society. Society, although also imperfect, is a stable repository of values derived from truth. These values guide conduct, and individuals can pursue their own interests appropriately only to the extent that they act consistently with these values and thereby contribute to the common good represented by society as a whole. Therefore conservatives believe that the law represents the distilled, collective wisdom of society codified specifically to guide conduct. Law is thus both a way of representing truth and morality and a means for guiding individuals in society's norms. Police, courts, and institutions of correction all exist to uphold law and the social norms it represents.

Because the common good is well served by bringing individuals into line with the social temper, conservatives do not oppose the rehabilitative function of justice. In practice, however, they strongly favor the retributive function, believing that rehabilitating criminals to act consistently with social norms is basically a side effect of punishing them for the crimes they have committed. Unless society punishes criminals swiftly and surely, the moral authority of society is undermined, the purposes and applications of law remain unclear, and public safety is ill served. Retribution expresses society's moral outrage at crimes, inculcates some criminals with society's norms, and protects society from those criminals who remain incorrigible. The primary duty of the system of justice and public safety services is to provide for the well-being of actual and potential victims of crime, not to aid criminals. This duty is so profound that the system must be highly directive toward the real and alleged criminals with whom it comes into contact. Not they but the society the system represents constitutes the real clients of the system, and in any case criminals have largely forfeited their moral standing in society. Therefore in terms of human services theory conservatives insist that the system of justice and public safety services cannot act collaboratively with criminals, seeking to involve them as active partners in determining their futures. It must instead act unilaterally and directively toward criminals in administering retribution and inculcating society's norms, although it necessarily acts collaboratively with society in upholding those norms that society determines, especially as codified in law. Furthermore, this duty is so profound that conservatives believe the system of justice and public safety services is unique among the six human services systems. It is the one system that cannot be left even in part to voluntary or private initiatives. In protecting society against crime the system must be public, even-handed, and universal. Dealing with the consequences of the imperfections of human nature must be done publicly if society is to uphold its norms and prevent chaos. Because neither human nature nor society is perfectible, conservatives believe that the system will always be necessary and necessarily public.

Conservatives comprise the first group of critics of juvenile courts, those who have argued on moral grounds that society should first seek to punish, not aid, transgressors against its well-being. For this reason alone conservatives have remained highly skeptical of the traditional ideology of juvenile courts that stresses rehabilitation. The dilemma for conservatives lies in the fact that during the twentieth century most have accepted the idea that there are real distinctions to be made between children and adults because children often are not responsible for their actions in the same sense as adults. Retribution may shape the behavior of children but before they reach a certain stage of understanding children have little grasp of the moral dimensions of either their acts or the punishments they receive. If the moral purpose of retribution is thus lost on young children, the real purpose of their contact with juvenile courts must then be to encourage them to act consistently with society's norms. Is the real purpose then not rehabilitation? Should courts not then help them come to understand and accept that society's norms represent the best interests of all individuals? Once conservatives have accepted in practice any distinctions between children and adults, they have undercut a basic reason for their skepticism of the traditional ideology of juvenile courts.

In fact, most conservatives are in favor of modern and presumably enlightened methods for dealing with both criminal and status juvenile offenses. In modern America there is no conservative movement to treat adults and children indiscriminately. Conservatives accept the belief that because of their ages and circumstances beyond their control most juveniles are not wholly responsible for their actions and few are incorrigible, but they also insist that the primary purpose of juvenile courts must remain the same as the purpose of other courts: upholding law and promoting public safety. Therefore the societal model that conservatives advocate is based on the idea that despite age or understanding juveniles must still be brought in line with the social norms represented by law. Only after this purpose has been fulfilled can juvenile courts be concerned with acting in the best interests of juveniles. In practice the best interests of juveniles are almost always fulfilled when juveniles have been brought in line with social norms. Thus the societal model is intended to bring juvenile offenders to justice before the law; for those not acquitted or otherwise dismissed, punishment should be applied appropriately. Appropriate punishment may include any number of modern and enlightened forms of correction such as confinement in an institution for juveniles that provides counseling, education, vocational training, and other potentially rehabilitative programs. The basic conservative concern about the traditional ideology of juvenile courts is that it reverses proper priorities. Conservatives believe that in attempting to act in the best interests of juvenile offenders and provide therapy before providing justice, traditional courts have often lost sight of their duty to uphold law and social norms. Because of the courts' confusion their best efforts have often failed to rehabilitate juvenile offenders and protect the interests of society.

A secondary but also important conservative concern about traditional juvenile courts is the intrusiveness of their procedures into the private lives of citizens. Especially in the case of status offenders courts have been empowered to probe into virtually all details of the private lives of children and their families and to exert authority to alter substantially these lives even in the absence of criminal activities. In general conservatives are not against juvenile courts acting decisively under appropriate circumstances to provide constructive solutions to the problems of status offenders and thereby to reduce the probability of future crime or blighted lives; however considerable disagreement exists among conservatives over the limits of the intrusive powers of the juvenile court. Most conservative advocates of the societal model do not want courts to be the sole interpreters of society's norms; therefore most want juvenile courts to use restraint and exert their intrusive authority only when the oldest and surest traditional means of inculcating social norms such as family, school, church, and community have clearly broken down. Most conservatives argue that juvenile courts have helped break down these traditional means for inculcating society's norms in children when they have acted too intrusively in accordance with the liberal ideology of the early juvenile court movement. Thus the societal model upholds society's norms but at the same time places limits on the courts' role in attempting to act as the sole social arbiter of these norms. Most conservatives agree, for example, that juvenile courts should uphold law but not intrude unduly into the legitimate prerogatives of parents to guide the upbringing of their children. For these reasons many conservatives have welcomed the limitations placed on juvenile court proceedings by the *Gault* decision, and some even support the otherwise liberal child advocacy movement, at least to the extent that it focuses on limiting the power of government to interfere with the directive traditions of society itself. Only a small minority of conservatives of the extreme "get tough on crime" or "law and order" persuasion advocate virtually unlimited authority for the entire system of justice and public safety services on the grounds that only by granting such authority can society protect itself from crime and uphold its norms.

The conservatives' societal model of juvenile justice therefore sees society as the great repository of truth and values that have been translated into guides for action by being codified into laws. The primary function of juvenile courts under this model is to provide justice and public safety by upholding laws. The most effective way of protecting society and inculcating social norms is to provide retribution to juvenile offenders. While recognizing the real differences between children and adults, juvenile courts should mete out retributive justice in appropriate and humane ways that are also potentially rehabilitative. The coercive authority of juvenile courts is not absolute, but should be limited so as not to break down the traditional means by which society has inculcated children into its norms.

This model is consistent with several American social norms. It is consistent with the belief that government has an obligation to assist the helpless and the weak. Real and potential victims of crime need to be protected by the government's upholding of law, and juvenile offenders are recognized as relatively helpless and weak compared to adults and therefore deserving of a special court system. This model is also consistent with the belief in government of shared responsibility. Although conservatives believe that juvenile justice is part of the one human services system that cannot be left to private-party or marketplace decision-making, they believe the intrusive power of juvenile courts should be limited and society's traditional forms of social controls left as fully intact as possible. Finally, the societal model is consistent with the belief in progress through resolution of problems by science and technology to the extent that conservatives believe the findings of modern social science can help improve the workings of the juvenile justice system. Although conservatives believe neither human nature nor society is perfectible, they believe there is still much to learn and much room for improvement in how juvenile courts and institutions of correction carry out their tasks. The societal model therefore seeks to improve, not to abolish, the workings of the juvenile court system, and conservatives do not wish to return to the nineteenth-century practice of treating children and adults indiscriminately. They do wish, however, that juvenile courts properly prioritize the retributive and rehabilitative functions of justice.

The liberal perspective examined. The child-centered model of juvenile justice advocated by liberals is shaped by their general beliefs as applied to the system of justice and public safety services. Liberals believe that society does not embody any fixed and final truths. If there are such truths, they have not yet been discovered or at least there is no widespread consensus on what they might be. Therefore liberals believe that the highest values for society and individuals are realized in the process of healthy growth. Final ends are indeterminant and values derive from the process itself. The development of individual and collective social intelligence as

FIGURE 8–2.   Chart showing the forces impinging on juvenile courts—and on their traditional role of acting in the best interests of juvenile offenders—as interpreted by the conservatives' *societal model* and the liberals' *child-centered model*.

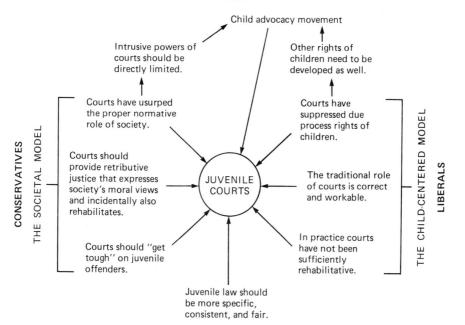

tested by the guiding of healthy growth is the surest way to realize value. Therefore liberals believe that the law represents a means of promoting the healthy growth of both individuals and society. As society's norms codified to guide conduct, law can promote the development of individuals who in turn promote constructive social change through democratic participation in society. As society's norms thus change, the law itself will change to promote more effectively further healthy growth for both individuals and society. Neither human nature nor society is in any final sense perfectible, but both can develop toward increasingly higher levels. Police, courts, and institutions of correction all exist to contribute to this process.

Because the common good is well served by promoting individual development, liberals strongly favor the rehabilitative function of justice. They see rehabilitation as merely a way of extending the normal nurturing and educative capacities of society to those individuals who have somehow been deprived of them and who, suffering from arrested development, have violated society's norms. According to liberals society gains little from punishing criminals unless they are also rehabilitated. There is little evidence that retribution alone is an effective deterrent to crime. Because society does need to be protected from criminal activities, forms of punishment such as incarceration can be justified, but society is not well protected in the long run unless criminals are rehabilitated so that they too can someday contribute to the continuing well-being and development of the social order. In extending the nurturing and educative capacities of society to criminals, society only appears to make criminals the clients of the system of justice and public safety services. The real clients remain the society at large, which protects its collective interests by attending to the needs and interests of all its citizens, even those of its lowest moral status. Effective rehabilitation ultimately requires criminals to guide their own development intelligently, even though they may not be able to do so initially. However, in terms of human services theory liberals insist that the system can eventually act collaboratively with criminals, involving them as active partners in determining their own futures and even the future of society itself. To become rehabilitated criminals must come to understand that actions one undertakes for one's own interests can still be moral acts if they also benefit society, but this understanding is impossible without some experience in collaborative action. Were the system of justice and public safety services sufficiently successful in rehabilitating criminals and were society itself sufficiently successful in otherwise extending its nurturing and educative capacities to all citizens, the reasons for the existence of police, courts, and institutions of correction would cease. Although this will not actually happen in the foreseeable future, liberals believe that the system of justice and public safety services is the one human services system that could cease to exist if society were to develop to a sufficiently high level. In the meantime the system must remain public, even-handed, and universal to protect the public interest most effectively and to rehabilitate those citizens who have violated society's norms.

The child-centered model of juvenile justice advocated by liberals is based on these beliefs and is consistent with the original ideology of the juvenile court movement. Prominent in this model is the idea that children should not be treated as adults. Although even hardened adult criminals are seen as potentially capable of rehabilitation, children are far more so. Because of their age, developmental status, and dependency on parents or other adults, children are malleable. Most of their lives stretch before them. Those children who come into contact with juvenile courts because of crimes or status offenses are far more accurately seen as victims of circumstances than as blameworthy. Why punish them, treat them similarly to adults who can better control their actions, or otherwise mingle them with adult criminals when their basic problem is having been deprived of proper upbringing and moral guidance? Seen in this light the duties of juvenile courts necessarily include exercising the lawful interests of government to direct the upbringing of children for their own best interests.

The liberals' child-centered model stresses engaging individual children in understanding and resolving their specific problems to promote their healthy development. All the modern tools of diagnosis, casework, therapy, counseling, and the like are used by juvenile courts and special institutions of correction to help attain this goal. The healthy development of real or potential juvenile offenders rehabilitates them for constructive life in society at large and so serves the best interests of both individuals and society. However, the dilemma for liberal advocates of the child-centered model is a practical one, for despite the dominance of the ideology of their model in the system of juvenile justice in America throughout the twentieth century, results have fallen far short of hopes and expectations. These shortcomings cast doubts on the workability of the child-centered model, however worthy its intent. Liberals are quick to suggest that the shortcomings may be due to actual practices of juvenile courts being inconsistent with their ideology. They point out that when the workings of any system fail to live up to the highest goals and expectations, the wise course of action is to improve practices, not to abandon worthy goals. They hold that the child-centered model remains a viable way of embodying America's highest aspirations for rehabilitating juvenile offenders.

Some liberals remain in favor of the traditional practice of juvenile courts to act extralegally as long as such actions are undertaken in the best interests of juveniles. They argue that juvenile courts are not like other courts that are simply concerned with weighing evidence presented in adversarial proceedings and passing judgments and sentences; juvenile courts must themselves gather as much information as possible about the entire lives of children to understand specific children's problems and fulfill their obligation to make the best possible dispositions of individual cases. Other liberals remain in favor of such intents but still wish to restrict the extralegal activities of juvenile courts. These liberals largely comprise the second group of critics of juvenile courts who stress the need to protect the due process rights of children to best serve their interests. Because juveniles may disagree with courts about what their best interests are or how they can be upheld, juveniles should have the same rights as adults to present evidence, contrary opinions, and the like. In fact these liberals argue that the best interests of children can be served only when the abilities of juvenile courts to control children's lives are not unlimited, for only under such circumstances can children be seen as active collaborators in decisions that affect their lives. The good intentions of courts are not sufficient, and the upholding of due process rights for juvenile offenders provides circumstances more conducive to their healthy development than when courts may be completely directive. These beliefs correspond with the liberal focus in the child advocacy movement on broadening the rights of children and making children increasingly responsible for intelligently directing their own lives. Especially since the *Gault* decision and the development of child advocacy, this point of view has predominated among liberals. Thus the child-centered model of juvenile justice that is reflected in contemporary liberal thought stresses due process rights of children and limits the intrusive prerogatives of juvenile courts to probe and direct the private lives of children and their families.

The liberals' child-centered model of juvenile justice is consistent with many of the same American social norms as the conservatives' societal model, although the reasoning of liberal and conservative advocates is sometimes quite different. The child-centered model is consistent with the American belief that government has an obligation to assist the helpless and the weak. Both liberals and conservatives agree that juveniles are deserving of a special court system because their age, developmental status, and dependency make them relatively helpless and weak compared to adults, but liberals stress the obligation of juvenile courts to promote individual development and conservatives the obligation to protect society. Both models are consistent with the belief in progress through resolution of problems by science and technology, for both liberals and conservatives believe that modern social science can help improve the workings of the system of juvenile justice. Both also wish to preserve and improve that system. Liberals, however, suggest that such progress can extend to constructive changes in society itself, whereas conservatives believe progress is limited to improving the system's functioning within the prevailing social order. Both models are likewise consistent with the belief in government of shared responsibility. Liberals believe that government responsibility should ultimately be shared with the people (whence initially it is derived) to provide opportunities for helping people become better able to participate intelligently in collaborative governing. The limited authority of all forms of government, including juvenile courts, reflects the liberal beliefs that authority derives from individuals and that individual development is the force that drives shared, collaborative social change. In contrast conservatives stress that because the limited responsibility of all forms of government is necessary to protect society's traditional forms of social control and maintenance, the authority of juvenile courts should thus be limited.

The child-centered model of juvenile justice reflects basic American social norms and liberal ideology stressing the value of the rehabilitative function of justice. Although liberals do not wish to change that ideology, they have historically been disappointed by practical difficulties in the workings of the system of juvenile justice in the United States and have generally supported recent developments providing due process rights for juvenile offenders and otherwise limiting the potentially intrusive powers of juvenile courts. Despite practical difficulties, liberals generally remain confident that practical improvements will demonstrate that the present system of juvenile justice is both workable and desirable: It should be improved but its basic liberal ideology should remain unchanged.

Future Directions

Both conservatives and liberals recognize the need for a separate system of juvenile justice, both give general support to the present structure of the system, and both see the need for specific improvements in practices. Given these facts, there is little likelihood of major, fundamental changes in the system but considerable likelihood of gradual, evolutionary changes. Debates about the retributive versus the rehabilitative functions of justice in themselves will likely have little impact on the actual operations of juvenile courts because the same sentences can often be viewed as retributive or rehabilitative depending on the perspective of the viewer. For instance, conservatives want sure and speedy retribution but also enlightened sentences that are humane and potentially rehabilitative; liberals want humane rehabilitation but also sentences that will surely protect society from future crimes. Public attention will likely continue to focus on the efficacy and humaneness of specific practices.

Many of the evolutionary changes of the 1960s and 1970s reported by Serrill (1979) have continued into the 1980s and show little sign of altering direction. This evolution seems to be the result of the conflicting forces described in this chapter. Serrill suggests that the public perception of the increasing rate of juvenile crime (an increase between 1960 and 1975 of 283 percent in the number of juvenile arrests) and its increasing seriousness (the percentage of shoplifting and car theft decreasing, the percentage of robbery and murder increasing) spawned a "get tough" movement that strenuously urges retributive justice. This force has been balanced by the child advocacy movement, itself spawned by public concern for children's rights to due process and bolstered by public revulsion against intolerable conditions discovered in many juvenile institutions. Both forces have placed considerable pressure on the practices of juvenile courts (although less so on traditional rehabilitative ideology), with judges accused of either being too lenient and losing sight of their duty to protect society or too harsh and sentencing juveniles to inhumane institutions. These balancing forces prevented sudden shifts in any direction by the system during the 1960s and 1970s, and as a result many conservatives and liberals have joined in attempts to rewrite juvenile law to be more specific, consistent, and fair, whether its intent is retribution or rehabilitation. The major outcome of this coalition has been for juvenile courts to deal more severely with serious juvenile criminal offenders but less severely with status offenders. Evolution has been toward continuing expansion in the rights of due process for juveniles and a continuing decline in the number of juveniles in institutions of correction (from forty-three thousand in 1965 to twenty-six thousand in 1979) despite an increase in the number of serious offenders (Serrill, 1979, pp. 20, 22, 24). This trend has continued in the 1980s but at a much slower rate, even though it has been abetted by recent thinking of social scientists and lawyers that has generally been consistent with the conservative perspective. For instance, citing studies done by Patterson (1980), Hirschi (1983) suggests that retribution is necessary for rehabilitation, for even problem children who have not yet committed criminal misdeeds "must be *punished* for their misdeeds if they are to learn to live without them" (p. 53 [emphasis in the original]). Walkover (1984) sees juvenile courts as increasingly emphasizing procedures of due process, accountability of all but very young offenders for their crimes, and punishment, and therefore concludes that the proper function of juvenile justice is punishment but that nonculpable children should be protected from the state. "This, in sum, is the received wisdom of the last twenty-five years of juvenile sociological and jurisprudential study" (p. 562).

Still, in the absence of a major social revolution, unforeseeable shifts in basic American beliefs, or another *Gault* decision, conservative and liberal forces on juvenile courts likely will remain balanced and evolution of the present system of juvenile justice toward improved practices for juvenile courts will continue. Evolution will remain slow, for neither conservatives nor liberals know how to improve practices and conclusive evidence is unlikely to emerge. In the meantime debates will continue about the relative merits of retribution and rehabilitation but as in the past will likely have little real influence on the actual workings of juvenile courts. After more than eight decades of existence juvenile courts and their workings are thoroughly ingrained in America's system of justice and public safety services, a system of human services built on some of the deepest beliefs of Americans as codified in law. Although now a practical necessity in modern society, juvenile courts are part of the human services system least amenable to planned or sudden changes. Practices will improve but these improvements will continue to take place more by evolution than design.

STUDY QUESTIONS AND ACTIVITIES

1. Who are the clients of the system of justice and public safety services? How can the system benefit clients with whom it has never come into contact? For whom it has never assessed specific needs? Define crime. Should the system be directed primarily at preventing crime, ameliorating the results of crime, or punishing criminals?

2. What are laws? Why do developed societies need written laws? Explain how laws are potentially liberating. Explain how they are potentially coercive. List specific examples of how laws fulfill each of the following purposes: protecting ownership, defining the parameters of private and public property, regulating business, raising revenue, providing redress for broken agreements, upholding social institutions, regulating relations, protecting public interests, providing for needed change, and preserving order. Explain the difference between civil and criminal law. Why do conservatives and liberals agree on how the coercive power of law should be legitimated but disagree on how it should be exerted?

3. How do police organizations differ from military organizations? Why are police organizations in the United States decentralized? List specific police organizations that exist in the United States and the activities that each undertakes. What differences exist between these organizations? Why do some police organizations concentrate on crime, order, and law and others on social services? Why do many citizens hold ambivalent attitudes toward police activities? In what senses do these activities represent the front line of the system of justice and public safety services?

4. In what ways do courts provide the same services as police? Define justice. Explain the basic functions of courts. What are the relationships between the judicial, executive, and legislative branches of government? Why do courts not rule on hypothetical matters? Why do they rely on legal precedents? How does the United States have a dual system of courts? Explain the difference between trial courts and appellate courts. Explain the meaning of due process of law. List the due process rights that apply to criminal cases. How might due process rights apply to civil cases? What is the difference between determinant and indeterminant sentences?

5. Do institutions of correction deserve the negative criticism they have received in American society? Collect and carefully weigh relevant data on this question, including descriptions of life inside minimum and maximum security prisons and institutions for delinquent youths. Explain the differences between the four basic purposes of incarceration: deterrence of crime, protection of society, rehabilitation of criminals, and retribution against criminals. Why does debate usually focus on rehabilitation versus retribution? How can retribution be rehabilitative? Can rehabilitation be retributive? Under what circumstances?

6. How do juvenile courts differ from courts for adults? Why has there histor-ically been a gap between expectations for juvenile courts and their perfor-mance? How would you evaluate the performance of a juvenile court? Define status offenses. What lawful interests of the state do juvenile courts rep-resent?

7. Find historical examples of how children in various societies have been sub-ject to virtually absolute control by their parents. Is there a middle ground between this kind of control and children being treated as adults by the state? If so, when did it develop? Why? What information can juvenile court judges use in making their decisions? What other resources do they have at their disposal? Describe and evaluate the two basic ideological criticisms of juvenile courts. Describe the *Gault* decision and its relationship to the child advocacy movement.

8. Why do both conservatives and liberals wish to preserve the juvenile court system? What criticisms of it do they share? According to conservatives, what is the relationship between truth, society, values, and law? Why do they be-lieve the system of justice and public safety services must be public and uni-versal? Explain the societal model of juvenile justice. What is the relationship between the societal model and retribution? Why does the societal model place limits on the actions of juvenile courts?

9. According to liberals, what is the relationship between society, law, and change? Why do they believe that rehabilitation protects society more surely than retribution? Why do they believe the system of justice and public safety services is potentially contingent? Explain the child-centered model of juve-nile justice. How is this model consistent with the early juvenile court move-ment? Which American social norms support both the societal and the child-centered models? Why? Which social norms support one model but not the other?

10. Why will debates about retribution versus rehabilitation likely have little influ-ence on future changes in juvenile courts? Why will such changes likely be evolutionary rather than rapid? Explain how common efforts by conser-vatives and liberals during the 1960s and 1970s resulted in juvenile courts' treating criminal offenses more severely and status offenses less severely. How could the number of juveniles in institutions of correction have declined markedly if courts have treated criminal offenses more severely? In what ways are juvenile courts a necessity in modern society? In what ways will they be a necessity in the future?

REFERENCES

Bersoff, D. N. (1976). Child advocacy: The next step. *New York University Educational Quarterly,* *8* (3) 10–17.

Bortner, M. A. (1982). *Inside a juvenile court: The tarnished ideal of individualized justice.* New York: New York University Press.

Bronars, J. R. (1979). Children's rights and intellectual freedom. *The Educational Forum, 43,* 291–298.

Gold, M. (1977). Crime and delinquency: Treatment and prevention. In *Encyclopedia of social work* (17th issue, vol. 1, pp. 218–228). New York: National Association of Social Workers.

Hirschi, T. (1983). Crime and the family. In J. Q. Wilson (Ed.), *Crime and public policy* (pp. 53–68). San Francisco: Institute for Contemporary Studies.

Patterson, G. R. (1980). Children who steal. In T. Hirschi & M. Gottfredson (Eds.), *Understanding crime* (pp. 73–90). Beverly Hills, CA: Sage.

Platt, A. M. (1969). *The child savers: The invention of delinquency* (pp. 137–175). Chicago: University of Chicago Press.

Reid, S. T. (1982). *Crime and criminology* (3rd ed., pp. 20–44, 318–361, 396–433, 473–517). New York: Holt, Rinehart & Winston.

Ryerson, E. (1978). *The best-laid plans: America's juvenile court experiment* (p. 15). New York: Hill & Wang.

Serrill, M. (1979, June 23). The search for juvenile justice. *Saturday Review*, pp. 20, 22, 24.

Walkover, A. (1984). The infancy defense in the new juvenile court. *UCLA Law Review, 31,* 503–562.

SELECTED
BIBLIOGRAPHY

Achenbaum, W. (1978). *Old age in the new land: The American experience since 1790*. Baltimore: Johns Hopkins University Press.

Advisory Committee on Child Development. (1976). *Toward a national policy for children and families*. Washington, DC: National Academy of Sciences.

Alan Guttmacher Institute. (1976). *11 million teenagers: What can be done about the epidemic of adolescent pregnancies in the United States*. New York: Author.

Alan Guttmacher Institute. (1981). *Teenage pregnancy: The problem that hasn't gone away*. New York: Author.

Albrecht, G. L., & Higgins, P. C. (Eds.). (1979). *Health, illness and medical care*. Chicago: Rand McNally.

American Humane Society. (1978). *National analysis of official child neglect and abuse reporting*. Denver: Author.

Ball, R. M. (1975). *Social Security—Today and tomorrow*. New York: Columbia University Press.

Bane, M. J. (1976). *Here to stay: American families in the twentieth century*. New York: Basic Books.

Bell, D. (1973). *The coming of post-industrial society: A venture in social forecasting*. New York: Basic Books.

Bell, D. (Ed.). (1980). *Shades of Brown: New perspectives on school desegregation*. New York: Teachers College Press.

Bernier, N. R., & Williams, J. E. (1973). *Beyond beliefs: Ideological foundations of American education*. Englewood Cliffs, NJ: Prentice-Hall.

Biegel, D., & Naparstek, A. (1982). *Community support systems and mental health: Practice, policy and research*. New York: Springer.

Binstock, R. H., & Shanas, E. (Eds.). (1985). *Handbook of aging and the social sciences*. New York: Van Nostrand.

Bishop, J. (1977). *Jobs, cash transfers and marital instability: A review of the evidence*. Madison, WI: Institute for Research on Poverty.

Bortner, M. A. (1982). *Inside a juvenile court: The tarnished ideal of individualized justice.* New York: New York University Press.

Broudy, H. S. (1981). *Truth and credibility: The citizen's dilemma.* New York: Longman.

Burr, W., Hill, R., Nye, I., & Reiss, I. (Eds.). (1979). *Contemporary theories about the family.* New York: Free Press.

Butts, R. F. (1978). *Public education in the United States: From revolution to reform.* New York: Holt, Rinehart & Winston.

Callahan, R. (1962). *Education and the cult of efficiency.* Chicago: University of Chicago Press.

Campbell, A., Converse, P. E., & Rodgers, W. L. (1976). *The quality of American life: Perceptions, evaluations, and satisfactions.* New York: Russell Sage Foundation.

Clifford, G. J. (1975). *The shape of American education.* Englewood Cliffs, NJ: Prentice-Hall.

Coleman, J. S., et al. (1966). *Equality of educational opportunity.* Washington, DC: U.S. Government Printing Office.

Cremin, L. A. (1961). *The transformation of the school: Progressivism in American education, 1876–1957.* New York: Vintage Books.

Cremin, L. A. (1976). *Public education.* New York: Basic Books.

Downs, A. (1981). *Neighborhoods and urban development.* Washington, DC: The Brookings Institute.

Duignan, P., & Rabushka, A. (Eds.). (1980). *The United States in the 1980s.* Stanford, CA: Hoover Institute.

Education Commission of the States. (1983). *School finance reform in the states.* Denver, CO: Author.

Egan, J. J., Carr, J., Mott, A., & Roos, J. (1981). *Housing and public policy: A role for mediating structures.* Cambridge, MA: Ballinger.

Ehrenreich, B., & English, D. (1979). *For her own good: 150 Years of the experts' advice to women.* Garden City, NY: Anchor.

Empey, L. (Ed.). (1979). *The future of childhood and juvenile justice.* Charlottesville, VA: University Press of Virginia.

Fischer, L., & Sorenson, G. P. (1985). *School law for counselors, psychologists and social workers.* New York: Longman.

Fox, D. M. (1967). *The discovery of abundance.* Ithaca, NY: Cornell University Press.

Fox, F., & Cloward, R. A. (1979). *Poor people's movements: Why they succeed, how they fail.* New York: Vintage Books.

Franklin, A. W. (Ed.). (1978). *The challenge of child abuse.* New York: Grune & Stratton.

Frieden, B. J., & Kaplan, M. (1975). *The politics of neglect: Urban aid from Model Cities to revenue sharing.* Cambridge, MA: The MIT Press.

Furstenberg, F. F. (1976). *Unplanned parenthood.* New York: Free Press.

Galper, J. (1975). *The politics of social services.* Englewood Cliffs, NJ: Prentice-Hall.

Garms, W. I., Guthrie, J. W., & Pierce, L. C. (1978). *School finance: The economics and politics of public education.* Englewood Cliffs, NJ: Prentice-Hall.

Gartner, A., & Riessman, F. (1977). *Self-help in the human services.* San Francisco: Jossey-Bass.

Golembiewski, R. T., & Wildavsky, A. (1984). *The costs of federalism.* New Brunswick, NJ: Transaction Books.

Gottlieb, B. (1981). *Social networks and social support.* Beverly Hills, CA: Sage.

Haar, C. M. (1975). *Between the idea and the reality: A study in the origin, fate and legacy of the Model Cities program.* Boston: Little, Brown.

Hands, A. R. (1968). *Charities and social aid in Greece and Rome.* New York: Cornell University Press.

Hartman, C. W. (1975). *Housing and social policy.* Englewood Cliffs, NJ: Prentice-Hall.

Hirschi, T., & Gottfredson, M. (Eds.). (1980). *Understanding crime.* Beverly Hills, CA: Sage.

Horton, G. T. (1975). *Readings on human services planning.* Arlington, VA: Human Services Institute for Children and Families.

Human Resources Development Center. (1980). *Paraprofessionals in deinstitutionalized settings: A systematic study of effective use and potential.* New York: National Child Labor Committee.

Janowitz, M. (1979). *Social control and the welfare state.* New York: Harper & Row.

Joint Economic Committee. (1982). Social Security and pensions: Programs of equity and security. In U.S. House of Representatives, Committee on the Budget, *Impact of the*

Omnibus Reconciliation Act and the proposed fiscal year 1983 budget cuts on entitlements, uncontrollables, and indexing. Washington, DC: U.S. Government Printing Office.

Kadushin, A. (1980). *Child welfare services.* New York: Macmillan.

Kahn, A. S., & Kamerman, S. B. (1975). *Not for the poor alone.* Philadelphia: Temple University Press.

Kamerman, S. B., & Kahn, A. J. (1976). *Social services in the United States.* Philadelphia: Temple University Press.

Kamerman, S. B., & Kahn, A. J. (1977). *Social services in international perspective.* Washington, DC: U.S. Government Printing Office.

Kamerman, S. B., & Kahn, A. J. (Eds.). (1978). *Family policy: Government and families in fourteen countries.* New York: Columbia University Press.

Keith-Lucas, A. (1972). *Giving and taking help.* Chapel Hill: University of North Carolina Press.

Kempe, C., & Helfer, R. (Eds.). (1972). *Helping the battered child and his family.* Philadelphia: J. B. Lippincott.

Keniston, K., & the Carnegie Council on Children. (1978). *All our children.* New York: Harcourt Brace Jovanovich.

Kirst, M. (1985). *Who controls our schools? American values in conflict.* New York: W. H. Freeman.

Leiby, J. (1978). *A history of social welfare and social work in the United States.* New York: Columbia University Press.

Levine, D. U., & Havighurst, R. J. (1984). *Society and education* (6th ed.). Boston: Allyn & Bacon.

Lewis, D. (Ed.). (1981). *Reactions to crime.* Beverly Hills, CA: Sage.

Luker, K. (1975). *Taking chances: Abortion and the decision not to contracept.* Berkeley, CA: University of California Press.

MacIntyre, S. (1977). *Single and pregnant.* New York: Prodist.

Merchant, C. (1980). *The death of nature: Women, ecology and the scientific revolution.* New York: Harper & Row.

Moore, K. A., & Caldwell, S. B. (1976). *Out of wedlock pregnancy and childbearing.* Washington, DC: The Urban Institute.

Moroney, R. M. (1978). *The family and the state: Considerations for social policy.* New York: Longman.

Morris, R. (1979). *Social policy of the American welfare state.* New York: Harper & Row.

Mosteller, F., & Moynihan, D. P. (Eds.). (1972). *On equality of educational opportunity.* New York: Random House.

Muse, D. N., & Sawyer, D. (1982). *The Medicare and Medicaid data book, 1981.* Baltimore: Health Care Financing Administration.

National Center on Child Abuse and Neglect. (1978). *Child abuse and neglect in residential institutions.* Washington, DC: U.S. Government Printing Office.

National Center for Health Statistics. (1982). *Health, United States, 1982* (DHHS Publication No. 83-1232). Washington, DC: U.S. Government Printing Office.

National Commission for Children in Need of Parents. (1979). *Who knows? Who cares? Forgotten children in foster care.* New York: Author.

Paul, J. L., Neufeld, G. R., & Pelosi, J. W. (Eds.). (1977). *Child advocacy within the system.* Syracuse, NY: Syracuse University Press.

Pearce, D. (1978). *The feminization of poverty—Women, work, and welfare.* Unpublished manuscript, University of Illinois, Chicago Circle, Department of Sociology.

Pemberton, S. M. (1981). *The federal government and equality of educational opportunity.* Lanham, MD: University Press of America.

Piven, F. F., & Cloward, R. A. (1971). *Regulating the poor.* New York: Random House.

Platt, A. M. (1969). *The child savers: The invention of delinquency.* Chicago: University of Chicago Press.

Public Health Service. (1981). *Better health for our children: A national strategy* (DHHS Publication No. 79-55071, Vol. 4). Washington, DC: U.S. Government Printing Office.

Ravitch, D. (1983). *The troubled crusade: American education, 1945–1980.* New York: Basic Books.

Reid, S. T. (1982). *Crime and criminology* (3rd ed.). New York: Holt, Rinehart & Winston.

Reiss, I. L. (1980). *Family systems in America.* New York: Holt, Rinehart & Winston.

Reissman, F. (1962). *The culturally deprived child.* New York: Harper & Row.

Reissman, F. (1969). *Strategies against poverty.* New York: Random House.
Reverly, S., & Rosner, D. (Eds.). (1979). *Health care in America.* Philadelphia: Temple University Press.
Rimlinger, G. V. (1971). *Welfare policy and industrialization in Europe, America, and Russia.* New York: John Wiley & Sons.
Robin, G. D. (1980). *Introduction to the criminal justice system.* New York: Harper & Row.
Rossi, A. S., Kagan, J., & Hareven, T. K. (Eds.). (1978). *The family.* New York: W. W. Norton.
Rossum, R. A. (1978). *The politics of the criminal justice system: An organizational analysis.* New York: Marcel Dekker.
Ryerson, E. (1978). *The best-laid plans: America's juvenile court experiment.* New York: Hill & Wang.
Schorr, A. L. (1980). *". . . thy father and thy mother . . .": A second look at filial responsibility and family policy.* Washington, DC: U.S. Department of Health and Human Services.
Schussheim, M. J. (1974). *The modest commitment to cities.* Lexington, MA: D. C. Heath.
Sechrest, L. B., White, S. O., & Brown, E. (Eds.). (1979). *The rehabilitation of criminal offenders: Problems and prospects.* Washington, DC: National Academy of Sciences.
Siedel, S. R. (1978). *Housing costs and government regulation.* New Brunswick, NJ: Rutgers University Press.
Silberman, C. (1978). *Criminal violence, criminal justice.* New York: Random House.
Skolnick, A., & Skolnick, J. H. (Eds.). (1980). *Family in transition.* Boston: Little, Brown.
Solomon, A. (1980). *Housing the urban poor.* Cambridge, MA: The MIT Press.
Stack, C. B. (1974). *All our kin.* New York: Harper & Row.
Steiner, G. Y. (1976). *The children's cause.* Washington, DC: The Brookings Institute.
Stephan, W. G., & Feagin, J. R. (Eds.). (1980). *School desegregation: Past, present, and future.* New York: Plenum.
Vardin, P., & Brody, I. N. (Eds.). (1979). *Children's rights: Contemporary perspectives.* New York: Teachers College Press.
Walton, J. (1971). *Introduction to education: A substantive discipline.* Waltham, MA: Xerox College Publishing.
Weicher, J. C. (1980). *Housing: Federal policies and programs.* Washington, DC: American Enterprise Institute.
Weicher, J., Yap, L., & Jones, M. (1982). *Metropolitan housing needs for the 1980s.* Washington, DC: The Urban Institute.
Wilensky, H. (1975). *The welfare state and equality.* Berkeley, CA: University of California Press.
Wilson, J. Q. (Ed.). (1983). *Crime and public policy.* San Francisco: Institute for Contemporary Studies.
Wilson, J. Q. (1983). *Thinking about crime* (rev. ed.). New York: Basic Books.
Wise, A. E. (1979). *Legislated learning: The bureaucratization of the American classroom.* Berkeley, CA: University of California Press.
Wolfe, S. (Ed.). (1983). *Handbook of health care services.* New York: McGraw Hill.
Woody, R. H. (1984). *The law and the practice of human services.* San Francisco: Jossey-Bass.
Zackler, J., & Brandstadt, W. (Eds.). (1975). *The teenage pregnant girl.* Springfield, IL: Charles C. Thomas.

INDEX